Capturing the Commons

Capturing the Commons

DEVISING INSTITUTIONS

TO MANAGE THE MAINE LOBSTER

INDUSTRY

James M. Acheson

University Press of New England

HANOVER AND LONDON

Published by University Press of New England,

37 Lafayette St., Lebanon, NH 03766

© 2003 by University Press of New England

Printed in the United States of America

5 4 3 2 1

Library of Congress Cataloging-in-Publication Data

Acheson, James M.
Capturing the commons : devising institutions to manage the Maine
lobster industry / James M. Acheson.
p.   cm.
Includes bibliographical references and index.
ISBN 1—58465—317—5 (cloth : alk. paper)
1. Lobster industry—Government policy—Maine—Citizen participation.
2. Lobster fishers—Maine. 3. Lobster fisheries—Maine.
4. Fishery policy—Maine. I. Title.
HD9472.L63 U52 2003
338.3'725384—dc21   2002153372

To Ann, with love and appreciation

Contents

Illustrations

Figures

Maps

Tables

Illustrations

Acknowledgments

The data on which this book is based were gathered during the course of a number of research projects stemming back three decades. My first field research with the lobster industry in 1971 was sponsored by a grant from the National Marine Fisheries Service. From 1977 to 1979, I was Principal Investigator on a large National Science Foundation–funded project entitled "University of Rhode Island–University of Maine Study of Social and Cultural Aspects of Fisheries Management in New England Under Extended Jurisdiction." During these projects, I did extensive fieldwork in Maine lobster fishing communities and became familiar with the institutions of the industry, the territorial system, attitudes toward management, and differences in the views of fishermen and biologists.

Between 1993 and 1996, I participated in four research projects that expanded my knowledge in various ways. In 1993, I joined University of Maine colleagues Jim Wilson, Peter Kleban, Ralph Townsend, and Raymond O'Connor, who had received funds from the University of Maine Sea Grant Office to study the "Management of Chaotic Fisheries." While I was a latecomer to the project, my participation gave me a chance to interview fishermen on their ideas about lobster biology and the oceans, and to explore the ways in which fisheries were managed in other cultures. In 1994, I was P.I. on a project entitled "History of Lobster Management Legislation," financed by the University of Maine Lobster Institute, during which I gathered data on the history of state management. Russell Hall, a graduate student in the history department at the University of Maine, helped with the archival work. In 1993, I joined economist Jim Wilson and biologist Bob Steneck, both of the University of Maine, in a project designed to develop Amendment 5 of the Lobster Management Plan for the National Marine Fisheries Service; and in 1997, I worked with Jim Wilson and Bill Brennan, former Commissioner of Marine Resources, on a project entitled "Maine Fisheries Licensing Scheme" (financed by the Maine Department of Marine Resources).

I am especially indebted to the University of Maine Sea Grant program for sponsoring a project entitled "Case Studies in Co-management" on which Jim Wilson and I are co-Principal Investigators. This project financed my work from 1996 to 2001, and provided information that has been used in virtually every chapter in this book.

I thank several people and groups of people whose help contributed to this book in different ways. I am indebted to the hundreds of fishermen who agreed to be interviewed in depth and who answered questionnaires. Several have been especially helpful, and some have helped with a variety of projects over the course of years: Ted Ames, Doug Anderson, Charlie Begin, Doug Boynton, Jimmy Brackett, Richard Carver, Dan Cheney, Rusty Court, Blaine Davis, Eddie Drisko, Karl Ilvonen, Chad Hanna, Dan Miller, Russ Nisbet, John Olson, Arthur Pierce, Woody Post, Ken Prior, Brian Sawyer, Oscar Simpson, Myron Sprague, Tim Staples, Sherm, Shermy, and Alfred Stanley, Jan White, and Bert Witham. Norman Davis, Phil Davis, and Maynard Winchenbach, all now deceased, gave me invaluable information during the early years of my studies.

My knowledge of the politics of lobster management has been greatly enhanced by interviews and phone calls with Pat White, David Cousens, and Eddie Blackmore of the Maine Lobstermen's Association; Junior Backman of the Downeast Lobstermen's Association; Bill Adler of the Massachusetts Lobstermen's Association; and three people who have served as commissioner of the Maine Department of Marine Resources: Robin Alden, Spencer Apollonio, and Vinal Look. Zone Chairmen Norbert Lemieux (Zone A), Jon Carter (Zone B), Gerald Weed (Zone C), and Lyman Kennedy (Zone F) helped me understand the Maine co-management experiment as it developed. Special thanks are due David Black (Zone D), Larry Knapp (Zone E), and Jim Alwin (Zone G), who agreed to be interviewed repeatedly.

Conversations with Laura Taylor, Chris Finlayson, and Penn Estabrook of the Department of Marine Resources, Senator Jill Goldthwait, and Representatives David Etnier and Chester Rice of the marine resources committee of the legislature filled various gaps in my knowledge about state government and lobster management.

Over the course of years, I learned a great deal from lobster biologists, including Jim Thomas, Jay Krouse, and Carl Wilson of the Maine Department of Marine Resources; Tom Morrissey and Mike Fogarty of the National Marine Fisheries Service; Douglas Pezzak of the Canadian Department of Fisheries and Oceans; and Bob Bayer of the University of Maine. Their conversations and articles helped more than they know. Leslie Scattergood, who worked for the Department of Marine Resources beginning in the 1930s, and Dr. Richard Judd of the University of Maine contributed to my understanding of the history of the industry. Mary Ann Bates, now deceased, a student who went on to become a professional anthropologist, worked on several of my early projects and added insights about the intricacies of kinship and community in coastal towns. I owe a special debt to six people with whom I have worked closely on various research projects and articles in the past few years: Terry Stockwell, Maine Department of Marine Resources; biologist Robert Steneck, University of Maine; Bill Brennan, former commissioner of the Department of Marine Resources and member of the Regional Council; geography Ph.D candidate Jennifer Brewer (Clark University and University of Maine), and economist Roy Gardiner (Indiana University). Last but not least is economist Jim Wilson, University of Maine, with whom I have collaborated on several projects going back several decades now.

I owe an intellectual debt to anthropologists Robert Merrill and F. G. Bailey, who sparked my interest while I was in graduate school about the ways in which humans make decisions under various kinds of social and cultural constraints, a concern that is woven through this book.

I was fortunate to be able to spend the 2000/2001 academic year as visiting research professor at the Workshop in Political Theory and Policy Analysis at Indiana University. Lin and Vincent Ostrom and their colleagues in the workshop proved to be very stimulating people with similar interests to my own. The entire manuscript was written during this year in Bloomington.

Lin Ostrom, Jim Wilson, Terry Stockwell, Bill Brennan, and Spencer Apollonio commented on one or more chapters. Fishermen Myron "Sonny" Sprague, Doug Boynton, Phil Reed, and Bert Witham reviewed and commented on sections. Mike McGinnis, Indiana University, provided valuable insights on the whole manuscript. All these people had innumerable suggestions that improved the book.

Patty Zielinski, Indiana University, formatted and edited the bibliography. Steve Bicknell, University of Maine, drew all of the maps. Ann Acheson, a peerless copy editor and critic, prepared all the tables and copy edited multiple drafts of the book. Without her help, this volume would no doubt have taken a longer time to reach completion.

I would like to express appreciation to Phyllis Deutsch of University Press of New England for her helpful editorial comments and to Rachael Cohen, who did the final copy editing.

No pseudonyms are used in this book. All place names are actual. All named people whose verbal statements are included here have been contacted, and have given permission for their names and statements to be used.

J. M. A.

Capturing the Commons

CHAPTER 1

Introduction

*T*he twenty-first century is opening on the specter of worldwide environmental disaster caused by human beings. Stocks of fish, forests, grasslands, agricultural land, wildlife, air quality, and water quality have all been seriously degraded by overexploitation, pollution, or a combination of the two. Marine fisheries are in particularly poor condition. According to a Food and Agriculture Organization analysis, "sixty-nine percent of the fish stocks in the world are exploited at a level at or beyond the level corresponding to MSY [maximum sustainable yield]" (Garcia and Newton 1997: 14).

Environmental disaster is not inevitable, however. There are a number of cases where local-level communities and governments have been able to generate rules to effectively manage resources at sustainable levels (Anderson and Simmons 1993; Baland and Platteau 1996; Berkes 1989; Dyer and McGoodwin 1994; McCay and Acheson 1987; E. Ostrom 1990; Pinkerton 1989; Ruddle and Akimichi 1984). However, at this point it is not at all clear why some communities have succeeded in conserving the resources on which their livelihood depends when the vast majority have failed. This situation means that two of the most critical questions for resource management are: Under what conditions will people overexploit or conserve critical resources? Under what conditions will governments let them do either? Despite their centrality, the answers to these questions are not at all clear at this point. This book attempts to address these questions by focusing on the Maine lobster industry.

The Maine lobster industry is one of the most remarkably successful fisheries in the world today. Since the late 1980s, catches have been at record-high levels despite decades of intense exploitation. We have never produced so many lobsters. Even more interesting to managers is the fact that catch levels remained relatively stable from 1947 to the late 1980s. While scientists do not agree on the reason for these high catches, there is a growing consensus that they are due, in some measure, to the long history of effective regulations that the lobster fishing industry has played a key role in developing. There can be little doubt that the lobster industry has developed a strong conservation ethic, and that lobstermen have been very active in the political arena. Robin Alden, who was commissioner of the Maine Department of Marine Resources in the mid-1990s, noted that "to others,

1

lobstermen stand out among commercial fishermen as a group which abides by conservation rules and supports them—the only group which apparently has not yet depleted its resource . . . Most agree that lobstering is the only segment of the industry that is generally well organized politically" (Alden 1996).

In retrospect, those concerned with the lobster fishery have worked hard to maintain the fishery for themselves and future generations. To this end, they have developed several different kinds of rules to limit access to the resource and to control the fishery, a common-pool resource. They are truly "capturing the commons."

The rules developed are the result of the interaction between two different kinds of organizations: local communities of fishermen and those of the government.[1] This book is largely about the way that community-level groups and government organizations have negotiated rules for this industry. The actors who produced these rules were motivated by both altruism and self-interest. Some of the rules are informal ("decentralized"); others are formal laws and regulations (a "centralized" solution). Most were produced by political entrepreneurs bargaining over distributional issues. It would not be far wrong to say that rules are byproducts of contests over who gets the lobster.

These rules fall into four categories. First, the fishermen in each local area have developed traditional lobster fishing territories designed to reserve the lobsters in specific areas for people from a harbor or a few contiguous harbors. The territorial system is a decentralized system that is completely the result of long-standing competition between groups of lobster fishermen for fishing space. It is not recognized by the state, and maintenance of this system involves some illegal activity. The system of lobster fishing territories, which is described in chapter 2, is the baseline institution in that its existence allows other rules to be devised.

Second, in a few instances local groups of fishermen have been able to provide rules informally when the government could not or would not provide them. Of particular importance are the informal trap limit rules that four harbors were able to provide for themselves, which are described in chapter 3.

Third are the "centralized" laws of the state of Maine. These statutes, it should be noted, are largely the result of highly effective lobbying activities of the lobster fishing industry. In dealing with the state, the industry has proven very adept at persuading the legislature to pass laws it—or at least powerful industry factions— wanted. If the negotiations and political maneuvers between industry factions, the Department of Marine Resources, and the legislature were often rancorous and marked by hostility, the rules that have been produced appear to be effective in sustaining the resource. The development of state statutes is described in chapters 4 and 5.

Last, during the past twenty-five years the lobster industry has expended a lot of time and effort dealing with the federal government and its various agencies. Lobstermen have not been notably successful in influencing federal agencies and policies. Their effort has been devoted not so much to getting rules that they want as it has been to fighting off initiatives they believe would be harmful. In some cases, they have been able to secure rules that they can live with; in other instances, they have been forced to accept rules that they regard as less than desir-

Capturing the Commons

able. For much of this period, lobster management was in the hands of the New England Regional Council, which was not able to formulate a lobster management plan that could garner enough political support to be enacted into regulations. This long stalemate can only be described as a kind of policy failure. More recently, the industry and the Atlantic States Marine Fisheries Commission have been able to work together to produce a workable lobster plan that is more acceptable to the industry.

Behind the long-running dispute concerning the course of federal management is a difference in conception of the problem. The federal and state agency scientists have one view of the lobster, and the industry has another. This has led to differences in opinion about how to manage the fishery. As we shall see, neither side has a premium on truth. Many of the lobstermen's ideas about what controls the stock of lobsters can only charitably be called "folklore"; and the science behind the federal policy is a lot less "scientific" than the scientists would want to admit, and is quite politicized. Federal management and the problems of science are described in chapters 6, 7, and 8.

The conclusion (chapter 9) attempts to synthesize what we have learned from this case study and the way in which it contributes to our understanding of the conditions under which effective rules to manage natural resources will be generated. Two of the more central questions are: (1) What are the characteristics of local communities that give rise to rules to manage resources? and (2) What are the characteristics of governments that foster or inhibit the generation of such rules?

The process by which formal laws and regulations were developed for the Maine lobster fishery is an anathema to professional fisheries managers. Fisheries biologists firmly believe that science and scientists should have a lead role in developing regulations, and that "special interests" should be kept at bay (Rosen 1995).[2] In the Maine lobster industry, regulations were not the result of cool, detached debate in which the best scientific evidence was formulated into law. They came about as a result of a political process in which the fishing industry, state agencies, dealers, the Maine legislature, and later the federal government and conservation groups played roles. The process was marked by heavy lobbying pressure coming primarily, but not exclusively, from various industry factions. The negotiations and political maneuvers between these interested players were often decidedly unfriendly and acrimonious.

In the debate and maneuvering that took place, genuine concern for the welfare of the resource was mixed with brazen self-interest. If people in the industry were concerned with conservation, they were often more concerned that the resource be conserved for them. Bureaucrats were concerned about improving conservation efforts for the lobster resource when this did not result in undue political opposition or take too much effort. The Maine legislature, for its part, usually remained above the fray until the votes were counted. Periodically, however, it would act with unusual courage in the public good.

The problems of managing the lobster industry cannot be solved by blindly following the prescriptions of scientists. The problems with lobster science are all too real. Using state-of-the-art science has led scientists to recommend policies that the industry has opposed for very good reasons (Acheson and Steneck 1997). Unfortunately, the problems in the science cannot be cured by fine-tuning. The problems are far more basic, and suggest that we need a new approach to fisheries management.

What such a new approach to management might look like is suggested by the rules that have been put in place to manage the Maine lobster industry. The lobster industry has long promulgated laws that control "how" fishing is done, and which make no attempt to control the amount of lobster taken. We call this "parametric management" (Acheson and Wilson 1996; Wilson et al. 1994). Although this approach is not supported by fisheries scientists in general, it appears to work well in the lobster fishery. Similar kinds of rules might work in other fisheries.

The rise in catch levels that occurred beginning in the late 1980s has convinced the industry that the rules to conserve the fishery have succeeded. However, this impression is not shared by the press and public. Over the past fifteen years, a number of articles have appeared in the national press stating that the industry is on the verge of disaster and predicting even more dire things to come. Stories with titles such as "Where Have All the Lobsters Gone?" (Keiffer 1993), "The Lobster Business is Going to Pot"(*Business Week* 1984), "A Tale of Two Fisheries" (Tierney 2000) present the ostensible demise of the lobster as due to massive overfishing.

By 2000, the idea that the lobster fishery was in deep crisis appeared to be a well-accepted fact by the public. The Monterey Aquarium (California) put lobster on its seafood watch list, advising the public to stop eating lobster because it was worried "about overfishing and that the fishery could be on the verge of collapse" (O'Leary 2000).

These disaster stories are traceable, in most part, to the press and some of the government scientists. The press loves disaster stories, and a faction of scientists is all too happy to oblige it. The fact that the press and the scientists have presented the fishermen as a pack of villains who have devastated the lobster brood stock, while record-high catches are being produced and while members of the fishing industry have worked hard to make various conservation efforts effective, has done nothing to endear either to the lobster industry.

Rules, Institutions and Organizations

Most of the lobster fishing industry's efforts to control the resource and influence the environment in which lobster fishing takes place involve the generation of rules. While the generation of rules, norms, and institutions has never been the primary focus of attention for any social science discipline, the problem has been approached by people from virtually every social science over the course of several decades. In the 1960s and 1970s, anthropologists were making some key contributions to this field with the work of Bailey (1969), Barth (1981), Heath (1976), and Kapferer (1976). More recently, the most seminal work has been done by political scientists, economists, and sociologists interested in what is known as rational choice theory and the closely related fields of institutional economics and institutional analysis and development. People in these fields are generally known as the "new institutionalists." The analytical tools employed in this book draw heavily on the insights and concepts of this literature.

What are institutions? How do they work their magic? The new institutionalists explain the generation of institutions in terms of the rational or goal-oriented decisions of individuals. Decisions are defined as "rational" when individuals use the scarce assets at their disposal to achieve their aims most efficiently. In many situations, the outcomes for an individual are dependent on the choices and rewards of others. People choose to establish rules because rules make it possible to gain the benefits of coordinated activities. Conversely, individuals will tend to change rules or defect from them when it is in their best interest to do so.

The new institutionalists use the term "institution" to mean a rule or norm, either formal or informal, that can be enforced (E. Ostrom 1999b: 50). North (1990a: 3) defines institutions as the "rules of the game," and this definition is very similar to the one employed earlier by anthropologist Frederick G. Bailey in *Strategems and Spoils* (1969). In this book, I will use "institution" in this sense, although it is not the standard definition used by anthropologists or sociologists by any means.

Institutions are different from organizations. Institutions are rules and norms defining interaction and competition. Organizations are the units formed in accordance with these rules. According to North, organizations are groups of people whose interactions are regulated by rules that come into being to "achieve some objective" (1990a: 4–5). Lineages, firms, trade unions, political bodies, clubs, associations, and schools are all types of organizations.

Rules or institutions structure social interaction. They make the behavior of other humans more predictable and thus reduce risk and uncertainty. In an uncertain world, institutions provide a basis for making decisions with reasonable assurance because they help to ensure the actions of others. Institutions, in the words of John R. Commons, "secure expectations" (1934: 705). For example, a rule that one must drive on the right-hand side of the road gives drivers a high degree of certainty about what the drivers of oncoming cars will do. With such a rule, the risks of driving are far less than they would be in the absence of the rule. However, rules are not a universal panacea. As Elizabeth Colson has pointed out, "rules do not solve all problems; they only simplify life" (1974: 52).

Institutions are a substitute for information. In a world of perfect knowledge, we would have no need for institutions (Coase 1960). If a farmer knew what prices for crops would be at the time of harvest, he or she could make decisions about which crops to grow with vastly increased assurance of high profits. In the absence of such information, a farmer can reduce risks by selling the crop through the institution of the futures market to obtain a guaranteed price. This means that rules or institutions are more than constraints that limit choices. They also open opportunities. For example, a contract between buyer and seller specifying the price and delivery schedule of a raw material is a constraint on both parties to the agreement. However, an entrepreneur might be unwilling to produce a final product using this raw material in the absence of such a contract.

Institutions are rarely completely fair. They favor some people over others. Individuals are aware of this and attempt to devise institutions that will benefit them. In this regard, Jean Ensminger says that "the underlying assumption is that institutions directly affect economic outcomes (distribution and growth), that individuals realize this, and that they attempt to change institutions to serve their ends more effectively, whether these ends be ideological or materialistic" (1992: xiii). As we shall see, the politics of lobster management have been dominated by conflicts over rules to favor one industry faction or another.

The new institutionalists perceive property rights—bundles of rights over goods or real estate—as a key institution (North 1990a: 33). Property rights influence decisions concerning investment, conservation, and efficiency. In Eggertsson's terms, "It is obvious that the nature of control matters for economic actors: short-term control shortens the time horizon; uncertain control discourages potentially profitable projects; lack of control incites costly races for possession; restricted control allocates assets to inferior uses" (1993: 2). Secure property rights give the "owners" of resources incentive to conserve them and use them efficiently. Many of the rules devised for the lobster industry give fishermen property rights over the resource (such as territorial rules), and thus motivate fishermen to conserve.

One of the most important insights of the new institutional economics is that institutions stem from problems in markets. Basically, this approach assumes that people obtain the goods and services they want through transactions with others. They will use the institution of the market when it is working well, but when the price system is not working well, they are able to make arrangements with each other (that is, non-market institutions) to obtain the things they need (Coase 1937; Williamson 1975). In Arrow's terms, "there is a wide variety of social institutions, in particular generally accepted social norms of behavior, which serve in some means as compensation for failure or limitation of the market" (1971: 5). The new institutional economists have used this insight to account for the generation of a large number of different kinds of social arrangements, ranging from firms, markets, and property rights to clubs, families, and associations (Acheson 1994: 6–7). Some of these arguments about the generation of non-market institutions are of special interest to anthropologists. Robert Bates provides a particularly good account of the causes of market failure, and the types of non-market institutions that result from each (1994: 45–52). Janet Landa argues that markets and contract law regulate exchange in modern economies, but that ethnic trading networks are of critical importance in developing countries, and gift-exchange systems (for example, the Kula and potlatch) are the dominant economic institution in tribal societies (1997: 1–6).

Perhaps most important of all, the new institutionalists are committed to the idea that human behavior is strongly influenced by institutions, but that institutions do not determine all choices. Rather, they influence the costs and benefits of behavior and thus influence choices and strategies (E. Ostrom 1999b). In some instances, the costs (or benefits) of disobeying a rule are so high that choices are severely limited; in others cases, there is ample room for independent action.

Generating Institutions: The Problem of Collective Action

Questions about the generation of conservation rules take us into the middle of one of the most important debates concerning social life: How do norms and institutions come into being and change? Among social scientists, there is a consensus that rules make it possible for humans to coordinate their activities and achieve goals that they could not achieve alone. But simply because rules bring about collective benefits is no guarantee that they will be provided. The problem was first framed by Mancur Olson (1965), who pointed out that even if rules or other public goods would benefit all, they will only be provided if "special incentives" exist. The essential problem, he saw, was that there is no incentive for individuals to help to produce a public good since they will have the benefit of it regardless of whether they contributed to producing it or not. Since it is rational for every individual to "free-ride" on the efforts of others, the public good is not produced. Everyone has acted rationally, and yet they are all worse off than if they had cooperated. The solution is to provide either rewards or sanctions to overcome the "free-rider" effect.

More recently, rational choice theorists would phrase the problem of devising norms in terms of a collective action dilemma (Elster 1989: 17; M. Taylor 1990: 223). These are situations in which there is a divergence between the interests of the individual and those of the society. Most such dilemmas can be modeled as prisoner's dilemma games (M. Taylor 1990). The solution to such dilemmas is to establish rules constraining the behavior of individuals. In the absence of rules, rational action by the individual will bring suboptimal results or even disaster for the collectivity. In collective action dilemmas, it is not rational for individuals to cooperate, even though cooperation would bring positive results for all.

The poor results produced by "rational action" provide an incentive to enact rules and norms. In collective action dilemmas, as Coleman points out, the activities of one person produce externalities for others (1990: 251). That is, some individuals are permitted to foist some of the costs of their activities onto others. It is the existence of externalities that creates the demand for norms. People whose interests are being damaged by the activities of others have a strong incentive to produce rules to curb the damage, while those who stand to gain in the short run have a strong incentive to oppose such rules.

Common-pool resources, including marine fisheries, present a classic collective action dilemma. In the case of fisheries, it is in the self-interest of individual skippers to catch as many fish as possible. Thus they resist enacting rules to constrain exploitive effort, even though such rules would result in a healthier breeding stock, increased catches, lower prices for consumers, and a sustainable industry. In most fisheries, the conditions necessary for the generation of norms have been largely absent, with the result that large numbers of fish stocks are dangerously overexploited. Such failures to solve the collective action problem have been documented in great detail in the literature on fisheries and common pool resources (Acheson 1989a; Hardin and Baden 1977; McGoodwin 1990). The lobster fishery is different in that it has repeatedly solved the collective action dilemmas it has faced. Repeatedly, it has gone to the government to enact formal rules, and small groups of fishermen have devised informal rules to constrain themselves.

Collective action dilemmas have received an enormous amount of attention from social scientists, primarily because they describe so many of the most vexing problems plaguing humanity. Elster and Taylor go so far as to say that "politics is the study of ways of solving collective action problems" (M. Taylor 1990: 224).

Among rational choice theorists, there is a consensus that rules to constrain individuals will improve outcomes in collective action dilemmas. However, these theorists do not agree on the conditions under which such rules are generated (M. Taylor 1990: 224–5). It is clear that people will not cooperate to produce rules or other kinds of public goods if those who did not sacrifice to produce them get most of the benefits. Curbing "free riding" is essential. For this reason, there is a consensus that people will be able to provide themselves with rules and institutions if the group is small, if people know a good deal about each other's past performances, if the game is played repeatedly, and if the rules can be enforced (Coleman 1990: 254, 272; Elster 1989: 41; Knight 1992: 48–64, 174–78; North 1990a: 12, 32–36; E. Ostrom 1990: 71–72, 189; M. Taylor 1982: 50–51; Wade 1994: 215). In such circumstances, people know who is likely to cooperate, and can monitor behavior and sanction shirkers.

However, a very large number of variables have been mentioned as facilitating the production of norms and rules, including homogeneity, social capital, community, trust, political entrepreneurship, discount rate, group size, ability to change the rules, and others (E. Ostrom 1990: 188; 2000a; 2000b; M. Taylor 1990: 224–25). In addition, several different theories have been developed concerning the process by which norms or rules are produced, including those of Jack Knight (1992), David Lewis (1969), Douglass North (1990a), and Robert Sugden (1986).

Much of this book is devoted to explaining how the Maine lobster industry solved a variety of collective action dilemmas at several different levels. A complicated set of factors is involved in the production of rules in the Maine lobster industry. All of these variables have been mentioned in the literature at some point, but the exact combination of those variables appears to be unique. As we shall see, political entrepreneurship and distribution fights both play a key role in producing rules to govern the Maine lobster industry.

Common Pool Resources, Public Goods, and the Management of Natural Resources

Another perspective on the problem of managing natural resources, including the lobster fishery, is gained by looking at the types of property rights and goods involved.

Economic theorists define four different kinds of goods: private goods, toll goods, public goods, and common-pool resources. These are defined by combinations of excludability and subtractability. *Excludability* refers to ease with which

Figure 1.1

A Classification of Goods

		Subtractability	
		Low	High
Excludability	Difficult	Public goods	Common-pool resources
	Easy	Toll goods	Private goods

Source: Ostrom, Gardner and Walker (1994:7).

others can be kept from using the resource. *Subtractability* refers to the degree to which use by one person subtracts from someone else's ability to use the resource. The classification of types of goods is contained in figure 1.1.

Understanding the production of each type of good poses substantial challenges. This task is made more difficult by the fact that each of these types of goods differs from the other, and there are also several different varieties of each type. This volume is devoted to understanding the management of the lobster, which is a common-pool resource. However, some aspects of the lobster territorial system and the services of the agencies charged with managing the lobster are best considered to be public goods.

Privately owned resources are subtractable, which means that they can be depleted. However, such goods have a private owner who can exclude others from using these resources. Since it is not in the rational best interest of an owner to damage his own property, most renewable resources owned privately are used efficiently and conserved (Acheson 1989a; McCay 1992).

Toll goods are characterized by excludability and non-subtractability. A toll road, for example, can only be used by those who pay for the privilege, but the use by one person does not prevent another from using the highway.

Public goods are characterized by difficulties of exclusion, but are not subtractable. Police protection and military defense are classic examples. One person's enjoyment of police protection does not subtract from the protection afforded other citizens. However, once such goods are provided, they benefit everyone in the society whether they have paid for them or not. As a result, the provision of public goods poses a collective action dilemma. Such goods might benefit the community as a whole, but an individual has little incentive to invest in them. Where public goods are concerned, the incentive to free ride is irresistible. Thus, if public goods are to be provided, there must be some means of forcing users to pay their fair share of the costs of producing and maintaining such goods. For this reason, most public goods are produced by the government, an organization capable of using force to end free riding.

Many renewable resources, including fish, oceans, rivers, air, and unowned rangeland, are *common-pool resources* (CPR). Such resources, including the Maine lobster fishery, have a number of characteristics that pose special difficulties for management. Common-pool resources are subtractable, so that harvesting by one person reduces the amount of a good that can be taken by others. Moreover, it is difficult to exclude others from using them. As a result, in the absence of enforceable rules, such resources are subject to escalating abuse as increasing numbers of people enter the industry and compete to take the CPR before someone else does. Here again, a collective action dilemma exists. It is all too rational for individuals to over-exploit such resources, even though this is detrimental to the interests of the larger society (and to individuals in the long run).

As is the case in all collective action problems, the solution is to make rules to constrain people. In the case of fisheries, the rules would presumably control exploitive effort in order to produce a sustainable output of the resource.

Several different solutions to CPR problems have been proposed in the literature. Hardin (1968) saw the solution as top-down management by the government, which might have to be imposed by autocratic means. Several economists who have studied the "common property" problem have proposed to manage such resources by simulating property rights through the use of licensing, limited entry, individual transferable quotas, and the like (National Research Council 1986). Such rules give users some of the rights associated with private property. A number of anthropologists and other social scientists have described a variety of systems that have been managed by local-level communities or groups of private citizens (Anderson and Simmons 1993; Baland and Platteau 1996; Berkes 1989; Dyer and McGoodwin 1994; McCay and Acheson 1987; National Research Council 1986; E. Ostrom 1990; Ruddle and Akimichi 1984). Co-management is another viable option (Pinkerton 1989; Pinkerton and Weinstein 1995). However, it should not be thought that the above list is exhaustive or that these different approaches are mutually exclusive. As we shall see, management of the Maine lobster industry involves all these approaches.

Several statements about the management of CPRs can be made with some certainty, however. First, many different combinations of rules and strategies can be used to govern CPRs. The only real constraint is that the rules devised must be congruent with the "physical environment and characteristics of the community" (McGinnis 1999: 8). This means that there are no general solutions to CPR problems. The rules used to govern the Maine lobster industry are unique to that industry. However, some general observations and principles about resource management can be learned from the lobster case.

Second, market solutions cannot be used to govern common-pool resources, including the lobster. The fact that the lobster CPR is subtractable means that fishermen can and do foist externalities onto others in the industry—that is, some of the costs of producing fish are assumed by others. As Bates (1994) points out, externalities are the primary cause of market failure. This means that all of the institutions used to govern the Maine lobster industry are non-market institutions of one sort or another.

Moreover, since users of CPRs are not paying all of the costs of production, they have a tendency to overinvest, or overcapitalize, in equipment to harvest the resource (Acheson 1989a). In the lobster industry, this overcapitalization has taken the form of larger, better-equipped boats and a massive increase in the number of traps. It took more than forty years to pass rules to control trap escalation.

Third, scholars generally agree that rules to govern CPRs cannot be devised unless access to the resource is controlled somehow. Groups who appropriate resources cannot be expected to constrain themselves if the benefits go to free riders who do not make a sacrifice to conserve the resource. The Maine lobster industry uses several means to control access to the resource.

Without rules to control entry, a CPR becomes an "open-access" resource. Open-access resources are always overexploited, since anyone can exploit them and no one has any incentive to invest in them. As a result, the term "open-access resource" has long been synonymous with resource destruction.

Defining Success

There is no consensus in the literature on how to define a successful fishery management program. It is tempting to say that policies are successful when conservation rules are generated that conserve the stocks. The difficulty with such a definition is that oceans are so complex that it is virtually impossible to be able to know with certainty exactly what effect a rule has on stock levels. In this regard, Singleton points out that anthropologists tend to define resource policy success in terms of policies that prevent unsustainable exploitation levels. The problem with this definition, she writes, is that many factors can affect sustainability, including a host of environmental factors. Thus, a resource may succeed or fail for reasons that "would be unrelated to institutional design" (1998: 26).

As a result, two criteria need to be used in defining the success of a fisheries management program. First, the people involved need to be able to solve the collective action dilemmas they face to devise the conservation rules they want. In this respect, the lobster industry and state government agencies certainly have been successful. Second, those rules must have a positive effect on fish stocks. It is difficult to ascertain what the effect of the lobster regulations has been, and there is a good deal of debate about this topic. Growing evidence indicates that many of the rules that the industry believes are most important do, in fact, help to conserve the lobster, but the case cannot be considered "proven" in any absolute sense.

Methodology

Most of the data on which this book is based were gathered over the course of thirty years of research with lobster fishermen. Throughout my research, I have concentrated on the mid-coast region, the area from Casco Bay to Penobscot Bay (see map 3.1).

Anthropology has a long and proud tradition of fieldwork. Most of the data used in this book I obtained using qualitative data collection techniques, including direct observation, open-ended interviews with key informants, and semi-structured interviews. These are standard data gathering techniques used in anthropology. I also did archival research in the Maine State archives and the

Fogler Library of the University of Maine. I made good use of articles in *Commercial Fisheries News,* whose reporters did a first-rate job of recording events as they developed. Their accounts were particularly useful in jogging my memory about events I had lived through, but that had become vague in all too short a time.

Most of the time, I was an observer of the lobster management process. However, my perspective on the politics of management was enhanced by various jobs and contracts, and by participation in a number of committees and commissions. I worked for the Fisheries Management Division of the National Marine Fisheries Service in Washington, D.C., in 1974 to 1975. I was one of the consultants who wrote Amendment 5 for the Regional Council in 1993 to 1994. In 1995 and 1996, I was a member of the zone management law implementation committee, which planned the Maine lobster zone management system. In 1998, I served on the "Sub-Zone Taskforce" established by the Maine Legislature. From 1997 to the present (2002), I have served on the social science advisory committee of the New England Regional Fishery Management Council. Currently, I am on the Atlantic States Marine Fisheries Commission (ASMFC) American lobster socioeconomic subcommittee. My participation in the political process is described in more detail in the chapters that follow.

Periodically, I have also gathered data using survey research techniques. Data from three survey projects proved to be especially valuable in eliciting information about attitudes toward management. One was done in 1973 in which 144 fishermen were interviewed; the second, called the Lobster Zones Questionnaire Project, was conducted in the summer of 1998 and was financed jointly by our Sea Grant–sponsored study of co-management and by the Maine Department of Marine Resources. This questionnaire was sent to half of the lobster license-holders in Maine and was completed by 1,140 fishermen (Acheson and Acheson 1998). Data from these surveys have been used in chapters 5 and 6. The third was a 1994 survey of fishermen about the factors influencing catches. Chapter 6 is largely based on the results of that survey.

On occasion, I used formal statistical analysis. In one study, I analyzed the factors influencing trap catches using regression techniques (Acheson 1980). Robert Steneck and I completed a number of statistical analyses of catch and effort data gathered by the State of Maine (see Acheson and Steneck 1997). These data are referred to in this book, but not used extensively.

The techniques I used varied over the course of time as the objectives of my research changed. During the 1970s and early 1980s, I was primarily interested in understanding the basic institutional structure of the industry, especially the harbor gangs, territorial system, and aspects of kinship and community. During this period, I lived in a fishing community for two years, rode a lot of fishing boats, and spent hours talking to fishermen in their homes and on the docks.

All of the data on territoriality (chapter 2) were obtained by in-depth interviews with key informants in the late 1970s and again in the late 1990s. In these interviews, fishermen were asked directly about fishing locations, harbor boundaries, the history of their fishing territory, the problems of territorial defense, and other questions. These data were recorded in notebooks and on standard

Capturing the Commons

oceanographic charts. (Currently I have over 130 maps produced by fishermen stored in two large cases.) Some of the most useful data on the territorial system came as a byproduct of interviews about other subjects over the course of many years. Obtaining accurate information on the territorial system posed many difficulties, since it touches on events that involve some illegal activity.

All of the data for chapter 4 regarding state laws and some of the data on the history of federal management in chapter 7 were obtained by archival research.

In the 1990s, as my interests turned to the politics of management, I spent increasing amounts of time interviewing industry leaders, legislators, zone chairmen, and bureaucrats, and attending various meetings concerning the politics of the industry. At this point, I expanded my attention to cover the entire coast, the Maine government, and the federal agencies concerned with managing fisheries in New England.

In short, the information on the industry was obtained through a variety of techniques, including unstructured interviews and participant observation, survey research, quantitative methods, and archival research. All are standard techniques in the social sciences. As do all anthropologists, I relied heavily on participant observation and unstructured interviews. These techniques produce data that is less neat, but far richer and more illuminating than data stemming from survey research (Bernard 1988).

I collected virtually all of the data in this book myself. There are some exceptions. I obtained information on catches, numbers of license holders, number of traps, and the like from the official figures published by the Maine Department of Marine Resources (1999). Moreover, I was fortunate to receive help from three graduate students who were hired to help with specific projects. Jennifer Brewer, a graduate student in geography at Clark University and the University of Maine, collected a good deal of data on the changing territorial system in the summer of 1998. Russell Hall, a history graduate student at the University of Maine, helped gather the archival data on which chapter 4 is based. Teresa Johnson augmented field data on the Penobscot Bay region.

One the whole, fieldwork in Maine proved very easy, particularly in comparison with the places anthropologists normally work. One can drive to every town, it is safe to drink the water, everyone speaks English, and there are no armed dissident political factions. Members of the lobster industry proved intelligent, well-informed, and willing to talk about their industry.

The Maine Lobster Industry: General Information

More lobsters are caught in Maine than in any other state in the United States, amounting to approximately 60 percent of U.S. lobster landings. Although 60 percent of the total North American lobster catch is landed in Canadian ports, lobsters are still strongly associated with Maine, and Canadian-caught lobsters are frequently marketed as "Maine lobster." Since the 1950s, lobster has been the most valuable fishery in Maine. In 2000, lobster sales totaled $186.1 million.

Lobster fishing is not concentrated in any one area. Every harbor along Maine's convoluted coast has a few lobster boats, and most have a lobster dealer who buys from local fishermen. In 2000, Maine issued 6,884 lobster licenses. Most people fish alone or go with one helper. The lobsters are sold to private dealers who have docks in virtually every harbor along the coast or to one of the seventeen cooperatives (Acheson 1988: 84– 90).

TECHNOLOGY

The lobster fishery is an inshore trap fishery. With the exception of a few boats fishing in offshore waters, it is a day fishery conducted by small boats that leave port in the early morning and return in the afternoon. In 1998, a lobster fisherman used an average of 570 traps that he tended alone or with the help of one helper called a "sternman." Most full-time fishermen use boats 33 to 38 feet in length that are made of wood or fiberglass, and powered by gasoline or diesel engines. Boats are usually equipped with a compass, hydraulic trap hauler, VHF radio, depth finder, Loran C, and, increasingly, radar and GPS systems. The vast majority are equipped with flowing seawater tanks or barrels to store the catch and keep the lobsters in good condition.

Many part-time fishermen use boats that are virtually identical to those used by full-timers. Others use outboard-powered skiffs ranging from 14 to 20 feet long. These skiff fishermen normally fish only in the summer months in sheltered bays and inlets near shore.

Before 1980, the vast majority of traps used were made of wood. Now most are 4 feet long and made of vinyl-covered wire. Both wire and wooden traps are equipped with funnel shaped "heads" made of nylon netting, designed to make it easy for lobsters to enter the traps but difficult to find their way out. Lobsters are attracted into the traps by bait that consists of dead fish. In past decades, the most common type of bait was fish frames (everything minus the fillets) from fish-packing plants; however, for the past twenty years, the most common bait has been herring remnants, which are placed in bags (so-called "bagged bait") and tied in place.

Lobster traps are attached to a Styrofoam buoy that floats on the surface by a rope made of nylon or polypropylene, called "warp," which is usually measured in fathoms (i.e., 6-foot increments). Most fishermen use toggles, made of bottles or Styrofoam, to keep the warp line off the bottom where it might become entangled. The length of the warp varies from 10 fathoms to 60 fathoms depending on the depth of water in the location being fished.

BIOLOGY

The American lobster (*Homarus americanus*) is found in the waters off the Atlantic coast of North America from Newfoundland to Virginia. Although adult lobsters

Capturing the Commons

can be found in waters ranging from 6 to 1,200 feet deep, lobsters are most concentrated in coastal waters of the Gulf of Maine at depths less than 150 feet. Although lobsters live on all bottom types, they prefer areas with boulders, especially where there is a good deal of kelp in which to hide (Bologna and Steneck 1993; Cooper and Uzmann 1980). In the winter, many lobsters move onto muddy bottom where they can dig burrows in which to hide.

Lobsters grow by molting. Early in their lives, they molt several times per year, while in later stages molting occurs only once each year or every other year. During molting or "shedding," the lobster shell splits along the bottom of the carapace, and the lobster wiggles out, leaving the shell intact. Within a few days, the new shell begins to harden again, but for a period of weeks the shell is soft, rendering the lobster more vulnerable to predation and attack. Although lobsters can molt in any month, the vast majority do so in the mid-summer months.

Lobster biologists and fishermen measure lobsters on the carapace—from the eye socket to the back of the body shell. Scientists record carapace lengths in millimeters. The law reads in inches. In this volume, the sizes of lobsters will be described in terms of carapace length measured in inches.

It takes approximately seven years for a lobster to grow from larval stage to a carapace length of 3.25 inches—the current minimum size that can be harvested legally in Maine. During the earliest larval stages, lobsters float through the water column for a period of several weeks before settling to the bottom. Adolescent-phase lobsters are between 1.57 and 3.54 inches long. They forage actively at night, but hole up during the day since they are subject to predation by large fish. Lobsters in the reproductive phase (over 3.54 inches) are subjected to far less predation and migrate considerable distances. They are most abundant in deep water and offshore areas (Skud and Perkins 1969). Very large lobsters (over 5 inches) have no natural enemies and may live as long as one hundred years (Cooper and Uzmann 1980).

In the Gulf of Maine, most female lobsters do not mature sexually until they are over 3.15 inches (late adolescent phase), and 50% are not mature until they reach 3.5 to 3.7 inches (reproductive phase) (Krouse 1972, 1973). Fecundity increases with size. When females first become mature at 3.25 or 3.50 inches, they can extrude a few hundred eggs. A single large female (with a carapace over 5 inches) can exude as many as one hundred thousand eggs. Lobsters mate right after mature females have molted, when their shells are soft and they are defenseless. Once the eggs are extruded from the lobster's body, they remain attached to her abdomen for a period of months until they hatch. Lobsters in this reproductive stage are called "berried" or "egged" lobsters.

Since lobsters require highly saline water, they are not found in numbers far up rivers or in estuarine areas with large influxes of fresh water. The life cycle of the lobster is affected by water temperature more than any other factor. Temperature affects larval settlement, molting, migration, growth, and hunger, which, in turn, affects willingness to crawl into traps.

Lobsters are generally highly sedentary. Early work in the 1950s showed that the vast majority of tagged lobsters were caught within 2 miles of the place where they were released. However, more recent studies show that some "extensive localized movement occurs" (Krouse 1977: 6). Under some conditions, lobsters migrate for long distances (Cooper and Uzmann 1971). In the Gulf of Maine, these migrations generally move in a southwest direction following the coastal currents. Moreover, Pezzack's work shows that large lobsters generally migrate offshore into deeper water (Pezzack and Duggan 1986).

Lobsters eat a wide variety of living and dead organisms. Their preferred diet probably consists of small crustaceans, mollusks, and fish, although marine worms make up a significant part of the diet in some situations. Lobsters are also capable of filtering plankton from water, and thus can live for considerable amounts of time in traps that have been abandoned. Lobsters are also cannibalistic, and will attack smaller and soft-shelled members of their own species. For this reason, fishermen put rubber bands around the claws of the lobsters they catch, and dealers separate out soft-shelled from hard-shelled animals and remove injured lobsters.

HARVEST HISTORY: BUST AND BOOM

Maine lobster catches have varied greatly over the past 120 years. Between 1880 and 1912, they ranged from a low of 11.1 to a high of 24.5 million pounds (Maine Department of Marine Resources 1995). After World War I, catches dropped precipitously and remained low until World War II, forcing large numbers of fishermen out of business. Throughout the lobster "bust" of the 1920s and 1930s, catches hovered between 5.5 and 7.1 million pounds annually (see table 1.1). From 1947 to 1988, catches were considerably higher and very stable, averaging about 20 million pounds.

Since 1990, lobster catches have steadily increased, and have been over 30 million pounds every year; in 1999, the Maine catch had risen to 53.1 million pounds; and by 2000, catches totaled 56.7 million pounds. In summary, at the present, the lobster industry is experiencing a boom. Catches have never been so high at any period. However, the severe lobster stock crash in the years of the "lobster bust" in the 1920s and 1930s should not be forgotten. There is no consensus on the reasons for either the "bust" or the "boom," and, as we shall see, this has had an effect on policy.

From 1930 to 1999, the number of traps used has steadily increased. Whereas 1931 saw only 210,000 traps in the water, in 1999 fishermen used 3,043,154 traps, an increase of over 1,400 percent (table 1.1). This increase in the number of traps was made possible by the adoption of a number of innovations over the past fifty years, including larger boats, hydraulic trap haulers, better trap-construction materials, and electronics that make it possible to locate traps more easily (Acheson 1988). There was a slight decrease in trap numbers in 2000.

At the same time, the number of lobster licenses has remained far more stable. From 1900 to 1930, the number of lobster licenses ranged from a low of 2,541 in 1902 to 3,291 in 1916. From 1950 to the present, the number of licenses varied from a low of 4,654 in 1951 to 10,455 in 1975, with an average of 6,721.

Capturing the Commons

Table 1.1

Official State Figures on Lobster Catch and Numbers of Traps and Licenses, 1880–2000

Year	Catch (lbs)	No. traps (thousands)	No. licenses	Year	Catch (lbs)	No. traps (thousands)	No. licenses
1880	14,234,182	104	2,763	1924	5,513,002	154	
1886	23,004,765			1925			
1887	22,916,642	109	1,906	1926			
1888	21,694,731	107	1,967	1927			
1889	24,452,111	121	2,080	1928	7,100,332	211	
1890	20,001,555			1929	6,620,615		
1892	17,642,677	153	2,628	1930	7,750,682	205	
1894		200		1931	5,365,466	168	
1897		234	2,436	1932	6,056,932	208	2,927
1898	12,267,498	279	3,103	1933	5,897,685	180	2,956
1899	12,718,136	335	3,116	1934	5,377,278	183	2,925
1900	14,406,201	327	3,105	1935	7,687,200	185	3,102
1901	13,982,964	304	2,788	1936	5,120,386	185	
1902	14,324,348	298	2,541	1937	7,348,500	186	
1903	13,115,709	268	2,558	1938	7,659,200	258	3,592
1904	12,083,554	264	2,509	1939	6,625,409	260	3,722
1905	11,137,947	256	2,562	1940	7,643,005	222	3,717
1906	15,014,147	305	2,672	1941	8,937,182	194	3,648
1907	17,397,342			1942	8,403,793	187	3,511
1908	17,635,980			1943	11,468,025	209	4,239
1909	16,954,270			1944	14,056,795	252	4,926
1910	19,936,542			1945	19,129,019	378	6,241
1911	16,189,224			1946	18,755,798	473	6,574
1912	16,298,370			1947	18,277,093	516	5,338
1913	8,116,776			1948	15,923,053	439	5,345
1914	8,632,915			1949	19,267,000	462	5,424
1915	11,535,800			1950	18,346,000	430	5,152
1916	10,155,047		3,291	1951	20,750,000	383	4,653
1917				1952	20,027,000	417	5,032
1918				1953	22,286,000	490	5,497
1919	5,793,784		3,867	1954	21,638,000	488	5,794
1920				1955	22,705,000	532	6,051
1921				1956	20,523,000	533	5,492
1922				1957	24,293,000	565	6,068
1923				1958	21,301,000	609	6,236

Table 1.1

Official State Figures on Lobster Catch (continued)

Year	Catch (lbs)	No. traps (thousands)	No. licenses	Year	Catch (lbs)	No. traps (thousands)	No. licenses
1959	22,317,000	717	6,488	1980	21,971,000	1,846	9,200
1960	23,999,000	745	6,636	1981	22,591,000	1,825	8,548
1961	20,904,000	752	6,472	1982	22,833,000	2,143	8,891
1962	22,068,000	767	5,658	1983	21,967,000	2,340	8,895
1963	22,798,000	731	5,695	1984	19,538,000	2,175	8,730
1964	21,407,000	754	5,803	1985	20,184,000	1,766	7,879
1965	18,857,000	789	5,802	1986	19,703,000	1,995	8,875
1966	19,910,000	776	5,613	1987	19,732,000	1,909	8,730
1967	16,483,000	715	5,425	1988	21,656,000	2,053	8,804
1968	20,497,000	747	5,489	1989	23,477,000	2,001	7,215
1969	19,829,000	805	5,750	1990	28,076,000	2,130	6,708
1970	18,167,000	1,180	6,316	1991	30,836,000	2,015	6,940
1971	17,552,000	1,278	6,702	1992	26,879,000	2,012	6,162
1972	16,252,000	1,448	7,045	1993	29,976,000	1,806	6,176
1973	17,039,000	1,172	7,894	1994	38,951,000	2,356	6,503
1974	16,452,000	1,790	10,525	1995	36,525,825	2,408	7,690
1975	17,012,000	1,771	10,455	1996	36,222,628	2,605	7,010
1976	18,996,000	1,750	9,041	1997	47,022,555	2,590	6,400
1977	18,482,000	1,739	8,827	1998	47,030,750	2,825	6,863
1978	19,126,000	1,723	8,712	1999	52,614,536	3,043	6,704
1979	22,130,000	1,810	8,600	2000	57,400,000	2,780	6,884

Conservation Laws

In Maine, one must have a license to fish for lobsters. The basis of lobster management has long been size limitations and regulations designed to protect reproductive or "berried" (egg-bearing) females. At the present time, it is illegal to take lobsters under 3.25-inch carapace length and over 5-inch carapace length, a form of
"slot limit," called the double-gauge law. The minimum size measure protects the
juvenile lobsters and the oversize or 5-inch law protects the large reproductive-size
lobsters. One cannot take egg-bearing lobsters. Another law designed to protect
the reproductive stock is the "V-notch" law. Fishermen catching an egg-bearing
lobster may voluntarily cut a notch in one of the side flippers of the tail, or telson.
Such V-notched lobsters cannot be taken by anyone else as long as the notch
lasts—at least two molts. The V-notch law has received massive support from the
industry, with the result that very large numbers of V-notched females—proven
breeding stock—can be found in the Gulf of Maine.

Capturing the Commons

In addition, Maine law specifies that lobsters may only be taken in traps, which are a highly selective gear. One can pull a trap to the surface, select out the undersize, egged, V-notched, and oversize lobsters. These prohibited lobsters can be put back in the water, where they float back to the bottom unharmed. Traps must have a state-issued trap tag with the fisherman's number. Moreover, each trap must be equipped with an escape vent $1^{15}\!/_{16}$ inches wide to allow sub-legal lobsters to escape, as well as a biodegradable panel, designed to self-destruct over time, to prevent lobsters from being trapped for very long periods in lost or "ghost" traps.

In 1995, the legislature passed the zone management law, which greatly changed many aspects of lobstering. This is a true co-management law, giving the industry control over some important aspects of management. The law divides the coast into zones run by zone councils elected by lobster license-holders. Under this law, an apprenticeship program has been established for the state, and different trap limits and limited entry regulations have been established in different zones.

All of these laws are strongly supported by the lobster fishing industry.

Beginning in the 1960s and continuing through the 1970s, the U.S. Congress passed a number of laws regulating the environment. Four of these were to have a profound impact on the management of fisheries. The most important were the Fisheries Conservation and Management Act (FCMA), which went into effect in 1977 (Public Law 94-265), and the Sustainable Fisheries Act of 1996 (Public Law 104–297), which essentially updated and strengthened the provisions of the FCMA. These laws resulted in actions by agencies of the federal government that the industry opposed. The Congress also passed the Endangered Species and Marine Mammal Acts, but these have had less effect on the lobster industry to date. However, as we shall see, they could pose an extreme threat to the industry in the near future.

Annual Round

The activities of lobster fishermen vary greatly from one season to another. The patterns of fishing activity are influenced by the biology of the lobster, the weather, involvement in other fisheries, and markets.

From the middle of January to mid-March, lobster fishing is at its annual low point. The stormy weather destroys a lot of traps, and makes it very difficult to pull traps often. Moreover, traps are relatively unproductive at this time of year, since the low water temperatures make lobsters inactive and thus far less likely to be caught. Since the best fishing at this time of year is in deep waters 3 to 10 miles from shore where inversion layers keep the water relatively warm, fishermen must spend a lot of time getting to and from the fishing grounds, where they are exposed to the full force of the wind. The only attractions of winter fishing are the fact that the price of lobster is at its annual high and gear tangles are less likely since there are few traps being fished. Despite the high price, many fishermen have only a small number of traps in the water that they pull only a few days each month when the weather permits. Others quit lobster fishing entirely. Some go shrimping or scalloping, while others devote most of their time to building traps and repairing gear for the next season.

As the water begins to warm in the middle of April, lobsters become more active and begin to migrate toward shore. As the weather improves, fishermen place more traps in the water, and pull them more often. The month of May sees an increase both in catches and in traps hauled. Unfortunately, prices usually drop precipitously in May due to a short-term glut of lobsters.

Catches fall dramatically during June and July because large numbers of lobsters are molting and hiding in the rocks at this time. Many fishermen take all of their traps out of the water during these months and spend their time painting their boats and repairing their gear.

During late July and early August, the fishery picks up momentum. More lobsters are available since a new year class has molted into legal size, and lobsters are active in the warm water. Moreover, the price of lobster is relatively high because of the increased demand at the height of the summer tourist season. The weather is usually cooperative and only rarely do fishermen lose days due to storms. Fishermen put more of their traps in the water and fish them hard. One of the few negative sides of the summer fishery is congestion. Since large numbers of lobsters are in shallow water, almost all traps are crowded together in the narrow band of water close to shore or near shoals. Congestion is further increased by the large number of skiff fishermen who enter the fishery at this time of year.

The fall and early winter are the most productive time in the lobster fishery. Catches are very good at this time of year, and fishermen generally put out all of the traps they own. Many sternmen are hired during this period. Between late August and November, approximately two-thirds of the entire year's catch is produced. Unfortunately, immediately after Labor Day prices generally fall to their lowest levels of the year due to high supply and lowered demand as the tourist hordes leave Maine. During this period, very large numbers of lobsters are bought by pound operators, who store them for a few months and then make their profit on the annual price rise.

As fall progresses, the weather becomes increasingly stormy. By November, fishermen are beginning to be forced to stay ashore on bad days. However, there are compensations for the worsening weather. The price of lobsters usually rises steadily throughout the fall. Moreover, trap congestion is less because lobsters begin to move into deeper water where there is more space to fish, and the storms have driven people with skiffs or small inboard-powered boats from the fishery.

Late in December and early in January, the water cools, catches decline, and fishermen pull all or most of their traps out of the water. Those who remain in the fishery place their traps in deep water and do not pull them often.

The Social Environment

Lobstermen are a part of a complicated subculture and social structure. The industry has rules that everyone is expected to obey, its own standards of conduct, and its own mythology.

Capturing the Commons

Lobster fishermen are first and foremost members of families and communities. For many, the town contains the most important social units in their lives. Most of the important social contacts are within towns, and the attention of the inhabitants is focused on their home communities to a large extent. It is no exaggeration to say that much that gives life its meaning is tied up with the local community and the social units it contains.

The most important social units are families. Within every community are a number of old established families with histories in the local area that, in some cases, go back before the American Revolution. Every individual in such families is involved in a thick network of ties created by descent and marriage that convey some tangible assets (Acheson 1988: 35– 42). Much of the social life of these communities revolves around "family activities." Clubs and voluntary associations are of secondary importance.

Beyond the realm of kinship, some of the most important people in a lobster fisherman's life are those who fish from the same harbor. Such social groupings, while they are recognized by everyone in the lobster-fishing industry, have no universally accepted name. People refer to the "Stonington bunch" or the "Monhegan fishermen" or the "Portland gang." I have referred to these groups as "harbor gangs," although this term is only rarely used by the fishermen themselves (Acheson 1972). (In Maine parlance, the term gang does not connote a criminal conspiracy as it does in much of the rest of the country. It is a synonym for "group" or "set.")

Many aspects of the environment within which lobster fishermen work are influenced by membership in a harbor gang. Fishermen identify with a particular harbor gang and are identified as members of it. Members of harbor gangs obtain a great deal of valuable information from one another about fishing locations and innovations. They also depend on each other for assistance in times of emergency at sea. This is one of the reasons that people in a harbor gang keep their radios on the same channel. Perhaps most important, lobstering is territorial; membership in a harbor gang gives access to lobster fishing territory. I will discuss this in detail in the next chapter.

A harbor gang is also a reference group. It is the yardstick by which one measures success. A lobster fisherman competes with members of his own gang. A person is a good fisherman or a bad fisherman in comparison with others in the local lobster fishery. The opinion of people in different harbor gangs does not count for much, because people from different harbor gangs do not know each other that well. Furthermore, lobstermen do not compare themselves to skippers of scallop, groundfish, or herring boats even though they might live in the same town or next door. Such men are in other fishing industries, and are playing a different game by different rules.

Lobster fishermen in the same harbor gang ordinarily have long-term, multi-stranded ties with one another. Most live in the town where the harbor is located. Many are members of long-established families with a variety of kinship ties to each other. Members of harbor gangs in the same generation have grown up together, have gone to the same schools, and have been members of the same sports teams and clubs.

The amount of interaction among fishermen varies considerably. Within each gang, some fishermen belong to cliques of friends and relatives who sometimes spend hours each day talking on the docks, visiting each other's homes, radioing each other at sea, or helping each other with tasks. Others remain quite solitary. As might be expected, some of these individuals are relatively marginal to the gang, but others are very popular and are considered to be important members.

Every member of a harbor gang knows every other member by sight and reputation. In the small gangs, fishermen know a good deal about each other's behavior and monitor each other constantly. In the larger gangs, the scrutiny is less intense, but fishermen are never completely anonymous and have difficulty keeping much secret.

In all harbor gangs, fishermen are expected to obey certain rules. People are expected to obey the conservation laws and avoid molesting the traps of other men. Everywhere, it is considered poor form to place traps in places where they will become entangled with those of others. Harbor gangs also have local rules. For example, on Monhegan Island one does not leave one's skiff or fishing equipment for long periods on the only beach on the island, where it will impede the activities of other fishermen. In Stonington, fishermen do not leave their boats at the town wharf overnight where they will make it impossible for vessels to use the wharf in emergencies. Some harbor gangs also have informal trap limits.

Fishermen are capable of putting intense pressure on each other to conform to group norms. Young fishermen who inadvertently cause problems by clogging docks with their traps or leaving their skiffs in places that bother other people are usually corrected verbally. Older fishermen who violate local rules repeatedly are treated much more roughly. In some cases they are sanctioned in meetings with other fishermen, in other cases by screaming matches or fist fights. In all cases, fishermen who gain the reputation of violating serious norms such as molesting the gear of other men or stealing lobsters from their traps or violating the conservation laws will be seriously punished. In some cases, they will be driven from the business.

Lobstermen often have little or no contact with other lobster fishermen from other harbor gangs, even when the harbors are only a few miles distant. This is the result of a coastal geography with long peninsulas making transportation difficult, as well as a history of inter-gang competition for lobster fishing territory. Members of different harbor gangs tend to think of each other in terms of stereotypes, which can range from relatively benign to very negative (Acheson 1988: 51).

One's standing in the harbor gang is determined both by fishing success and by adherence to valued norms of the community (see Acheson 1988: 52–63). Fishermen with high prestige usually are called on to assume leadership roles in the political affairs of the gang. They are elected to political offices in organizations influencing lobster fishing, and they tend to represent the harbor gang in dealings with all kinds of outsiders. They are treated with deference and their opinions are

Capturing the Commons

sought by others. Their influence on lobster politics is far out of proportion to their numbers.

Members of harbor gangs can be very competitive, and as in all small groups, they strive to ensure that other members conform to expectations. As we shall see, these characteristics of harbor gangs have an important influence on the politics and the ability of lobster fishermen to devise rules for their industry.

CHAPTER 2

Spatial Strategies and Territoriality

*T*he state of Maine is currently home to several different ocean tenure systems that operate at different scales and involve different principles. One territorial system exists at the local scale and is defined by local practice. Another exists at the level of the state and is codified into state law. Still a third has been imposed by the federal government after 1977 and the passage of the Fisheries Conservation and Management Act, which gave federal authorities power to manage the fisheries out to 200 miles. In this book, we will be primarily concerned with changes in the local-level system. The term "territoriality" is used here to refer to the local-scale system. Of secondary concern is the state system, which has had some effect on the local-scale system, especially in law enforcement. (We will discuss the territorial system operating at the federal scale in chapter 8.)

According to the law of Maine, all of the oceans, lakes, and rivers are public property. Ocean waters are held in trust by the state for all citizens. All ocean beaches to the high tide mark are owned by the state, and all citizens have legal access to them.[1]

In the lobster fishery, a different tradition prevails. Here, local fishing territories are the rule. To go lobstering, one needs a state license, which ostensibly allows a person to fish anywhere in state waters. In reality, more is required. One also needs to gain admission to a "harbor gang" that maintains a fishing territory for the use of its members. This means that two different groups with different kinds of authority have laid claim to the same inshore waters.

In the Maine lobster fishery, potential conflict between these two systems is kept to a minimum by the people involved, who avoid actions that would directly challenge those in the other system. Among state fishery officials, there has been a tacit acceptance of the traditional territorial system. Everyone knows it exists, but it has generally been accepted as long as violence and destruction of property are kept to a minimum and do not come to public attention. When they do, those cutting traps are prosecuted in court, long-standing tradition aside. In this sense, the lobster industry has operated as what Bailey (1969) calls an encapsulated political system—a system within a system—in which both public officials and lobster fishermen made accommodation to each other. Both sides historically have treated the territorial system like a skeleton in the closet; everyone knew it was there, but no one wanted to admit to its existence.

In recent years, the local-scale territorial system of the Maine lobster industry has undergone a number of important changes. Some have stemmed from technological and economic factors. Others have resulted from new management laws and enforcement activities of the government.

Harbor gangs are quite small. Many harbors contain as few as six or eight boats, and it is a rare harbor that has as many as fifty. The territories are small as well. The largest are no more than 100 square miles in area, and not all of this area is productive of lobsters. It is rare that a lobsterman will work more than 15 miles from his home harbor, and most are usually within 6 or 7 miles of their harbors even in winter. This means that a lobster fishermen spends his entire working life crisscrossing one small area of bottom that he fishes with a few others whom he knows quite well. In this respect, the lobster fishery differs radically from the groundfishery, where boats regularly make trips all over the Gulf of Maine, sometimes traveling more than 1,000 miles on a trip, and from sword-fishing boats that regularly fish between Cape Race, Newfoundland, and the Flemish Cap, halfway to Europe.

Each harbor where boats are moored normally has its own harbor gang and fishing territory. Usually there are as many territories in a township as there are harbors. The town of Saint George, for example, has four separate lobster fishing territories: Wheeler's Bay, Tenant's Harbor, Muscongus, and Port Clyde. A few of the largest harbors in the state have two gangs; for example, Friendship, has one group that fishes the Georges Island area and another that fishes more to the westward in Muscongus Bay. Unoccupied islands are usually incorporated into the territory of adjacent mainland harbor gangs, but occupied islands further offshore usually have separate territories designated by the island name.

When talking to people who are not in their harbor gang, fishermen will describe territories in very general terms. They will talk about territories along shore in terms of bays, mouths of rivers, or townships. Offshore they will speak of islands, channels, or ridges. Actual territorial boundaries are far more precise, and are demarcated by very small geographical features familiar only to people with an intimate knowledge of the area. Along shore, boundaries are marked by such small features as coves, trees, houses, or a rock formation on an island. Offshore, lines are defined in a number of ways. Some are described in terms of two or more visible landmarks. Others are defined in terms of underwater features such as the edge of a gully. Increasingly, they are marked off with Loran, radar, or GPS (geographic positioning systems). For example, when fishing along shore, the fishermen from Pemaquid Harbor can go no further east than Pumpkin Cove on the east shore of Pemaquid Point. The eastern line of Green Island is an imaginary line that runs north and south through a buoy in the middle of the channel. The eastern boundary of Metinic Island is a line running from Two Bush Lighthouse to Home Harbor, a small harbor on Hewett's Island further to the north. Part of the offshore boundary of Tenant's Harbor is defined in terms of the 12780 Loran C line. Seen on a chart, these fishing territories rarely have neat, regular geometric shapes. Usually they appear to be areas defined in terms of irregular lines of different lengths and shapes intersecting each other at odd angles.

Most territories are contiguous, so that one can go from one part of the territory to another without running across areas fished by other harbor gangs. However, in some parts of the coast, winter fishing grounds offshore are separated from inshore summer fishing grounds by territories fished by other gangs. This appears to be true particularly in lower Penobscot Bay.

Knowledge of territorial boundaries is a highly localized phenomenon in that fishermen know only those boundaries that affect them directly. People from Boothbay Harbor, for example, know the line between their area and Little River, but they do not know much about the lines between South Bristol and Pemaquid Beach to the east, or between Five Islands and Bay Point to the westward, even though those harbors are within 7 miles of Boothbay. In part, this lack of awareness is the result of the geography of the region. Communities are on long peninsulas, making contact by road difficult. In part, it is due to the lobstermen's general reluctance to talk about territoriality.

In general, demarcation of territorial lines varies with distance from shore. Close to shore, boundaries are known to the yard. In summer, when people are fishing close to shore, care is taken to place traps on one's own side of the line. Further offshore, people from several different harbors are normally fishing in the same area. Boundaries are less precise and not defended as vigorously. If one goes offshore far enough, there is no sense of territoriality at all. Fifteen miles from land, one can usually place traps where one wants. In great part, this pattern is connected to the amount of competition for fishing space. In the summer, when lobsters are concentrated close to shore, a large number of traps are in use within relatively little fishing area, due to the influx of hundreds of part-time skiff fishermen. "Shedder bottom," or summer fishing in shallow water, is a scarce resource, and people are prone to protect it. In mid-winter, when lobsters are best caught in deep water miles from shore, competition for fishing space is not keen. There are far more square miles of offshore fishing ground, full-time fishermen are using fewer traps, and the stormy weather has driven fishermen with small boats out of the fishery entirely.

However, where one fishes is not determined by the territorial system alone. It is influenced by the costs and benefits of territorial defense, in combination with costs of transportation and the revenues to be earned in various fishing locations. In mid-winter, when lobsters are concentrated in deep waters, the distance fishermen will go to place traps is strongly influenced by transportation costs. At this time of year, they regularly find it worthwhile to go 18 or 20 miles toward open ocean. Going much farther than this is not considered to be profitable, given the relatively low catches. The choice of offshore fishing locations is not strongly influenced by political considerations, for such areas are open to fishermen from all harbors and one is not likely to lose traps in territorial defense forays.

In the summer and early fall, trap placement is primarily determined by territorial rules. At this time of year, fishermen place traps in shallow water (i.e., "shedder bottom") within a few miles of the mouth of their home harbor and avoid

Capturing the Commons

going into areas controlled by other harbor gangs to avoid conflict and trap losses. Even though transportation costs to some of this desirable area would be very low, the costs in terms of trap losses and conflict would be very high. As a result, trap placement cannot be explained in terms of proximity to one's home harbor. Fishermen from Pemaquid Harbor, for example, regularly place traps 18 miles at sea in mid-winter but cannot place them in the South Bristol "gut" less than 2 miles from home (see map on page 49).

Members of a lobster gang ordinarily are allowed to fish anywhere within the territory controlled by that harbor, with some notable caveats. People are expected not to dump their gear on top of gear placed by other fishermen. Those who have placed their gear first in an area are ordinarily thought to have usufructory rights; others cannot enter the area until someone else leaves. In addition, older, high status fishermen have their favorite spots, which they may have been fishing for years or decades. Many of these are highly productive areas. Others, especially younger, less experienced fishermen, are well advised to stay clear of such places. Some part-timers are quite restricted in where they can place traps. I know two who place traps only in the coves in front of their cottages. They have been told that their traps are safe in those locations, but may be molested if they are placed elsewhere.

Boundary Defense

When a person or a group decides to defend "their" fishing territory against incursion, they will usually warn the interloper. Sometimes, the interloper is threatened verbally or abused in some way, but more usually there is some molestation of his gear. Sometimes two half hitches of rope are tied around the spindles of the offending traps; in others, bottles are left in the trap with notes; sometimes the heads in the traps are cut out; in still other cases, the traps are pulled, the legal-sized lobsters are taken out, and the doors of the trap are cut off. In other instances, buoys of the offending traps are tied together. In many cases, interlopers will move their traps when pointedly warned in this way. If the violation continues, the defenders may decide not to take further action or they may decide to sanction the interloper further. When they decide further action is warranted, they almost always will destroy the offending traps. This is normally done by pulling the trap, putting the warp line and buoy inside the trap and pushing it over the side. Sometimes the trap is pushed over in deep water where chances of finding it are slim. In such instances, the owner may never be certain what happened to his traps. Sometimes traps are destroyed in ways that advertise the fact that destruction has been purposeful. Buoys and warp lines may be cut off by the dozens and can be found floating all over the bay for days. Traps may be cut in half using a chain saw or wire cutters. When these traps are pulled, there is no mistaking what has happened.

Cutting traps is a very effective way of defending fishing areas. People do not have to resort to more severe sanctions. There is no practical way of protecting traps in the water. Moreover, removing traps not only removes the symbol of someone else's incursion into your territory; it also limits the intruder's ability to reduce the defender's catch, the prime goal.

When trap-cutting incidents occur, they are usually kept quiet. Those doing the trap cutting rarely advertise their "skill with the knife" to prevent retaliation by the victim and prosecution. Destroying other people's gear is illegal and can lead to a stiff fine and even a loss of license. Cutting other people's traps is considered somewhat shameful, even though it is considered justified in many cases. In the past, people whose traps were cut did not complain much either. Often they were not sure if their traps were deliberately destroyed or had fallen victim to the weather or a passing boat. One fishermen said, "when traps are cut all you have is a lot of hearsay." Even when they are certain that their traps had been purposely destroyed, they could only guess who was responsible, and rarely had any evidence. Increasingly, however, victims of trap cutting are going to the police and wardens to seek redress.

Certain factors work to increase friction between men in different harbor gangs and thus stimulate trap cutting; other factors serve to keep conflict in check. Virtually every day, someone in a harbor gang has traps missing. Sometimes this is due to the weather or from being cut off by the propellor of a passing boat. In other cases, traps are deliberately destroyed by other fishermen. Some will cut traps out of frustration with trap tangles caused by people placing traps too close to their own. Competition and past feuds are the root of other incidents.

Much friction between harbor gangs is caused by "pushing the lines," the practice of maintaining fishing area by using all of their territory or perhaps a little more. "Use it or lose it is the rule in lobster fishing," one man explained. Even after a peripheral area has ceased to be productive, fishermen will leave a few traps there to strengthen their claim to the area.

In most cases, people touch each other's traps only with great reluctance, knowing that their own gear is vulnerable. They are fully aware that a person whose traps have been cut will often retaliate, often against the wrong person. Such trap-cutting incidents can quickly escalate into a costly and comic vendetta, with fishermen blindly retaliating against the innocent and guilty alike. As a result, when people defend a fishing area, they use a good deal of care not to provoke a massive or violent response. "The secret of driving a man from your area," one man explained, "is to cut off just one or two traps at a time." This makes fishing in the area unprofitable, but does not make the intruder mad enough to risk a feud, particularly since he can never be certain who is responsible.

However, once or twice a decade, somewhere along the coast, a full-scale "lobster war" will break out in which dozens of fishermen will destroy hundreds of traps, and even burn wharfs and sink boats. Such incidents are gleefully reported in the press, with the result that the entire industry has had an unsavory reputation. Such incidents serve as a warning to people in the industry. Thoughtful fishermen realize that no one gains from such "wars," and they would certainly not want to be caught up in one under any circumstances. As a result, they are becom-

Capturing the Commons

ing increasingly rare. As anthropologist Evans-Pritchard (1940) pointed out a generation ago, the threat of a feud can be very effective in maintaining peace.

In the Maine lobster industry, the territorial system has long been a part of the social organization of the industry. Everyone understands the norms concerning where they can fish, and most of the time they obey them. As a result, there is very little trouble.

Nucleated and Perimeter-Defended Areas

In Maine at the present, two different kinds of lobstering territories exist, which I call nucleated and perimeter-defended territories (Acheson 1975b; 1988). They differ in the amount of boundary permeability permitted and the ease of entry into harbor gangs.

Most of the harbors in the state exhibit nucleated territoriality, including virtually all of the harbors on the mainland. In these territories, the sense of ownership is very strong close to the mouth of the home harbor where the boats are anchored, but grows progressively weaker the further from the harbor one goes. Intruders placing their traps close to the harbor mouth will quickly lose them. Several miles from shore, the sense of territoriality is weak and a good deal of "mixed fishing" takes place. Entry into these harbor gangs is relatively easy.

Perimeter-defended areas are found off a few islands and a few mainland areas, especially in Penobscot Bay. Here the territory is defined in terms of the peripheral boundaries, which are known to the yard and defended vigorously. In these areas, the sense of ownership remains strong out to the perimeter of the territories. Little or no mixed fishing is permitted. Entry into the harbor gangs controlling these perimeter-defended territories is much more difficult.

Nucleated areas have far larger territories, and the gangs controlling them have more fishermen than those in perimeter-defended areas. For example, thirty full-time boats fish from New Harbor; sixty from Boothbay; and forty-five from Tenant's Harbor. Friendship and Stonington, two of the largest ports in the state, have over two hundred boats in each. By way of contrast, the perimeter-defended area of Monhegan Island currently has twelve lobster boats, Green Island has nine, and Criehaven has eleven.

There are also important differences in the social organization of the gangs having these two different types of territoriality. People in perimeter-defended areas interact a good deal and know each other very well. These are primary groups in which everyone has a number of ties with the other fishermen and their families. On the permanently occupied islands, there is a strong sense of community. In nucleated areas, there is far less interaction. Many fishermen may know only a few other fishermen well, and have little to do with most of the members of the gang. In time of need, many members have only a few people they can call on for help. As we shall see, these differences have important implications for changes in territoriality and territorial defense.

Entry into Gangs. Since the entire coast is fished by the men from one harbor gang or another, a person has to gain entrance to such a group before he can go fishing at all.

Anyone seeking to go lobstering in nucleated territories will experience some hostility from those already established in the business. Most fishermen will have some of their gear molested for a few months after they start, but in some cases the harassment can continue for one or two years. A couple of established fishermen laughingly said that this amounts to a kind of initiation. Newcomers rarely think this is funny, especially since their position is apt to be very precarious. More than a few have become discouraged and have been driven out of business by people from the gang they are seeking to enter. After a time, most newcomers are accepted into the gang and the harassment gradually stops. Some people never really are accepted and remain marginal for years.

The hostility to newcomers is understandable. More fishermen in a harbor gang means more competition and fewer lobsters for those established in the business. Arthur Pierce of Sebasco Estates pointed out, "Like any business, no one likes to see competition." Moreover, novice fishermen do not know local practices, are bound to make mistakes, get their gear tangled with those of others, and may even need to be rescued on occasion.

The amount of harassment a person experiences depends greatly on personal characteristics. Age at time of entry, family background, residence, and willingness to abide by local norms are critical. A person will experience less resistance if he comes from the local community, is a member of an old established family with a long history of involvement in the fishery, and has other older relatives in the harbor gang. Such a person almost inherits a position in the harbor gang. His entry will be made easier if he begins fishing as a youngster in a skiff in the summer and then becomes a full-time fisherman after high school or college.

A person will have the most difficulty entering a harbor gang if he moves into the area from out of state, if his family has no connection to fishing, and if he begins fishing in middle age. He will almost certainly be treated very roughly if he begins fishing a large number of traps, and has another source of income. Such a person is regarded as an "outsider" with no rights to the local resources. He also is viewed as a "hog," taking more than his share at the expense of people who have no other way of earning an income. More important, he has no allies in the local community.

Perhaps the single most important factor influencing entry into a harbor gang is willingness to abide by local norms and the conservation laws. A person who molests other people's gear, takes lobsters from their traps, or sells short lobsters will not last long in the industry, regardless of family ties or age.

In most cases, part-time fishermen will have a more difficult time in gaining acceptance than full-time fishermen despite the fact that full-time fishermen use more traps and take more lobsters. The hostility directed at part-timers stems in great part from the fact that they are seen to be competing unfairly. They already have one job, usually one giving good benefits, and yet are taking lobsters from someone who has no other source of income. In addition, they are not as dependent on the industry, with the result that many have a more cavalier attitude toward local norms and practices.

Fishing rights in nucleated areas are usufructory to a large extent. If a person moves away from town and stops fishing, his claim to fishing rights becomes progressively weaker. His children will have a more difficult time entering lobster fishing than if he were an active member of the harbor gang. If he stays away from town for more than a few years, he might have a difficult time rejoining the harbor gang.

In the years before and after World War II, it was far more difficult to enter lobstering. People from out of town were not permitted to join a harbor gang, and men from non-fishing families were harassed more. It was not at all uncommon, according to older informants, for aspiring lobster fishermen to be told that they were not welcome, either in verbal confrontations, by letters, or by obvious and hateful harassment, such as having garbage dumped in their boat. Even hiring people from other communities as sternmen was frowned upon, out of fear that such people might find their way into the harbor gang eventually. John Olson from Cushing recalls that when he hired a sternman from an island community decades ago, he was invited to a big meeting of fishermen from his home harbor and pointedly asked to fire the man. He did not do so, and he was ostracized by several people for months. Rejection of newcomers to the fishery was often buttressed by an ideology stressing that resources, including land, jobs, and fishing area, should be reserved for people from old established families from the local community.

Over the course of the past half century, it has become easier to enter harbor gangs of nucleated areas. Many people have entered the industry who are not from lobster fishing families, and a lot of people "from away" have succeeded in becoming lobster fishermen. Several factors have made people more tolerant of new entrants. Educational levels are higher. People know more people from other communities due to school consolidation, and the ideology that fish resources are reserved for people from old established fishing families seems increasingly antiquated and provincial. Virtually every harbor has several lobster fishermen who live in other towns. In the 1990s, virtually anyone will be accepted eventually who makes friends in the community, does not violate local fishing norms, and begins fishing in a way that does not greatly affect the amount of lobsters available to others.

As a result of a relaxation of the barriers to entry in nucleated areas, the number of active fishermen in every harbor has grown. For example, David Cousens, President of the Maine Lobstermen's Association, reports that when he began fishing thirty years ago, "There were fifteen people fishing in the South Thomaston area; now there are almost sixty."

Territorial Defense. In nucleated areas, incursions into the area normally fished by another gang meets with no automatic response. Sometimes when traps are placed in areas that are considered to belong to another gang, the intruders get away with the incursion for a long time. In other cases, intruders are sanctioned quickly. Two factors strongly influence how intrusion is treated. The first concerns how many traps are being placed and where they are placed. People can sometimes place a few traps in fishing locations at the outer limit of the territory of a neighboring gang, and have little difficulty for months. People might grouse, and some of the intruder's traps might disappear when they become entangled with those of men who consider the territory their own, but no attempt will be made to repel this person. On the other hand, placing a large number of traps deep in the territory of another gang will usually provoke a reaction.

Second, some people are permitted to fish in areas where others from the same gang cannot go without courting trouble. Those with a lot of potential allies can get away with incursions better than those who are not in position to get support from many others. For this reason, older respected fishermen from large, well-established families can get away with incursions better than younger fishermen, unpopular men, or newcomers. No one wants to court trouble with a respected leader of a harbor gang who can bring to his aid six or eight kinsmen and friends. Such a person is not only apt to be able to defeat his adversaries, but may be able to brand his enemies as unsavory criminals and troublemakers. Another factor that allows people to fish a wider territory is family and friendship ties. One person from Portland fishes very close to a Casco Bay island, in an area most islanders see as theirs exclusively. He explained, "They [the islanders] are not going to bother me. My wife came from [name of island] and my brothers-in-law fish on the island. We are on good terms."

Last, people who have changed harbor gangs are often still allowed to fish in the area of their original harbor gang. One man who used to fish out of Pemaquid Harbor moved his boat to South Bristol and began to sell his lobsters in South Bristol. Although most people now consider him a South Bristol fisherman, he continues to fish an area that Pemaquid Harbor fishermen consider their exclusive area. To date, he has not been bothered.

In much of the area fished by people from nucleated areas, mixed fishing is allowed. But "mixed fishing" does not mean open access. For example, the area around the Western Egg Rock in Muscongus Bay is fished by people from New Harbor, Round Pond, Bremen, and Friendship. But fishermen from Cushing or Boothbay would certainly court trouble if they fished there. Moreover, in harbors where a good deal of "mixed fishing" is allowed, people usually cannot place traps around the harbor mouths of other harbor gangs. This is an area that is normally fished exclusively by other harbor gangs. For example, the people from South Bristol share most of John's Bay with the fishermen from Pemaquid Harbor, but the South Bristol men cannot go beyond Beaver Island, about one-half mile from the anchorage in the Pemaquid River, and the Pemaquid Harbor fishermen cannot fish in the "Gut," the narrow body of water where the South Bristol fishermen anchor and which is their exclusive area.[2]

The social organization of the gangs fishing most perimeter-defended areas is very different from that of the nucleated areas. These gangs are operating under conditions that have made it possible to develop rules and practices concerning fishing that confer joint benefits on the gang as a whole. The rules concerning territory are different; they have developed strict rules limiting entry to their harbor gangs; they are better able to defend their fishing territory; and some have developed informal trap limits. In this chapter, I describe the territorial rules and the defense of those territories. The next chapter will cover the complicated circumstances allowing these gangs to develop rules for mutual benefit.

One of the primary characteristics of perimeter-defended areas is the strong defense of the island's boundaries. Interlopers placing traps within the borders of such areas are almost certain to lose traps very quickly to the harbor gangs owning these areas, who traditionally have shown little tolerance for those who violate their boundaries. In these areas, little mixed fishing is the rule.

Part of the defense strategy of these islanders is to make sure that their territory is utilized out to the borders so not a lot of space is available for additional traps. Unused bottom is an open invitation for others to move in. If others move into your area, it is advisable to deal with the situation immediately. One person explains, "Once you have lost bottom for a year or two it is hell to get it back. It is the young guys who cannot remember who are the problem. They say 'but we fished there the past two years.' They can't remember you have been there for the past fifty. Old guys will not defend it against them and so it goes [i.e., is lost to another gang]."

Some fishermen defending perimeter-defended areas show little remorse about cutting traps of interlopers. One said: "When you go over the line, they put two half hitches on the spindle of the buoy. This means take them out of there. If you do not want to lose your traps, move them. If you do not move your traps, it is your own fault."

There is a feeling among all concerned that if the people "owning" perimeter-defended areas are not going to permit any fishing in their area, they should not expect a share of the fishing area outside of it. Still, in a number of cases, gangs from perimeter-defended areas insist on maintaining exclusive fishing rights to the area within their boundaries and still fish in deep water, outside the boundary, in the winter. One island fisherman admitted to fishing outside the boundaries of his perimeter-defended area even though his harbor gang has made no claim to the territory. He said, "We have taken the area over, and they have not pushed us back." He admits they would probably abandon this area if anyone seriously opposed them.

In perimeter-defended areas, the sense of ownership of fishing area is far stronger and more permanent than in nucleated areas. On most of these islands, land ownership combined with generations of use conveys fishing rights, in the local culture, if not in the eyes of the law. There is a tradition that people who own the land have a right to the "short warp" fishing near shore. Since virtually all of these fishermen own land or houses on the island, in their view they have rights to the waters near the island. Even if a member of a perimeter-defended area is not currently fishing, his rights to fish remain. He owns land, after all. Islanders worry that in selling land to "summer people," they and their kinsmen will lose fishing rights, which they regard as an insurance policy of sorts. Interestingly enough, if land is sold to an outsider, the new owner may be permitted to go lobster fishing, although this is not always the case. Lobstering rights are not automatically transferred in a deed.

Those fishing perimeter-defended areas have a strong historical sense. In their view, they are carrying on the traditions of their grandparents and even great grandparents. As in many communities, longevity gives sanctity to norms. One island fisherman voiced this sentiment well when he said, "my family has owned this island since before Maine became a state, and the state isn't going to take these waters away from us." Cultures, as all anthropologists know, are very persistent.

As a result, people will buy islands, in great part, to get the fishing rights ownership confers. One person I know, who lives in the Rockland area, bought a small island in the Muscle Ridge channel in the 1970s. "I can go fishing off the island in the summer, and it is a good investment," he said.

Entry into Gangs. It is vastly more difficult to gain entrance to the harbor gangs exploiting perimeter-defended areas. This is to be expected, given the fact that the objectives of territorial defense and barriers to entry are linked. The objective of maintaining strict boundaries around an ocean area is to keep the number of fishermen low to decrease competition. There is no sense incurring the costs of defending such a territory against incursions of other harbor gangs if anyone can join your own.

Every perimeter-defended territory has developed a set of rules restricting membership in the gang. They are highly restrictive and make it impossible for most people to enter the gang. As we will see in the next chapter, the rules governing entrance to these gangs vary considerably from one perimeter-defended area to another.

Territorial Defense. Several factors have aided the men fishing island territories in maintaining their exclusive areas. The primary factor is an ability to convince island fishermen to cooperate in organizing an effective defense. While the social organization of these islands varies somewhat, a number of factors make the defense of their island territories especially effective. The island gangs are able to organize a large number of people to defend their territory. While the number of people on the island may be small, the number of people they can muster on the line may be far larger than those wishing to invade their area. The islanders are often well led, and they have a long-term strategy that everyone in the team supports. In many cases the leaders are older men, usually respected highliners, who can persuade or bully others into doing what they want.

In addition, these gangs are small, so it is easy to monitor the activities of gang members. There is also a strong sense of community and people are very dependent on each other. Moreover, these islands are very dependent on the lobster fishery. On many islands, it is literally the only way to make a living. Many islanders are quick to say that if the lobster fishery fails, the permanent community of these islands would cease to exist. Within these harbor gangs, it is not wise to get the reputation of not doing one's share to defend the most valuable resource the island has—its lobster fishing territory.

All of these characteristics of island communities make it very difficult for fishermen to free-ride on the defense efforts of others. People are fully aware that their participation is crucial in defending the territory. One person said that one time a person who had been doing more than his share to maintain the territorial boundaries came to him and said, "I am tired of doing the dirty work. I want some help or I am all done. One or two of us came to the rescue. If that hadn't been enough, we would have got one or two more. We keep coming together [in a coalition] until you get what you need to do the job [i.e., drive off intruders]." They have been most successful.

In summary, the people in perimeter-defended areas have been able to solve two collective action dilemmas, which the people fishing nucleated territories have been unable to handle. They have been able to generate rules and practices that limit entry to their harbor gangs. They have also been able to organize the defense of their territory. In both cases, the incentives to be "free riders" are strong. As we will see in the next chapter, the same variables that aid these island harbor gangs in coordinating the defense of their lobster fishing territory and limiting entry to their gangs also help them to solve the collective action dilemma posed by the trap limit.

In the past, distance and the costs of transportation protected island areas to a large degree. However, with the advent of larger and faster boats, this is no longer true. In this regard, it should be noted that some of the perimeter-defended islands are currently unoccupied, and the men exploiting the island waters find it worthwhile to travel back and forth every few days or even every day. Distance does not deter them, even though it adds to their costs of doing business.

Economic and Biological Effects of Territoriality

A study done in 1973 and 1974 of a large number of traps hauled by twenty-eight fishermen from three nucleated harbors (Port Clyde, New Harbor, and Friendship) and three perimeter-defended harbors (Green Island, Metinic, Monhegan) revealed a number of biological and economic differences. While these differences have been reported in detail elsewhere (see Acheson 1975b; 1988: 152–58; McCay and Acheson 1987), a brief summary of these results is warranted.

The limited entry rules found in perimeter-defended areas in combination with spirited defense of boundaries has resulted in fewer boats fishing in these areas, and more fishing area per boat. For example, in 1988 in Port Clyde there were thirty-nine full-time boats, with .8 square nautical miles per boat. Green Island had eight boats with 1.4 square nautical miles per boat (Acheson 1988: 154).

In addition, a number of favorable biological effects are observed in perimeter-defended areas. Lobster fishermen in perimeter-defended areas catch more lobsters per unit of effort than people in nucleated areas, and those lobsters are larger. In every season of the year, the pounds of lobster caught per trap, the size of those lobster, and the pounds per trap per set over day are greater in perimeter-defended than in nucleated areas (see Acheson 1988: 155–58). These figures indicate that the breeding stock and stock density are larger in perimeter-defended areas than in nucleated areas.

These differences in productivity have economic implications. The larger number of pounds of lobster produced per trap means that the average trap hauled in a perimeter-defended area produces more revenue for its owner than one pulled in a nucleated area. It also means that people fishing perimeter-defended areas trap a larger number of big lobsters, which bring a higher price per pound, since they can be sold as "dinner lobsters" to upscale seafood restaurants.

What produces the favorable biological and economic effect in perimeter-defended areas? Without doubt, one cause is the limited entry rules and defense of territory, resulting in fewer fishermen and more space per fisherman. In addition, several of the perimeter-defended areas, including all of those in the sample, have self-imposed trap limits (discussed in the next chapter). Since each fisherman in perimeter-defended areas has more productive bottom and the same number or fewer traps than people in nucleated areas, it is not surprising that the average number of pounds per trap is higher than it is in mainland harbors where trap congestion is a serious problem. This may result in less exploitive pressure on the lobsters. In perimeter-defended areas, lobsters are older and thus larger when they are caught, and more survive to the size where they can extrude eggs.

Another factor that almost certainly plays a role in producing the favorable biological effects observed in perimeter-defended areas is the tendency for more large lobsters to migrate to deep water than smaller lobsters. This differential migration almost certainly helps to explain the larger number of big lobsters in perimeter-defended areas that have more deep waters, as well as the larger number of egged lobsters. However, there is no reason to think that migration affects the stock size. The larger stock sizes observed in perimeter-defended areas are almost certainly due to lower fishing pressure.

One of the most basic tenets of rational choice theory is that rules are devised to give people the benefits of coordinated action. The differences in catches, incomes, and catch per unit of effort of fishermen in perimeter-defended and nucleated areas have been reported in detail elsewhere (Acheson 1988: 155–58). The figures described there strongly suggest that both economic and biological benefits are conferred by boundary rules and limited entry rules on perimeter-defended islands.

Over the course of the past hundred years, all lobster fishing boundaries have moved, some far more than others. In Penobscot Bay, there has been relatively little movement. David Cousens, President of the Maine Lobstermen's Association, who fishes from South Thomaston, said "none of these lines have changed appreciably in the past eighty years." In the area from Muscongus Bay to Casco Bay, substantial boundary movement has occurred rapidly.

Technological changes opened the possibility for boundary changes. As rowing dories and sailing vessels were replaced by larger boats with gasoline-powered engines, the distance people could travel increased, along with the number of months they could fish. Powered trap haulers (1930s and 1940s) made it possible to fish more traps over a far wider area, while depth finders, coming on the scene in the 1950s, made it possible to learn the bottom. Radio gave people advanced warning of storms. By the middle of the twentieth century, it was possible for large numbers of fishermen to exploit waters miles from their home harbors efficiently during the winter months in reasonable safety. While the new technology increased the area a person can fish, this does not explain why people are allowed to fish large areas along the mainland, and are more restrained in the more eastern areas around Penobscot Bay. The technology is the same along the entire coast.

The differential breakdown of boundaries is a side effect of the competition of groups of fishermen for fishing space, which results in changes in territorial lines. A change in boundaries occurs when individuals or a group, usually from one harbor, successfully invade a place that had been fished by people from another. Boundary changes occur at varying rates of speed, and involve different amounts of violence

At times, very rapid boundary movement can take place without violence. This has occurred in several instances when island residents have moved to the mainland and decided not to defend island areas. In those cases, the traditional island areas are incorporated into the areas of nearby mainland towns. In the 1950s, the Loud's Island area was incorporated into the Round Pond and Bremen areas; and Teels Island was sold to an outsider and its traditional fishing ground was appropriated by men from Port Clyde and Cushing.

In other instances, boundaries move as a result of slow, long-term incursions of a group of fishermen into the area held by another. Until the 1980s, fishermen from Back Narrows on the upper Damariscotta River defended an area in the upper river that they fished exclusively. Fishermen from South Bristol did not fish above Fort Island. In the 1990s, the Back Narrows fishermen began to fish further down the Damariscotta River in areas that had been fished only by men from South Bristol and Little River, and the South Bristol fishermen began to place traps far up the river. This was accomplished with virtually no trap molestation by either side. In the summer of 2000, it was reported that two men from South Bristol were placing traps all the way to the town of Damariscotta, some 12 miles north of South Bristol. This means that all boundaries have disappeared in the Damariscotta River, at least temporarily.

In some cases, invasions of territories meet with very stiff resistence and a good deal of violence ensues. In the 1950s, six men from Tenant's Harbor decided to fish in the area of one of the perimeter-defended islands in Penobscot Bay. They deliberately set traps over the boundary line. When their traps were cut off, they retaliated in kind. After several forays in which dozens of traps were lost (duly reported in the press), the islanders retreated a few hundred yards and a new boundary was established.

Not all attempts to increase fishing areas succeed. For decades, repeated forays have been made against some of the boundaries of perimeter-defended areas. To date, the owners of these island territories have been able to repel every invasion, sometimes at considerable cost, maintaining their boundary intact.

Boundary movements are rarely the result of actions taken by individuals acting completely alone. To be sure, individuals get into small fracases all the time. Some people seem to have a penchant for trouble, continually crowd others, and push boundaries. It is a rare day when at least one fisherman in a harbor gang does not suspect that some of his traps have been molested in some way. Sometimes they retaliate. Although such small-scale disputes are widely noted on the local level, they are apt to result in stalemates with little effect on boundaries.

Boundary movement, when it occurs, is almost always the result of actions by groups of individuals. One group of fishermen will move into the area fished by another, and that other group is not successful in defending its fishing area, or decides not to defend it. I will call these groups of fishermen who are competing for territory "political teams" after Frederick G. Bailey (1969). It is very difficult to obtain accurate information on these groups, since they are involved in conflict and a certain amount of illegal activity. Some aspects of such teams are apparent, however.

Political teams of lobster fishermen are apt to be fairly small. Most involve three to eight fishermen; only very rarely can fifteen or twenty coordinate their actions for long. There is a strong tendency for such teams to be composed of young fishermen who are as much interested in raising hell and excitement as they are in the more serious side of political conflict at sea. Older men might instigate fights, but they rarely are in the thick of them.

There are, however, major differences in organization and duration of these groups. In many harbors, when political teams are formed at all, they tend to be groups of friends or acquaintances from one harbor gang who get together to engage in one or two forays with short-run goals in mind (such as driving one person from their area). If such a group has a leader, he is apt to have no resources that give him the ability to reward or sanction his followers. It is not at all uncommon for groups to agree on a course of action, only to discover that many individuals have defected, leaving one or two to make the threats and cut the traps. In some cases, people find out that they have been abandoned by their teammates before any illegal activities take place. However, there are cases when people have cut traps, in the firm belief that others were going to follow suit, only to find that they and perhaps one or two other "suckers" have done the dirty work, and that all the blame is theirs.

In other cases, fishermen are able to form much more cohesive teams to advance their political interests. These groups are able to coordinate their activities over the long run. They aid each other in forays. They are able to accomplish feats in a few hours on one night that would be impossible for a single person. They can aim a coordinated attack against one "enemy" fisherman, with devastating results for that person. Participants maintain a blanket of silence about the activities of the group, spread favorable rumors, and some have even gone so far as to provide alibis for each other. They can pool information about the activities of their enemies and help to guard each other's gear. A person who takes on one member of such a group will find that he must deal with several enemies. Perhaps most important, such teams provide friendship and support in a time of stress.

These more permanent teams are apt to be found in gangs fishing perimeter-defended islands, which have a number of social characteristics that facilitate coordinated activity. As we will see, these include the small size of the gangs, effective leadership, the dependence of island families on each other, a strong sense of "community," and high dependence on the lobster resource.

This is not to suggest that the only effective coordinated teams are found on islands. In the past, well-coordinated teams have successfully held fishing territories in the upper reaches of three rivers in mid-coast Maine. These teams tended to be composed of kin, and were very dependent on the area for their livelihood since they had small boats and could not fish outside the estuary.

The decisions of these teams to defend their territory or invade those of others is made with the costs and benefits in mind. Fishing territory is very valuable, but holding what one has or gaining new territory usually involves conflict, which can be very expensive. Several factors influence the costs and benefits of territorial defense and incursion.

First is the size and effectiveness of teams. Teams can help to monitor each other's traps and reduce trap losses. In addition, members of such groups are able to spread the risks and costs of boundary defense. If you are one of two people cutting traps to hold a line, you are very vulnerable, and all retaliatory efforts will be aimed at you. As one person from a perimeter-defended island explained the situation, "You need more than one person doing it [defending the lines]. Otherwise one person is a scapegoat and takes a beating." The size and cohesion of the team strongly affects the cost of conflict measured in terms of trap losses. If you are a member of a large and effective group, your losses will be far less than if you are an individual involved in a conflict. One individual attempting to oppose a coordinated group faces impossible odds.

Second is the value of the contested area. Some fishing grounds are more productive, acre per acre, than others. Some are far more crowded. The rewards are far higher to the individual to remove a competitor from an overcrowded, highly productive ground, because this will increase one's own catches. The rewards are far less for removing a competitor from an unproductive ground with few people fishing it. Here, removal of competitors will not increase the productivity of one's own traps by very much. For these reasons, people will sacrifice more for "shedder bottom," which is both scarce and productive, than for winter fishing bottom, which is neither.

Rewards are also strongly influenced by the number of months one can fish, and this in turn depends on the variety of areas held. If one has access to several types of fishing bottom at varying depths, one can fish throughout the year. Gaining access to a piece of bottom that permits one to fish more months per year is especially valuable.

Third is the cost of transportation, which is affected not only by the distance from one's home harbor, but also by the technology in use. Going to a distant spot always is more expensive in time and fuel than travel to a nearby spot. It obviously cost far more in time to go to a certain spot in the 1920s when boats were powered by one-cylinder engines capable of making 4 knots per hour than it is now when boats can cruise at 20 knots.

The fourth factor influencing territorial defense and incursion is the cost of monitoring one's gear, which is greatly affected by distance from one's home harbor. If traps are placed very close to shore, people on shore can see who is pulling them. That is impossible if traps are more than half a mile out. Moreover, it is easier to monitor one's traps close to home because the area is being used continually by boats from one's own harbor, and boats from other harbors are very conspicuous. Monitoring one's own gear is harder in more distant areas. Boats from a number of harbors have a right to fish in "mixed fishing" areas in the middle of bays, and boats from an even larger number of harbors can fish in offshore areas.

Fifth is the probability of being apprehended by the Marine Patrol. Being convicted of molesting the gear of other fishermen can bring a heavy fine and the loss of one's license. In the past, the consequences of prosecution were far less than they are now. As we shall see, this has increased the costs of territorial defense.

However, the decision to defend or invade another area is not always a matter of rational analysis of costs and benefits. Feelings of ownership, honor, revenge, and a lust for power enter in. When people are very angry, they will sometimes take actions that are very costly. In other cases, people will get worn down with hatred and conflict and acquiesce out of fatigue.

Changes in Territoriality: Three Stages

STAGE I: ORIGINS OF THE SYSTEM

The territorial system in Maine at present is the result of a long historical process in which some territories have remained intact, while other have been consolidated into larger nucleated territories. The way this system evolved is the result of changes in the factors affecting the costs and benefits of territorial defense and incursion.

Fifty years ago, lobstering was done only in the summer in very small territories occupied by small groups of men. In great part, this pattern is traceable to the technology then in use, which made it difficult to fish in distant waters, and unnecessary to do so. Since lobstering was done from a small dory or a sailing sloop between 18 and 30 feet long, fishermen could not fish in the stormy winter months far from home. Even in the summer, men placed their traps close to their home harbors to minimize travel time. Travel to and from fishing grounds even 3 to 5 miles distance could take several hours per day. If there was no wind, or if one had to tack upwind for long distances, it could take even longer. At that time, there was no need to fish a large area. One could only tend a small number of traps since they had to be pulled to the surface by hand or by using the old-style gasoline-powered winches. The average fisherman only had a hundred traps, and many could not tend even that number. Moreover, the fact that one could only learn the bottom by using a handline further limited the amount of area a person could know and use efficiently.

While there is no record of how the territories came into being, information from a few older informants gives us some inkling about the process. Several informants said that lobster fishermen usually used a small area near their home harbor or near an island they owned. They used the same waters for years on end and defended them vigorously. "My grandfather had his own little patch," one said, "and he didn't go outside of it." Another said that each of the islands between Georges Island and the mainland had a camp on it where the island's owner (or the person who rented fishing rights) stayed during the summer. They fished no more than a mile from the island, and others were advised to stay out of their little kingdom. One of these islands were owned by the X family and "you did not fool with old Henry X much." From comments such as these, it is reasonable to assume that fishermen got to know the area where they fished well, came to feel dependent on it for their income. At some point, usufructory rights strengthened into a sense of ownership, giving people justification for defending the area against the incursions of others. One old man said of the fishermen he knew as a boy in the 1920s: "Since a man's whole income was dependent on a small area, they felt justified in keeping other people out. They had their own areas after all." The generation of people who started the territorial system probably felt the same.

However, the evidence is inconsistent regarding the feelings of territoriality and the amount of violence involved in defending these areas. One person said that his grandfather "used to row to an island in upper Muscongus Bay where he would live in a camp and fish for lobsters all summer. He never mentioned any lines or territories."

In the minds of these informants, ownership of fishing area was tied to legal ownership of land. Almost certainly these small areas were adjacent to the fisherman's own property, and legal ownership over the land was extended to include nearby waters. Older informants also have said that "these areas were owned by one man or small groups" [of kinsmen], and "fishing rights were inherited along with [legal title to] the land."

Apparently the territorial system was well established before 1900. A 1907 newspaper article entitled "Clans of Lobstermen Threaten Bloodshed" (Anonymous 1907) describes the events that took place when interlopers on two mainland boats came to Monhegan and set traps in island waters for two days. The Monhegan fishermen were so infuriated that "no stranger dares venture ashore." The article goes on to say that "the Monhegan fishermen have always looked upon lobster fishing around the island as their exclusive right." The article leaves little doubt that the Monhegan fishermen in the past had defended their territory by cutting traps. "In some mysterious manner, their lobster warps would be cut and their pots would be lost, and altogether the damage to their gear would be more than the lobsters taken would pay for."

In a few instances, enough historical data exist so that we can be sure that some of these small perimeter-defended areas have lasted from the early decades of the twentieth century to the present. The area around Pond Island, Little Pond Island, and Camp Island was fished in the 1920s by George Lurvey, a veteran of the Spanish-American War. Lurvey owned Little Pond Island and Camp Island, and made arrangements with the owner of Pond Island, a dentist from New York, to fish around that island as well. When Lurvey died in 1947, Little Pond Island and Camp Island were inherited by his stepson, Leon Bosse, who purchased Pond Island as well. Bosse fished the territory of these three islands himself until he lost his license in a territorial skirmish. At this point, he allowed other fishermen from nearby harbors to fish in the territory and collected a percentage of their catch, locally called "freight money." These fishermen lived in camps on Pond Island in the summer. In 1972, these islands were bought by Richard Carver, who has owned them ever since. Carver allows two friends to fish the islands area, which they maintain jointly, and he does not charge them any "freight money" for the privilege. Carver points out that his associates do not have access to other lobster fishing areas and thus it is in their best interest to help to maintain this fishing territory. Over the century, the boundaries of the island's territory have contracted somewhat, but there is no good record of how much. The current boundaries are defined by reference to points on nearby islands and the mainland, and Carver believes this is how the boundaries have always been defined (see Map 2.1). The area enclosed by the solid line on Map 2.1 is fished only by the three Pond Island fishermen; the area enclosed by the dashed line is a mixed fishing area where traps are placed by fishermen from three other nearby harbors, as well as by the Pond Island fishermen.

In short, the first fishing territories were small, close to shore, fished mainly in the warm months of year, and vigorously defended by their owner or owners, who were usually close kin. Much of this pattern has persisted to the present day in the perimeter-defended areas, and in some of the mainland harbors on the shore of Penobscot Bay. On the mainland, especially in the mid-coast area, this pattern has completely broken down. Very small territories have been combined into larger territories whose boundaries are not vigorously defended and where most ocean area is fished by people from at least two harbors. In Muscongus Bay, Casco Bay, and the area in between, most lobstermen fish much of the year in zones where mixed fishing is allowed. In short, the territorial pattern that we see at present has resulted from the fact that perimeter-defended areas have been maintained in some areas, and have been amalgamated to form nucleated territories in other

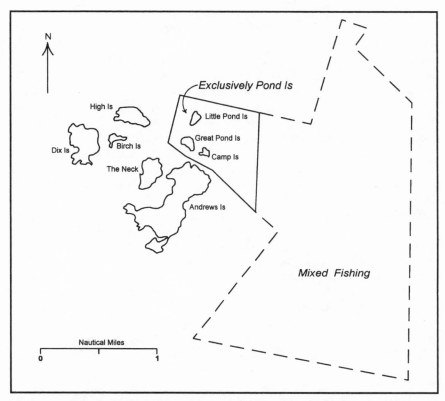

Map 2.1. Pond Island lobster fishing area, 2001. The area enclosed by the solid line is fished only by the three Pond Island fishermen; the area enclosed by the dashed line is fished by the Pond Island fishermen and men from three other harbors.

places. What we need to understand is the factors producing this differential breakdown of territorial boundaries.

STAGE II: CONSOLIDATION OF FISHING TERRITORIES

In the mid-coast area, where the coast is strongly convoluted and formed into deep bays, the traditional areas of communities on open ocean have been under considerable pressure from people in the towns further up rivers and bays. In the World War II era, fishermen from towns on the outer ends of peninsulas (e.g., Port Clyde, New Harbor, Boothbay Harbor) were able to fish at least nine months per year. They had ample "shedder bottom" to occupy them in the summer and access to deeper waters further offshore where they could catch large amounts of lobster in the fall and spring. By way of contrast, fishermen from towns up bays and estuaries such as Bremen, Searsport, and Wiscasset had to restrict their fishing to the summer months when they could catch lobsters in the shallow waters adjacent to their home harbors. During the latter part of the twentieth century, fishermen from such bay communities have been purchasing boats capable of going to open ocean. If these people are going to fish on a year-round basis, they must fish in deep water. This means that they had to invade what were formally exclusive territories of towns such as New Harbor, Little River, and Five Islands on open ocean. Those from river communities were willing to sacrifice a great deal to gain access to deep water. The alternative was to be bottled up in the small traditional territories adjacent to home harbors, where they could fish only a few months each year.

For the fishermen in invaded areas, it was not worthwhile to repel the invaders. It is true that invasion meant that people from harbors on open ocean had more competition in the middle of bays where they fish in the fall and spring. Some of them complain about getting smaller yields as a result. However, an attempt to stop people from upriver from invading would mean a full-scale war, involving large financial losses. Even though there was a good deal of bitter talk, those from open-ocean harbors felt it was better to mix than fight.

In Muscongus Bay, for example, fishermen from up-river towns moved into the lower bay over the course of two decades beginning in the late 1950s. In some cases, their incursions were relatively peaceful; in others some small-scale trap-cutting took place. During the 1950s, fishermen from Bremen had small skiffs that they used in the Medomak River. In the 1960s, a number of Bremen fishermen bought larger boats, and larger gangs of traps. When the permanent inhabitants of Loud's Island moved to the mainland, the Bremen fishermen saturated the ocean area near the island with so many traps that they gained access to the area that had been fished exclusively by the islanders. Then they pushed further south into the middle of Muscongus Bay in the fall and winter, moving into an area that had long been fished jointly by people from New Harbor and Round Pond. Their move to the south was stopped once they reached the Monhegan line, a perimeter-defended area.

The Bremen fishermen were generally happy with the results, since they gained a good deal of fishing ground without having to resort to much violence. The people from towns on the ends of peninsulas who were invaded had a different point of view. They were quite bitter about seeing areas that they had fished opened to mixed fishing with people from up river, but they did not find it worthwhile to defend these areas. Their response was to move up river in the following decades. Their rationale is that if men from places such as Bremen and Friendship are permitted to come down to fish in the middle of Muscongus Bay and the open ocean to the south, they, in turn, should be permitted to fish further north in the upper reaches of the Bay. Accordingly, New Harbor and Round Pond fishermen began to move their traps north of the traditional line in the summer months to gain access to more shedder bottom. Interestingly enough, this has met with very stiff resistence from the Friendship and Bremen fishermen. In the late 1990s, the area around Jones's Garden Island has become a very contested piece of bottom. The irony of the situation has not been lost on one New Harbor fisherman who said, "What is good for the goose is not good for the gander. It is okay for them to come down here [to the southern part of the bay] in the fall, but it is different when we go up there in the summer. One guy from Friendship is the worst. He puts an enormous gang of traps off here [New Harbor] in the fall, but he is the first one to cut us when we go up there [north of the old New Harbor line] in the summer."

In other estuaries, the same process has occurred, but with less violence. Fishermen from Five Islands and South Bristol are fishing much further up the Sheepscot and Damariscotta Rivers, respectively, while men from up-river communities are able to come south and fish in open ocean in the fall and winter.

In these areas, an increase in areas where mixed fishing is allowed resulted from conflicts between gangs wanting to increase access to bottom that would allow them to fish more months of the year. Here again, the success of invasion attempts depends on the organizing ability of a team and their willingness to incur losses. One fisherman ruefully recalled his unsuccessful attempt to defend the Sebasco Estates territory from incursions by men from West Point. "The two areas merged because they [West Point] pushed and we didn't stop them. I spoke to people [to get them to defend the area]. But other people let me do it [cut the offending traps]. I took the hit. So I gave up and said I'd come down here. I was the only one being open with it. I felt they should leave us alone where we hadn't bothered anyone. Up in the river gets lobsters first so we had it good when they didn't. They would come up, but when ours quit, they didn't want us down there." The Sebasco fishermen did finally succeed in pushing into West Point territory in the fall. As a result, both areas have merged for all practical purposes.

Much less mixed fishing occurs in mainland harbors in Penobscot Bay. In towns such as Spruce Head and Tenant's Harbor, people can fish near their home harbors in the summer, and then go out in the middle part of the bay to fish in their winter fishing grounds there. This gives them both shoal water and deep water, so that fishermen from these communities can fish all year round without having to enter the territories of islanders in the Muscle Ridge Channel or in the middle of Penobscot Bay (e.g., Vinalhaven, Green Island, etc.). Although the waters of the islands are attractive to mainlanders, they are never faced with the alternatives of ceasing operations during certain seasons or entering waters adjacent to other mainland harbors or the islands. Since lobstermen in these areas are not forced to violate boundaries to make a living year round, the mainlanders have not been so desperate that they have been willing to assume the cost of invading other areas. Thus, boundaries have been easier to defend, so that the amount of territory fished exclusively by men from each harbor remains relatively large.

As a result, the perimeter-defended areas have remained the exclusive fishing ground of gangs fishing off those islands. To be sure, the lines of these island areas are tested every year by mainlanders placing traps over the boundary. There have also been a numbers of more serious attempts to invade these island areas, some of which have resulted in the boundaries being changed to give mainlanders more fishing area. However, the perimeter-defended areas still exist even though some of them contain less fishing area than formerly.

In the 1980s and 1990s, a number of changes took place that are having a marked effect on the territorial system.

Trap Escalation. Since the 1930s, the number of traps in use has steadily increased. In 1960, there were 745,000 traps in use; by 1980 the number had more than doubled to 1,846,000; by 1999, the number had increased to 3,045,000 traps. This increase in traps has continued even after trap limits were imposed beginning in 1995. As we shall see in chapter 7, this increase in traps is due to a complex combination of technical, social, and economic factors.

The increases in traps have led to increasing trap congestion. Trap congestion is especially bad in the nucleated territories on the mainland, which have experienced an increase in fishermen, as well as the use of more traps per capita on the average in recent years. Fishermen from mainland harbors have felt under considerable pressure to increase the area they fish to avoid places so saturated with traps that they become entangled and catches are lowered. The perimeter-defended areas around islands have not experienced such an increase in trap numbers. Here the number of traps in use has increased, but not to the same degree. As a result, islanders do not feel the same pressure to increase the area they fish.

Law Enforcement. Since 1970, fishermen have become less willing to cut traps because they fear prosecution. Industry members have become better educated and more committed to conservation and law enforcement. They are more likely to report infractions, including trap-cutting incidents, to Marine Patrol officers. The Marine Patrol force has become ever more professionalized and effective in prosecuting violations of the laws. Officers interviewed report that 90 to 95 percent of the people they arrest are convicted. Being convicted of cutting traps brings a very heavy fine and potentially the loss of one's lobster-fishing license for up to three years. Still, it is very difficult to get evidence on trap cutting, which means that a fisherman is not likely to be successfully prosecuted if he does cut traps and takes some precautions while doing so. Several Marine Patrol officers and fishermen said that what deters trap cutting is not so much the certainty of being caught as the huge losses that will occur if one is convicted of cutting traps. In an era when large numbers of full-time fishermen regularly earn gross incomes of over $150,000, fewer are willing to risk the prospects of prosecution for the more ephemeral benefits of enforcing territorial boundaries. One man from an island whose territory was being invaded by mainlanders was heard to remark, "In the good old days we would have taken care of the problem with the knife, but this isn't the good old days." As a result , most of the Marine Patrol officers interviewed say that the number of trap-cutting incidents has decreased. One officer, who appears to be typical, reports that in his district, there were about "twenty-five trap cutting incidents twenty years ago; now there are about twelve."

Ecological Changes and the Location of Lobsters. Ecological changes also have altered when and where lobsters can be profitably caught. In the past, winter was a very unproductive time to fish. Many lobsters were in near-hibernation, and so few crawled into traps that many people did not fish at all in the mid-winter months. In the recent "boom period," a large enough number of lobsters can be caught in deep water on mud bottom to make it profitable to fish in the winter. To be sure, winter fishing is still not as productive as summer fishing, but now many fishermen with large boats find it worthwhile to fish 10 and 15 miles from land where very few, if any, fishermen went before.

These factors have resulted in two kinds of changes in the territorial system. First, fishermen with large boats and big gangs of traps are finding it worthwhile to exploit offshore, deep water areas more. For example, people from Spruce Head are fishing large numbers of traps during the winter south of Matinicus Rock, some 30 miles from their home harbor. Boats from Portland and other towns in Casco Bay have been going to offshore areas southeast of Cape Elizabeth.

No attempt has been made to incorporate these areas into the traditional fishing areas. The offshore areas have always been open to all. They remain so. The reason is that the cost/benefit ratio does not make it rational to try to establish territories in these offshore areas. The usual way to defend territorial claims is by trap cutting, and this is becoming increasingly risky and unprofitable. These offshore areas are exploited, typically, by people from several harbors. If fishermen from one harbor attempted to drive out people from the others, a major and very costly battle would likely result, which would almost certainly result in intervention by the Marine Patrol force and police. Moreover, little can be gained by driving other fishermen out of such areas. Traps are placed so far apart that tangles are not frequent, and the traps of other people do not reduce your own catches greatly, if at all. As a result, the size of the traditional fishing areas has not expanded. What has increased greatly is the size of the exploited area that is open to all fishermen from all harbors. An increasing number of fishermen are spending a lot of time exploiting waters that are claimed by no harbor, where they do not have to worry about infringing on territorial boundaries. More than one fishermen has said that they like this situation.

Second, in inshore areas, the amount of area where mixed fishing is allowed has increased. The increases in the number of traps in use and the larger and faster boats have resulted in more fishermen placing traps in waters that were the exclusive zone of other harbors or in areas where people from other harbors practiced mixed fishing. An increasing number of these incursions have been successful due to changes in the cost/benefit ratios faced by aggressors versus defenders. People who invade other areas have much to gain from greater access to increased bottoms at certain times of year, and the chances of facing effective resistence are less than they were in the past. The people whose boundaries have been violated have less to gain from a successful defense, in comparison with the possible losses, which can include loss of license, a fine, or even time spent in jail. As a result, the areas held

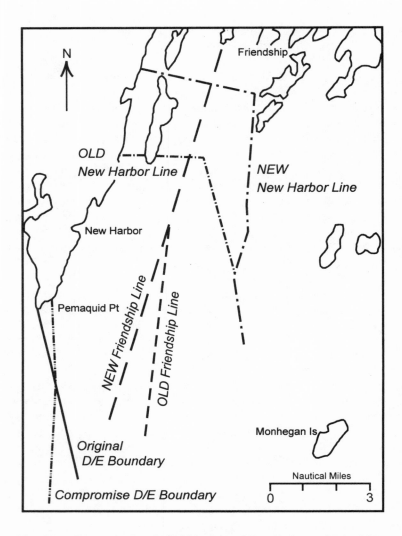

Map 2.2. Changes in the mixed fishing area of New Harbor and Friendship between the 1970s and the late 1990s. Over the course of thirty years the size of the mixed fishing area of both Friendship and New Harbor has increased. New Harbor fishermen now go farther north in the bay; Friendship fishermen are permitted to fish farther to the west. Fishermen from Round Pond and Bremen fish in these same waters, but, in the interest of simplifying the map, their boundary lines are not shown here. The D/E boundary line is an official line established in 1997 as part of the Zone Management process. With the exception of the D/E zone boundary, all of the lines shown on this map delineate nucleated fishing area boundaries. They represent the farthest point that most fishermen from a given harbor can place traps without getting into trouble.

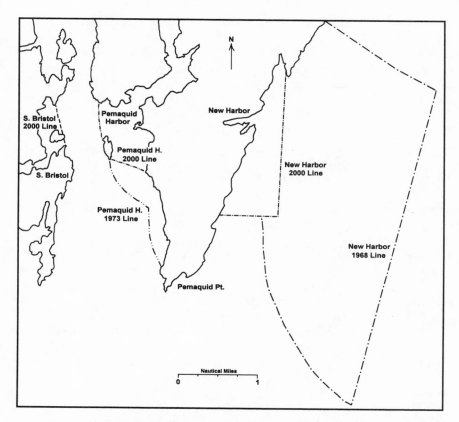

Map 2.3. Changes in the small, exclusive areas fished by New Harbor, Pemaquid Harbor, and South Bristol, 1968 to 2000. Only a fraction of the area exploited by fishermen from nucleated harbors is held for their exclusive use. In most harbors (for example, New Harbor and Pemaquid Harbor), these exclusive zones have decreased markedly in the past thirty years. In a few instances, exclusive areas have not decreased much, as in the case of South Bristol, whose fishermen currently have much the same exclusive area at the mouth of their home harbor as they had thirty years ago.

exclusively by individual harbor gangs has decreased, and areas that used to be fished by two harbor gangs are now used by three or four (see maps 2.2 and 2.3).

This is not to suggest that boundaries demarcating the exclusive area held by harbors are undefended. Fishermen have had some nasty fights over such incursions, such as the one currently going on in Muscongus Bay over the area north of Jones' Garden. Even further offshore, incursions into areas where mixed fishing is permitted meet with substantial resistence. In the mid-1980s, a group of fishermen from Cushing, Friendship, and Port Clyde began to place traps in an area in outer Penobscot Bay southwest of Matinicus. People from Tenant's Harbor, Wheeler's Bay, and Martinsville, who had been fishing this area jointly for a long time, got together with some of the intruders and forcefully said that their incursion could not continue without trouble. A line was drawn, primarily by negotiation, establishing a boundary running southeast from Mosquito Head just south of the 12810 Loran C line. Boats from Cushing, Friendship, and Port Clyde do not come north of that line. What is unusual about this case is that a boundary line was established by negotiations rather than trap cutting. I suspect that many more boundary disputes will be handled in this way in the future. It is also one of the few cases I know about where people from two or more harbors have been able to get together to defend a boundary.

The Islands. Increasingly, island territorial boundaries are under pressure as large numbers of mainland fishermen from crowded mainland harbors feel compelled to seek additional fishing grounds further from their home harbors. They have successfully invaded parts of the territory of various islands, with the result that the boundaries of those islands have moved somewhat. This is true even in perimeter-defended areas, which have been successfully defended for so many years. The eastern boundary of Metinic has been moved to the west by a quarter of a mile, reducing the area fished by the men on that island; the eastern Green Island line is under assault, and may well move somewhat to the west, while the men from Wheeler's Bay and Spruce Head have successfully pushed a wedge-shaped area into an area that hitherto had been fished by men from Matinicus and Vinalhaven. In all these cases, the incursions have ceased to be opposed by the defending islanders and are likely to be permanent. On some of these islands, a bunker mentality has begun to develop as the islanders face constant attempts to invade their areas while fear of prosecution hinders defensive efforts.

Lobstermen from Swan's Island and Monhegan have succeeded in defending fishing areas by the novel ploy of going to the government. In 1984, Swan's Island, under increasing pressure from mainland fishermen and experiencing increasing trap escalation itself, was able to persuade Commissioner of Marine Resources Spencer Apollonio to make the traditional fishing area of Swan's Island a "conservation zone."

In 1995, Monhegan was also successful in obtaining a conservation zone. By the 1980s, men from mainland harbors were regularly fishing well to the south of Monhegan in waters where previously only Monhegan islanders had fished, and by 1995, fishermen from Friendship began to fish large amounts of gear. The Monhegan fishermen attempted to drive off the invaders using traditional means. Many Friendship traps disappeared in a series of "killer fogs." The Friendship fishermen retaliated in kind, and one Monhegan boat was also sunk under conditions that the sheriff's department ruled "not accidental" (Kyle 1996: 1). The Commissioner of Marine Resources attempted to settle the feud by establishing a conservation zone around Monhegan with rules that would permit Friendship fishermen to fish in these waters if they abided by Monhegan rules. The agreement broke down when the Monhegan fishermen proved unwilling to let the Friendship fishermen into Monhegan waters under any condition.

In 1998, after three years of serious conflict with fishermen from Friendship,

Capturing the Commons

and endless debate in the newspapers and on docks, the Monhegan fishermen were successful in lobbying the legislature to establish a conservation zone, with special rules establishing a special trap limit and local apprenticeship program.

However, the establishment of the Monhegan conservation zone was to have one very serious consequence, namely that it ended the possibility of other conservation zones being established in other areas. The contest between Monhegan and Friendship was so protracted, bitter, and divisive, that the legislature established a special commission to recommend some way to handle other requests for conservation zones or sub-zones with special rules and boundaries. This "Sub-Zone Task Force" issued a report stating that "sub-zones were to be discouraged at this time" (*Commercial Fisheries News* 1998b: C21).

Thus, the conservation zones established around Swan's Island and Monhegan stand alone. These two islands have defended their traditional fishing areas by successfully lobbying the legislature to formalize their traditional territories, thereby handing over the onerous job of enforcing the boundaries to the warden force. In the immediate future at least, other islands will not have this option.

Territoriality in 2000: A Nickel Overview of the Central Coast

Over the course of the twentieth century, spatial strategies and the territorial system have undergone substantial change. An increasing number of fishing areas have been consolidated, boundaries have moved so there is much more area where mixed fishing is allowed, and much more lobster fishing area is outside the area where territoriality exists.

However, enormous variation exists in the amount of change that has occurred in various parts of the coast. In Casco Bay, the territorial system has been changed greatly. Many areas have been consolidated, and "mixed fishing" is permitted in much of the bay. No impediments at all remain to placing traps in the deep water outside the bay, save for the formal zone boundaries. Yet, even here there are places one cannot place traps without courting trouble. On the offshore islands (e.g., Long Island, Chebeague, Cliff), shedder bottom is still defended by the islanders, and small exclusive areas are maintained and defended by their traditional owners in the upper reaches of some of the rivers. There is still a boundary between Harpswell and the Casco Bay islands. Fishermen from Harpswell do not go west of Whaleboat Island, and those on the islands do not go to the east of it. In the eastern part of the bay, Harpswell, Bailey's Island, Cundy's Harbor, and Sebasco Estates all defend areas close to their harbors, but fish together in the fall and winter in the outer part of the bay.

In the central coast, most of the inshore fishing grounds have been consolidated into areas where mixed fishing is allowed. (Again, these areas are not open to just anyone.) In fact, people from places such as Port Clyde, Cushing, Friendship, Bremen, New Harbor, Pemaquid, South Bristol, Little River, Boothbay Harbor, Southport, and Five Islands have no area that they fish exclusively, except small areas very close to the mouths of their home harbors. In the deepwater areas offshore, no territorial boundaries are defended at all (see map 2.4).

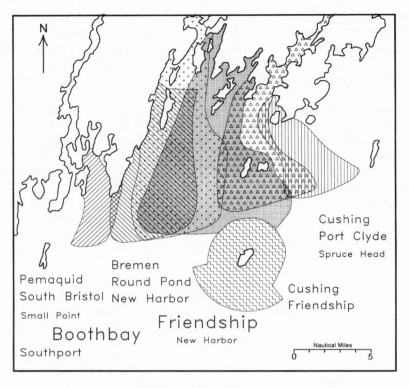

N

Cushing
Port Clyde
Spruce Head

Bremen
Round Pond
New Harbor

Pemaquid
South Bristol New Harbor

Cushing
Friendship

Small Point

Boothbay

Friendship

New Harbor

Southport

Nautical Miles
0   5

Key to Inshore Areas:

Pemaquid / S. Bristol   Cushing

New Harbor / Round Pond   Port Clyde

Bremen   Monhegan Is

Friendship

Key to Offshore Areas:
Harbor names indicate where concentrations
of lobstermen place traps.

Map 2.4.   Nucleated fishing areas of Muscongus Bay area (Mid-Coast Region), 2000. Several different types of informal territoriality are exhibited in this map. Some exclusive areas show clearly, as is the case of Bremen, Friendship, and Cushing. The territories indicated as "inshore areas" are nucleated areas. The boundaries represent the farthest point most fishermen from those harbors can go without courting trouble. Monhegan's area is an official "conservation zone" where, according to state law, only Monhegan fishermen are permitted to put traps. In the past, Monhegan held a perimeter-defended area. The "offshore areas" indicate where lobster fishermen place traps in the cold months of the year. But these waters are open to people from all harbors, even though they are generally exploited only by people from mainland harbors in the vicinity. The word "Cushing" indicates where a concentration of fishermen from that town place traps in the winter, but this area could be fished by people from Bremen if they wanted to go that far from their home harbor.

In the upper reaches of Penobscot Bay, much the same pattern persists. Here, most of the area is fished by men from at least two harbors. In the summer, small areas along shore are defended by people from adjacent harbors. In the fall and winter, however, people range far and wide. Many from Belfast and Searsport regularly fish 15 miles down the bay in the region near Great Spruce Head Island and Butter Island, just to the north of Vinalhaven.

The exception is the area at the mouth of Penobscot Bay, where a large number of perimeter-defended areas have been maintained and successfully defended for generations. Islands such as Criehaven, Green Island, Little Green Island, Metinic, Monhegan, and the islands in the Muscle Ridge channel all maintain large areas where people from those gangs fish throughout the year. Those boundaries are defended. There are areas south of Penobscot Bay and further offshore where "mixed fishing" is allowed, but the proportion of mixed fishing to exclusive area is much smaller in this area.

The Construction of Territoriality

In the 1970s when I first began to interview people about spatial strategies and territoriality, people would admit with little urging that such a phenomenon existed. Some were openly boastful about the role they played in territorial defense and incursions into the areas of other harbor gangs. Others would talk in general terms about "lines" and fishing "areas," but were less than helpful when it came to describing the seamy side of territorial defense. In the summer of 1998, when graduate student Jennifer Brewer and I began to gather data on territoriality again, many people, especially in the central and southern regions, were quick to tell us that there were no boundaries and that territoriality had disappeared. Several weeks of intensive interviewing convinced us that the territorial system was very much in existence. In some places it had changed, but in others it is virtually the same as it was in the mid-1970s.

Territoriality is not only a system of rules and practices; it also has an ideological side. This ideology is a contested construction. That is, the way people select facts about territoriality and interpret those facts is influenced by their own interest to one degree or another. Wishful thinking, attempts to be totally accurate, and strategic reporting all influence the stories we heard about territoriality. There was also a normative aspect to such reports. Reports about territoriality reflected what people thought was "right" and what "should be." Reports were also influenced by knowledge of the increased law-enforcement efforts, which they knew made boundary defense more difficult. To a large extent, people generalized from what they knew about, namely the conditions in their own local areas.

There was a marked difference in the reports of people from areas where nucleated territoriality existed as opposed to perimeter-defended areas. People in nucleated areas played down territoriality. Some even said there was no territoriality. These people are impressed with the fact that more mixed fishing area exists now, and that fishermen are spending a lot more time in open ocean areas where there are no feelings of ownership. They also know that some people can exploit areas where others from the same harbor cannot go so that, in their minds, "there are no lines." Others said there were no lines, meaning that there should be no lines or that they hoped there would be no lines. Of course, it is one thing to say that people are fishing more area offshore where there is no territoriality, that there is more "mixed fishing," and that boundary defense is more costly. It is entirely another to insist that no territoriality exists at all.

Some in the same harbor would report boundaries encompassing far more area than others reported. On the whole, these were older fishermen, who were reporting how the situation might have been once, and hopefully would be again.

Fishermen from up-river towns, who had to fish in the middle of bays in the winter, would almost inevitably report that the "boundaries are weakening" or that there were no territories. This is a rationalization for their own actions, which involve fishing in areas others considered their own. Men on the ends of peninsulas were far more prone to insist that territoriality existed, and to describe their own harbor area in generous terms with relatively little mixed fishing area. In several instances, it was obvious that such descriptions were part of an ideology justifying defending territorial lines that were under pressure from people up river. After all, an area over which they had "rights" was being invaded by people who had no "right" to be there.

Political considerations played a role as well. People's descriptions were tailored to their political agendas. They did not want a report that supported a legislative effort of which they did not approve. Time and again, we heard "this isn't going to be used to make a law is it?"

People in perimeter-defended areas, without fail, emphasized that the territorial system was alive and well. They emphasized the longevity of this system, and linked their rights to ocean area to the ownership of island land. Their reports were clearer and definitive. They had boundaries, they had always had boundaries, and they defended them. Their reports were not clouded by issues such as "mixed fishing" and the fact that some people could not go where others could. Sometimes the political agenda that lurked under the surface of these reports came to the fore. They said that they hoped that their perimeter-defended boundaries would endure. After all, islanders had no other way to earn a living and they were doing a good job conserving the resource. We were assured that only they limited entry, and had trap limits imposed through "gentlemen's agreements."

The islanders' reports were clouded by what was a siege mentality. They said they hoped they would always have these territories, but they were clearly worried about the increasing incursions by mainland boats and that the Marine Patrol force was making defense difficult. They tended to slide over the fact that their boundaries were sometimes defended by illegal actions.

The information we obtained on territoriality and boundary defense was complicated, and contradictory in many cases. It is an area where more research needs to be done.

Conclusion

The Maine lobster fishery is a common-pool resource. Like all common-pool resources, the lobster fishery faces two problems: It is difficult to limit access to the resource, and subtractability exists so that use of the resource by one person results in less of the resource for others users (Ostrom, Gardner, and Walker 1994: 7).

The common-pool status means that the lobster industry lies somewhere between open-access regimes on one hand and private-property regimes on the other. It is not like the private-property regimes where a sole owner has the right to appropriate all of the resource and a strong incentive to protect that resource and invest in it. But it is also not like open-access regimes where a complete lack of property rights leaves the resource open to exploitation by anyone and everyone, leading to massive overexploitation. In these common-pool arrangements, people have some ability to control access and can, with difficulty, erect rules to restrict exploitive effort. In the Maine lobster industry, the harbor gangs have been able to reserve portions of the ocean for their own use and have been able to limit entry to their own "gang" to one degree or another. This certainly decreases competition for lobster and increases the catches per unit of effort for those who are admitted to the common pool (i.e., gang). In the absence of these rules, the catch per trap would be less. These rules give some, but not all, of the benefits associated with private property.

However, all of the institutions concerning territoriality are under assault, particularly in the nucleated areas comprising most of the state. In the nucleated areas, the barriers to entry have been lowered, with the result that it is far easier to join these harbor gangs. The costs and benefits of territorial defense have altered, with the result that traditional territorial lines are retracting so that there is more area where "mixed fishing" is allowed. There is also a lot of fishing now being done in open ocean where no territoriality exists at all.

However, the people in perimeter-defended areas have their own problems. The cost of maintaining these areas has become higher as ever-increasing numbers of boats from the mainland continually push the island lines and increased law enforcement makes illegal acts of boundary defense more risky. Swan's Island and Monhegan have resorted to lobbying the legislature for laws to establish conservation zones, which protect their traditional fishing area. Other islands have seen their fishing area shrink due to the incursion of people from crowded mainland harbors.

The future of the perimeter-defended islands is a matter of some debate. Some think the perimeter-defended areas are essentially undefendable now. One island fisherman said that "if anyone wanted to fish [name of island] they could. If I cut someone off, then they would get a warden and I would lose my license. Tradition and respect for others is all that maintains these lines now."

There are many in Maine who believe that we are witnessing a fundamental change in the traditional territorial system. Some think the system will no longer exist in a few years.

As we shall see, these changes in the territorial system have resulted in political pressure for formal laws. In the past, who could fish for lobster and where they could fish were dependent on rules and arrangements generated informally by groups of fishermen and harbor gangs. Increasingly, these same issues are being determined by the power of the state of Maine. Informal rules are giving way to formal rules.

CHAPTER 3

The Island Game: Informal Rules and the Factors Producing Them

Some of the island areas in Maine have been far more effective in providing rules for themselves than nucleated areas on the mainland have been. As we have described, they have been effective in organizing the defense of territorial boundaries, and they have limited entry to their harbor gangs. Some of these island areas have also been able to provide trap limits for themselves. Why should this be so? What characteristics do these islands have that allow them to succeed in providing such rules? What do these cases tell us about the central issue of the conditions under which norms are generated? In this chapter, I will attempt to answer these questions by focusing on the circumstances that allowed fishermen on four of these islands to provide trap limits for themselves. However, some attention needs to be paid to territorial defense and limited entry, since all three problems are interconnected.

Since the mid 1950s, many lobster fishermen have wanted trap limits. The proponents of trap limits argue that having a maximum number of traps that can be fished substantially cuts operating costs, reduces trap tangles, and promotes equity among fishermen. (The incentives to obtain trap limits will be discussed in greater detail in chapter 5.) Legislators, responding to the wishes of their constituents, put in trap limit bills, but every one was defeated. By the late 1960s and early 1970s, fishermen were badly frustrated with the stalemate in the legislature. A number of groups of fishermen along various parts of the coast were talking seriously about imposing trap limits on themselves by informal means. Only five island communities succeeded in doing so: Monhegan, Swan's Island, Criehaven, Metinic, and Green Island, and most of these were still in effect in 2001. Green Island and Criehaven have provided trap limits informally by "gentlemen's agreements." Monhegan and Swan's Island have had them formalized by the state of Maine. No other individual communities tried to establish an informal trap limit except for Pine Point (on the mainland), which had a limit for a few years that then failed. The state legislature was not able to pass a statewide trap limit rule until 1995 as part of the zone management law, after decades of stalemate (see chapter 5).

The difficulties in establishing a trap limit are traceable to the fact that a trap limit poses a typical collective action dilemma. It is rational for individuals to increase the number of traps they fish, even though a rule limiting trap numbers would benefit everyone. A person with a higher percentage of the traps on the bottom will catch more lobsters than someone who has a smaller percentage, assuming that skill and other factors remain equal. Even in the face of an agreement, fishermen have strong motivation to cheat, since people who have more traps than their fellows will earn more. What this means is that the five island communities that have imposed trap limits on themselves have overcome a collective action dilemma. How have they been able to succeed?[1]

The Islands

The islands off the coast of Maine were visited by some of the earliest explorers of the New World. Beginning in the early seventeenth century, the rich fishing grounds attracted Europeans who first visited Maine's islands in the summer to dry cod for shipment to Europe. By 1750, many islands were occupied year round. The late 1880s saw approximately 1,100 islands with permanent settlers, who were engaged in both farming and fishing. In the 1880s, tourist hotels and cottage colonies created additional economic opportunities. Shortly after the turn of the twentieth century, island populations began to fall rapidly. The mainland held many attractions. Only the largest islands had stores, schools, and post offices, and none had electricity. Everything has to be transported to an island by boat, and on many islands a supply of water is always problematic. At present, only eleven islands along the Maine coast are permanently occupied. Lobster fishing and tourism are the mainstays of their economies.

This chapter describes the circumstances surrounding the provision of trap limits on four islands. The institutions underlying the trap limits are quite different, and the trap limits have not all been equally successful by any means.

MONHEGAN

Monhegan Island is approximately 1¼ miles long and is located 12 miles from the nearest point on the mainland. It has the longest and most distinguished history of any of the islands, having been visited by John Cabot in 1497 and by a number of famous explorers in the sixteenth century, including Verrazano, Francis Drake, and Jacques Cartier (Proper 1930). Sir Fernando Gorges established a settlement on the island in 1616 (Proper 1930: 109). It has been continuously occupied since the late 1600s. For many decades, all of the fishermen who exploit the waters around Monhegan have lived on the island.

Monhegan's current fishermen are scarcely isolated rustics. The island has long supported an artist colony, and it has been a tourist mecca, drawing thousands of

Capturing the Commons

visitors every summer, when there are daily boats coming to Monhegan from Boothbay Harbor, New Harbor, and Port Clyde. In the winter, only seventy or eighty people remain. Most of these are members of fishing families.

Since the turn of the twentieth century, there have been twelve to fifteen boats on Monhegan, whose crews have the most unusual annual round of any on the coast. In 1907, they lobbied the legislature for a law making it illegal to fish in the waters within 2 miles of Monhegan in the summer and early fall. In 1948, they succeeded in convincing the legislature to change the law making it legal to fish within 2 miles of Monhegan from January 1 to June 25. This means that Monhegan fishermen are fishing for lobsters only in the winter when prices are at their annual high. During the summer months, they go to work in the booming tourist industry or in other fisheries, while the wardens protect their boundaries from the incursions of fishermen from the mainland.

On Monhegan, the sense of community is very striking. Literally everyone knows everyone else. No one is anonymous, and no one's business remains secret for long. One fisherman was heard to remark, "My life is an open book. I hope other people find it entertaining." Interaction is facilitated by the fact that all the houses and tourist hotels are clustered around the harbor in an area about half a square mile. There is only one dock, one harbor, one store, and a small restaurant. Since only two short gravel roads pass through the settled area and no car ferry services the island, there are few vehicles. Everyone walks. On a trip to the store and the wharf to meet the mail boat, one can see a sizeable percentage of the island's inhabitants.

People are expected to sacrifice a good deal of time and effort for the community. Literally all of the adults take on a job to help the community or assume an office in the town government, usually without pay. The offices of zoning officer, tax assessor, fire marshal, road commissioner, and a dozen others are filled essentially by volunteers. People do not really run for these offices; the decision about who will do what is made in a less formal way. By law, town meetings are held annually, but the real decisions are made beforehand by a process of talking things out. The only time a town meeting will be contentious, one person said, is when "people have not had time to talk things over."

On Monhegan, ritual events are very important. Christmas is a very important time. The entire town meets in the school and presents are exchanged between a high proportion of the population. "Trap day," the first day when fishing is allowed, brings the entire community together in joint effort. Every able-bodied person helps the fishermen lug traps to the wharf and put them on the boats.

On Monhegan, gossip, slander, and ostracism are usually quite successful in forcing people into line with the expectations of the community. One local fisherman said, "small communities periodically create witches. I was the local witch once and I have watched two other people get the treatment." Still, on Monhegan, people try to get along with others and do not make accusations against others lightly. Feuds in small communities can cause a lot of problems, especially since it is impossible to avoid contact and the inhabitants are so dependent on each other for help and essential services.

Lobstermen on Monhegan hold formal meetings of the captains to make decisions concerning fishing and the harbor gang. These meetings are held in the fish house of one of the fishermen on the waterfront, which serves as a kind of community center for the fishermen. No one besides captains are allowed entry, and what transpires in these meetings is kept secret. Even sternmen are excluded. It is here that issues are aired, strategy discussed, and problems ironed out. Any of the captains can call a meeting. It is in these meetings that territorial defense is coordinated, although the specifics of these decisions are never revealed. Decisions are made democratically and a consensus generally emerges, although it can take some time and much talking.

Members of the Monhegan harbor gang expect a good deal of cooperative behavior from each other. People are expected to help other fishermen in time of need, keep skiffs off the beach everyone uses, and move traps off the wharf as quickly as possible. On occasion, when someone is sick or has boat troubles during the start of the fishing season, fishermen will decide to postpone "trap day" until that person is able to go fishing again.

The harbor gang also maintains a great deal of social control over its members. One is expected to be a "good fisherman." Anyone caught molesting another's gear or violating the state conservation laws will be severely sanctioned by other fishermen on the island. One fisherman said, "our punishment for taking short lobsters is much worse than the state's." One is also expected to do one's share in defending the island's fishing boundaries against the incursions of mainlanders.

To ensure that they will become assets to the island's fishing community, a person wanting to fish on Monhegan must first serve an apprenticeship by working as a sternman for a member of the harbor gang for several years. They will be allowed to set traps only if they pass muster. Even then, a person can be rejected for failure to live up to important norms.

Social control in the harbor gang is facilitated by the fact that most of the fishermen on Monhegan have not been there long, which has increased the leadership power of a few older fishermen from long-established island families. Four or five of these men have had enormous influence on what happens in the island's fishing community.

On rare occasion, very direct means are used to drive unwanted fishermen from the island. In past decades, two fishermen who had been accused of violating lobster conservation laws were made to feel very unwelcome on Monhegan. Both were called to special "captains'" meetings, and according to one person who was present, told "Pull up your gear, you are all done here." Whether these people had really violated the lobster laws or not is debated by some. There is some suspicion that they were disliked because of other personal characteristics, and that they were reported to a Marine Patrol officer—and even framed—as a means of getting rid of them.

For our purposes, the most important decision was the institution of a six hundred-trap limit in 1974. The Monhegan fishermen were persuaded to establish a trap limit by two successful island fisherman who argued that the trap limit in the Canadian Maritimes had been a resounding success. But another factor was a desire to avoid competition. One man said, "some of the older fishermen were getting a little too much competition from the younger men and they didn't like it." The trap limit reduced the ability of younger men to earn more by working more gear. Two fishermen with a lot of gear opposed the establishment of the trap limit, but they were persuaded to try the limit after a time.

The Monhegan gang has had little problem with enforcement. A couple of fishermen said that five or six years after it was established the trap limit "kind of faded," but none of the kinds of public accusations and recriminations were aired that are so dangerous in a small community. About 1982, all of the fishermen agreed to reinstate the limit. No further defections from the norm have occurred, and a six hundred-trap limit remains in effect.

Monhegan islanders have imposed on themselves the strictest conservation rules in the industry. Since 1907, they have had a six-month season formalized by law. They have also had the informal trap limit and an informal apprenticeship program. In 1998, in the aftermath of years of territorial disputes with Friendship fishermen, the Monhegan islanders persuaded the legislature to establish a conservation zone around the island, which included a six hundred-trap limit, where only people who lived on the island could fish. This law established a zone 2 miles wide around the island (except on the southwest, where a 3-mile boundary exists). In this conservation zone, a six hundred-trap limit holds, and fishing is only permitted from December 1 to June 25. The number of licenses issued is limited to the number of licenses issued for Monhegan in 1997. In addition, only fishermen who have passed a special apprenticeship program on Monhegan can obtain a commercial lobster license to fish in the island's waters. According to the law, aspiring fishermen must spend 150 days on a Monhegan boat, and once they pass the apprenticeship program, they cannot go fishing in Monhegan waters until one of the fishermen on the island ceases to fish (Kinzie 1998).

Passage of this law was the result of the coordinated efforts of the fishermen on the island, and other island inhabitants, who spent over two months lobbying legislators in Augusta (Griffin 1998). In this effort, they were well led by fishermen Doug Boynton and Sherm Stanley, who literally lived in the state capital for weeks to buttonhole as many members of the legislature as they could. Despite massive opposition by fishermen from the mainland, the Monhegan conservation zone law passed easily. Prominent legislators said that they supported Monhegan's efforts because of the island's long history of effective conservation, and because failure to do so would reinforce fishermen who had overexploited their own inshore territory and were rapidly escalating the numbers of traps they fished. The sponsor of the bill, Senator Jill Goldthwait, urged senators to "support the people who have been doing it the right way for many generations" (Kinzie 1998). The legislature may have also been responding to the concerns of conservationists and the press, because most press coverage seemed to favor Monhegan.

Criehaven is about 1.25 miles long and contains some 750 acres of land. In 1799, the island was owned by Alexander Nichols, and by 1850, twelve people lived on the island. One of these settlers, Robert Crie, soon came to dominate the life of the island. He was the largest farmer on the island, with some 210 acres of farm land; by the 1870s he branched out into fish packing. He built a wharf and warehouses along the harbor where he conducted his business (McLane 1982: 37). He also divided up about 5 acres of land he owned along the harbor into 25- by 100-foot strips and gave them to his workers. This incentive was designed to keep a work force for his fish plant and to help keep the total island population large enough to maintain a post office, school, and store.

Few tourists visit Criehaven. The Crie family sold only a few pieces of land, and only a few cottages were ever built. Most of the land on the island has been kept in a wild state by the two families that bought the Crie estate.

By the 1920s, Criehaven began to decline. Some time before 1920, the fish-packing business established by Robert Crie went out of business, and all of the fishermen turned to lobstering. In 1925, the islanders gave up township status and became a plantation. The school was closed in the mid-1930s; the store and post office were gone by the 1960s.

The fishermen began to leave the island before World War II to take up residence on the mainland. They commuted to their fishing grounds around the island; during the days they were fishing, they stayed in the small houses they maintained there. They have continued this pattern to the present. Most of these houses they bought or inherited from the original owners who had received their land from Robert Crie.

After World War II, returning combat veterans were determined to improve the island's fisheries. Oscar Simpson and Phil Reed, two men from old established island families, took a leadership role. In the late 1940s and early 1950s, they carried on a campaign to persuade the rest of the fishermen that all would be better off if they limited the number of people allowed to fish for lobsters in the island's territory and established a trap limit. After much discussion, it was decided that the number of fishermen would be limited to those who owned the original eleven pieces of shore property on the harbor deeded by Robert Crie to his workers. Only these "berth owners" would be allowed to fish in the island's territory. These berths could be sold, and the new owner would not only own the land, dock, and house, but also rights to fish in the island's territory.

Then the Criehaven fishermen agreed on a trap limit. Consensus was helped along by the activities of one man with a pension and a huge gang of traps. One of the leaders kept pointing out that the average fisherman could not compete with a person with extra income. A trap limit, he said, would be fair to everyone and allow all to make a living. In the early 1950s, the eleven Criehaven lobster fishermen had instituted another rule that only 175 traps would be fished in the shallow water near the island to avoid trap congestion during shedder season. Later, the rule was changed to specify that only 300 traps could be used at any time of year; and still later the trap limit was changed to 600 traps.

Until very recently, the Criehaven gang has had little difficulty maintaining these rules and their rights to the island's territory. The island's territory has been established for a long time, and as one man pointed out, "everyone knows what the rules are." The fishermen held meetings twice a month to iron out problems. A couple of summer people with houses on the island did have to be prevented from going lobster fishing. One person who bought a house assumed that he would be allowed to go lobster fishing. A special meeting of the fishermen was held, and he was pointedly told that owning a cottage would not entitle him to go fishing. He left the island and sold the property. There have also been some incursions from nearby Matinicus, but no major "cut wars" have occurred.

However, there are signs that the solid front of the Criehaven gang may be breaking down. All of the fishermen and their families have lived in various towns on the mainland for so long that the families, at least, do not consider themselves islanders. At no time in the year do the families of Criehaven fishermen get together for any event, and they do not depend on each other at all. The fishermen themselves interact far less than their predecessors did. The bimonthly fishermen's meetings have not been held for the past several years. By 1996, only two of the original eleven fishermen who established the "berth" system after World War II were still fishing, and most of the other "berths" had been sold to people with no connections or family ties to the island. The year-round island community has not existed for several decades, and the sense of community appears to be waning rapidly.

This decline in social solidarity has resulted in an increased willingness to deviate from the rules. Some fishermen are unwilling to defend a part of the territorial lines that are being breached by men from another harbor. In addition, at least four are not abiding by the six hundred-trap limit. They were not sanctioned severely for several years, because it was recognized that cutting off their gear or a physical confrontation would result in a great deal of bitterness, retaliation, and an irreparable fissure in the "gang." Each person owns a berth and that gives them fishing rights.

Still, the fishermen who were abiding by the trap limit were very disappointed with the inability to a maintain consensus on the trap limit, and continued to fish six hundred traps. Finally, in 2000, several men decided to sanction those who were violating the trap limit. A verbal confrontation turned violent and resulted in a fight involving a melee between two fishermen, one wielding a pitchfork and the other a gaff. The one violating the trap-limit rule was convicted, but his conviction was overturned by the State Supreme Court after he argued that he was "acting in self-defense, contending he was under siege by other lobster fishermen on Criehaven who felt he was violating their locally imposed rules by using too many lobster traps" (Sharp 2000).

So far, the limited-entry program has remained intact, and the fishermen have been able to defend their fishing territory. Together, these institutions have made it possible to make a good living with fewer traps and avoid the aggravating tangles that have become endemic in mainland harbors. When berths on Criehaven become available, men from the crowded mainland harbors compete to get them, despite the fact that they cost in excess of $250,000 each. In the view of Phil Reed, who fished on Criehaven for decades, this system was brought about by one person. He said, "If it hadn't been for Oscar Simpson, Criehaven would never have been as it is today."

GREEN ISLAND

Green Island lies about 9 miles from the western shore of Penobscot Bay. It is an 82-acre, flat, treeless island, which was used seasonally for hay and pasture in the early nineteenth century. Some time after 1850, half of the island was bought by a members of the Witham family; and in the early 1900s the Witham family bought the other half. The land on the island has remained in the hands of various Withams ever since, and the island's fishing territory has been the family's exclusive domain for well over one hundred years (McLane 1982: 32).

Only a small number of people have ever lived on Green Island. In the latter part of the nineteenth century and first half of the twentieth century, a few members of the Witham family lived on the island and fished. After 1900, when faster, gas-powered boats became standard, they tended to live on the mainland most of the year, and inhabited the island only during the summer when they were fishing. Since the 1960s, all of the family members have lived on the mainland and commuted daily to the island to fish. They continue this pattern to the present. In 2000, nine Withams fished in Green Island waters. They live in Rockland, Tenant's Harbor, and other towns in Knox County. All of them moor their boats in Tenant's Harbor.

The Withams are very proud of their family and its historical connections with Green Island. Fishing is more than a way to make a living. It is a valuable heritage, and one they want to preserve for their children. The fact that in recent years four of the sons of various fishermen have decided to enter lobster fishing and continue the family heritage is a source of some satisfaction to the older fishermen.

Those fishing around Green Island are engaged in a family fishing enterprise. They love the island and value it greatly; and they want future generations of family members to be able to enjoy it as well. However, they do not really constitute a community. No one lives on the island year round, none of the family members cooperate in any activities on the island, nor do they maintain any improvements on the island, such as a common road or wharf. The fishermen's nuclear families, which live in various mainland towns, never meet together, nor do they have any rituals. Six family members do own camps on the island, but most of these are only occupied for a few weeks in the summer.

Moreover, interaction among the fishermen is limited. The Green Island fishermen themselves only talk on the dock before or after they go fishing. They do not meet on any regular basis. However, they do get together when an issue of some kind arises that involves the island or fishing. In recent years, informal meetings have been held involving state rules, environmental regulations, and boundary incursion. However, such meetings are quite rare in most years.

The Green Island fishermen have been very successful in controlling entry to their island territory. For the past several decades, only members of the Witham family who own land on the island itself are allowed to fish in the island's waters. In some periods, when not enough family members were fishing to use the fishing area and defend the lines, the family resorted to allowing a select few other fishermen to live on Green Island in camps in the summer and to fish off the island. These fishermen agreed to sell all their lobsters to a dealer in Rockland (usually Witham Brothers); the dealer would pay a set fee per pound caught, called "freight money," to the Witham family. This "freight money" was put in a special account and divided up among all family members who owned land on the island or was used to reimburse people who lost traps in defending the island's boundaries. The practice of charging "freight money" was stopped in the early 1970s when the older generation died.

For the past fifty years, the number of people fishing Green Island waters has remained constant. In the mid 1950s, nine boats were fishing off the island; in 2000, there are still nine vessels.

The Withams have been very successful in maintaining their exclusive fishing rights to the island's traditional territory. The defense is buttressed by the local ideology that asserts that the people who own shore land have fishing rights in the waters adjacent to their property.[2] In their view, the island and its waters have been theirs for a long time. No one is going to take them away easily. The importance of maintaining their territorial rights is one thing this gang agrees on.

However, they have been less successful in maintaining their trap limit. In the early 1970s, the members of the Witham family fishing around Green Island decided to maintain a five hundred-trap limit. At that time there appeared to be consensus. The trap limit seemed to work well from 1972 to about 1974. Then the norm came completely unraveled within a matter of a few months. One person decided he did not want to abide by the informal trap-limit agreement and put in more traps. Another discovered this fact, and rather than trying to sanction the defector, he too began to fish more than five hundred traps. When a third fisherman followed suit, the defections from the local trap limit became public knowledge and everyone began to order more traps. No one ever made any serious attempt to punish those who violated the norm because no one believed the defectors could be persuaded to obey the norm once they had decided to break it. There was never any question of rejecting the defectors from the Green Island territory. After all, they were family members, they owned land on the island, and they were entitled to fish there. However, some bad feeling resulted from the incident.

Since the 1970s, the number of traps the Green Island fishermen use has varied considerably. After the mid-1970s, the number of traps in use grew, and by 1997 individuals were fishing between twelve and sixteen hundred traps each. Since that time, they have reduced the numbers fished to avoid being in violation of the regulations of the zone they are in. In 2000, most were using eight hundred traps each, the maximum allowed by the zone regulations.

Swan's Island, with some 8,000 acres, is the largest in the group. The island was visited every summer by the Penobscot Indians until well into the twentieth century; and it was used by European fishermen as a fish-drying station in the seventeenth century if not before (Simpson 1960: 183; Westbrook 1958: 30–34). After the American Revolution, Massachusetts sold off chunks of Maine to entrepreneurs, with the provision that they attract settlers and develop the lands they received. Swan's Island was sold to James Swan, a friend of George Washington, Henry Knox, and Marquis de Lafayette, who set about attracting settlers to his proprietorship island by promising them 100-acre plots. Swan left the island in the hands of an agent; went broke; and spent many years in debtor's prison. The settlers were able to obtain legal title to the land Swan promised them, after literally decades of legal wrangling (Simpson 1960: 186; Westbrook 1958: 42–44). Most of the permanent residents of the island are descendants of these people.

In the nineteenth century, agriculture and groundfishing were the mainstays of the island's economy. After 1900, lobster became the most important fishery (Simpson 1960: 187–88; Westbrook 1958: 69–75). The last farms disappeared after World War II. On Swan's Island, the tourist industry has never achieved the prominence it has on Monhegan. There are, however, a good number of old farms that have been bought up by "summer people," and cottages line the shore in places. In 2000, the population was listed at 327 by the U.S. Bureau of the Census, but in the summer an estimated 1,000 people are on the island on any given day.

There are three settlements on Swans's Island. Many of the people live in Minturn and around Burnt Coat Harbor on the south end of the island; another small cluster of houses is in Atlantic on the north side of the island. However, many people also live in houses stretched along the 15 miles of road on the island or down driveways in isolated parts of the island. On Swan's Island, the population and services are scattered enough so that everyone owns a car. People regularly travel to the mainland to shop and obtain medical and legal services using the car ferry owned and operated by the state of Maine.

The lobster fishermen sell their catches at the cooperative and to two private dealers; a number have their own private wharfs. The largest employer on the island is Atlantic Salmon of Maine, a salmon aquaculture operation employing eight to ten people.

As in most small, isolated communities, a good deal of interaction takes place among the people on the island, and a distinct sense of community has developed. All of the permanent residents know one another, and everyone knows what other people are doing. A couple of people have said that Swan's Island is just a "big family." In fact, most of the permanent residents are members of one of the seven extended families that settled the island. Social life in the community revolves around family get-togethers, church suppers, meetings of the Odd Fellows, suppers at the Odd Fellows hall, and baseball games. Usually a group of people will get together once a year to put on a play. Others volunteer a good deal of time to the historical society, library, or town politics.

However, on Swan's Island it is possible to lead one's own life and remain remarkably uninvolved with community events. One person said some families are quite "independent." They are friendly enough, but mind their own business and sell their own lobsters on the mainland to make a few extra dollars. Another said, "Some people just work every day, and spend what little time they have with their family watching TV. You really do not see them that much."

The ability to remain detached is facilitated by the physical layout of Swan's Island. The population is scattered, and the widespread use of cars isolates people. Moreover, the island has no ethic of universal community service. Some people serve the community; others are content to let them. One person said, "it is the same small group of people who take responsibility for making sure things run." One person served as a selectman for twenty-five years, and is now on the school board.

The number of lobster fishermen has grown greatly in the past few years. Swan's Island certainly does not have a limited-entry program. One knowledgeable person said about fifty lobster fishermen fished from Swan's Island in 1980 (thirty-five full-time); today there are eighty-five or ninety boats, and at least fifty of these are owned by full-time fishermen. A few islanders have said that the island waters are reserved for "natives" of Swan's Island, and most of the fishermen do come from the seven old island families, or have married into such families. However, this doesn't do much to limit the number of fishermen. Virtually anyone from Swan's Island who wants to fish can do so, and a few "transplants" and "off islanders" have been successful in establishing themselves in the fishery as well. New fishermen on Swan's Island, like new fishermen in any harbor, go through a period of harassment, but no serious attempt has ever been made to limit the numbers of fishermen.

However, Swan's Island has been quite successful in maintaining its traditional territory and establishing a trap limit. The Swan's Island trap limit began in 1984 when the Commissioner of Marine Resources was persuaded to enact a regulation making Swan's Island a "conservation zone." That is, boundaries were agreed upon, and all those who fish within those boundaries must fish under a certain number of traps or face prosecution. The conservation zone is administered by a committee of four fishermen elected by the lobster license holders on the island. The number of traps permitted has varied somewhat. In 1984, the trap limit was 600; then it was lowered to 400 for a two-man boat and 300 for a man fishing alone; in 2000, it is 475 for everyone.

The Swan's Island conservation zone was brought about largely by one man, Sonny Sprague, who was aided by a few other highly regarded fishermen, who had long been "sick of the crowding and never being able to find a place to set traps." In 1978, after a series of statewide trap-limit bills had died in the legislature, Sprague and a few others became determined to obtain a local trap limit. He spent the next six years arguing and negotiating.

Most of the island's fishermen came to favor the conservation zone and trap limit when Sprague convinced them that such a law would allow everyone to make a good living, while reducing congestion and costs. Nevertheless, a small group of determined Swan's Island fishermen fought against the plan, and they remained bitterly opposed to it years after it passed. Persuading fishermen from other nearby harbors to go along with the trap limit was more difficult, since many of them perceived that they might lose fishing territory. In deference to them, the north side of Swan's Island was excluded from the conservation zone, and a provision was included in the plan allowing people from the mainland to go fishing in the zone if they are willing to abide by Swan's Island's stringent trap limit. Spencer Apollonio, the commissioner, signed the regulation creating the zone in 1984 only after years of talking convinced him that such a law would cap fishing effort and that most of the fishermen in the region would go along with it. The conservation zone and trap limit have been in effect ever since.

There is a good deal of support for the conservation zone and trap limit on Swan's Island. In 2000, sixteen years after it was established, most fishermen agree that the conservation zone and trap limit have benefitted everyone. Swan's Islanders say that a trap limit helps to limit gear tangles, reduces bait and trap expenses, and minimizes the jealousy that is so prevalent in other harbors. Their willingness to support the conservation zone is enhanced by the fact that it helps to maintain their fishing territory. Fishermen also feel that the conservation zone will help conserve the lobster resource in the long run. Sonny Sprague said that one of the major objectives of the conservation zone was to preserve the fishery for the next generation. He said, "The lobster fishery is the only thing that keeps Swan's Island alive as a year-round community. If it goes, the community would die as a year-round population."

The conservation zone has had two different kinds of problems. First, fishermen from the increasingly overcrowded harbors on the mainland have been placing more and more traps close to the Swan's Island lines. "We are feeling squeezed," one Swan's Island fisherman said. Second, fishermen on the island do not have universal agreement about how many traps should be used. Some people would like to fish more than the allowed 475, both to make more money and to help hold their fishing territory against the encroachments of the mainlanders. These men have been lobbying to change the number of traps to 600. Early in 2000, the administrators of the Swan's Island conservation zone held three meetings at the Odd Fellows hall to settle this matter. The proposal to change the trap limit from 475 to 600 was defeated by a vote of the fishermen.

The Marine Patrol has had relatively few problems in enforcing the Swan's Island conservation zone rules. In the eighteen years since the conservation zone was passed, only approximately eight cases have come to court. Some people from other harbors have been prosecuted for placing traps in Swan's Island waters; others from the island itself have been prosecuted for setting more traps than they were allowed under the trap limit regulations.

Analysis of Factors Promoting Informal Trap Limits

A complicated set of variables played a role in producing the trap limit on the four islands described above.

Knight (1992) argues that all rules and norms come about as a result of conflicts between factions over the distribution of valuable goods and services. This insight sheds a good deal of light on the factors producing trap limits. In all cases, the trap limits were the result of distributional battles within the harbor gangs between people with different interests. The limits were put in place by coalitions who wanted to use smaller numbers of traps to constrain those who were using more. These coalitions were led by skilled fishermen who could earn a good living using few traps; they were joined by others who, for one reason or another, could not fish large numbers of traps. One objective was to cut costs and control the increasingly troublesome gear congestion. Another goal of those with small numbers of traps was to increase the proportion of traps that they had on the bottom so they would get a "fair share" of the lobsters.

On Monhegan and Criehaven, those wanting to fish more traps acquiesced with good grace. On Swan's Island they did not, causing a rift in the fishing community that took years to heal. In the case of Green Island, everyone supported the move to a trap limit initially. The unraveling of the rule began when younger fishermen, who wanted to fish larger numbers of traps, defected. When it proved impossible to sanction them, the informal trap limit broke down completely. In this case, those who wanted to fish more traps ultimately forced their agenda on other gang members to the detriment of the trap limit.

However, if a distribution fight is all that is required to establish a trap limit, then many harbors would have them, since those favoring some control on the number of traps are in the numerical majority in many places. Clearly more is involved.

SIZE

Rational choice theorists generally agree that it is easier for groups to generate norms and rules if the group is small. In small groups, where people know what each other are doing, it is easier to monitor each other's behavior and detect cheating; there is an increased likelihood that sanctions will be imposed on those who violate rules (Coleman 1990: 260ff, 272; Knight 1992: 176–80; North 1990a: 12; E. Ostrom 1998: 2; M. Taylor 1990: 244; Wade 1994: 215). In small groups, each person's contribution is a larger percentage of the whole, making free riding more costly, and individuals have more incentive to cooperate since gross and average benefits of cooperation increase as group size decreases (Elster 1989: 33; R. Hardin 1982; Libecap 1989).

It is significant that Monhegan, Green Island, and Criehaven are very small; each has between eight and twelve fishermen. Swan's Island, by way of contrast, with some fifty full-time fishermen, is much larger, but since all the fishermen live permanently on the island, they can still monitor each other relatively closely.

A trap limit cannot come about in the absence of both limits on entry and territorial control. Like any rule, a trap limit can only be applied within the territory of a group willing to enforce it. A rule cannot apply generally. For this reason, trap limits cannot develop in areas under the control of two or more gangs where there is a lot of mixed fishing. Why should a person from one gang obey a local trap limit when he is fishing a few yards from someone from another gang who has inundated an area with traps? Obeying a trap-limit rule under these circumstances puts one at a disadvantage.

At the same time, it makes little sense to have a trap limit where it is possible for others to enter the harbor gang in large numbers. The objective of a trap limit is to gain the benefits of lower congestion and costs, when all members of a gang lower the number of traps they have in the water. If everyone in a harbor gang lowers the number of traps they own, while others are allowed to join the gang, the result can be more traps and more congestion, not less. For these reasons, trap limits are found only in perimeter-defended areas where boundaries are well defended and substantial barriers to entry exist.

On these islands, varying mechanisms are used to control access to the island's waters and to defend boundaries. On Criehaven, rights to fish are obtained by purchasing a berth; on Green Island, such rights are conveyed by family membership and inheritance. On both these islands, the island's fishing territory is defended by the threat of illegal activity, which is legitimized in the eyes of the island fishermen by the fact that they have legal property rights on the island. On Monhegan, entrance to the harbor gang is attained by moving on the island, serving an apprenticeship, and being judged acceptable by the established fishermen. On Swan's Island, fishing rights are obtained by virtue of being a member of an established island family. On Monhegan and Swan's Island, the island's fishing territory is specified in law and maintained with the help of the state's Marine Patrol.

All four islands have perimeter-defended territories that give rights over ocean areas that have many of the attributes of private property (Ostrom, Gardiner, and Walker 1994: 7ff). A number of analysts have stressed that property rights lower transaction costs and help secure the benefits of investments (Acheson 1994; Libecap 1989: 12–15; North 1990a: 33, 52). Both E. Ostrom (1992: 69) and Wade (1994: 215) argue that people will not assume the costs of producing rules to manage resources in the absence of such rights.[3]

The importance of controlling territorial boundaries and entry to harbor gangs vastly increases the problem of generating informal trap limits since it means that a *three-tiered collective action problem* is involved. Organizing a group to claim and defend a territory is one collective action problem. Generating a rule to limit entry to gangs is another. Producing a trap limit involves the third collective action problem. Solving the trap-limit collective action problem depends on having solved the first two collective action dilemmas. Such multi-tiered collective action problems have been noted in the literature before (see Hechter 1990: 246).

Capturing the Commons

Some social scientists argue that the time horizon that users of resources act under affects their behavior. If people value future income streams from a resource highly, they will be motivated to maintain the resource in the long run. Such people, who have low discount rates, will be much more willing to conserve the resource for their own gain in the future or even for their children. If they discount the future highly, they want to obtain all they can from the resource as quickly as possible, since future income will be small or not come at all (E. Ostrom 1990: 34–37, 188, 206–209; 1998: 2– 4; Singleton 1998: 24). People who have a high dependence on the resource are more likely to have a low discount rate. If the resource is overexploited and destroyed, they have no way to earn a living in the future, and the community dies (E. Ostrom 2000a: 34).

There can be little question that people in these four perimeter-defended areas are highly dependent on the lobster industry. Lobster fishing is the primary way of making a living on Monhegan and Swan's Island. There is no other way of making a living from the investment made in Green Island and Criehaven. As expected, the people fishing in the waters of these islands place a high value on future income from the lobster industry, indicating a low discount rate. Time and again, they stressed that they were willing to make sacrifices to preserve the resource for the next generation. Repeatedly, they stressed the history of the island and the role of their family in that history. They said they wanted enough of the children to be able to earn a living on the island so that the island community would not die. They were willing to control how the fishery is conducted to ensure the long term well being of future generations and their community.

COMMUNITY AND SOCIAL CAPITAL

Recently, a number of scholars have argued that one of the most important factors allowing some groups to develop rules to solve collective action dilemmas is a sense of community and the social capital that is found in communities (Singleton 1998: 23–24; Singleton and Taylor 1992). Communities, in this sense, are small groups whose members have intense face to face interaction and multiplex ties. They have a relatively stable membership, share a set of beliefs and values, and expect to continue interacting with each other over a long time span (Agrawal and Gibson 1999: 640; Singleton and Taylor 1992: 315). In small communities, where people interact a great deal over time, they have developed common norms, networks, and sentiments. This "social capital" makes it easier to obtain consensus (Coleman 1994: 190). In such communities, everyone knows the reputation of everyone else; they know who to trust and who is likely to violate rules. Perhaps most important, they have reciprocal relationships with a number of other people, which increases what Singleton and Taylor call their "mutual vulnerability." That is, they are dependent on each other for a variety of things of value, which other people can withhold if they are angry or displeased. This renders people in small communities more vulnerable to sanctions (Singleton and Taylor 1992: 315). Elinor Ostrom (1998: 3) puts much of this in a nutshell when she writes: ". . . reciprocity, reputation and trust can help to overcome the strong temptations of short-run self-interest." She summarizes the importance of community and social capital for developing rules to manage common-pool resources by saying:

> In such situations, individuals repeatedly communicate and interact with one another in a localized physical setting. Thus it is possible that they can learn whom to trust, what effects their actions will have on each other and on the CPR, and how to organize themselves to gain benefits and avoid harm. When individuals have lived in such situations for a substantial time and have developed shared norms and patterns of reciprocity, they possess social capital with which they can build institutional arrangement for resolving CPR dilemmas. (E. Ostrom 1990: 183–84)

The existence of a community itself will not guarantee that rules can be generated to solve collective action dilemmas. Rather, such communities have characteristics that make the negotiations to establish norms less costly, and hence increase the probability that such rules will be provided. Taylor and Singleton (1993: 196) argue that the existence of community makes it easier to overcome the transaction costs that are incurred in developing norms. E. Ostrom echoes this theme (2000a: 45).

POLITICAL ENTREPRENEURS

In all four cases, *political entrepreneurs* played a critical role in generating these local trap limits. Highly successful fishermen worked for months or even years to persuade fellow fishermen in their own harbor gangs and others that a trap limit would be advantageous. They succeeded, at least with the people who were fishing or wanted to fish moderate-sized gangs of gear. As do all political entrepreneurs, these people did more than work for the public good; they also offered information, expertise, and resources (M. Taylor 1990: 233–34). More important, they changed people's beliefs about trap limits.

Towns without Informal Trap Limits

None of the towns on the mainland have developed informal trap limits. Data presented here on four of these communities—Spruce Head, Pleasant Point (Cushing), New Harbor, and Boothbay Harbor—reveal that they have a very different set of characteristics than the islands that have developed trap limits.

These mainland communities have larger populations and are spread over far larger areas. The smallest is Spruce Head, with a population of 719 permanent inhabitants; the largest is Boothbay Harbor, with 2,334 in the 2000 U.S. Census.

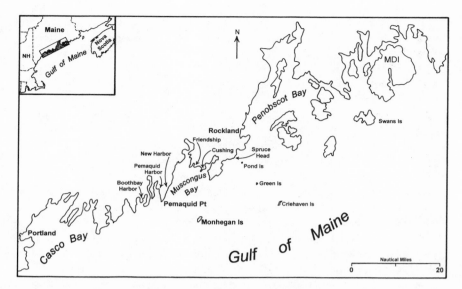

Map 3.1. Location of selected communities with and without informal trap limits.

Moreover, the population of these towns, like all towns along the Maine coast, explodes in the summer months. The shorefront property of all of these townships is lined by cottages, which are sometimes only a few feet apart. No good summer census exists, but there is no question that the summer population of these communities is several times what the winter population is. In the summer months, it is estimated that Boothbay Harbor has at least 10,000 people while Cushing has an estimated 2,000.

Nevertheless, three of these four communities have retained a decidedly rural and quiet atmosphere. These towns are down peninsulas, and their inhabitants do most of their shopping and obtain services in the nearby small cities along U.S. 1, such as Brunswick, Bath, Damariscotta, and Rockland. None of these towns except for Boothbay Harbor has many service businesses. New Harbor, for example, has an area in the middle of town (it would be too much to call it a "downtown") with a moderate-sized food store, a store selling groceries, gas, and short-order food, a hardware store, two restaurants, a bakery, and four gift shops and art galleries serving the tourist trade. Spruce Head and Cushing offer far fewer services. The exception is Boothbay Harbor, which is one of the tourist meccas and yachting centers along the Maine coast. Here, there are four boat yards in the harbor and immediate area that build a variety of different kinds of boats, a yacht club, and other establishments catering to the boating trade. The harbor itself is lined with motels, restaurants, and stores of various kinds catering to the summer tourists. In the summer, the downtown district throngs with people on foot, and the automobile traffic creeps through town. Finding a parking place in Boothbay Harbor can be very difficult. In addition, Boothbay Harbor has a small hospital, a large senior citizen's residential complex and nursing home, a number of professional offices, a Coast Guard Station, the Department of Marine Resources laboratory, and the Bigelow Laboratory for Oceanographic Research.

In all of these communities, employment is far more varied than it is on the islands. In Boothbay Harbor, the tourist and service industries are the largest employers. In New Harbor, Cushing, and Spruce Head, the lobster fishery employs more people than any other single industry in the community, but a substantial number of people are employed in service industries or in jobs in nearby cities (including Bath Iron Works and a cement plant in Thomaston). In some of these communities, the number of lobster fishermen is far outstripped by retirees who have no job at all.

All four of these harbors have nucleated territoriality. Most of the area exploited by people from these harbor gangs is fished jointly with men from one or more other harbors. To be sure, each of these harbors has a small area very close to the harbor mouth that its harbor gang fishes exclusively in the summer months. In Boothbay Harbor, these exclusive areas are literally in the heads of Linekin Bay, Lobster Cove, and Boothbay Harbor itself. The exclusive area of New Harbor is approximately 1.5 square miles of the estimated 55 square miles of territory. In Spruce Head, the exclusive area is a bit larger, but not much.

Moreover, in harbors such as these, efforts to limit entry have largely broken down. In the past, the vast majority of fishermen came from the town itself, and most people attempting to join these harbor gangs from other towns were rebuffed. Even people who moved into the community from outside had a difficult time going fishing. This situation has changed in the past twenty years. Now the vast majority of people who come to live in the community, learn the local norms, and begin lobster fishing on a small scale, have been able to enter the lobster fishery. In 2001, a sizeable number of fishermen in all four harbors either live in other towns or have moved into town from elsewhere. In Boothbay Harbor, for example, an estimated half of the fishermen did not grow up in Boothbay Harbor; and at least a third of those fishing out of Boothbay Harbor live in the nearby towns of Boothbay, Edgecomb, or Southport. In Cushing, the situation is similar, with people fishing from Pleasant Point who live in Thomaston and a few from the towns of Hope and Union, which are 20 miles away inland. Still, as we discussed in the last chapter, these communities are not completely open access either. In recent years, two fishermen from Augusta who went fishing from Boothbay Harbor in a fashion that offended many local fishermen lost so much gear that they finally decided on another line of work. The same thing has happened in virtually every harbor with nucleated fishing areas along the coast.

In all of these four harbors, the amount of interaction among fishermen is far less than it is on the islands. In these harbors, fishermen know each other at least by reputation, and they all know who the "high-liners" and potential troublemakers are. A good deal of interaction takes place on the radio. Boothbay Harbor fishermen monitor two channels; the younger men, who are more verbose, tend to use channel 10, while the older fishermen use 77. But there are no meetings that all the lobster fishermen attend, and many fishermen in these harbors do not know each other well. One fisherman from Boothbay Harbor who had served as president of the local cooperative said he knew all of the lobster fishermen in Boothbay Harbor who had boats over 30 feet long. "I know who they are, but I can't recall the names of all of their boats or what their [buoy] colors are." This conspicuously leaves out the numerous men with small boats, who include virtually all of the "part-time" fishermen. When I asked him how many of the Boothbay Harbor fishermen he talked to over the course of the year, he estimated that he talked to about three-quarters of them. However, he admitted he did not know many of these men well or "what they were thinking." Contrast this with Monhegan Island, where fishermen all meet together on numerous occasions—sometimes more than once a week—in the fish house of one of the lobstermen.

Characteristics of Harbors with and without Informal Trap Limits

Informal trap limits are the result of a rare set of conditions that are found on only a few islands. I argue that they came about where political entrepreneurs were able to mobilize an effective following within a harbor gang to win a distributional conflict against those who wanted to fish large amounts of gear. It was worthwhile to accept the transaction costs involved in this contest where the gang has a lot of exclusive fishing area, where entry into the harbor gang is strictly limited, and where the discount rate is low. Small gang size, social capital, and a sense of "community" aided the groups in gaining consensus and keeping people from defecting from the norm.

Virtually none of the other harbors along the coast have harbor gangs with the characteristics necessary to produce trap limits informally. In many harbors, those wanting to fish small or moderate amounts of gear have been effectively opposed by those wanting to fish more. Even on some of the islands with perimeter-defended areas, attempts to establish trap limits informally are stymied by powerful coalitions of men wanting to fish a lot of gear. A resident of one such island, who requested anonymity, said that "the ones that could have helped [impose a trap limit] are the biggest pigs in the bay." Some islands have all of the characteristics that would support the institution of an informal trap limit except for political control by a group wanting such a limit. On these islands, nothing happened. This reinforces the idea that a distribution fight and control by factions in favor of trap limits are key variables in producing informal trap limits.

More important, in mainland harbors with many part-time fishermen, the full-time fishermen have little incentive to establish trap limits, since their response to an increasing part-time population has been to put more gear in the water to maintain catch levels.[4] In the words of fisherman Arthur Pierce, when the "part-timers come in, the full-timers build up their gangs to keep ahead—to maintain a lead in the competition for lobsters. If you have a string of traps and the part-timers move in, your string will catch a lower number of pounds of lobster per

Table 3.1

Characteristics of Harbors with and without Local Trap Limits

	Monhegan	Criehaven	Green I.	Swan's I.	Spruce Head	Cushing	New Harbor	Boothbay Harbor
				Area				
Territory type	Perim.-defended	Perim.-defended	Perim.-defended	Perim.-defended	Nucleated	Nucleated	Nucleated	Nucleated
Local trap limit (historic)	600 (1974)	175 (inshore)	500 (1970s)	600 (1984)	None	None	None	None
Local trap limit (current)	600	600	None	475	None	None	None	None
Total boats	12–15	11	9	50	100	55	58	120
Sense of community	High	Medium, live on mainland, but family	High	High	Low	Low	Low	Low
Group decision making	Freq. mtgs. of captains	Earlier, 2×/mo, all fishermen? Now infrequent	No regular joint decision making	No regular joint decision making	None	None. Very infrequent meetings	Only co-op meetings	No joint decision making
Monitoring	Very high	High	High	Medium	Medium/low	Medium/low	Medium/low	Low
Dependence on resource	High	High	Medium	High	Medium	Medium	Medium	Low
Conformance w/current trap limit	High	4 of 11 not conforming	Broken down	High	N/A	N/A	N/A	N/A
State laws on local trap limit and area boundaries	Conservation zone; 6 mo.season	None	None	Conservation zone (8 in court)	None	None	None	None
Limited entry	Yes; residence	Yes; berth owners only	Yes; island owners only	Yes; old families mainly	No	No	No	No

trap. To make a living, you have to increase the number of traps you fish." The influx of part-time fishermen, especially in the western part of the coast, has resulted in massive trap escalation, with full-time fishermen commonly fishing more than eighteen hundred traps prior to the recent imposition of the statewide twelve hundred-trap limit. Casco Bay, where much of this escalation has occurred, became known facetiously as the "Bay of Pigs." Here, virtually all full-time fishermen have opposed trap limits because such rules work to the benefit of their competition, the part-timers, by increasing the percentage of traps that they have on the bottom.

Moreover, none of the harbors on the mainland have perimeter-defended areas. The existence of nucleated territoriality in these areas means that members of a gang who imposed a trap limit would be competing with people who are not constrained by such a rule. The alternative would be to organize two or more adjacent gangs to establish a trap limit. The transaction costs of such an attempt would be enormous.

The large size of mainland harbor gangs, along with weak community ties, exacerbates the problem of establishing trap limits. The large harbor gangs on the mainland have less capacity to come to consensus and sanction violators of norms.

It may be possible to generate self-imposed ("decentralized") trap limits on the mainland, but clearly the transaction costs of doing so would be much higher. Only one mainland harbor has succeeded, and their trap limit rule did not last long. Palmer (1994: 246) reports that this rule lasted for only a few years before it broke down. A summary of the characteristics of harbors with and without informal trap limits is contained in table 3.1.

Three Collective Action Dilemmas

The four perimeter-defended islands described here have been able to provide several different kinds of rules for themselves: territorial rules, limited entry rules, and trap limits. All of these posed collective action dilemmas. In all cases, people had strong motives to defect from the norm.

Are there factors that have been instrumental in allowing these islands to produce and maintain all three kinds of rules or rules in general? Are the factors responsible for the production of trap limits the same as those allowing these communities to generate rules concerning limited entry and territorial defense? In answering these questions, it needs to be noted that the factors responsible for generating these rules are not the same as those responsible for maintaining them.

There is no doubt that distributional concerns are the primary motive behind establishing the trap limits, and that these rules were established by negotiations orchestrated by political entrepreneurs. Establishing trap limits would make little sense in the absence of territorial boundaries and limited entry. These institutions prevent the benefits of trap limits from being captured by fishermen from other harbors.

Although we have little information on the motives of those establishing territories and limited-entry rules in the nineteenth century, it is very likely that distributional concerns played a strong role. After all, both territorial defense and limited-entry rules are ways of increasing catches for a group of fishermen in a particular location. However, in interviews concerning territorial defense and limited entry, two additional factors came to the fore, namely a low discount rate and dependence on the resource. People made it plain that they had few if any other ways to make a living on these islands, and that they needed to preserve these resources for themselves, if they were to make a living, and for future generations, if the community was to survive. I suspect these factors played a strong rule in motivating the establishment of territories and limited-entry rules.

What maintains these rules once they are established? A clue is contained in the fact that not all of the harbors have been equally successful in maintaining these three types of rules. Swan's Island has been able to maintain its trap limit and traditional territory by lobbying the Department of Marine Resources to establish a conservation zone. It has not been able to limit entry into the harbor gang, and there is not universal compliance with the trap-limit regulations. Green Island has done a good job of territorial defense and limiting entry. However, its trap limit broke down completely after a few years. Criehaven has limited entry to the eleven people who own berths, but this gang has experienced some defections from the trap-limit rule, and some members have clearly been free-riding on the willingness of others to defend the traditional territory. Of all of the islands, only Monhegan has been able to limit entry, maintain territorial defense, and maintain its trap limit. What is it about Monhegan that has allowed it to be more successful in solving its collective action dilemmas than the other islands?

Monhegan has succeeded in maintaining all three rules because of its very strong sense of community. It is a small, year-round community where intense interaction aids in developing common goals and values, allowing people to reach consensus more easily. The ability to sanction defectors is enhanced by the ease with which the behavior of others can be monitored and by their high degree of dependence on other islanders, making them "mutually vulnerable."

Swan's Island, by way of contrast, is also a year-round community. However, its population is larger and more spread out, and there is much less interaction between inhabitants. Its fishing community has developed factions, and some people are defecting from the trap-limit norms.

Green Island and Criehaven have little sense of community, the fishermen and their families do not interact much, and they have not developed much social capital. The ability to sanction defectors is undermined by several factors. The fishermen and their families all live on the mainland, adding to the cost of monitoring each other's behavior, and making them less dependent on each other. Moreover, the idea that only those who own land have the right to fish off these islands makes it very difficult to sanction island fishermen who violate rules. After all, they own land or berths on the island and have a right to fish there. This ideological commitment, however, does reinforce the local limited-entry rules.

If this analysis is correct, two factors play a key role in establishing rules: distributional concerns motivate people to want rules, and political entrepreneurs are the means by which they are negotiated. A strong sense of community appears to play a key role in maintaining rules once they are in place.

CHAPTER 4

The Genesis of State Laws
for the Lobster Industry

The state statutes governing the lobster industry came about during three periods spanning the past 120 years. The first of these was the 1870s and 1880s,
when the first conservation laws were enacted. The second was the early 1930s,
when the double-gauge law was enacted. The third is the current period, from 1977
to the present. In 1977, the federal government had gained the power to regulate
fisheries and this strongly influenced the legislation, even state laws, passed in this
period. During this period, the Maine legislature passed the escape-vent law, and
in 1995, it enacted the zone management law, which radically changed many aspects of governance of the industry.

These laws were put into place over the course of the past 120 years by political
processes that do not fit neatly into any one theoretical mold. Complicating the
picture are the complex and changing roles played by factions in the lobster industry, the bureaucracy, and the Maine legislature. Changes in lobster stock sizes and
catch levels also had a major effect on the legislation that was passed. Catches were
relatively high in the 1880s, although they had been much higher previously (see
table 1.1). Catches languished in the early years of the twentieth century and then
declined disastrously in the years between World War I and World War II. Since
World War II, catches have been very stable, save for the past twelve years when
they have increased to record highs.

Emergence of a Conservation Ethic

A major factor influencing legislation has been attitudes toward conservation in
the industry and among the public. In the late nineteenth and early twentieth centuries, massive violations of the then-existing conservation laws occurred in the
lobster industry. Throughout the early decades of the twentieth century, it was
common for people to take home short lobsters to feed the family. A very large
number of fishermen and dealers were involved in the lively and remunerative
"short-lobster" trade, whereby untold amounts of illegal-sized lobsters were

shipped out of state (Judd 1988: 612). Zenas Howe, the Massachusetts Fisheries Commissioner, reported that illegal lobsters from Maine were arriving in Boston by the boatload in the 1930s (Correspondence of the Commissioner 1931e). In addition, it was not unheard of for fishermen to smash up short lobsters caught in their traps to serve as bait (Clifford 1961: 124). Even worse, many used stiff brushes to scrub the eggs off berried females, and sold them. The biologist Rathbun was horrified at the "wholesale slaughter of females with eggs, which has always been going on" (Rathbun 1887: 697). Other biologists made similar comments (Cobb 1901: 124; Herrick 1911: 370).

In the early 1920s, violations of the lobster conservation laws were so severe that Commissioner Crie closed the entire lobster fishery along the central coast for a period, convinced that only drastic action would change attitudes and practices (Clifford 1961: 204; Martin and Lipfert 1985: 55). His action had little effect. In the early years of the century, people in the industry did not consider violation of laws as very serious offenses. A conspiracy of silence surrounded the illegal lobster trade, and fishermen did very little to aid law enforcement. Commissioner Crie pointed out that the wardens could do little without the cooperation of the fishermen and that, "It has been my experience in the past that almost every man, woman, and child in your county were in favor of the illegal traffic in lobsters" (Correspondence of the Commissioner 1932a). Fishermen considered it "alright to save shorts to eat" and large numbers did so regularly (Correspondence of the Commissioner 1931b). Sometimes when people were convicted of taking "shorts," judges allowed them to retain their licenses (Correspondence of the Commissioner 1932b). Biologist Leslie Scattergood, who went to work at the Boothbay Harbor laboratory of the Department of Marine Resources in 1939, said in a 1996 interview that, in the 1920s and early 1930s, "violation of the lobster laws was like rum running. It was against the law, but everyone was doing it." Even in the fishery agencies, conservation wasn't taken very seriously. Les Scattergood tells of being invited to the house of the commissioner of the state agency charged with managing marine resources in a mid-Atlantic state where the commissioner's wife served her guests illegal-sized lobsters.

The period between 1930 and 1960 saw the beginning of a marked change in attitudes toward conservation. By the end of the 1930s, Leslie Scattergood reports that "large-scale violations had ceased." This change in attitudes is reflected in the correspondence of Commissioner Crie, who began to receive reports of illegal activity from fishermen. Walter Donnell of York Village wrote the commissioner complaining that "Mr. Underhill the warden at Saco knows all about who is dealing in shorts, but why don't he stop them. He will catch someone once in a while with some shorts up here, but the ones he catches are only fishermen with a few traps" (Correspondence of the Commissioner 1932c). The change in attitudes and practices was brought about by the disaster of the 1930s as much as anything. Increasingly, people became convinced that those violating the conservation laws were doing far more damage than they had thought previously.

In the years since World War II, a marked conservation ethic has grown in the industry. By the 1990s, the lobster conservation laws became almost self-enforcing.

The Genesis of State Laws 81

Moreover, as we shall see, the leadership of the industry associations are very much concerned with conservation legislation. They spend a major part of their time working to pass legislation that will benefit the resource and the lobster industry in the long run. In short, the last seventy years has seen the industry go from a time when illegal activity was well accepted to a time when the industry is a strong supporter of effective conservation legislation and law enforcement (Clifford 1974: 146).

Minimum Size Limit and Protection of Egged Females: 1870s and 1880s

Until the middle of the nineteenth century, lobsters were caught for local consumption, but no commercial lobster industry existed (Martin and Lipfert 1985: 9–11). The commercial development of the industry had to await two technical developments in the 1840s: the invention of the lobster smack, a sailing vessel with a circulating seawater tank, allowing shipment of live lobsters to the cities along the north-Atlantic coast; and the invention of canning (Cobb 1901: 243– 44; Martin and Lipfert 1985: 13).

After 1840, the commercial lobster industry expanded rapidly. Untold millions of live lobsters were shipped to destinations such as Boston and New York. The first lobster cannery was established in 1842, and by 1880 twenty-three plants in Maine were packing lobster (Rathbun 1887: 690). In this period, the vast majority of lobsters caught were canned.

In the 1840s and 1850s, lobsters were plentiful, and the size was very large (Martin and Lipfert 1985: 43). However, by the late 1860s there were clear signs of trouble. The catch was the same, but the numbers of fishermen and traps had increased markedly, resulting in a clear reduction in both the average size of lobsters caught and the catch per unit of effort (Cobb 1901: 244, 255–56; Herrick 1911: 367– 69; Rathbun 1887: 701–708). After 1880, catches declined to the point where the operation of some of the canneries had to be curtailed early in the season for a lack of lobsters to pack (Cobb 1901: 256).

Everyone concerned with the industry agreed that something should be done to protect the resource, but the solutions proposed by the canners and live-lobster industry differed significantly (Rathbun 1887: 725).

The fishermen and dealers engaged in the live-lobster trade blamed the canners. There can be no denying that canning was very wasteful. Canners made a practice of transporting lobsters in "dry smacks," which killed a lot of the catch (Cobb 1901: 250). It took about 5 pounds of raw lobster to obtain 1 pound for packing. Moreover, although the canneries took all size lobsters, they preferred small ones, because they could be had at a cheaper price per pound (Mattocks n.d.). Several reports indicate that canners regularly processed lobsters weighing as little as half a pound or less (Cobb 1901: 256; Martin and Lipfert 1985: 42). Such practices were detrimental to the live-lobster industry. Since the stock-in-trade of the fresh-lobster dealers and fishermen were large "dinner" sized lobsters destined for restaurants in the large cities of the East Coast, it was in the interests of this part of the industry to protect small lobsters until they grew to a size where they could be sold on the "live market."

Thus, the battle lines were drawn between the canners and the live-lobster industry. The laws that ultimately emerged were the result of a twenty-year struggle for control of the resource. Much of the ammunition for that battle was supplied by European lobster biologists, who recommended that the problems in the lobster industries of their own countries could be cured with various types of regulations on size, season, and protection of breeding stock (Rathbun 1887: 711–25).

Interestingly enough, it was the canners who lobbied the Maine legislature for the first "conservation laws," to defend their interests (Judd 1988: 605). In 1872, a law was passed forbidding the taking of egg-bearing females (Legislative Documents 1872). In 1874, the canners lobbied the legislature again, with the result that fishing for lobsters less than 10½ inches (head to tail) was prohibited from October 1 to April 1 (Laws of Maine 1874). These so-called "conservation" laws were designed to curtail the activity of the fresh-lobster industry, but did little to change the practices of the canneries. The law prohibiting the capture of egged females did not affect the canners since they used lobster too small to extrude eggs, while the seasonal size minimum left the canneries free to take all sizes of lobsters during the summer canning season, and made the state responsible for protecting the lobsters when the canneries were processing vegetables. Not too surprisingly, the devastation to the resource continued.

The live-lobster industry lost the first battle, but they won all the rest. After 1870, the live-lobster trade expanded enormously because of the market expansion facilitated by the arrival of the railroads, which allowed long-distance shipment of iced lobsters, and because of the development of the lobster pound (a fenced-in portion of the ocean) where live lobsters could be stored for months. As increasing numbers of fishermen supplied the live market, their dependence on the canneries decreased, especially in the western part of the coast where access to rail service was better. The political power of those involved in the fresh-lobster market grew correspondingly.

Those in the live-lobster trade knew that the existing legislation worked to the benefit of the canners and did nothing for conservation. They wanted a law prohibiting the canneries from slaughtering millions of small animals, so that the lobsters could grow to a size at which they could be sold in the live trade. One fisherman called the existing laws a "farce," and called for a "law to protect the small and soft lobsters the entire year" (Rathbun 1887: 727). Many echoed his sentiments, and the legislature was soon besieged with requests and petitions from fishermen's groups for legislation to protect small lobsters.

In 1879, it was made illegal to can lobsters from August 1 to April 1 (Laws of Maine 1879). In 1883, it was made illegal to catch any female lobster "in spawn or with eggs attached, or any young lobster less than nine inches in length [i.e., total body length, head to tail]" between April 1 and August 1 (Laws of Maine 1883). These pieces of legislation changed the distribution of the lobster catch considerably, since they made it illegal to take the small and cheap lobsters on which the canners depended, effectively reserving the lion's share of the catch for the live-lobster industry.

The canners and the fishermen along the eastern coast who sold to the canneries fought back. They opposed the minimum size measure and repeatedly petitioned the legislature to allow canning to continue unencumbered. Their propaganda claimed that it was the lobster pounds, not canning, that were causing the depletion of the resource.

The live-lobster industry continued its assault unabated. In 1885, its lobbying efforts resulted in a law effectively reducing the canning season to three and one half months (Laws of Maine 1885); and in 1889, the law was changed to make it legal to take lobsters as small as 9 inches in total length only from May 1 to July 1 (Laws of Maine 1889). These laws made canning so unprofitable that the canneries began to close (Cobb 1901: 256–57). Many went to Canada. In 1895, the legislature passed a law increasing the minimum legal size to of 10½ inches at all times of year; this law apparently forced the last of the canneries from the state (Judd 1988: 606; McFarland 1911: 233).

Although both canners and the fresh-lobster industry lobbied for legislation to reserve much of the catch for themselves, the rules they put in place were designed to protect juvenile lobsters and egg-bearing females. To this day, efforts to conserve the lobster still depend on size regulations and protection of the breeding stock.

The Export Ban and Seasonal Laws: 1900 to 1925

In the first two decades of the new century, little was done on the legislative front. During these years, the industry did engage in lobbying for two kinds of bills. Neither lasted.

Fishermen in a large number of coastal towns petitioned the legislature for closed seasons on lobsters in the waters where they fished. The first such law closed Pigeon Hill Bay in Milbridge and Steuben to fishing in the summer (Laws of Maine 1899). Similar laws were enacted in other towns. In 1907, Monhegan Island successfully lobbied for a law to close fishing within 2 miles of the island from June to November (Laws of Maine 1907b). In 1911, fishermen from Winter Harbor lobbied the legislature to enact a law making it illegal to catch lobsters in the waters of Winter Harbor in the summer (Laws of Maine 1911); and in 1915, similar legislation was passed establishing closed seasons in Cutler, Trescott, Lubec, Jonesboro, Roque Bluffs, and Machias Bay (Laws of Maine 1915a, 1915b, 1915c). A few years later, such laws were passed for Criehaven and Petit Manan Point (Laws of Maine 1925, 1931). By the late 1930s and 1940s, the fad had passed and most of these laws were repealed.

We know very little about the reasons these laws were passed or why they were repealed. The surviving legislative record reveals little about the rationale for such laws. In one or two cases, it was mentioned that the goal was to protect the lobsters in the summer months when they were molting. However, it is very likely that those advocating such rules had other, more practical motives in mind. The only one of these laws that has survived to the present is the Monhegan season law. If we can judge from this law, the goal was to preserve the lobsters for a particular group of people to take at a time convenient for them. This law effectively prevents mainland fishermen from exploiting the lobsters around Monhegan in the height of the summer season when Monheganers are occupied with the tourist trade, and allows Monhegan fishermen to take them in the winter when prices are highest and they have no other available source of income. It is very likely that similar motives prompted the passage of other season laws in other towns.

John Olson of Cushing, who began lobster fishing in 1934 when he was twelve years old, recalls conversations with older fishermen on this issue. He believes these laws were designed to raise income to fishermen and shippers by lowering mortality rates. At this time, lobsters were transported to market in smacks with flowing seawater tanks. In the summer, there would be a high mortality rate on shedders and soft-shelled lobsters transported in this way. The law against taking lobsters in the summer months conserved the catch until the fall when they could be shipped with much less loss of life. When refrigeration was widely adopted in the late 1930s and 1940s, the mortality due to shipping dropped dramatically, and these laws became unnecessary.

Another legislative initiative in these years was the move to prohibit the export of live Maine lobsters, fueled in part by a fear of "trusts" (i.e., corporations) who were suspected of planning to hijack most of the supply, and the interests of Maine's growing tourist and hotel trade, whose well-advertised outdoor lobster "bakes" depended on a supply of cheap lobsters. The lobster dealers opposed the ban since they depended on out-of-state markets for much of their income, especially in the cold months of the years when tourists were scarce and the hotels were closed. Their allies were the fishermen from eastern Maine, where the tourist trade was undeveloped. Together they managed to defeat the export ban in the legislature (Judd 1988: 614–16).

In retrospect, neither the efforts to establish town closed-seasonal laws nor the export ban had any lasting impact on the industry. However, they call attention to the willingness and ability of groups of fishermen in certain towns to lobby effectively for legislation they believe will conserve the lobsters and further their own economic interests.

The Double Gauge: 1915 to 1933

The end of canning and the passage of these first size laws and season laws did not see an improvement in the prospects of the lobster industry. Catches continued to decline. From 1900 to 1920, the average catch was 13.2 million pounds, close to half of what it had been in 1889 (Maine Department of Marine Resources 1995). Both fishermen and biologists recognized that the industry was not what it had once been (Cobb 1901: 241; Rathbun 1887: 707). The consensus among biologists was that additional regulations were needed, over and above the of 10½-inch minimum size limit and the prohibition against catching gravid females that had been passed in the 1880s (Kelly 1990: 3). As early as 1910, biologist George Field argued that catches would not begin to rise until the larger, more prolific breeding stock was protected (Martin and Lipfert 1985: 51). However, most people in the industry were strongly opposed to raising the minimum size, seeing clearly that such an increase would cut their catches by increasing the number of lobsters that had to be thrown back, and would produce large lobsters that would have to be sold at such high prices that Maine would be effectively closed out of much of the national and international markets. In retrospect, it is hard to argue with the reasoning of either side.

Francis Herrick proposed a compromise solution, namely, a double-gauge law specifying both a minimum size to protect small lobsters and a maximum size to protect larger, proven breeding stock. This would focus all fishing on lobsters that were large enough to make a good meal (i.e., dinner-sized lobsters), but were small enough so that they could not usually extrude eggs. Herrick originally thought the minimum should be 9 inches and the maximum 11 inches (Herrick 1911: 382).

Lack of consensus resulted in the legislature doing little beyond changing the way lobsters were measured, thereby retaining in effect the 10½-inch minimum gauge (Laws of Maine 1907a). Lobsters were to be measured on the carapace rather than in terms of total length. Thus a lobster with a total length of of 10½ inches became a lobster with a of 4¾-inch carapace, measured from the tip of the rostrum to the end of the body. This is a 3.65-inch lobster measured from the eye orbit to the back of the shell. For many, this was the worst of all possible worlds. Fishermen had dubbed the of 10½-inch measure the "poverty gauge," since it outlawed the vast majority of the lobsters they caught (Acheson 1992: 155). They agitated against this law continually. The biologists were openly contemptuous, since this law put all the fishing effort on the large, reproductive-size lobsters. Biologist Francis Herrick minced no words. He said the law was "unscientific," "defective," and "bound to fail" (1911: 369, 371). The disrespect with which this law was held almost certainly exacerbated the problem of enforcement. Fishermen, after all, are not prone to obey laws they consider ineffective and counterproductive.

In 1915, conditions in the industry were serious enough that the legislature appointed a commission to study lobster regulation (Legislative Record 1915a). Dr. Francis Herrick was called to testify, and strongly urged the commission to recommend a double-gauge law for the long-run welfare of the industry and the state (Legislative Record 1915b; Martin and Lipfert 1985: 55). The commission recommended passage of the double-gauge law, but after representatives from coastal counties talked with their constituents, no bill favoring the double gauge was sent to the floor of the legislature (Legislative Record 1915c).

The basic cause of the impasse was a conflict of interest between industry factions. In general, fishermen from the western counties wanted to lower the minimum size from of 4¾ inches on the backshell (10½ inches total body length) to 9 inches total body length. They found allies among dealers and hoteliers who wanted to increase their share of the national markets, where small or "chicken" lobsters from Massachusetts and Canada had proven all too popular. However, most of the fishermen along the central and eastern parts of the coast did not favor a small gauge, since they believed it was nothing more than a ploy by the dealers to import large amounts of small Canadian lobsters and undercut the price received by Maine fishermen (Correspondence of the Commissioner 1933a).

They couched their case in terms of conserving the reproductive stock.[1] It was to take a disaster to break the impasse.

In 1919, catches declined sharply, and they remained at record low levels throughout the 1920s and well into the 1930s.[2] Once the Depression began, prices for lobster fell drastically, even though catches were also very low. The incomes of fishermen were so low that 32 percent left the industry between 1928 and 1932 (Acheson 1992: 157– 60; Correspondence of the Commissioner 1933b; Maine Department of Marine Resources 1995). The disastrous conditions continued for years (Correspondence of the Commissioner 1931a; 1931b; 1931c; 1933c). The fishery was not to recover until World War II.

Horatio Crie, who was the Commissioner of Sea and Shore Fisheries and a very able politician, played a key role in all of the attempts to alleviate the situation. Crie attacked the problem by urging the people of Maine to eat "lobsters twice a week" to strengthen demand (Correspondence of the Commissioner 1931d). In addition, he and Senator William White strongly supported a bill in the U.S. Congress that would have prohibited the importation of "cheap" Canadian lobsters, which were thought to be depressing the Maine prices (Correspondence of the Commissioner 1933b; Elden 1931). President Roosevelt refused to support this effort on the grounds that the Canadians might retaliate by imposing tariffs on the importation of U.S. goods and products. The U.S. Congress did not pass these bills. In addition, Crie and industry leaders attempted to generate higher prices for lobsters by initiating an advertising campaign and by introducing three bills in the U.S. Congress levying tariffs on imported Canadian lobsters (Correspondence of the Commissioner 1931d; 1933d; 1933e). This did little for sales. When it became obvious that these efforts had failed, Crie and his ally in the legislature, Senator Look, turned their attention to passing a double-gauge law (Correspondence of the Commissioner 1933f). Crie pointed out that the double-gauge law would protect small lobsters, conserve the large reproductive-size lobsters, and allow Maine fishermen to catch smaller, more marketable lobsters than the current law allowed. It would also, he argued, keep out 40 percent of the Canadian lobsters that were currently flooding the U.S. market (Elton 1933a). In short, Crie argued that the double-gauge law would be good for both conservation and sales.

In 1933, Crie began a whirlwind campaign to rally support for the double-gauge law. He announced his support in all the coastal newspapers; he sent letters explaining his position to fishermen and the congressional delegation (Correspondence of the Commissioner 1933f; 1933g); and he had his wardens try to convince fishermen to sign petitions favoring the double gauge (Correspondence of the Commissioner 1933h).

But no consensus emerged. A questionnaire that Crie sent to all lobster license holders revealed that the industry was badly split on the issue (Elton 1933b). Judd reports that "1,166 respondents favored the double-gauge law, and 1,068 were satisfied with the existing limit" (1988: 622). Most of the support came from the western coast, and most of the opposition from the east (Acheson 1997: 12).

The debate became nastier, and the correspondence reveals a good deal of bitterness and frustration on all sides (Correspondence of the Commissioner 1933h). In the regular session of the legislature, efforts to reduce the legal minimum size to 9 inches (overall) and to establish a double-gauge law were both voted down (Elton 1933a: 8).

In December 1933, the Maine legislature met in special session to deal with a number of issues concerning the deepening economic crisis. Another double-gauge bill was proposed as the solution to the lobster industry's problems. On December 11, 1933, Commissioner Crie spoke in favor of the bill, emphasizing the need to preserve the industry by protecting the large, reproductive animals. He promised "if a double-gauge measure is passed . . . that you will see the lobsters continue to increase from year to year and no one will ever have to feel disturbed about the depletion of the lobsters on the Maine Coast so long as a double-gauge measure is enforced" (Crie 1933:2).

A few days later, with almost no publicity or debate, the Maine legislature narrowly passed the bill (Elton 1934). It provided for a 3¹⁄₁₆-inch minimum and 4½-inch maximum carapace measure. It was truly a radical piece of legislation, one of the few double-gauge laws in the world (Legislative Document 1935), and it remains the backbone of lobster conservation efforts in Maine to this day.[3]

Reaction in the industry was decidedly mixed. Some groups went on record as favoring the law (*Portland Sunday Telegram* 1933). The opponents were so unhappy that they decided to try to have it overturned by a referendum, but did not obtain enough signatures to have it put on the ballot (Correspondence of the Commissioner 1934). The opponents of this law remained bitter for decades, convinced the Crie had sold out their interests to the dealers.

Economic conditions played a role in the passage of this legislation. The industry and legislature were more willing to consider radical solutions after years of economic decline. However, the bill would likely not have passed into law were it not for Crie's political entrepreneurship. His open advocacy of the bill, his enlisting of support from key legislators, and his speech to the legislature before the final vote were all crucial. Most important were his lobbying efforts with the industry. In the last analysis, the double-gauge law passed because of a coalition between the proponents of the bill in the industry, Commissioner Crie, and powerful members of the Maine legislature, such as Senator Look, who were concerned with marine resources. When this coalition went into action in 1931, twenty years of gridlock gave way in less than eighteen months. In essence, Crie and Look had negotiated a deal in which they gave their support to an industry faction favoring a smaller minimum-size limit to increase markets, in exchange for that faction's support of a maximum-size measure protecting the more prolific large lobsters.

The V-Notch Program: 1917, 1948, and Building

The current V-notch law states that lobsters with a V-shaped notch cut into one of the side flippers may not be taken. Fishermen take advantage of this law by cutting

Capturing the Commons

V-notches in the egg-bearing females they catch to prevent them from being taken by other fishermen once their eggs have dropped off. They are considered proven breeding stock.[4] Many lobster fishermen consider this the most important conservation measure in force today. In their view, it has resulted in a very large brood stock, which ensures an adequate number of eggs in the water. It has tremendous support in the Maine industry at present. However, it is important to realize that the V-notch program is voluntary. The law prohibits fishermen from taking berried females, but no law makes it mandatory for them to put a notch in the tail. Large numbers of fishermen do so to preserve the breeding stock. (It should be noted that a 2002 proposal makes V-notching mandatory in coastal waters of Maine, New Hampshire, and northern Massachusetts.)

The V-notch program builds on a law that was designed to subsidize pound owners. By the World War I era, there was a general consensus that the preservation of the industry depended on protection of the breeding stock, and that additional conservation laws were needed to accomplish this task. While the legislature refused to pass the double-gauge law in the 1915 and 1917 legislatures, it was persuaded to compensate by establishing a program whereby egged lobsters would be purchased by the state, whose officers would punch a hole in their tails and release them (Legislative Record 1917). Fishermen were forbidden to take lobsters with punched tails (Kelly 1990:3), and they were not allowed to sell the berried lobsters they caught to the state. Only pound owners could do so (Maine Commission of Sea and Shore Fisheries 1926: 16). Biologist Leslie Scattergood said in an interview, "this law was passed primarily to stop pound owners from scrubbing the eggs from lobsters that had extruded eggs while they were in the pounds." Pound owners had bought these lobsters from fishermen and felt that they had a right to sell them, even though it was illegal to do so once they had extruded eggs. The "punched-tail" law or "seeder program" was an effort to bribe pound owners to obey the law. By the mid-1930s, however, the "seeder program" had expanded to the point where the state of Maine was purchasing "60,000 pounds of seed lobster, from the fishermen through dealers, at market prices" (Maine Department of Sea and Shore Fisheries 1936: 11). These lobsters were punched on a tail flipper, and most were released where the warden had purchased them, but others were used in the hatchery at Boothbay Harbor.

Only a few minor changes were made in the laws concerning egged lobsters from 1917 to the present. In 1948, the law was changed to state that egged lobsters would be marked by cutting a V-shaped notch in the tail, rather than being marked by a round hole punched in the tail. In addition, egged lobsters would only be purchased from people licensed by the commissioner, a change designed to aid enforcement efforts (Laws of Maine 1947).[5] In 1973, the law was changed to specify that the V-notch was to be placed in the "right flipper next to the middle flipper" (Kelly 1990: 4).

The big change in the V-notch program took place on the informal level, when increasing numbers of lobster fishermen took advantage of the law to conserve the resource by voluntarily cutting notches in the tails of the egged lobsters they had caught. Eddie Blackmore, president of the Maine Lobsterman's Association, said that it was the young veterans returning from World War II who were responsible for the change: "We decided that if we were going to keep it [the fishery] going, we needed to do something to replenish the supply." One of the primary ploys they used was to take advantage of the V-notch law by *voluntarily* cutting notches in the tail flippers of egged lobsters. Former Commissioner Vinal Look points out, "there was never a law that stated that fishermen could not cut V-notches in the tails of egged lobsters." It became increasingly popular to do so. It is one of those cases, perhaps rare, where a formal law was turned into an informal norm.

The current V-notch law receives a mixed reaction from observers of the industry. On the whole, lobster fishermen consider this the most important conservation measure in force today. In their view, it has resulted in a very large brood stock, which ensures that there are an adequate number of eggs in the water. However, federal and state biologists are not convinced, for reasons we will explore in detail in chapters 6 and 7. As a result, they have worked long and hard for passage of a federal fisheries management plan that would not include either a V-notch or an oversize measure. As we shall see, this resulted in a battle over the V-notch lasting more than twenty years, which greatly influenced the course of lobster management.

The Escape Vent: 1978

From 1976 to 1978, a great deal of interest arose within the bureaucracy and the industry for establishing an escape-vent law. Such a law would specify that a space be built into each trap, by one means or another, to allow small, sub-legal lobsters to escape from the traps before they were hauled up. This would reduce the amount of time it took fishermen to clean out their traps. It would also reduce the numbers of lobsters killed or mutilated, since small lobsters are eaten by larger lobsters in the traps and by large fish after they are thrown overboard and are on their way back to the bottom; molting lobsters are also eaten by any hard-shell lobster in the trap. In addition, lobsters tend to hang on to the traps, and regularly have claws pulled off by fishermen who are attempting to remove them and throw them overboard. An escape vent would reduce the numbers mutilated in this way.

By the mid-1970s, the escape vent was an idea whose time had come. Massachusetts and Newfoundland had established such laws in the 1970s (Martin and Lipfert 1985: 109). In the United States, state and federal biologists were very interested in reducing mortality on sub-legal lobsters. In the mid-1970s, the entire research staff of the Maine Department of Marine Resources became strong advocates (Krouse and Thomas 1976). Spencer Apollonio, who was commissioner at that time, recalls that "Cecil Pierce of Southport developed a plastic vent. We [the DMR biologists] tried it out in a tank, and it clearly worked. The DMR then made the escape vent mandatory by regulation," and within a year, a proposal for an escape vent became part of the proposed Federal American Lobster Management Plan (*Maine Commercial Fisheries* 1978c).

Some fishermen, at least, saw virtue in escape vents. A few scattered along the coast had already been placing escape vents in their traps. "High-liner" (highly successful fisherman) Jimmy Brackett of Pemaquid Harbor said that "one of the secrets of success was to have one lathe on the bottom of the trap with a large space" to reduce the amount of work cleaning out small lobsters from traps and to increase the catch of legal-sized lobsters. Eddie Blackmore, president of the Maine Lobstermen's Association, recalls, "after I had escape vents in all my traps I was saving an hour a day pulling [hauling traps] and two to three gallons of gas." In the debate that followed, some of these men became the strongest advocates of the escape vent.

In 1976, Representative Lawrence Greenlaw of Stonington introduced a bill in the legislature mandating an escape vent (Greenlaw 1978). This produced a good deal of heated discussion in the industry and the legislature. Greenlaw withdrew the bill in the face of opposition led by Representative Bonnie Post of Owls Head, who, speaking for the fishermen in her district, argued that the escape vent was something that fishermen should do for themselves, and that in any case, the issue needed more study before it should be enacted into law. In the meantime, a sizeable number of fishermen began to support the idea of an escape vent. Eddie Blackmore strongly endorsed the idea, and the Maine Lobstermen's Association worked for the bill on the local level.

In the next session of the legislature, Representative Post introduced an escape-vent bill. Different people have different memories of the hearings that were held up and down the coast concerning this bill. What is apparent is that the bill had many enemies in the industry, but a good deal of strong support as well. Commissioner Spencer Apollonio, who moderated many of these meetings, recalls that a lot of opposition to the bill occurred in scattered locations, particularly in the Rockland area and parts of the eastern coast, but no well-orchestrated attempt was made to scuttle it. It passed in the legislature over moderate opposition in 1978 (Laws of Maine 1978), and went into effect in 1979. Twenty years later, the escape vent has tremendous support in the industry. Eddie Blackmore said this "is probably the best single thing we have done in the past fifty years." Although the law was modified in 1987, and again in 1992, basic support for the law has never wavered (Jones 1985a; Kelly 1990: 12–14).

In retrospect, the escape-vent law passed so expeditiously because it was strongly supported by the Department of Marine Resources, the leadership of the Maine Lobstermen's Association, and a majority of the fishermen, as well as by members of the legislature's committee on marine resources. In this respect, it is perhaps unique in the history of the industry.

The Players, Alliances, and Maine Lobster Legislation

History did not repeat itself. Each law involved different issues and different players who had varying amounts of power and very different goals. The genesis of the first conservation legislation in the 1870s and 1880s was the result of what Judd (1988) has called "commercial rivalry" between lobster canners and the live-lobster industry, each of which proposed legislation reserving the resource for itself. Conservation was a slogan, not an important goal. In this contest, scientists and the bureaucracy played little role. The double-gauge law of 1933 came about in the middle of the most serious crisis the lobster industry and the nation had ever faced. The industry was badly split on the issue of the double gauge. Under these conditions, Commissioner Crie, who was very much influenced by scientists, and his legislative allies were able to persuade the legislature to pass this controversial measure with the long-term good of the resource in mind. Legislation for the escape vent was passed with the support of the Maine Department of Marine Resources bureaucracy, the marine resources committee of the legislature, and a sizeable faction in the industry led by Eddie Blackmore, then-president of the Maine Lobstermen's Association (MLA). For all parties, conservation was a primary concern.

Despite these differences, some common elements can be found in the processes producing these laws. Without question, fishermen have had more influence over legislation than any other group. Vinal Look, former Commissioner of the Department of Marine Resources, said that "the legislature has never passed an important regulatory bill without substantial support from the industry." This means that anyone wanting to understand the development of lobster legislation at the state level must focus on the strategic choices of various groups of fishermen and the process of negotiations among them. The industry has long been interested in conservation, especially in recent decades. But where industry is concerned, conservation is of less importance than distributional issues.

The legislature and the Department of Marine Resources (DMR) had a strong influence on the legislation that emerged. While the legislature and DMR often have different goals, they have one dominant interest that distinguishes their actions from those of the industry: an interest in conserving the resources of the ocean that they hold in trust for the public. It is a responsibility they have taken very seriously. To be sure, the legislature is always careful to assess public support and the interests of their constituents, but in the last analysis, conservation has been a primary emphasis. This is, perhaps, only to be expected. All governments have an interest in promoting economic growth, both to increase revenues to the state and to build political support in order to stay in power (Knight 1992: 191).

Second, the actions of the government changed outcomes. To be sure, neither the DMR nor the legislature could dictate rules that had little or no industry support. However, agents of the government could and did enter into coalitions with various industry factions to raise the support they needed to pass certain pieces of legislation. In these cases, the agents of the government had enough power to insist that bills be altered in ways that met their own agenda. The double-gauge law, for example, was the result of an alliance between Commissioner Horatio Crie and a faction of the lobster industry in the western counties, which wanted a smaller minimum gauge. Neither could have attained their goals in the absence of the other. Commissioner Crie was able to use industry support for a smaller minimum-size measure to pass a double-gauge law, which protected both juvenile and reproductive-sized lobsters.

Forty-five years later, Commissioner Spencer Apollonio and MLA President

Eddie Blackmore worked hard to ensure passage of the escape-vent law. The law almost certainly would not have passed had these men pulled in different directions. Recently, Commissioner Robin Alden and her allies in the legislature were able to use strongly divided industry opinion on trap limits and entry controls to fashion the zone management law and apprenticeship program.

Scientists played a decidedly secondary role in the generation of conservation legislation at the state level. Pronouncements by scientists concerning industry problems were certainly not enough to ensure that remedial legislation was forthcoming swiftly. Richard Judd points out that "there was no simple one-to-one correlation between biological necessity and conservation law" (1988: 598).

Scientists have, however, been a primary source of management ideas and data. The original size-limit laws, the laws protecting egg-bearing females, the double-gauge law, and the escape-vent law originated with European scientists. Sometimes it took decades for these management ideas to be enacted into law. The double gauge was proposed by biologists just after the turn of the twentieth century, but no law was enacted until 1933. The idea of a trap limit has been bandied about for over thirty-five years. Ideas of scientists were eventually incorporated into state laws, but only after powerful factions in the industry realized that they could be used to further their own agendas. This underlines the fact that "scientific facts" are often little more than ammunition that can be seized on by contestants when it serves their interests.

Conservationists are latecomers to the game. As we shall see in chapter 6, they entered the fray only in the 1990s in an effort to force federal agencies to enforce federal legislation. They played no role in producing any state legislation.

Analysis of Factors Promoting Laws at the State Level

A number of factors have had a marked influence on the development of statutes and regulations in the Maine lobster industry. While all of them have been discussed by rational choice theorists and others interested in the production of norms, they fall into no well-integrated theoretical mold.

DISTRIBUTION FIGHTS

Jack Knight has hypothesized that most institutions come about as a byproduct of conflict over resources (Knight 1992: 123–32). This hypothesis explains most, but not all, of the state lobster laws. The first minimum-size measure and prohibition on taking egged females, the double-gauge law, and trap limits all came about as byproducts of negotiations over distributional rewards.

The first size regulations and prohibitions against taking egg-bearing females were instituted during the course of a battle between the canners and the live-lobster industry over control of the lobster supply. At first, the canners succeeded in persuading the legislature to pass seasonal rules and size regulations to constrain the live-lobster industry and reserve the catch for themselves. After 1879, the live-lobster industry succeeded in lobbying for laws that ultimately made it impossible for the canners to stay in business. The live-lobster faction won because they had more support in the public, the press, and the legislature.

The same overriding distributional concerns dominated the long battle for the double-gauge law. Here, the fight was between a faction composed of fishermen in the western part of the coast, dealers, and hotel owners who all wanted smaller, cheaper lobsters (i.e., 9 inch lobsters) to expand their markets, and a faction of fishermen primarily in the eastern part of the state opposed to lowering the gauge to prevent a flood of lobsters from Canada, which they thought would benefit the dealers. Neither side had the resources to gain an advantage until Commissioner Horatio Crie, an able political entrepreneur, and members of the marine resources committee formed a coalition with the industry faction wanting a smaller gauge, in exchange for their support for the double gauge.

In both the case of the first conservation laws of 1870s and 1880s and the double-gauge law, fishermen in the eastern part of the state were pitted against those in the west. In this contest, the fishermen in the east were at a distinct disadvantage, since there are fewer fishermen east of Penobscot Bay. More important, only two counties lie along the eastern coast and six in the west. Since this disparity gives fishermen from the western part of the coast more influence in the legislature, they were able to force through rules in their favor.

In the case of all three of these laws, multiple solutions could be found to the problem (i.e., multiple equilibria), each of which would benefit one industry faction more than another by allocating to it an increased part of the catch. People in the industry were, of course, fully aware of this fact and fought strenuously in the legislative arena for laws that would benefit them. The faction that ultimately succeeded was the one that had the most resources in terms of numbers of votes and power in the legislature. In every case, this meant forming a coalition with agents of the government, who had their own agendas. The laws that emerged were compromises, incorporating features desired by powerful industry factions to gain control over the lobster resource and features that agents of the government were able to insert in the bill.

The processes by which these three lobster regulations have been generated serve as a reminder of one of the most basic axioms of the new institutional economics and rational choice theory, namely that regulations are rarely neutral; they usually help some people more than others. "Individuals realize this, and they attempt to change institutions to serve their ends more effectively" (Ensminger 1992: xiii).

SOCIAL CONVENTIONS

The escape-vent and V-notch laws came about as the result of an entirely different process. The interactions that generated these rules are best modeled as pure coordination games of the type described by Lewis (1969) and Sugden (1986). These rules benefitted everyone in the industry and served the cause of conservation as well.[6] The process by which these laws were passed was far less acrimonious than that resulting from the distribution battles described above.

Beyond these similarities, the circumstances surrounding the passage of the escape-vent and the V-notch programs were quite different. The escape-vent law came about through formalization of an existing practice; the V-notch law took advantage of a formal law to build a conservation program by decentralized means.

Support for an escape-vent law came about very quickly in the 1970s, since the DMR bureaucracy, members of the marine resources committee of the legislature, and a sizeable majority of the fishing industry led by MLA President Blackmore were well disposed toward it. Many people in the industry supported the proposal, influenced by the fact that some "high-liners" had tried escape vents and found them advantageous. In a sense, the passage of this law was tantamount to the formalization of an informal practice. Many laws are, in fact, generated in this fashion (Knight 1992: 85).

The V-notch program is an informal institution building on the possibilities presented by a formal law. The original law was designed to save a few thousand seed lobsters. Fishermen saw the possibilities inherent in this situation and proceeded to V-notch very large numbers of the egged lobsters they caught in the interests of conservation. Their voluntary activities have made the program far more effective than its originators ever dreamed in 1917.

POLITICAL ENTREPRENEURSHIP

Political entrepreneurs played a crucial role in the development of some of the most important lobster conservation laws. The double-gauge law would not have been passed were it not for Commissioner Crie; Commissioner Apollonio and MLA President Eddie Blackmore played a key role in lobbying for the passage of the escape-vent laws. As we shall see, political entrepreneurs were crucial in the development of other rules. These people wielded no unusual power, nor could they provide rewards; rather, they were critical in changing people's attitudes toward legislation by pointing out to various groups the benefits to be gained. In this regard, Taylor argues that the ability to change attitudes is the most important function of political entrepreneurs (M. Taylor 1990: 233–34).

DISCOUNT RATE AND THE CONSERVATION ETHIC

All of those playing a role in producing lobster legislation are motivated, at least in part, by a concern for the long-run well-being of the resource. Their motives differ somewhat, however. "Conservation" of the resource has been the holy grail for the scientists, who are dedicated to preserving the ecosystems of the earth and ocean. The legislature and bureaucrats, by way of contrast, tend to think in terms of preserving a valuable industry and the incomes of voters. Periodically, the industry will set aside distributional concerns and support legislation to protect the lobster stocks. In the last seventy years, this has happened increasingly as the industry has developed a conservation ethic. However, the motives of the industry are clearly more commercial. They know that if the resource is destroyed, it cannot provide them with an income stream in the future. They have a low discount rate because they value that income stream.

The political support for every law discussed in this chapter has been wholly or partially motivated by a concern for ensuring the well-being of the lobster stock In some cases, such as that of the escape vent, a concern with conservation is the primary motive of all concerned, bureaucrats, legislators, and industry alike. In other instances, only some of the parties involved are motivated by a sense of stewardship. In the fight for the double gauge, only Commissioner Crie and a few legislators were concerned about the resource.

CHAPTER 5

Co-management in the
Maine Lobster Industry

Co-management of the Maine lobster industry came about with the passage of the so-called "Zone Management Law," enacted by the Maine legislature in the spring of 1995 (Public Law 1995, Chapter 468). This arguably was the most important piece of legislation concerning the lobster industry passed in the twentieth century. This very wide-ranging law changed many aspects of the governance of the lobster industry. It established an individual trap limit of twelve hundred traps by the year 2000, a trap tag system to identify owners of traps, an apprenticeship program for new entrants into the lobster fishery, and eligibility criteria to qualify for a commercial lobster and crab license. Most important, it was designed as a true co-management law, giving the lobster industry control over managing certain aspects of the lobster fishery, while retaining most authority for management in the hands of the Department of Marine Resources and the legislature. This law established a framework by which the commissioner of Marine Resources could create lobster policy management zones. These lobster zones are managed by an elected council of lobster license holders. The councils were empowered by the 1995 law to propose three different kinds of rules for their zones: the maximum number of traps each license holder is permitted to fish (a trap limit), the number of traps that may be fished on a single line, and the time of day when lobster fishing will be allowed. If the proposed rules are passed by a vote of two-thirds of the license holders in the zone, the zone council is obligated to convey the results of the referendum to the commissioner of Marine Resources. If the commissioner judges them to be "reasonable," he or she can use his or her regulatory power to establish the rules as departmental regulations enforceable by the Marine Patrol (Alden 1995: B4; Jones 1995b: A8). In 1999, the zone councils were given an additional right—namely they were empowered to make proposals to limit the entry of new fishermen into their zone as older license holders retired. Again, the commissioner can transform these proposals into regulations.

Why did the legislature pass such a law? Co-management, after all, is a radical concept. One reason, in brief, was that a few powerful people in the legislature and bureaucracy saw co-management as the wave of the future. More important, members of the marine resources committee of the legislature saw that a co-management law could be framed in such a way as to solve some problems that had stymied the legislature for decades, namely the need for a trap-limit law and limited entry (Sonnenberg 1991).

Shortly after the trap escalation began in the 1950s, people in the lobster industry began calling for a trap limit. The proponents argued that a limit would confer benefits on all. A fisherman would catch as many lobsters if everyone were restricted to the same number of traps, and he would garner substantial savings, in that he would have to build, bait, and tend fewer traps. Moreover, fishing a smaller number of traps, it was argued, would permit fishermen to use smaller and less costly boats that could be operated by a single person, rather than larger vessels requiring crews of two and three people. Perhaps most important, a trap limit would also alleviate the problems of trap congestion and gear tangles, which had become very severe.

From a theoretical point of view, lobster fishing presents a situation in which there should be a considerable demand for rules limiting effort. As Coleman points out, "the demand for a rule will rise when an action by one actor imposes externalities on other actors" (1990: 251). Lobster fishermen impose two kinds of external costs on each other: (1) the lobsters one person catches cannot be caught by others fishing in the same area; (2) traps can become entangled, and the number of tangles increases with the number of traps in an area. Nevertheless, it proved very difficult to get a trap-limit bill passed.

The first effort to pass a trap limit was made in the late 1950s. Representative Chester Rice avers that one or more trap-limit bills had been introduced in every one of the last fifteen sessions of the Maine legislatures. One of the most important efforts was the Jackson bill of 1974, which came close to passing. This law would have combined a trap limit with limited entry and zone management. The Maine Lobstermen's Association proposed bills calling for trap limits and limited entry in 1979 (Billings 1979), in 1985 (Billings 1985a), and again in 1991. All of these were defeated. The basic problem was a lack of agreement in the lobster industry, which quickly resulted in a lack of political support for these bills in the legislature.

Efforts to establish a trap limit have always foundered on two issues. First, there is a strong feeling that a trap limit will do no good unless it is coupled with a limit on licenses (limited entry). The logic is that a trap limit will not relieve congestion if new fishermen can still come into the industry, bringing with them thousands of new traps. However, limited entry has always been received with ambivalence because such legislation would mean prohibiting young people from entering the lobster fishery, one of the few employment possibilities available in many coastal towns (Acheson 1975a: 663– 65).

Second, and more important, the majority of fishermen agree that there should be a limit on traps, but no one agrees on what the limit should be. Part of the problem is that the average number of traps fished varied widely from one part of the coast to another. A trap limit that would have been acceptable to people in eastern Maine, where six hundred traps was considered a large number, would be completely unacceptable in an area such as Casco Bay, where fishermen commonly had over eighteen hundred traps. Moreover, within each town the so-called full-time fishermen generally fish far more traps than the "part-timers," who have other jobs. Thus, attempts to establish trap limits engender two sources of conflict: between different areas of the coast, and between full- and part-time fishermen in any single harbor (Acheson and Wilson 1996). This has resulted in a lack of consensus in the industry and a general lack of support for any trap-limit proposal in the legislature.

Moreover, the conflict over trap limits is exacerbated by the fact that such limits have severe distributional effects. Trap limits do not constrain all fishermen. They force those fishing over the allowable maximum to reduce the number of traps they fish. This is likely to affect the big fishermen, and may not force the small or average fishermen to make any changes at all. In the process, however, the percentage of traps small fishermen have on the bottom is increased relatively, giving them a higher percentage of the catch. From this perspective, a trap limit is a means by which small fishermen can constrain big fishermen and lower their proportion of the catch.

This lack of consensus on the trap limit and legislative fears about limited entry translated into a lack of political support for any specific bill. The result was stalemate for several decades.

However, the pressure on the legislature to pass such a bill was unceasing (Acheson 1975a: 666). Representative David Etnier said, "I would go to Five Islands and places in my district and all I would hear is 'Why don't you do something for us? Why can't we get a trap limit?'"

By the 1990s, other forces and ideas were gaining momentum that were to result in a trap limit in the aftermath of other legislation. There was a good deal of interest in co-management. Many people interested in fisheries management had become convinced that standard ways of managing fisheries were failing, and that new approaches needed to be tried. Over the course of twenty years, a sizeable body of literature has been produced documenting the local-level conservation rules found in a large number of fishing communities (Acheson 1972; 1975b; Anderson and Simmons 1993; Berkes 1989; McCay and Acheson 1987; E. Ostrom 1990; Pinkerton 1989; Ruddle and Johannes 1985). In 1993, the idea began to float around the Maine fishing industry and marine resources committee of the legislature after a session on co-management at the Maine Fishermen's Forum organized by Jim Wilson of the University of Maine. I was one of the participants.[1]

Perhaps most important, the legislature and Maine fishermen had some experience with aspects of co-management. As early as 1974, lobster fishermen became familiar with the idea after an unsuccessful effort by Representatives Greenlaw and Jackson to pass a bill dividing the coast into zones with different trap limits and limited-entry provisions. Then in 1994, the Maine legislature passed a sea urchin management law dividing the industry into two zones with different management rules. In addition, in 1994, Amendment 5 of the American Lobster Management Plan had divided federal waters into zones and established "Effort Management Teams" (EMTs) composed of industry members to make management recommendations for each zone (see chapter 6).

In the spring of 1995, the legislature was under some pressure to pass a law reducing effort to bring Maine into line with the "federal lobster measures proposed by the effort management teams" that had been established by the New England Regional Council (Plante and Jones 1995). Accordingly, a bill was prepared, which would be sponsored by Rep. Chester Rice, proposing a four-year moratorium on new state lobster and crab licenses. It would also contain a trap limit of twelve hundred, which would be reduced to eight hundred traps over a period of years, to be in accord with federal rules for the zone beyond the 3-mile line (so-called exclusive economic zones, or EEZ). It also had a number of other provisions, such as a prohibition on lobster fishing on weekends during the summer (Plante and Jones 1995). A controversial part of the bill was a provision to grant licenses only to people who had been active in the fishery and had caught lobsters in the 1993/1994 season, which would eliminate hundreds of inactive or part-time fishermen.

In the early spring, the prospects for a trap-limit law did not look bright because there was a good deal of opposition from the fishermen in Casco Bay and the Downeast Lobstermen's Association, which had very different ideas about limited entry and trap limits.

However, Robin Alden herself, who was confirmed as commissioner of Marine Resources in February 1995, worked hard to overcome opposition to the bill. She had become increasingly interested in co-management after having served previously on the regional council and being editor of *Commercial Fisheries News* for twenty years. Both of these experiences gave her insight into the problems inherent in the "top-down" federal management system.

In April 1995, the cause of co-management received another boost during hearings held by the legislature's joint standing committee on marine resources concerning a number of bills sponsored by the Maine Lobstermen's Association. I was one of a number of academics, industry representatives, and agency scientists who testified. Several of us supported the co-management concept, arguing that if fishermen had management authority they would impose on themselves those conservation rules that they believed were effective in conserving resources, and that were in their own best interests. This would foster a sense of stewardship and reduce enforcement costs. Several others said similar things.

By June, the bill was framed in final form (Jones 1995a), and in July, at the end of the legislative session, the bill passed (Public Law 1995, Chapter 468; Jones 1995b).

In retrospect, the law was framed in a way that allowed the legislature to navigate several shoals and snags. It produced what a large number of fishermen wanted, a trap limit, but it contained a mechanism for coming to grips with one of the major stumbling blocks for trap limits, namely strong disagreements about how many traps would be permitted, by allowing fishermen in different areas of the coast to establish their own limits. The law also addressed the need to couple a trap limit with limited entry by passage of the apprenticeship program. This provision was designed to slow entry into the industry in a way that would increase the sense of stewardship, while at the same time ensuring that all people who really wanted to go lobstering could get a license eventually. This reassured those legislators and industry people concerned with the all-too-real problem of a lack of alternative economic opportunities in small fishing towns, especially in the eastern part of Maine.

The law had another virtue from the point of view of the legislature. By giving the zone councils power to make recommendations on trap limits, fishing time, numbers of traps on a line (and, later, limited entry), the legislature was divesting itself of several vexing, long-term problems. All of these rights given to the zone councils involve very contentious issues.

The law received a mixed reception in the industry. Officers of the Maine Lobstermen's Association lobbied for it. They had initially wanted a trap limit and limited-entry law, and the zone management bill contained no limited-entry provision. However, Pat White of the MLA supported it as a means to obtain a trap limit. Once the law was passed, the leadership of the Maine Lobstermen's Association worked hard to see it implemented.

Others were much less enthusiastic. When the law passed, a group of fishermen from eastern Maine and Casco Bay filed a lawsuit seeking to nullify it. This suit was later judged to have no merit (*Bangor Daily News* 1996; Jones 1996e). Many full-time fishermen all over the state were leery of the law, since they believed it would favor the part-time fishermen who would have a majority of votes. Some part-time fishermen (with other jobs) were fearful that the full-time fishermen would pass laws restricting the time when fishing could be done, such as prohibiting fishing on Saturdays or after 4:00 P.M., which would force them from the industry.

Many observers of the industry, including some experienced politicians, were convinced that the law was desperately flawed. I recall a conversation with a former legislator who had served several terms on the marine resources committee. He said, "This law is designed to fail. You can't expect lobster fishermen to cut their own effort. If this law passes, you will have a big dog fight up and down the coast."

Seven years after the zone management law was passed, it is clear that the criers of doom were wrong. The legislature framed a law allowing lobster fishermen to generate rules curtailing their own exploitive efforts for the long-term benefit of the fishery. They took full advantage of that opportunity. The co-management law has clearly been a success so far. By the summer of 1998, all seven of the zones had passed trap limits of six or eight hundred traps. By January of 2001, five of the seven zones (zones B, D, E, F, and G) had established limited-entry rules for their zones.

Implementation of the Law

Despite the predictions of disaster, implementation of the zone management law went ahead rapidly after its passage in June 1995. In the fall of 1995, an implementation committee was appointed by the commissioner to convert the legislation, which had been framed in general terms, into regulations, a workable management program (Jones 1996a).[2] The law merely stated that the commissioner was empowered to divide the coast into zones led by a zone council, and that the councils could put referenda on three kinds of regulations to their constituents for a vote. The law said nothing about how many zones were to be established, where the zone boundaries would be, how representatives to the zone council were to be chosen, or what the bylaws of the councils were to be. These recommendations were made by the implementation committee.

By February 1996, the implementation committee had produced a report containing a set of guidelines that gave shape to the zone council system and the entire co-management effort (Jones 1996a). It recommended that five zones be formed, which were to be divided into electoral districts containing approximately one hundred lobster license holders each. Since there were approximately seven thousand license holders, each zone would have approximately fourteen hundred license holders and fourteen districts. Thus, each zone council would have approximately fourteen members. These council members would presumably know the fishermen in the district well and be able to represent their viewpoints in the council.

It was determined that each license-holder would be able to cast one vote in the elections for representative to the zone council and a single vote in each referendum regardless of how many traps he fished. The committee considered giving fishermen different numbers of votes depending on how many traps they fished. It hardly seemed fair that an amateur with five traps would have the same voting power as a full-time fisherman with more than one thousand traps. This suggestion was forwarded to the Attorney General's Office, which ruled that it would be unconstitutional. One person was to have one vote. But as we shall see, a great deal of trouble between part-time fishermen and full-timers might have been avoided if some kind of weighted voting system had been put in place.

In order to avoid conflict over boundaries, the committee made initial recommendations on where the boundaries of the five zones should be. They were deliberately placed to divide areas with different fishing practices, and where traditional boundaries had already been established. In addition, the committee recommended that license-holders could fish in multiple zones, but that they would have to abide by the rules of the most stringent zone. Thus, if a person choose to fish in waters of a zone with one thousand traps and in another with an eight hundred-trap limit, that person could only have eight hundred tags.

The implementation committee choose not to deal with two issues of importance: the apprenticeship program and the zone council bylaws. It was decided that the apprenticeship program would be developed at a later date. This was such a sensitive issue that attempts to specify how a person would pass an apprenticeship might jeopardize the entire zone management effort. The committee recommended that the bylaws for each zone be written by an interim zone council composed of members appointed by the commissioner (Jones 1996c: 22a; Jones and Plante 1996: A17).

In Maine, hearings must be held before commissioners of government departments before the commissioner can promulgate regulations. Accordingly, hearings were held in seven locations up and down the coast in January and February of 1996. At these hearings, which were chaired by Professor Jim Wilson of the University of Maine, a good many questions were asked about the specifics of the plan and the governance structure, but the general tone of the comments was very favorable to the idea of local level management. The implementation committee edited its plan, and the final version was presented at a session of the Fishermen's Forum on March 2, 1996. The earlier part of the meeting was dominated by a series of fishermen who objected to various aspects of the plan. However, the feelings of the majority of those in the industry in attendance showed when fisherman Ted Bear gave a speech at the end of the meeting strongly supporting the idea of local-level management. He received thunderous applause. We on the committee were much relieved.

After these hearings were finished, the recommendations of the implementation committee were made department regulations. They became the operational rules defining the way the co-management law in Maine works. In retrospect, virtually all of the recommendations of this committee survived intact. There are two exceptions: (1) The implementation committee recommended that sub-zones could be established. In the fall of 1998, the Sub-Zone Taskforce, commissioned by the legislature, recommended that "sub-zones would be discouraged." (2) The implementation committee had initially recommended that five zones and zone councils be established; after the hearings were held in January and February, it was decided to establish seven zones.

In the spring of 1996, the commissioner had appointed the interim zone councils (Jones 1996d); and by April 1997, these interim zone councils had completed their job. They established the voting districts; established the initial boundaries for those zones; approved the bylaws for the zone councils; and organized the election of permanent zone council member (Jones 1997c: 18a).

Establishing voting districts went smoothly in most cases. The rules established by the implementation committee were that one representative to the zone council was to be chosen for every hundred license holders. This caused no problem except for the permanently occupied islands, several of which wanted their own representative even though they had far fewer than one hundred members. This issue was settled by vote. In Zones B, C, and F, islands were given their own representatives, while in Zone D, they were not.

The individual zones' bylaws were not written by the zone council members. The Zone G bylaws were written by a lawyer, and the two DMR resource coordinators each wrote different sets of bylaws for the other councils. In 1999, after a Zone G lawsuit, the Department of Marine Resources hired a lawyer to produce a standard set of bylaw for all zones, one they hoped would avoid the pitfalls that would lead to more lawsuits.

The Work of the Permanent Zone Councils: Legislative Dominos

TRAP LIMITS

The permanent zone councils began operation in the late spring of 1997. While it became apparent that the zone councils had a variety of different concerns, two

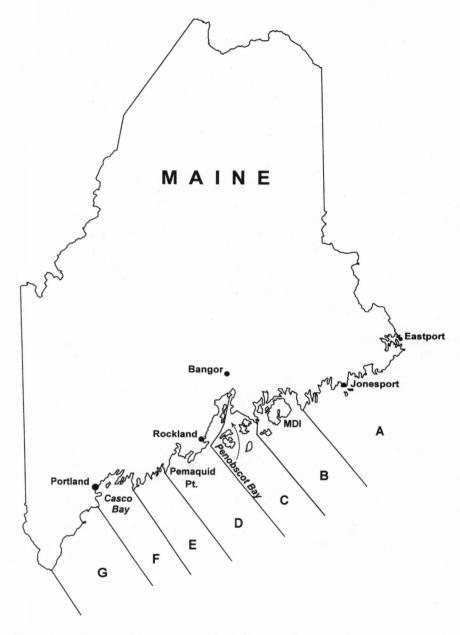

Map 5.1. Lobster management zones, March 1997. In 2002, the zone management boundaries are the same as they were in 1997 when they initially were established, though most have been moved slightly. See map 2.2 for changes in the Zone D/E boundary line.

issues came to demand most of their attention initially. First, the commissioner of Marine Resources involved the zone councils in the right whale issue, which involved a lawsuit brought under the Marine Mammal Protection Act that threatened the entire lobster industry (DMR News 1997: 4B). Even though the zone councils were not empowered to deal with such issues, they devoted considerable time to lobbying industry members to frame an industry-wide response. (The right whale issue will be discussed in greater detail below.)

The second concerned trap limits. In August 1997, the Zone E council voted to submit a referendum to establish an eight hundred-trap limit by 1998, a seven hundred-trap limit by 1999, and a six hundred-trap limit by 2000; in September the Zone G council voted to have a similar referendum, which would establish a build-down to establish an eight hundred-trap limit by 2000 (*Commercial Fisheries News* 1997b: B5). Both of these referenda passed easily. The rest of the zones followed in the next few months. By the summer of 1998, all of the zones had held referenda in which trap limits were passed (DMR News 1998b).

The vote in favor of trap limits was overwhelming in all cases. In Zone E, the trap limit passed with 80 percent of those casting ballots voting "yes"; in Zone G, 81 percent voted "yes" on the first ballot, and 82 percent voted "yes" to a more stringent trap limit later in the fall of 1997 (Jones 1998c: 14a). In Zone D, the trap limit vote "passed by 77 percent of the votes cast" (DMR News 1998a). In Zone A, the trap limit passed with 88 percent of the vote; in Zone B, 94 percent voted "yes" to a trap limit; and in Zone C, the trap limit passed with 82 percent voting in favor (DMR News 1998b). Despite the huge plurality, the losers, who were generally men fishing a lot of traps, took their defeat very hard, and caused several different kinds of problems.

Two political forces were involved in producing trap limits within the zones. The first was the desire of a large number of small and medium-sized fishermen for a trap limit. These men had grown tired of watching "big fishermen" or "hogs" take a disproportionate amount of the lobsters and cause huge trap tangles in the process.

The second was the threat of federal action. The Atlantic States Marine Fisheries Commission (ASMFC) announced one plan in 1996 that National Marine Fisheries Service (NMFS) officials claimed was inadequate (Plante 1997c). Empowered by the Sustainable Fisheries Act, the NMFS prepared its own lobster management plan in 1997 and 1998, which proposed a drastic build-down to 472 traps over the course of five years. The councils and their constituents strongly favored the ASMFC plan and devoted considerable time and effort lobbying for it. As a result, Zones B, C, D, and F deliberately framed their trap-limit referenda to coincide with the recommendations of the Atlantic State Marine Fisheries Commission, which had proposed a twelve hundred-trap limit in 1998; a one thousand-trap limit in 1999, and an eight hundred-trap limit in 2000 (Jones 1998a). By framing their referenda in this way, they hoped to ward off more drastic action by the NMFS. David Black explained the proposed referendum in Zone D by saying, "We are going along with the ASMFC. These are the trap limits which will probably be enacted anyway." The zone councils were not responding just to their constituents. They were responding to a plan at the federal level, one that they hoped would pass.

The passage of trap limits greatly exacerbated the animosity and conflict between big and little fishermen. If the little fishermen had felt put upon by the big fishermen before the trap limit, it was the big fishermen who felt victimized after the trap limits were passed. Trap limits, after all, constrain only the big fishermen.

Even more galling to the big fishermen was the fact that many small fishermen began to increase the numbers of traps they fished after the trap limit went into effect. In the views of some observers of the fishery, the trap limit was not so much a maximum number of traps; it had become a goal to achieve. The situation was made even worse by the fact that many commercial fishermen were moving into the lobster fishery on a full-time basis, attracted by the record high lobster landings achieved in the late 1980s and the 1990s, while landings in most other fisheries declined. In 1978, approximately 20 percent of all lobster license-holders were considered full-time fishermen, while by 1997, an estimated 58.3 percent earned 75 to 100 percent of their income from the lobster fishery, attesting to the huge growth in the numbers of full-time fishermen (Acheson and Acheson 1998: 11). In short, although lobster catches increased phenomenally in the past decade, the established "big" fishermen saw a disturbing proportion of that increase going to people with small and medium-sized operations and to newcomers to the industry, at a time when they were forced to reduce the amount of gear they fished. Under these conditions, it is scarcely surprising that many big fishermen were angry, feeling that the trap limit was working against them and benefitting their competitors.

The big fishermen first fought against trap limits using strategies that were largely ineffective. In Zones C and F, where many of the zone council members were big fishermen, the zone councils refused for months to put a trap limit out to referendum. They finally agreed to hold a referendum in the spring of 1998 in the face of pressure from a large number of their unhappy constituents and the threat of oncoming ASMFC rules. It took months of agitation by their constituents to force them to take this action. In Zone F, the council insisted on linking a trap limit with limited entry. Lyman Kennedy, at the 1998 Fisherman's Forum, swore that he would not support a trap limit until the state government limited the number of fishermen. He relented only when limited-entry legislation began to be discussed seriously.

In Zone G, four big fishermen sued the state over the trap-limit referenda that had been passed in that zone. In September 1997, the Zone G council proposed a referendum for an eight hundred-trap limit to be accomplished in three years (by 2000). This passed, with 81 percent voting in favor. Later in the fall, a group of Zone G fishermen, who had wanted a six hundred-trap limit all along, presented the Zone G council a petition with over two hundred signatures for another referendum for an eight hundred-trap limit to begin earlier, in March 1998. When this referendum also passed with an 82 percent vote in favor in November 1998, a handful of irate fishermen complained to a legislator who tried mightily to persuade the governor and the commissioner of Marine Resources not to accept the referendum as "reasonable" and therefore not adopt a new regulation. After much divisive politicking, the acting commissioner stood behind the second vote for an

Capturing the Commons

eight hundred-trap limit to begin in March 1998 (Jones 1998a: 16a.). At this point, a group of four fishermen from the towns of Kittery and Saco, who each had well over eight hundred traps, each hired a lawyer to sue the Department of Marine Resources in order to rescind the trap limit, on the grounds that it was enacted in the course of an illegal vote. They argued that the second vote violated the bylaw of Zone G, which stated that no referendum could be held on the same "issue" within a two-year period. The essence of the suit was that the Zone G council had violated the bylaws when it passed two trap-limit referenda within a three-month period. In July 1998, a superior court judge issued a consent order prohibiting the DMR from enforcing the trap limit endorsed by the second referendum, and gave an opinion favoring the four plaintiffs. This meant that the trap limit remained at twelve hundred in 1998, one thousand in 1999, and eight hundred in 2000 (Jones 1998b: 9a). Most fishermen in Zone G were very disappointed. Jim Alwin, the Zone G chair, said, "Most of Zone G is feeling that the results of a legitimate election had been thwarted by a small handful of big fishermen. They had money to hire a lawyer."

In Zone E, the big fishermen attempted to nullify an earlier vote establishing a six-hundred-trap limit by holding another referendum. In November of 1998, the fishermen of Zone E again voted overwhelmingly to uphold the six hundred-trap limit. Many of the big fishermen in Zone E, including Larry Knapp, the zone council chair, were very disappointed. However, Terry Stockwell of the DMR said that an analysis of the vote revealed that eighty-one of the big fishermen from the Boothbay region did not vote. I suspect, despite all their vocal opposition to the six hundred-trap limit, that they were very ambivalent about fishing large numbers of traps, and were hoping that the trap limit would be upheld.

LIMITED ENTRY AND THE TRAP CAP

In the fall of 1998, the Lobster Advisory Council, an industry group advising the Maine Department of Marine Resources and the legislature on policy for the industry, got to work on serious legislative proposals to solve the problems posed by trap limits. First, several "tiered license" proposals were discussed. These proposals suggested the establishment of different classes of licenses based on financial dependence on the industry, each of which would have a different trap limit and a different vote in zone council elections. The purpose was to allow full-time fishermen to fish more traps than various kinds of part-timers and to have a greater voice in zone council elections. None of these license schemes ever came to fruition, primarily because it proved to be impossible to agree on the criteria for defining the different levels of licenses and how people could move among them.

In the winter of 1998/1999, the Lobster Advisory Council worked on two other ideas that eventually were passed into law by the legislature in June 1999. One was a trap-tag freeze, which essentially permitted people fishing under eight hundred traps to purchase only one hundred more trap tags then they were issued as of November 20, 1998. License holders fishing over eight hundred could fish no more traps (Public Law 1999, Chapter 397). The law that went into effect was to last until 2001, when it was to be sunsetted. In the fall of 2000, the Department of Marine Resources decided that this law should be continued as it was for a period of years to slow the build-up of traps, and accordingly recommended that the Lobster Advisory Council make this recommendation to the legislature. The other law established limited entry by zone (Public Law 1999, Chapter 508). Both of these laws had considerable support in the industry and were enacted with little difficulty. In the industry, support for these laws stemmed from both selfish and altruistic motives.

Both of these laws are designed to further the objectives of fishermen with large amounts of gear, namely stopping entry into the industry (especially in the overcrowded western zones) and preventing part-timers from building up the amount of gear they fish while full-time fishermen are forced to reduce their numbers of traps. They were, in the words of one full-time fisherman, "our solution to the part-timer problem." However, they were also motivated by the feeling that the industry genuinely needed to reduce effort.

Many in the industry, including the leadership of the Maine Lobstermen's Association, had long wanted limited entry coupled with a trap limit, and had introduced several bills into the legislature to obtain such legislation. Many fishermen, including officers of the MLA, were very unhappy that the zone management law did not include a limited-entry provision. In the words of one, when the legislature passed the zone management law, "it gave us only half the tool box we needed to do the job." In addition, they were unhappy that total trap numbers continued to increase even after the trap limits had been put in effect. It took very little for these people to put limited entry back on the table again in 1997.

In 1997, limited-entry legislation was introduced again at the urging of the MLA in the form of L.D. 1448. The legislature did not pass this bill, but rather passed a resolve that the limited-entry question be studied by the Lobster Advisory Council, which was to give a report on the subject to the legislature in February 1998.

In the spring of 1999, the marine resources committee and the Lobster Advisory Council produced a bill calling for limited entry by zones. The limited-entry law was passed by the legislature in June 1999 (Public Law 1999, Chapter 508). It greatly extended the powers of the zone councils. This law specifies that the zone council can make a recommendation to the commissioner of the Department of Marine Resources to limit entry by imposing a ratio of people allowed to obtain licenses for those that give up their licenses. A one-to-three ratio, for example, means that one person would be allowed to get a license for every three people giving up their licenses. If the commissioner agrees with the recommendation of the zone council, he or she can impose that ratio. If he or she does not agree, he can impose a different ratio or none at all.

The law specifies an elaborate procedure to be followed to avoid problems with the anti-trust laws. First, the zone council informs the commissioner of its intention to seek limited entry for its zone. At this point, the commissioner places a moratorium on the entry of new licensees into that zone. Then the zone council must take a "nonbinding survey" of zone license-holders concerning their desires for limited entry and the in/out ratio they would like, and the results of this survey are entered into the record (Amory 1999b: B6). Next, the zone council makes its recommendation to the commissioner on the in/out ratio it seeks, taking into account the results of the survey. The commissioner must hold a public hearing in the zone on the limited-entry proposal. Only then can the commissioner impose the limited-entry ratio using his or her regulatory powers. The bill further specifies that the commissioner must maintain a waiting list of people who want licenses in each closed zone. These people must have passed the apprenticeship program.

From early in the fall of 1999 until the summer of 2000, the zone councils wrestled with the issue of limited entry. Four zones, D, E, F, and G, voted to request limited entry. They began the process for limited entry in the fall of 1996, and the commissioner closed their zones to new entry at that time. They carried out their constituent surveys in the early winter.

In the meanwhile, with limited entry looming, the Department of Marine Resources had to wrestle with several problems. One was how to frame regulations to allow new fishermen to enter closed zones. That is, when an in/out ratio is passed, who gets in and how? Officials at the DMR decided that when limited entry was declared in a zone, fishermen with licenses would have a one-time opportunity to declare themselves as members of that zone. People without licenses could obtain licenses to fish in that zone in one of three ways.

Another decision had to be made concerning how many traps a person from one zone could place in another. There is little sense in closing a zone to new entrants and reducing the number of fishermen in that zone by an in/out ratio, if people from adjacent zones can place any number of traps in the waters of that zone. What would stop a person from Zone G from coming up to Zone D after it was closed and putting all their traps in Zone D waters? In order to solve this problem, DMR officials came up with the so-called 49/51 percent rule. This rule stipulates that licenseholders have to keep at least 51 percent of their traps in their own zone, and could place a maximum of 49 percent of their traps in the waters of another closed zone. This was a sensible solution to the problem, but one that was to have fateful consequences for boundary problems.

The four zone councils voted on limited-entry ratios in May and June of 2000 and informed the commissioner of their recommendations. The commissioner held public hearings on the proposed in/out ratios in the summer of 2000, and the rules went into effect in September 2000. The commissioner approved a one-to-one ratio for Zone D; a two-to-one ratio for Zone E; a three-to-one ratio for Zone F; and a two-to-one ratio for Zone G. Later in the fall, Zone B voted for limited entry and the commissioner approved a three-to-one ratio. Thus, by the end of 2000, five of the seven zones had established in/out ratios.

In general, the zone councils tried to follow the wishes of their constituents as expressed in the surveys. The problem was, the constituents had such a wide range of ideas about limited entry that any limited-entry ratio the zone council recommended would please only a minority. In Zone D, for example, the survey results, made available at the March 14, 2000, meeting, showed that 296 of 441, or 67 percent of those returning questionnaires, answered "yes" to the question "Do you favor more limits on entry into the lobster fishery for new Class I, II, or III license-holders in Zone D beyond the two-year apprentice program?" Of those who answered "yes," seventy-five said they favored a one-to-one ratio; sixty-five favored a two-to-one ratio; fifty-seven wanted a three-to-one ratio; nineteen wanted a four-to-one ratio; and eighty-two wanted a five-to-one ratio. Eighteen said they wanted some other ratio. In short, if limited entry came to a referendum, there were just barely enough in favor to pass, given the fact that referenda need to be passed by a two-thirds vote. Of those favoring limited entry, more license-holders favored a one-to-one or a five-to-one ratio than any other. Moreover, at the Zone D meeting on May 2, 2000, when the vote to recommend limited entry was to be taken, several fishermen gave strong speeches against any limited-entry provision at all because this would make it difficult for their children to enter the business. A couple of council members cautioned that the constituents in their districts favored limited entry because there was a real need to reduce the number of fishermen to reduce snarls and conserve the resource.

What does a zone council do with such information about the wishes of their constituents? After talking about the options for an hour, the Zone D council voted to recommend a one-to-one ratio to the commissioner. At the hearings that were held at the Samoset Hotel in July, the Zone D council was roundly criticized for not requesting a higher ratio to begin lowering the number of licenses in the zone. David Black, the Zone D chair, said he didn't even bother going to the hearing. He thought the council had done the right thing, and he knew that regardless of what they had recommended, criticism was inevitable.

In general, the commissioner gave the zone councils the in/out ratios they recommended. Of course, the commissioner had played no small role in persuading the councils to vote for low limited-entry ratios. During the spring, Terry Stockwell, the DMR resource coordinator, told the council members that the commissioner would not go along with a recommendation for an "unreasonable" limited-entry ratio. At those same meetings, Laura Taylor, assistant to the commissioner, presented figures showing that very high in/out ratios would result in people having to wait for decades to obtain a lobster license. As a result, Zones D, E, and G dutifully requested relatively low ratios such as one-to-one or three-to-one.

Zone F was an exception. In Zone F, where trap escalation had been the worst in the entire state, there was solid sentiment among full-time fishermen that numbers of fishermen would have to be curtailed if the number of traps was to be reduced. This sentiment was reflected in the council, where sentiment for high in/out ratios ran high. At the May 3, 2000, Zone F meeting when the limited-entry vote was taken, many council members said that they favored a high in/out ratio because the need to reduce fishermen and traps was still acute. One council member pointed out that the "Feds still say we are overfished. We need to bring the number of traps down." They were strengthened in this conviction by the news that people could become eligible for a license in a closed zone (that is, one with limited entry) three different ways. The news that any number of eighteen year olds who completed the apprenticeship program could get a first class license, regardless of whether the zone was closed or not, came as a surprise to all present. Representative David Etnier said he "had never heard of the eighteen-year-old rule." This clearly hardened their conviction to request a high ratio. Terry Stockwell told the council, "You should go with what you want for a ratio, but the commissioner will not approve a five-to-one ratio."

When the vote was taken, nine council members voted for a five-to-one ratio, four voted for a three-to-one ratio, and two voted for a two-to-one ratio. They also voted to turn down a motion to allow all those who had completed the apprenticeship program in Zone F to have licenses. All those at that meeting were convinced that the Zone F council was very serious about cutting effort and letting the chips fall where they may.

Late in the summer of 2000, after the hearings had been held on the Zone F council's recommendation, Commissioner La Pointe approved a three-to-one in/out ratio. He said that he would not support a five-to-one ratio, and he was as good as his word.

Support for limited entry varies considerably from one part of the coast to another. The sentiment against limited entry is especially strong in Zone A on the Canadian border. Most of the fishermen in this rural, sparsely populated area feel that there is no need for limited entry. Some feel they could use more fishermen; and the vast majority do not want to put up barriers against young people who might want to go fishing. Fishing, after all, is one of the few means of earning a living in this easternmost part of Maine. Several people said that if the youngsters cannot go fishing, they will have no choice but to move away and the communities, already struggling to maintain their populations, will die. There is nothing novel about this objection. It is one of the most common objections to limited entry in general (see Singleton 1998: 139).

In the more overcrowded harbors to the west, far more fishermen favor limited entry. Here, there is a strong feeling that there are too many fishermen and too many traps. Much of the problem stems from the entry of a lot of part-time fishermen and the trap escalation that has been particularly severe in this part of the coast. These differences are reflected in the in/out ratios that the various zone councils requested that the commissioner impose. In Zone F and G, more council members wanted a five-to-one ratio than any other; in Zone A, by way of contrast, the vast majority of the council members wanted no limited-entry rules at all. No one voted for a five-to-one in/out ratio.

The contrast from east to west is also reflected in the answers we received to questions concerning limited entry on our 1998 questionnaire. In response to the question: "Do you favor more restrictions on entry into the lobster business beyond the two-year apprenticeship program," only 35 percent in Zone A favored limited entry, while the percentage of those favoring it in the more westerly zones was much higher. In Zones E and F, the percentages were 66 percent and 65 percent, respectively. Interestingly enough, in 1998, a large percentage of fishermen in the middle of the coast (Zones C and D) favored limited entry. Yet two years later,

Table 5.1

Question: Do you favor more restrictions on entry into the
lobster business beyond the two-year apprenticeship program?

	Zone A		Zone B		Zone C		Zone D		Zone E		Zone F		Zone G	
	#	%	#	%	#	%	#	%	#	%	#	%	#	%
No	125	65	72	65	54	39	100	40	47	34	48	35	54	49
Yes	68	35	39	35	83	61	150	60	91	66	90	65	57	51
Total	193		111		137		250		138		138		111	

they were lukewarm toward the idea. The Zone C council tabled the limited-entry proposal, and Zone D requested and received from the commissioner a one-to-one ratio.

The 49 Percent/51 Percent Rule and Boundary Problems

The initial committee charged with implementing the zone management law thought no serious disputes would result from the establishment of zone boundaries, since these boundaries would coincide with existing informal territorial boundaries, and the rules made it possible for people to fish in two zones, providing they fish according to the rules of the most restrictive zone. But this committee had not contemplated the effect of limited entry. When limited-entry legislation was being discussed by the marine resources committee, several observers including the Deputy Commissioner of Marine Resources, Penn Estabrook, predicted that boundary problems would result. They were right.

Six of the seven zones have become involved in boundary disputes since the passage of limited-entry legislation (only Zone A has remained above the fray). These disputes all involve contests over access to lobster bottom, which followed on the heels of legislation. The exact cause was not the same in each zone, however.

The disputes between Zones C and D, and Zones F and G did not come to a head immediately, since these four zones had the same trap limit, leaving fishermen free to place traps where they had always fished. However, with the passage of the limited entry by zone law came the realization that boundaries would have to be made more impermeable. One could not have limited entry in a zone if licenseholders from adjacent zones could fish in that zone with impunity. Thus, the so-called "49/51 percent" rule was passed by the commissioner, limiting fishermen from one zone to placing a maximum of 49 percent of their gear in the area of another zone. This limited the activities of people from one zone who had "traditionally" fished a lot of gear in waters now belonging to another zone. Men from Portland (Zone F) who had long placed most of their gear in offshore waters east of Biddeford Pool and Kennebunk in the winter, now in Zone G, could no longer do so. It made it impossible for men from Spruce Head and Wheeler's Bay (Zone D) to place large amount of traps southeast of Matinicus (Zone C) where some had been fishing in the winter for years. Ironically, the majority of fishermen in all of these zones favored limited entry, but a few people who had been disadvantaged objected mightily and caused the problems.

In all of these cases, the DMR and the zone councils attempted to adjudicate the disputes by trying to devise new lines acceptable to all parties. They had little luck. The negotiations were complicated by the fact that all agreed that the zone boundaries should follow "traditional" fishing lines, and then tried to define their "traditional fishing grounds" in such a way as to give them strategic advantage in the negotiation. The large amount of area where mixed fishing is allowed made possible a number of interpretations.

Such problems have certainly dogged the negotiations over the Zone C and D boundary. This dispute appeared to be settled after a meeting in February 2000 in which the two zone councils agreed on a new line zigzagging the length of Penobscot Bay, involving a buffer zone. However, the agreement broke down when fishermen from Owls Head objected, insisting that the line be drawn to allow them to fish in a wedge-shaped area they had recently wrested from Vinalhaven and Matinicus. After thirty-one meetings with the DMR resource coordinator, the two zone councils could come to no agreement.

The zone bylaws state that zone councils can establish a new boundary line by majority vote. If a dispute over a boundary cannot be solved by the councils themselves, mediation will take place. If mediation fails, then the commissioner is empowered to establish a boundary unilaterally. Some of these boundary disputes have gone on for a long time. In some cases, such as the Zone C and D dispute, Commissioner La Pointe appears to be determined to force these fishermen to propose a zone boundary line agreeable to both sides. In other cases, he used his regulatory powers to impose a boundary. In the early fall of 2001, he established a new boundary between Zones F and G, which had been in contention over the boundary since 1997. Neither side is likely to be completely happy with the result, since the commissioner's boundary will allow Zone G fishermen to fish inside Portland harbor, well within the older Zone F boundary, while allowing the Zone F fishermen to fish two miles further to the west in offshore waters than was the case under the original Zone F and G boundary line.

In the winter of 2000, Representative David Etnier (of Harpswell) introduced a bill designed to solve boundary disputes stemming from the 49 percent/51 percent rule. This bill would have limited the authority of the zones and zone councils to the 3-mile zone. Outside 3 miles, traps could be placed anywhere, which would have allowed most people to continue fishing where they always had gone. This bill was passed in the House late in the spring of 2000, but was defeated in the Senate. Had it passed, it would have resulted in still other problems that would have demanded solution at a later date. For example, it would have made it possible for a person with a license in one zone to fish in any zone, providing that he only kept 49 percent of the traps within 3 miles and had 51 percent outside the 3-mile line. Such people could have circumvented the entire limited-entry program.

The dispute between Zones D and E stemmed from another cause—a difference in trap limits. Zone E passed a build-down of traps in 1997, which was more restrictive than the one passed by Zone D. (Zone E was to achieve a six hundred-trap limit by 2000; Zone D was to have an eight hundred-trap limit by 2000.) This meant that people from Zone E could fish to the east of the boundary (Pemaquid Point), but big fishermen from Zone D could not place traps to the west of that boundary. The Zone D fishermen were incensed over this turn of events, since it seemed unfair to them that they would be stopped from fishing in areas where they always had gone. The Zone D and E dispute simmered from 1997 to late in 1999. Two meetings were held to try to settle the dispute, but to no avail. Unfortunately, this dispute was especially bitter, since, in the words of First Selectman Bob Fossett, "It split the town of Bristol down the middle." It turned fishermen from Pemaquid Harbor (Zone E) against fishermen from New Harbor (Zone D), who had gone to school together and in some cases were close relatives. After months of wrangling, a meeting was held at the Bristol School on the evening of November 4, 1999. This meeting was called by the commissioner, who conveyed the word through intermediaries that he would consider the testimony given at this meeting and then make a final decision on the zone boundary. During the formal meeting, most of those testifying represented their side of the case. The only thing many seemed to agree on was that the whole zone concept was more trouble than it was worth and should be scrapped in its entirety. During the meeting, a proposed compromise line was suggested by Richard Cheney of New Harbor. The meeting broke up without the two sides being able to come to agreement. After the meeting, however, several fishermen from both sides continued to talk. Within half an hour, they had hammered out a compromise line, almost identical to the one proposed by Richard Cheney in the formal meeting. In the weeks that followed, several influential fishermen, including Brian Sawyer and Don Wotton of New Harbor, organized more meetings with the commissioner to iron out details and build support among the fishermen for the agreement. Early in 2000, a new boundary line involving a mile-wide buffer zone at Pemaquid Point was established by the commissioner, essentially formalizing the line agreed to by the local fishermen.

The problem concerning the Zone B and C boundary stemmed from an administrative error. Somehow this boundary was not drawn on official maps as originally envisioned by the zone council members who approved the boundary. It begins at Naskeag Point rather than Newberry Point, passes through the middle of the Swan's Island conservation zone, and ends at a place on the south that is in contention by fishermen. A new line was successfully negotiated by the two zone councils and approved by the commissioner in the summer of 2001.

All of these boundary disputes were caused by passing zone boundary rules that affected access to fishing areas. In the negotiations that followed, groups of fishermen and zone councils attempted to move them or maintain them with access to fishing bottom in mind. The single exception to this is the Zone B and C problem. Of all of these disputes, only the Zone B and C problem and the dispute between Zone D and E concerning the waters around Pemaquid Point were settled by negotiations between zone councils and fishermen themselves. The other disputes will likely not be settled until the commissioner forces the issue or makes the decision himself. Bottoms-up management has some limitations.

Capturing the Commons

Implementing the License Moratorium, Apprenticeship Program, and Trap-Tag System

The zone management law contained three other provisions that went into effect in the first few years after the law was passed: a license moratorium, an apprenticeship program, and a trap-tag system. While they were not as contentious as the trap-limit issue, they will have a radical effect on the way the lobster fishery is conducted.

LICENSE MORATORIUM

The license moratorium was designed to put a cap on the number of lobster licenses and to remove the inactive license-holders from the fishery. Under this provision, only people who could demonstrate that they were in the fishery in 1993 and 1994 were allowed to hold licenses in 1996. Unfortunately, this rule was implemented in a way that caused a lot of dissension. There was widespread perception among lobster fishermen that the moratorium was not working at all, and the rumor spread that a lot of people were entering the fishery by cheating. Certainly the criteria for obtaining a license were very loose. Laura Taylor, the assistant to the commissioner, said she was told "all you had to do was show any paper connecting you to the fishery and you were virtually assured of getting a license." A series of waivers of the requirements also allow sternmen and anyone over sixty-five years old who had any history of lobstering to be given a license. Moreover, some people who were denied licenses went to their legislators, who proceeded to intercede for their constituents with the Department of Marine Resources. Only after 1998 was the moratorium enforced stringently. After 1999, with the passage of limited entry by zone law, entry into the industry became much more difficult.

In spite of these problems, the moratorium clearly had some effect. The number of lobster licenses dropped dramatically after 1995. In 1995, there were 7,690 licenses, and in 1999, that number had dropped to 6,704 (see table 1.1). Under these conditions, why was the industry convinced that many new fishermen were entering the fishery? Part of the answer is that many fishermen who had lobster licenses became full-time lobstermen at this time. The perception that all was not well was exacerbated by the characteristics of these new entrants. As Norbert Lemieux, the Zone A chair, pointed out, some of these new entrants came from the dragger industry and had "no commitment to conservation."

The rumors that many new entrants were coming into the lobster fishery was to have one critical effect—it fueled support for the limited entry by zone law.

APPRENTICESHIP PROGRAM

The apprenticeship program went into effect in 1996. This program was designed to limit entry into the fishery, and in many quarters it was hoped that it would prove to be enough of a barrier that a limited-entry law would not be necessary.

When the law was passed, the implementation committee assumed that the apprenticeship program would include both a practical work requirement and an educational requirement. In fact, only a work requirement was implemented. To pass the apprenticeship program, an applicant must work for a minimum of two hundred days on a lobster boat. These days must be at least five hours long. The number of days must be certified by the captain of the boat; and every fifty hours also has to be certified by a warden. No more than 20 percent of these hours can be maintenance or yard work.

Commissioner Robin Alden formed a committee to implement the educational component of the program in 1997. I was charged with writing the plan. The plan I drew up called for a substantial course with sections on biology, laws, safety, navigation, and the like. The committee met once to discuss the draft plan, and then it was shelved (no great testament to my political skills). Fishermen in the eastern part of the state were opposed to an educational component, and DMR staffers opposed it because the agency did not have the financial resources to run the proposed course.

The apprenticeship program got off to a slow start. In February 1998, two years after the program began, only twenty people in the state had signed up for the program. By the summer of 2000, 280 people had joined the program.

In 2001, the apprenticeship program was given a strong boost by events in Zone C. A large number of fishermen in Zone C were leery of supporting limited entry because they did not want to make it impossible for young people to enter the industry. However, they also recognized that some limit on new licenses had to be devised. Gerald Weed, the Zone C chair, said the Zone C council feared that after the zones bordering Zone C (i.e., Zones B and D) had passed limited-entry ratios, Zone C would see an influx of new fishermen unless they did something. After months of talk, they had a local representative introduce into the legislature a bill to allow zones to have an expanded apprenticeship program as an alternative to having limited entry with an in/out ratio. This bill was modified to apply to Zone C only. The law allows the zones to enact by referendum four or five different optional ways of limiting entry via an apprenticeship program. These include extending the amount of time an aspiring lobster fisherman must spend in the apprenticeship program, a requirement to apprentice only in Zone C, and imposing an educational component. This law went into effect in September 2001. After much debate, two proposed rules were sent out for a referendum vote. One would make it mandatory for those seeking to fish in Zone C to apprentice in Zone C. The other proposed rule would allow only people with more than five years of experience to sponsor apprentices. The Zone C experiment will be watched carefully. If it succeeds, other zones might follow suit.

TRAP-TAG PROGRAM

The zone management law also specified that all lobster traps were to be equipped with tags with a number identifying the owner of the traps. These aluminum tags are purchased from the Department of Marine Resources each year for $.20 each. They must be attached to each trap in the water by March 1 (Stevens 1998). Since the intent of the trap-tag program was to make it possible to enforce the trap limit, a license-holder can only buy the maximum number of tags permitted by the trap-limit regulations of the zone of which he is a member.

The trap-tag provision went into effect in March 1996 (Jones 1996b). It made fishermen very uneasy. Many thought that federal or state governments might use the number of tags purchased to implement a trap "build-down." That is, they feared the government might rule that trap numbers would be cut by a certain percentage each year. Although Commissioner Alden assured fishermen that the trap-tag system would "never be used against them," many fishermen were very leery of having to document the number of traps they fished. Their suspicions were well founded, because the National Marine Fisheries Service lobster management plan, put forth in 1998, proposed exactly the kind of build-down many feared.

Many connected with the industry became convinced that trap-tag numbers gave no reliable indication of the actual numbers in use. Some said widespread cheating was taking place. Industry people said that people were buying a lot more tags than they used as a means of grandfathering themselves into the fishery. This, they asserted, makes it appear that far more traps are in use than are being placed in the water.

Our 1998 survey provides some data on the numbers of traps used and traps purchased. We gathered data on the number of traps fished, the number of trap tags purchased, the zone license-holders are in, and data on personal characteristics.

The data we collected show that the number of trap tags purchased was only a little larger than the number of traps in use. Table 5.2 shows that in the state as a whole, only 176,611 tags, or 6.9 percent of the total, were purchased but not used on traps. For some reason, the practice of purchasing "extra" tags is greatest in Zone B and least in Zone D.

Table 5.3 shows a wide variation among individual fishermen in differences

Table 5.2

Mean Tags Bought, Mean Traps Fished, and Estimated Unfished Traps per Zone, 1997

	Zone A	Zone B	Zone C	Zone D	Zone E	Zone F	Zone G	State
Mean tags bought	571	494	591	667	466	615	703	593
Meantraps fished	541	422	540	646	428	577	638	552
Percentage of difference	5.25%	14.57%	8.62%	3.15%	8.15%	6.17%	9.24%	6.91%
Total traps per zone[a]	376,309	213,649	420,267	620,832	213,257	504,757	206,804	2,555,875
Estimated unfished trap tags	19,756	31,129	37,951	19,556	17,381	31,144	19,109	176,611

[a] Information on total traps per zone (used in calculating estimated unfished trap tags) was provided by the Department of Marine Resources.

Table 5.3
Difference between Traps Fished and Trap Tags Purchased, by Zone, 1997

	Zone A		Zone B		Zone C		Zone D		Zone E		Zone F		Zone G		State	
	#	%	#	%	#	%	#	%	#	%	#	%	#	%	#	%
Fewer tags than traps	18	8.8	6	5.0	17	11.6	42	15.9	21	14.5	18	12.0	11	9.6	133	11.6
Equal tags than traps	96	46.8	52	43.3	54	37.0	115	43.6	47	32.4	70	46.7	49	42.6	483	42.2
1–100 more traps	63	30.7	35	29.1	36	24.6	71	26.9	48	33.1	43	28.7	22	19.1	318	27.8
101–300 more traps	24	11.7	19	15.8	31	21.2	29	10.9	23	15.8	15	10.0	24	20.9	165	14.4
Over 300 more traps	4	1.9	8	6.7	8	5.5	7	2.6	6	4.1	4	2.7	9	7.8	46	4.0
Total	205	100	120	100	146	100	264	100	145	100	150	100	115	100	1,145	100

between the numbers of tags purchased and numbers of traps fished. Forty-two percent of the fishermen on whom we have information fished the same number of traps and tags. A higher number (46 percent of the total) of people had more tags than traps. Sixty percent of these (318 of 529) had one hundred or fewer tags more than they had traps. Only a small minority (46 of the 529 or 8.7 percent) had three hundred or more tags than they had traps.

A relatively small number of fishermen (11.6 percent of the total number in the state) reported fishing more traps then they had tags for. Some of these men undoubtedly misread the question or inadvertently gave the wrong information. Others openly admitted that they were violating the law and fishing more traps than they had tags for. Their explanations ranged all the way from a lack of money to patriotism.

If these figures are at all accurate, there is no substance in the idea that the passage of a trap-tag program caused massive cheating or massive numbers of tags to be purchased that are not used on traps. For better or for worse, the number of trap tags purchased provides a reasonable estimate of the numbers in the water. However, some fishermen are clearly buying more tags than they use to better position themselves for a future that may see more stringent regulations passed.

Other Laws

In the period between 1995 and 2000, two pieces of legislation were passed at the state level that did not directly involve the zones and zone councils. One was the owner/operator law, which was framed by the Lobster Advisory Council and DMR officers and passed in 1998 by the legislature. It received a lot of industry support. This law required vessels used in the lobster fishery be owned and operated by the lobster license-holder (Public Law 1997, Chapter 693). This law was designed to prevent corporations such as Schaftmaster Corporation—based in New Hampshire and tending large numbers of traps in offshore waters, using big trawlers with hired captains and crews—from doing the same in Maine. The law also deals with the "two-boat problem," that is, individuals who had one boat in their own name and another in the name of another person, allowing them to operate as many complements of traps as they had vessels.

In 1999, the Maine legislature altered the trap-limit law to permit only a certain number of traps per boat (not individual). The intent of this law is to stop a fisherman from exceeding the maximum number of traps allowed in the zone by having a full set of traps in his name and a large number in the name of another license-holder. This was done in response to pressure from the ASMFC to keep Maine in compliance with ASMFC rules, and did not originate with the zone councils. However, this boat trap limit is difficult to enforce. It is legal, after all, for anyone with a license to own traps, including wives, children, and sternmen.

ZONE COUNCILS

In 1995, the zone management law created two legal units: the zone councils and districts within those councils. Subsequently, the Lobster Advisory Council, a unit that existed prior to 1995, was modified to serve as an intermediary body between the DMR and the zone councils.

Since 1997, when the first interim zone councils were appointed, the various units involved in the co-management process have developed ways to interrelate and do business that are becoming standard. Some of these practices are framed by the legislation itself, others by the regulations of the Department of Marine Resources, and still others are the result of more informal processes.

The key unit is the zone councils, which are composed of members elected by license-holders in each zone. The zone council members then elect a chair and a secretary. The chair runs the council meetings and is involved in all aspects of running the council. The secretary, as the name suggests, keeps the notes of the meetings.

For the past several years, zone council meetings are held every month during the fall, winter, and spring. The councils adjourn from June to September. The meetings are ordinarily held in public buildings in a central location in each of the zones. For example, the Zone F meetings are at the Yarmouth High School, Zone B meetings are at the Somesville Fire Station, while the Zone A meetings are in Machias, generally at the Bluebird Motel or the University of Maine at Machias campus.

Zone meetings are ordinarily held in the early evening, and last from two and a half to three hours. By law they are open to the public. However, meetings are ordinarily attended only by council members, the DMR resource coordinator, and perhaps ten to fifteen fishermen. Sometimes a member of the legislature, a member of the Marine Patrol, a biologist, or a newspaper reporter might also be present.

Meetings have a printed agenda that is made up by the council chair in consultation with the DMR resource coordinator. Most of the items on the agenda are put there by the two functionaries, although any member of the council can put an item on the agenda, and members of the public can suggest agenda items to be taken up at the next meeting. The agenda is typed by DMR personnel, put on the DMR web page, sent to the local newspaper, and distributed to council members. The chair of the council will sometimes give copies to others who show an interest in council affairs. The agendas usually begin with an introduction and a motion to accept the minutes of the previous meetings, and then take up old business and new business. In the meeting, reports are usually made on events at the state and federal level by DMR employees, usually the resource coordinator, and perhaps a member of the legislature who will give an update on laws pertaining to the lobster industry. At one or two times during the meetings, there will be a period when questions and comments from the audience are allowed. The meetings will end with a proposal to set the next meeting date.

The length of the agenda will depend on the issues at hand. Some agendas will have as few as ten items, including introductions and adjournment. Others can have as many as eighteen if a number of pressing issues are coming to a head.

According to the bylaws of the zones, zone council meetings are supposed to be run by Robert's rules of order. In some cases, Robert's rules are really used as intended, but in other cases meetings are run in ways that would make Robert blanch. As one person phrased it, "We run by Robert's rules of order except when we don't." Zone D meetings are always run according to the agenda, and people do not speak unless permitted to do so by the chair. Zone E meetings are always more chaotic, with council members and even members of the audience speaking at will.

In many cases, issues have been discussed beforehand and a decision has been made before the meeting. In such cases, the discussion can be perfunctory unless a surprise element is added to the conversation by a DMR employee, a legislator, or a members of the public. In other cases, there is little agreement, and long, protracted discussions can take place between council members. When contentious issues or important legislation are pending, discussions on an issue can last for several meetings.

Council members are elected for staggered three-year terms. When a vacancy occurs for a zone council position, the DMR notifies the voting district that nominations for the position will be accepted for a specific period of time. At the end of this period, the election date is set and ballots are mailed to each eligible voter in that district. The ballots are send to the DMR, which counts the votes and announces the winner.

ZONE DISTRICTS

The districts within the zones are far less organized. As envisioned by the implementation committee, the members of districts are supposed to convey their wishes and views to their council representative, who represents their views in the zone council. Unfortunately, no rules were generated to ensure this happens. Districts are not required to have meetings, and only a few of them, particularly in Zones G and D, do so. Many zone representatives take their job seriously, try to work for the best interests of their districts, and stay in touch with their district members by phone or radio. However, in most cases communication between districts and the councils is not what it should be. Fisherman Ted Ames, who has been very critical of the Zone C process, goes so far as to say that most council members do not even know who is in their districts (Ames 1999: 14C). In most zones, fishermen with something to discuss with the zone council bypass the districts all together and go directly to the zone council meetings.

As a result of these kinds of communication problems, the zone council process has come to rely on mail surveys to gather information on constituent wishes. Before every trap-limit referendum, each zone council, working with the DMR, mailed out a questionnaire to all of the eligible voters in each zone. The questionnaire was drawn up by members of the zone council, usually a subcommittee, and printed up and mailed to the voters by personnel of the DMR. The questionnaires were returned to the DMR, which tabulated the results and then gave the results and the questionnaires to the zone council chair. This procedure was so successful that it will likely be continued before any other referendum, even though it is not required by law or departmental regulations. However, a mail survey is required by law to be sent to all license-holders in a zone by the commissioner before any limited-entry regulations are promulgated. Surveys are well on their way to becoming part of the political culture of the zone management process.

LOBSTER ADVISORY COUNCIL

In 1996, the implementation committee envisioned the need for coordination between the councils. It recommended the legislature create a "council of councils" to adjudicate disputes between the zones and to act as an advisory board to the commissioner. The membership of this unit was to consist of two representatives from each of the zone councils.

The legislature never created such a unit. Instead, the Lobster Advisory Council, which had been created by prior legislation, was modified by legislation to serve this function. The Lobster Advisory Council consists of a representative from each of the zone councils, who is elected to this position by that zone council; three lobstermen at large representing the eastern, central, and western part of the coast; two lobster dealers, one from the east and the other from the west; and a public member. No DMR personnel or legislators sit on the Lobster Advisory Council. Normally the Lobster Advisory Council meets several times per year or monthly when important business is pending. The meetings are always held at the offices of the Department of Marine Resources in Hallowell, 2 miles from the state capital in Augusta. DMR employees do much of the staff work for the Lobster Advisory Council.

The purpose of the Lobster Advisory Council is to serve as an advisory body to the commissioner. When the zone management system was put in place, it was envisioned that the Lobster Advisory Council would be a conduit of information between the councils, the DMR, and the legislature, and serve as a means to resolve conflict between the zones. Instead, the Lobster Advisory Council has come to perform the function of a legislative advisory group for the commissioner and legislature. That is, legislation is suggested by the commissioner, and discussed in detail by the Lobster Advisory Council, which modifies drafts of bills. When the bill is complete, it is given to the marine resources committee of the legislature, which then puts it through the usual legislative process.

Since 1997, the Lobster Advisory Council has taken the lead role in framing all important legislation passed concerning the lobster industry. In 1997, it devoted many meetings to developing the owner/operator law. In 1998 and 1999, it spent the entire year discussing ways to deal with the inequities produced by the imposition of trap limits. The limited-entry law and the trap-cap law were the result of its deliberations on this problem. In 2000, it wrestled with the problem of extending the trap cap.

Implementation Problems

In the first three years, several kinds of problems came to the fore as the zone management law went forward.

One concerned a conflict of interest. Most of those zone council representatives are very conscientious. However, a number of those elected to the first zone councils in 1997 had no intention of serving their constituents in general, but rather chose to represent their own interests or those of a minority of their constituents. This caused serious problems in a number of zones. One zone had three problem representatives. One never came to meetings; another was a "big fisherman" who would not hear of any proposal to cut effort; the third was a "small fisherman" who vigorously promoted any and all effort reduction proposals, regardless of merit. The activities of these representatives resulted in a good deal of acrimony in this zone.

In one zone, a large number of big fishermen got on the council and did all they could to avoid holding a referendum on a trap limit, despite the fact that the majority of fishermen in this zone, as in all other zones, favored such a limit. The result was not only general unhappiness in that zone; their actions also fueled an attempt by fishermen from one of the islands in the zone to establish their own sub-zone.

In the second round of elections, in 1999 and early in 2000, many of these unpopular representatives were voted out of office. Some were self-serving; others had been ineffective. Neither group was able to deliver what their constituents wanted.

A second problem concerned the role of the Lobster Advisory Council. Many fishermen and Lobster Advisory Council members quickly came to feel that the LAC had become almost an arm of the commissioner—a tool in helping to implement top-down management. There was some justice in this complaint. The Lobster Advisory Council does not take the initiative in acting on proposals of the zone councils and fishermen. Rather, it studies proposals for legislation that the DMR has on its agenda, by a process of interacting with department personnel, scientists, academics, and members of the marine resources committee of the legislature. The proposed legislation is then directly communicated to the legislature and reported to the zone council members as a fait accompli. The zone councils and fishermen in the districts have little opportunity in the process to review, comment on, or modify the actions of the Lobster Advisory Council. The lobster industry is not ignored in this process. The two industry associations, especially the Maine Lobstermen's Association, have taken a special interest in the council process.

Since 1998, even members of the Lobster Advisory Council have come to feel used. In the fall of 2000, the Lobster Advisory Council was asked to approve a departmental initiative to request that the legislature extend the trap-cap law beyond 2001 when it was scheduled to be sunsetted. One member noted that the LAC had no opportunity even to tell anyone in the zone councils what was happening. He was not pleased. Many members have reacted by simply missing meetings. During 2000, a number of meetings of the Lobster Advisory Council did not have a quorum.

A third problem with the implementation of the zone management law is the proper role of the zone councils and the Department of Marine Resources. The DMR has become heavily involved in the operation of the co-management system. By law, the DMR must organize the hearings concerning limited-entry proposals, qualify people for licenses, and certify that people have completed the apprenticeship program. However, the zone councils have come to depend on the DMR staff to perform a variety of other tasks that are not specified in any law or regulation. Terry Stockwell, the DMR resource coordinator, and his staff help make up agendas for council meetings, advertise council meetings in the newspapers and on the web, organize and run the council elections, and administer surveys. To be sure, Stockwell consults continually with the zone council chairs. Even so, the zone councils have become so dependent on the DMR staff that they have probably lost more independence than they should have.

In 2000, the problem of too much state control was recognized and efforts were made to change the situation. The University of Maine Sea Grant program began to help the zone councils by providing secretarial services for the council meetings. Having a good record of meetings and decisions will help the councils in the future. Moreover, George La Pointe, the commissioner of Marine Resources, is seeking ways to help the Lobster Advisory Council develop agenda items to respond to problems and requests of fishermen. The objective, in the words of Terry Stockwell, is to put the "co" back in co-management.

Another problem is essentially cultural. Implementation of the zone management law at all levels has been hampered by long-standing social and cultural patterns, which have made it difficult for fishermen to communicate and cooperate with each other and to operate as intermediaries between fishing communities and the state bureaucracy.

If the zone council system is to work as envisioned, council members from all of the different harbors in the region must work cooperatively with men from their own council and others. They have no experience in inter-town cooperation The convoluted nature of the shoreline does not facilitate contact. Moreover, fishermen in different communities tend to view each other with some suspicion, which is not surprising, given the fact they are members of groups with a history of conflicts over fishing bottom. Most who have been elected to the zone councils have made a valiant effort to work together. Still, the past is difficult to overcome. Zone council meetings have been held in which council members from towns currently in territorial conflict would not even look at each other, much less speak to each other. The zone councils have managed to accomplish a good deal, but there can be no question that the traditional social organization of coastal Maine does not facilitate the business of the zone councils. It is something to be overcome, rather than a basis on which such cooperative endeavors can be built.

Zone council chairs and members also need to be politicians who are adept at dealing with highly controversial issues. Being effective on a zone council requires a lot of time, patience, flexibility, and negotiating skills, along with a willingness to learn the issues, the law, and the bureaucracy. One council member said, "I have learned more here about government than I did in my political science course." However, more than knowledge is required; council members need to understand two different subcultures and be able to work effectively in both. They need to understand their constituents and the intricacies of fishing, and at the same time work with state officials and legislators in negotiating solutions to complex problems. This is very difficult, given the fact that fishermen and bureaucrats have different world views, operate under different kinds of constraints, and have mastery of very different bodies of knowledge. In this respect, they are in a position analogous to that of the East African chief of the 1950s, between the British Colonial administration and the so-called "natives" on the ground (Fallers 1955: 290–305).

The skills required of zone council members have not been easy for many to learn. Despite the fact that lobster fishermen are small entrepreneurs and have a variety of skills, the vast majority have no training or background that has given them experience in running meetings, writing bylaws, proposing legislation, or negotiating creative management solutions. The fact that the zone councils have done so well is a testament to the efforts of the council members, the leadership ability of the council chairs, and the effectiveness of the DMR area coordinator.

Fatigue and burnout have also been problems. Council members have put in untold numbers of hours talking with constituents and attending meetings, to the detriment of family life and their business. One zone chair said that his income dropped by $10,000 during 1998. They have also had to deal with emotionally charged situations in which they have had to shoulder a good deal of blame for the results of the regulations they proposed. Every major legislative or regulatory push has come at the cost of months of tense meetings, confrontations, and conversations with angry constituents.

Actions at the federal and ASMFC levels have added a considerable burden to the zone councils and their members. During 1997 and 1998, for example, two competing plans were proposed for the lobster industry. One, as we have seen, was put forth by the ASMFC; the other by the NMFS. After months of talking, a consensus was reached in the Maine lobster industry to support the ASMFC plan, because it seemed more reasonable and effective. The zone councils were at the vortex of this struggle. They devoted considerable time and effort to support the ASMFC plan. They also took part in what proved to be very effective negotiations, which finally resulted in ASMFC plan being endorsed by the NMFS.

Adding to the confusion and stress was the right whale controversy (which will be covered in some detail in the next chapter). The problem stemmed from a series of suits between 1996 and 2000 to protect the right whale under the Marine Mammal and Endangered Species Acts. These caused a lot of work and soul-searching for the zone councils. In 1996, for example, a suit was brought under the Marine Mammal Act that claimed that right whales were being killed by being entangled in lobster gear (University of Maine 1996). In June 1997, the commissioner of the

Department of Marine Resources called on the lobster zone councils to help assess the sentiment of the fishing industry in an effort to frame its response to the National Marine Fisheries Service whale plan. In the months that followed, the zone councils devoted considerable time to the whale plan negotiations (*Commercial Fisheries News* 1997a). As we shall see, their efforts met with a good deal of success and resulted in a plan in which the DMR, the zone councils, and volunteer fishermen agreed to work with the Coast Guard to create a monitoring system to track and disentangle whales.

However, these activities took a tremendous amount of time and diverted the zone councils from doing what they were empowered to do. Knowledgeable observers in 1997 and 1998 thought the zone councils would be overwhelmed, and that these side issues threatened the very existence of the co-management experience in Maine. Attendance at meetings dropped, some zone council meetings were acrimonious and chaotic, and council members vowed not to run for re-election. Junior Backman, the DMR resource coordinator for eastern Maine at that time, said of the whale issue, "It was just too much. The zone councils didn't have the authority to do anything with the whale situation and it distracted them from what they could have done."

In the years that have followed, the zone councils have been called on to respond to a number of federal initiatives. This came at a cost in terms of burnout and conflict. It also resulted in the zone councils responding to pressures from the federal bureaucracy and not to their own constituents in the industry. This served to alienate them further from the rank-and-file fishermen.

In retrospect, federal intervention did have a positive result. It motivated large numbers of people to persist in their efforts to manage the lobster fishery. Spurred by the fear of draconian federal control, many remained involved in the zone management process long after they might have given up under ordinary circumstances. They volunteered to help monitor the whales, and the leadership of the industry increasingly devoted a good deal of time to the ASMFC process after 1997. As Larry Knapp, chairman of the Zone E council remarked, "either we manage this resource or they [the feds] will do it for us." As we shall see, by the year 2000, the activities of fishermen were to have a marked effect on the federal and ASMFC management process.

The Behavioral Response to the Trap Limits

When trap limits began to be imposed in 1997 and 1998, many observers of the industry, including the author, predicted that the number of traps in use would quickly stabilize and then begin to drop. In fact, the total number of traps in use rose. Official state statistics indicate that in 1994, the year before the trap limit went into effect, a total of 2,786,000 traps were in use in Maine (see table 1.1). For the next several years, the number in use increased, so that by 1999, 3,043,000 traps were in the water. Fishermen reported in our 1998 survey that they fished a mean number of 432.5 traps in 1990, 503.6 traps in 1995, 552.4 in 1997, and 571.1 in 1998.

Table 5.4

License-holders Changing the Number of Traps between 1995 and 1998

	Decrease ≥ 200 traps	Decrease 1–199 traps	Same number of traps	Increase 1–199 traps	Increase ≥ 200 traps
Number of respondents	160	19	260	350	266
Percentage of respondents	15.2%	1.8%	24.6%	33.2%	25.2%

Not all fishermen increased the number of traps they fished. The response was highly differential. However, the number of fishermen who reduced the number of traps fished are far outweighed by those who increased their numbers of traps. The result has been an overall increase in the number of traps in the state. As can be seen in table 5.4, of the 1,055 lobster license-holders interviewed on whom we have information, 616, or 58.4 percent, reported that they increased the number of traps they fished from 1995 to 1998; 260, or 24.6 percent, said that they fished the same number of traps they fished the year previously; and 179, or 17 percent, said they actually fished fewer traps than they did in the past year.

If we want to understand changes in the number of traps in use, we must explain why different sets of fishermen decided to increase or decrease the number of traps as they did. We will discuss the factors influencing fishermen to decrease the numbers of traps they fished first, and then the variables influencing people to increase traps.

FACTORS LEADING TO A DECLINE IN TRAP NUMBERS

Three different factors influence people to decrease the numbers of traps fished, which are relatively straightforward and easy to understand.

Trap Limits. A number of license-holders in the sample reduced the number of traps they fished because of the trap limit. When the zone management law went into effect in 1996, fishermen with more than twelve hundred traps were forced to begin to reduce the number of traps they fished in increments to meet the state-mandated limit. When the zone trap limits were announced in 1997 and 1998, more people had to begin to reduce the number of traps they fished. Still others, who favored a trap limit all along, reduced their number of traps by attrition, in the certain knowledge that more severe limits were coming and that it was nothing short of foolish to buy more traps under these circumstances. These people were making the kind of choice many observers had assumed would be general in the industry.

Age and Illness. Some fishermen in our survey said that they were entering retirement or semi-retirement and were reducing the number of traps accordingly. Others said that they had reduced due to their own illness or the illness of someone in their family. Those who are scaling down with retirement in mind will almost certainly never again increase the number of traps they fish. Younger people with injuries or illnesses are likely to increase the number of traps they fish once they recover.

Overcrowding and Shore-Based Jobs. Another set of respondents reduced the number of traps they fished because they had to devote more time to a full-time job and/or because of severe trap overcrowding. A few of them were leaving fishing altogether to enter another business or go back to school. Others said they were reducing the number of traps they fished since they were going back to "fishing singles" (i.e., fishing one trap on a line) as a means of coping with gear congestion. One man said, "I am getting a lot of overtime now [on his full-time job] and haven't got as much time for lobstering as I used to. With all the tangles it takes me longer to pull my gear than it used to. When fifty traps wore out last fall, I didn't replace them."

FACTORS INFLUENCING INCREASES IN TRAPS NUMBERS

Three different factors caused fishermen to increase the numbers of traps fished. These factors are less straightforward, more complicated, and more difficult to understand than those leading to decreases in trap numbers

Catches, Income, and the Increase in Full-time Fishermen. One dominant factor causing the increase in traps was the economic opportunities presented by lobster fishing. Very high incomes could be earned in the industry, which stemmed from record-high catches and high lobster prices. While no definitive study of lobster-fishing incomes has been done recently, a number of reliable sources report lobster fishermen catching over 40,000 pounds of lobster and grossing over $250,000 in the mid-1990s. In our survey, 264 license-holders of the 1,083 on whom we have information, or 24.4 percent, said that they caught over 25,000 pounds of lobster in 1997. Since the average price per pound received by lobstermen in that year was about $3.75, it is reasonable to assume that these men grossed over $93,750 during that year. Other estimates indicate that full-time fishermen with average-sized operations might gross $65,000 and have a net income (after taxes and expenses) of $40,000.

At the same time, conditions in other fisheries have been terrible. In Maine, catches of groundfish have plummeted in recent years, primarily due to overfishing, which has resulted in a sharp reduction in numbers of boats and people employed in that fishery (Murawski et al. 1997). Throughout the 1980s and 1990s, people switched from groundfishing into a variety of alternative occupations.

As a result, a large number of people who had been part-time lobster fishermen (or were completely inactive in the fishery) became full-time fishermen who used a lot more traps. Some of them had earned most of their income in shore-based jobs; others had been primarily in the groundfishery. When it became possible to earn high incomes in lobstering, these people gradually shifted their operations and devoted more months to lobster fishing and less time to other jobs or other fisheries. As a result, while the total number of licenses did not increase appreciably in the last twenty years, the number of fishermen whose primary target species is lobster has increased by leaps and bounds, particularly from 1990 to 2000.

The shift to full-time lobstering is reflected in changes observed in the percentage of income earned in lobstering over the course of time. A 1973 study of the lobster industry estimated that "less than a third of the licensed fishers could be considered full time" (Huq and Hasey: 1973: 1; Acheson 1975a: 661). By the mid 1990s, the majority of lobster fishermen had become full-time lobster fishermen and earned very little of their income in other fisheries or in non-fishing jobs. Our 1998 survey showed that over 50 percent of the license-holders in every zone reported earning between 50 and 100 percent of their income from lobstering (see table 5.5). Over 50 percent of the respondents said that they earned no income in any other fishery; and over 50 percent said that they earned nothing in any non-fishing job.

As people became more dependent on the lobster fishery, the number of traps they used increased. In the state as a whole, license-holders earning 75 to 100 percent of their income from the lobster fishery used an average of 732 traps, while those earning 50 to 74 percent of their income from lobstering used 535 traps, and those earning 25 to 49 percent of their income from the lobster fishery used only 311 traps on the average (table 5.6). Clearly, the move from part-time to full-time status is accompanied by a great increase in the average number of traps used.

Legislation and Uncertainty. In some part, the decisions of fishermen concerning the number of traps to fish was a response to a whole plethora of regulations and proposed regulations, and to uncertainty about what the future would bring. After 1995, federal, state, and ASMFC regulations came so fast that fishermen literally did not know from one month to another where they stood. Zone meetings became increasingly devoted to discussing ASMFC rules, NMFS plans, "whale-take reduction" strategies, lawsuits, and other issues. The trap-tag provision of the zone management law raised special anxieties. Many fishermen predicted that the trap-tag information would be used to limit or freeze the number of traps a person could fish. As one fisherman phrased the situation, "We are not sure who is going to be able to fish, where we will be able to fish, or how many traps we will be able to fish." As a result, revealed wisdom among many in the industry has been that fishermen who increased their trap numbers or bought more trap tags than they were using would be better off when the all-too-likely reduction in trap numbers was ordered. These people felt they were grandfathering themselves into the fishery. David Cousens, Maine Lobstermen's Association president, summarized the attitude of many of these men by saying, "Many guys figured it was now or never."

When we asked people why they had increased trap numbers, many were quite clear. One wrote: *"Federal laws. We are afraid of what they might do"*; another simply commented, *"Over regulation."* Still a third put down: *"To get the number of traps up. That way when the feds, tree huggers, and all the other groups that know nothing about lobstering put us on a limit of some kind, hopefully they will leave me enough to make a living, where 100 percent of my living comes from lobstering."*

Table 5.5

Percentage of 1997 Income Reported as Earned from Lobstering, by Zone

Percent of income	Zone A		Zone B		Zone C		Zone D		Zone E		Zone F		Zone G		State	
	%	#	%	#	%	#	%	#	%	N	%	N	%	N	%	N
0	11	5.5	13	11.1	7	4.8	18	7.2	12	8.4	21	14.3	7	6.2	89	7.9
1–24	27	13.6	15	12.8	14	9.6	29	11.5	21	14.7	28	19.0	15	13.2	149	13.3
25–49	18	9.1	14	11.9	13	8.9	22	8.7	9	6.3	9	6.1	3	2.6	88	7.9
50–74	38	19.2	12	10.2	22	15.1	25	9.9	20	13.9	12	8.2	12	10.6	141	12.6
75–100	104	52.5	63	53.8	89	61.4	162	62.5	81	56.6	77	52.4	76	67.2	652	58.3
Total	198	100	117	100	145	100	256	100	143	100	147	100	113	100	1,119	100

Table 5.6

Average Traps Fished in 1997, by Percentage of Income from Lobster Fishing

% income from lobstering	Zone							State avg.
	A	B	C	D	E	F	G	
0%	32	71	53	34	11	37	25	38
1–24%	218	93	169	136	143	134	169	152
25–49%	302	313	381	276	337	232	333	311
50–74%	553	552	501	590	347	553	651	535
75–100%	735	569	674	844	584	929	790	732

Competition. Typically in open-access fisheries, competition feeds on itself. This certainly occurred in the lobster fishery. Once some fishermen in a harbor increased their number of traps, others felt they were forced to follow suit or see the percentage of traps they had on the bottom decline, along with their incomes.

Moreover, the competition was spurred by concerns with prestige. "Highliners," very successful fishermen, receive a good deal of prestige in lobster fishing circles; and much approbation can be heaped on "poor" fishermen (Acheson 1988: 48–59). Under these conditions, keeping up with the competition maintains not only income, but also one's social standing.

REASONS TO CHANGE TRAP NUMBERS:
A SUMMARY OF THE DATA

How important were these various factors in influencing the decisions of fishermen concerning the changes in trap numbers? This is a difficult question; many fishermen were influenced by a number of variables. However, some indication of relative importance of these variables can be obtained from analyzing the answers to the survey question: "If you changed the number of traps you fished in the last five years, explain why you made these changes." The answers received are summarized in table 5.7.

People gave three reasons for decreasing the numbers of traps they fished: age or illness, the trap limit, and switch to a shore-based job. None of these factors motivated large numbers of fishermen, and all three appear to be of equal importance in motivating people to use fewer traps.

The responses to this question indicate that the most important factor influencing an increase in traps is an increase in economic opportunities in the lobster fishery brought about by high stock sizes and record-high catches. There was money to be earned in the lobster fishery, and people responded by putting more traps in the water to get higher catches and returns. They phrased the reasons for their actions in different terms. For example, 161 fishermen said they were "expanding [their] business"; another 139 said they were putting more traps in the water to get more income for "consumption purposes"; another 41 said they were

Table 5.7
Primary Explanation for Changing Numbers of Traps Used

Reason offered[a]	# respondents	% responses
Competition	130	11
Uncertainty due to laws and government action	61	5
Expanding business	161	14
Increase income for investment (new boat, etc.)	41	4
Increase income for consumption (bills, college, house)	139	12
Switching to lobstering from less desirable fishery	20	2
Switching to lobstering from shore job	31	3
Decrease due to trap limit	47	4
Decrease due to age or illness	77	7
Decrease due to overcrowding, or switch to shore-based job	72	6
Fishing about the same number	199	17
Other explanation or no explanation	167	15
Total	1,145	100

[a] Some are reasons given for increasing the number of traps fished; others are reasons for decreasing trap numbers.

expanding the number of traps they fished to get money for a "new investment" such as a boat. People who gave these three answers totaled 341, or 30 percent of the whole sample. Another 51 respondents, or 4 percent, responded by saying that they were moving into lobster fishing from other troubled fisheries or shore-based jobs.

Keeping up with the competition was the second-most important reason given for increasing traps: 130 fishermen, or 11 percent, gave this answer.

Sixty-one license-holders, or 5 percent of the total, responded that they increased the numbers of traps they fished due to the uncertainty brought about by regulation and government actions. The effect of actions of the government may be more important in motivating license-holders to increase traps than these numbers alone would indicate. General concern with actions of the government was laced throughout the questionnaire responses. When fishermen were asked "What is the most serious problem facing the fishing industry," a very large number said "the feds, the government." In this period, fishermen were very concerned with positioning themselves for an uncertain future.

The fact that fishermen chose to increase the number of traps they fished in the face of a trap limit is certainly counterintuitive. I was one of the many people who predicted that the number of traps fished would quickly decline when the trap limit was imposed. We were wrong. In retrospect, it is difficult to understand our lack of insight, particularly because all of the variables that have produced the increase in traps were present in 1995 when the lobster zone management law embodying the trap limit was passed.

Assessing Co-management: The View of Fishermen

Despite the problems and criticism, lobster fishermen on the whole supported the co-management effort. Their assessment of the way the zone management law was working is reflected in answers we received on our large-scale 1998 survey.

The answers to many questions revealed a good deal of support for the zone process, even though the survey was being conducted within months of the time when the zone councils had passed trap limits over the vociferous opposition of many "big fishermen." Answers revealed a good deal of support for co-management, as well as what fishermen thought were problems with the system.

Fishermen were generally in favor of the zone management law. Table 5.8 indicates that almost three-fourths of the fishermen surveyed were in favor of this law in 1995. When they were asked to rate it on a 1-to-10 scale, the mean rating was 5.8, which is a mildly positive assessment for the respondents as a group (table 5.9). A better indication of their assessment of the zone management law is the fact that 43.8 percent of the respondents gave the law a favorable rating (i.e., scores of 7, 8, 9, and 10), whereas only 26.9 percent gave it a negative rating (i.e., scores of 1, 2, 3, or 4). However, it should be noted that approximately 30 percent of the respondents had very strong feelings about the law. Some 15.8 percent gave it very negative ratings (i.e., ratings of 1 and 2), while 13.5 percent gave it very positive ratings (i.e., ratings of 9 and 10).

Fishermen thought that the most serious problem was too much gear in the water and too many fishermen (see table 5.10). There was also a concern with "feds/bureaucracy," which in many cases reflected fishermen's frustration and concern that their fate was in the hands of people who did not know much about the lobster or their industry. Smaller numbers saw the "part-timer/full-timer" conflict as the paramount issue. This issue, of course, is tied up with the effort to establish trap limits.

They were also overwhelmingly in support of the trap limits, which reflects the votes in all of the zones. Of the 1,145 people who answered the question "Are you in favor of the trap limit passed by referendum of the fishermen in your zone?" 685 or 60 percent said "yes" in one way or another, and only 203 or 18 percent were against the trap limit (see table 5.11). But the support for the trap limit is even stronger than these figures would indicate, since 90 of the people who said "no" were in favor of a trap limit, but wanted one that was more stringent one than the one passed by their zone referendum process.

Table 5.8

Question: Were you in favor of the zone management concept when the zone management law was passed in 1995?

	No	Yes	Total
Number	280	777	1,057
Percentage	26.5	73.5	100

Table 5.9
Question: Overall, how would you rate the zone management law?

Rating	Very neg.				Neutral				Very pos.		Total
	1	2	3	4	5	6	7	8	9	10	
Number	141	26	56	62	190	123	149	173	42	101	1,063
Percentage	13.3	2.5	5.3	5.8	17.9	11.6	14.0	16.3	4.0	9.5	100%

Note: Respondents were asked to rate on a 1 to 10 scale, with 1 being "very negative," 10 being "very positive," and 5 being "neutral." The mean rating was 5.8 (s.d. 2.68), which is a mildly positive assessment for the respondents as a group.

Table 5.10
Question: What is the most serious problem faced by the lobster industry?

Coded answer	# respondents	% responses
Too many fishermen	76	7
Too many traps	240	21
Overfishing	212	19
Lack of trap limit or correct trap limit	28	2
New entrants (draggermen switching over)	39	3
Part-timer/full-timer controversy	66	6
Feds/gov't. bureaucracy	206	18
Other	276	24
Total	1,143	100

Table 5.11
Question: Are you in favor of the trap limit passed by referendum of the fishermen in your zone?

Coded answer	# respondents	% responses
Yes, no explanation	471	41
Yes, with additional suggested rule	182	8
Yes, but not strict enough	32	4
No, no explanation	48	16
No, not strict enough	90	5
No, it only redistributes the traps	30	3
No, encourages buildup	24	3
No, we need limited entry too	11	2
Other responses	203	1
No response	54	18
Total	1,145	

Table 5.12

*Question: What is the most important problem facing
your zone management council at present?*

Coded responses	# respondents	% responses
Trap limit	146	11
Federal government	107	8
Lack of communication/cooperation	111	8
Over fishing	48	4
Licenses/license regulation	92	7
"Lack of concern for the future," "Greed," "Trap build-up"	128	10
Other responses	203	15
Don't know	61	5
No response	451	34
Total	1,347	

The answers to the question "What is the most important problem facing your zone management councils at present?" reveal a potpourri of concerns, ranging from actions the councils were considering or had undertaken, to the way the zone management system was operating (see table 5.12). Some gave answers that reflected a concern with issues the councils were dealing with in the summer of 1998. Large numbers of people were concerned with curbing the trap escalation, which was the most important issue being dealt with in the summer of 1998. Some called on the councils to enact trap limits; others were concerned about the motivation behind the trap escalation (e.g., greed, etc.). Others said they wanted a "tiered" license system as a means to handle the so-called "part-timer problem."

Still others recognized the problems that actions of agencies of the federal government were posing for the industry and the co-management system. Many made specific reference to the whale controversy and the lobster plans put forth by the NMFS and the ASMFC. Many of these people wanted less intervention or no intervention by the federal government on ideological grounds, reflecting a growing feeling in the country that too much power is being concentrated in the hands of the central government. But some of these people had very serious and sensible misgivings about the specifics of the plans being put forth by the NMFS on both the whale issue and lobster management.

Others were concerned with the operational problems the councils were facing. In this category is a concern with communication among the fishermen, the zone councils, and the DMR. This was clearly a way of saying that they did not feel they were being listened to by the zone councils and Lobster Advisory Council, whose attention was riveted on the threat of federal intervention.

The largest number of respondents did not answer the question. It is difficult to know how to interpret this. They may not have wanted to think about the problem, but it may also indicate that many respondents could not name a single all-important problem facing the zone council.

Table 5.13

Table 5.13
Question: What is the solution to this problem?

Coded responses	# respondents	% responses
Trap limit or trap freeze	351	31
Limited entry	166	15
Tiered licenses based on income	73	6
Leave us alone	105	9
Other conservation rules (seasons, V-notch, increase measure, increase vent, etc.)	119	11
Other	329	29
Total	1,143	

As might be expected, the answers lobster license-holders gave to the question "What is the solution to this problem?" were determined by what they had identified as the problem facing the zone councils (see table 5.13). Those who saw the proliferation of traps as the problem suggested trap limits as a solution. Those concerned with "over-fishing" or "too many fishermen" focused on the need for limited entry or tiered license solutions. The people identifying federal control as a problem wanted to be "left alone." The important point is that generally the respondents were not just aimlessly complaining and whining, they had an interest in the fishery and the co-management system, and they had a plethora of suggested solutions to the problems they had identified.

Surprisingly, when fishermen were asked if the zone councils should have additional authority, 64 percent (723 out of 1,135) said "no" (see table 5.14). The vast majority favored co-management, but thought that the zone councils had all they could handle temporarily. One person said, "once the trap-limit problem is settled, then we can think about expanding the powers of the zone councils." Another

Table 5.14
Question: Should the lobster zone management councils have additional authority?
(If "Yes," explain what additional powers they should have.)

Coded responses	# respondents	% responses
No	723	64
No response	199	18
Yes, to curb power of feds and the state	23	2
Yes, to give the fishermen more control	48	4
Yes, should have power enough to solve the problems they face	33	3
Yes, to control entry	51	5
Yes, other	58	5
Total	1,135	

Capturing the Commons

said, "They have enough on their plate to keep them busy for a while." Some of these respondents were against the whole concept of local control.

Those answering "yes" thought that the zone councils should be empowered to control entry into the industry and would be able to handle a variety of other problems. Some were very much in favor of local control, and wanted the councils to succeed so the federal government and state would have little excuse for exercising more control over their fishery.

CRITICISM AND THE THREAT OF POLITICAL ACTION

Despite the general popularity of the co-management effort, the law is unpopular in certain quarters. Criticism of all aspects of the zone management law was especially strident in eastern Maine, where it found voice in the statements and actions of officers of the Downeast Lobstermen's Association.

The marine resources committee heard more than its share of this criticism, and in 1999 they began to take it to heart. In November 1999, a meeting was held near DMR headquarters in Hallowell that was attended by members of the marine resources committee, the commissioner, George La Pointe, and key members of his staff, former commissioner Robin Alden, officers of the Maine Lobstermen's Association and Downeast Lobstermen's Association, and a couple of academics, including the author. The topic under discussion was how to improve the zone management process, but in the course of the meeting it became clear that Senator Jill Goldthwait, the Senate chair of the marine resources committee, was questioning the wisdom of the whole co-management effort. She hinted that she was thinking of introducing legislation to nullify the whole zone management law. I suspect that she was just calling the bluff of certain people who had been very vocal in their criticism of the zone management law, but it is also possible that she was serious. If the latter is the case, then the zone management effort in Maine might have had a very short life.

The Future of Co-Management in the Lobster Industry

Cultures are very persistent. Once rules and values are established, they do not change easily. Bob Dow, who was commissioner of the Department of Marine Resources in the 1950s, applied this principle to the lobster industry by saying in an interview: "When a new law is proposed, fishermen are against it. Once it has been in existence for ten years, fishermen will fight anyone who wants to change it." This underscores the idea that the co-management system is likely to be very vulnerable in the first decade or so of its existence. When it has become institutionalized, it will likely to be more impervious to change. The institutionalization process is likely to be helped along by the ASMFC, which has also endorsed zone management.

The fact that the zone management process has had tremendous success in producing trap limits and limited-entry rules will undoubtedly inspire people to maintain the co-management effort in Maine.

There are some issues and questions that will need to be faced in the near future that have profound implications for the way the co-management system in Maine will evolve.

First, the tension between full-time and part-time fishermen will have to be addressed. Large numbers of full-time fishermen feel seriously disadvantaged by the system because they can be outvoted by the part-timers. A tiered license system, which has been discussed by the Lobster Advisory Council on several occasions, could help to alleviate some of the fears of the full-time fishermen. However, a licensing system in which part-time fishermen received a smaller number of traps and a partial vote might also alienate numbers of part-time fishermen and raise constitutional questions.

Second, boundary problems have proven to be very severe and more intractable than anyone thought when the zone management law was proposed. It is beginning to appear that several of these will only be solved by forceful, top-down management by the commissioner.

A third issue is trap escalation. The primary reason the legislature passed the zone management law and the industry came to support it was the fact that it promised a way to produce trap limits, which, in turn would lead to a reduction in traps. The trap limits have not led to a quick reduction in numbers of traps used, and this had led a minority of fishermen to question the value of the whole co-management concept. If the number of traps continues to escalate along historical trend lines, the result could be a substantial unraveling of support for the law. In fact, trap numbers could climb in the immediate future. After all, in 1998, half of the license-holders were part-time fishermen (see table 5.5). If a substantial number of these become full-time fisherman, trap numbers would continue to go up.

I predict that the number of traps will fall some time in the future. The combination of the trap limit and limited entry will almost certainly bring a reduction in the number of traps over time. It is difficult to imagine how numbers of traps can continue to climb in the long run when the number of traps is capped at six or eight hundred and the number of licenses declines. It is possible that the number of traps is already beginning to decline, since the number in use in 2000 was slightly smaller than the number reported for 1999 (table 1.1). Moreover, even in the short run, these rules almost certainly have had an effect. Were it not for the trap limits and the moratorium on licenses, the boom in the lobster industry almost certainly would have attracted additional fishermen and motivated established fishermen to buy ever-increasing numbers of traps. As Terry Stockwell phrased the situation in 2001, "Lobster fishing has been phenomenal. I would hate to see how many traps we would have had in the water now had we not got started on trap limits in 1995."

Other questions facing the zone management system involve the proper role of the governance units in the co-management process. What rights should the councils have? How much time should be allocated to various tasks and processes? When should the commissioner be able to act unilaterally to promulgate rules for the co-management system? Under what conditions should the legislature be involved? Co-management, as the name suggests, indicates a system of shared governance in which all parties have duties and responsibilities. Those have not been specified well enough, and are still in the process of evolving.

Some functions are clearly best left to the government. Enforcement is one of these. No one has suggested that enforcement of formal zone regulations be left to the industry. There are always costs to sanctioning others. Maine fishermen know it is best to foist the costs of law enforcement onto officers of the government, and the same is true of fishermen of other societies. (e.g., see L. Taylor 1987: 304).

The councils also need some technical and logistical support. With that in mind, then-commissioner Robin Alden created within the bureaucracy positions for two full-time resource coordinators to work with the zone councils. However, the creation of such intermediaries had some serious drawbacks. In the first year after they were appointed, the coordinators became indispensable to the councils and their operations. Some observers felt that they did too much. But could the councils have operated without the resources of the DMR? It is very doubtful, in my opinion.

It would be possible to hire staff members for the councils (independent of the DMR), or have other firms or agencies run some of the surveys and elections for the councils. This would likely increase independence from the state bureaucracy, but it would also likely increase work for the council chairs and lead to problems of continuity when the council members rotated. Then there is the matter of money to finance such services. In Maine, this is often the deciding factor.

A closely related issue concerns the amount of power that the commissioner of the DMR should have to promulgate regulations affecting the co-management process without the zone councils or the Lobster Advisory Council ratifying them. Many problems might have been avoided if the zone councils and LAC had had a chance to discuss the implications of the 49/51 percent rule and eighteen-year-old license rule before they went into effect. But it is also clear that the commissioner needs some authority to promulgate rules, especially in cases in which the councils and LAC are unable to solve problems. A good case in point is the boundary disputes that have dragged on for years.

What is the future of the Maine co-management effort? To a large extent, the answer to this question depends on the activities of government at several different levels. If we have learned anything about co-management in general, it is that lack of support by government agencies can be the death knell of such programs (Jentoft 1989; McCay and Jentoft 1996). I have no doubt that the lobster zone management law would not have passed through the legislative process had it not been for the support of Commissioner Robin Alden. There can also be little doubt that an unsympathetic commissioner with good bureaucratic skills could have killed such a program, especially in the early stages before it has become institutionalized. Such a commissioner would find ample ammunition in the enabling legislation and the Maine APA (Administrative Procedures Act), which gives virtually all power for rule making to top state administrators.

In 1997 and 1998, federal intervention could have dealt the zone management process a mortal blow. There would have been little sense in the councils going through all of the *sturm und drang* of establishing 600- and 800-trap limits for the zones, only to have the National Marine Fisheries Service dictate trap limits of 475 for the fishery as a whole. When Zone E was wrestling with trap limits, and its council members were garnering a good deal of criticism for their efforts, one council member remarked, "If the feds are going to force a 475-trap limit on us, all we have done is create a lot of enemies among the neighbors."

Can the co-management system of Maine retain enough independence to continue? Neither the structure of state government nor the nature of federal legislation give us cause for much optimism. Neither does much to facilitate bottoms-up management. The structure of Maine government makes it possible, even mandatory, for the DMR to exert a good deal of control over the zone councils. The zone councils can only recommend rules to the commissioner, and then only in a very restricted sphere. Only the commissioner of the Department of Marine Resources can make these recommendations of the councils into enforceable regulations. The reason is the Administrative Practices Act of the State of Maine, which centralizes the decision-making authority for all state departments in the hands of the commissioner of that department. There is no provision in state law for a commissioner to delegate any authority. The "reasonable clause" of the APA makes it possible for the commissioner to change any rule suggested by the zone councils if he or she does not deem them "reasonable." In addition, all of the money to run the councils comes from the state, and is funneled through the Department of Marine Resources. As Ferejohn and Weingast point out, control over the purse strings leads inevitably to political control (1997: 12). This suggests that the APA will likely need to be modified, and that the zone councils should control their own funds if co-management in Maine is to achieve its full potential.

Even worse, if the state government is not supportive of co-management, federal legislation is downright antithetical to it. Federal legislation is leading in exactly the opposite direction it should be going if we want to develop co-management systems. Since the 1970s, the federal government has enacted a number of laws that influence fisheries management or restrict the freedom of fishermen to operate, including the Marine Mammal Act, the Endangered Species Act, the Fisheries Conservation and Management Act, and the recent Sustainable Fisheries Act. All of these laws give federal agencies a high degree of authority to enforce laws impinging on the fishing industry. These laws strongly shift the decision-making authority to people who have little direct knowledge of fishing, such as federal bureaucrats, judges, conservationists, and scientists. The capacity of these people to undermine the zone councils and their authority is very great indeed. Nothing in the law protects the zone councils or the Lobster Advisory Council from encroachment by these agencies (e.g., veto power), nor is there any way of constraining federal agencies.

Another threat to co-management is posed by the attitudes of the fishermen themselves. The future success of the co-management system will necessitate the continued support of the industry and the willingness of fishermen to sacrifice. Should that support wane, the co-management system could die quickly. Lack of support could stem from many sources. Running the co-management organization imposes high costs on chairs and council members in the form of time spent at meetings, responding to constituents, and sacrifice of income and time with one's family. Then there are the psychic costs imposed by the long negotiations and acrimony that occur when people attempt to generate rules to constrain exploitive behavior. Such costs can devastate local-level management efforts. In the past two years, a number of zone council meetings and Lobster Advisory Council meetings could not proceed because a quorum was not present. Some individuals have served one term on a zone council and have refused to run for a second term. The number of fishermen who take the time to come to council meetings is always very small. Many fishermen do not know what their zone councils are doing, and do not seem to care much. In this sense, of course, the co-management system suffers from the same problem that plagues most democracies. Most of the work is done by a small percentage of the total population.

A deeper problem is the willingness of fishermen to accept and utilize power. In the past five years, it has become apparent that a number of fishermen are solidly against bottom-up management. Table 5.8 shows that 26.5 percent of the fishermen were against the concept of co-management before the law was passed, and that 15 percent thought the zone councils were doing a very bad job after the law was implemented. To be sure, they are a minority, but their existence is troubling. Interviews with these people reveal that many are against government in general. Some of the older fishermen dream of the golden age of the 1950s and 1960s when there was minimal government control over fishing. Others rationalize their unwillingness to cooperate in the self-management effort in terms of an ideology emphasizing "independence." I suspect that they are the counterparts of the Nova Scotia fishermen who refuse to support cooperatives and fishermen's organizations due to an ideology of "rugged individualism" (Jentoft and Davis 2000).

Others seem to expect the government to tell them what to do. Many of these people, I suspect, long for a structured world and the security that comes from responding to authority. The military and large bureaucracies are full of such people. A world in which you have to make your own decisions is less certain, less secure. Freedom is empty; it provides no goals. One fishermen said "I'll obey the law and the governor, but not these guys" (i.e., the zone council). He apparently found disquieting the idea that fishermen on the zone council could make the rules .

Academics interested in co-management need to do more research on those who oppose self-governance. A good place to begin is the extensive literature on people who fit badly in democratic societies. A generation ago, several social scientists (e.g., Fromm 1941; Hoffer 1951) pointed out that there are people who long for certainty. These people are putty in the hands of charismatic demagogues. Their tendency is to undermine democratic institutions such as co-management structures.

Several different kinds of problems have been encountered in implementing the Maine lobster zone management law. Some of those could have been predicted given the literature on co-management; other problems appear to be unique to the Maine situation and would not have been predicted by the literature.

PROBLEMS FORESEEN IN THE CO-MANAGEMENT LITERATURE

Four obstacles to successful co-management governance structures have been identified in the literature on co-management. (1) Co-management can result in substantial conflict between groups of fishermen (McCay 1988: 334; C. Smith 1988: 134); (2) Co-management regimes can fail due to opposition by government officials (McGoodwin 1990: 192– 93); (3) Co-management organizations can be ineffective if they are given too little authority (Jentoft 1989), or do not receive technical help from government agencies with which they are supposed to coordinate; and (4) Co-management efforts can fail, if fishermen who have been competitors fail to work together in a common cause (McCay 1988: 334–35).

Let us take these issues in order.

Co-management can cause conflict. There can be no doubt that implementing the lobster co-management law has involved conflict. But the term "conflict" scarcely cuts to the essence of the issues in lobster management, nor does it describe what has occurred in the lobster fishery as the zone management process unfolded. Several different kinds of conflicts involve different parties and issues. More important, in each case, conflict is a mechanism by which people attempt to obtain rules in their benefit. Furthermore, attempts to solve a problem at one level have caused another kind of conflict at another level demanding still another solution.

Since their inception, the zone councils have been involved in three different kinds of conflict. First is conflict over the imposition of a trap limit between those with large number of traps and those with smaller numbers. Second, there were boundary conflicts over sub-zones and zone boundaries. Last, federal intervention involved the zone councils in two different conflicts with an unusual cast of allies and enemies. Efforts to protect the right whale under the Endangered Species Act pitted the National Marine Fisheries Service against the State of Maine and its lobster fishermen. Moreover, the threat of the National Marine Fisheries service to pre-empt the lobster management plan of the ASMFC involved the zone councils in still another conflict.

All of these disputes were dominated by distributional concerns that influence people's income. In all of these cases, people were entering the political arena in an attempt to frame rules that favored them.

Co-management regimes can fail due to opposition by government officials; and co-management organizations can be ineffective if they are given too little

authority or do not receive technical help from government agencies with which they are supposed to coordinate. These assertions, I believe, hold true in the Maine lobster case. I have no doubt that opposition by Commissioner Robin Alden or key members of the marine resources committee of the legislature could have killed any possibility of the lobster zone management bill being passed into law. Opposition by federal officials could have dealt the zone management process a mortal blow. If federal management had imposed a 475-trap limit, it would have undermined the authority of the councils, making the entire zone management process an exercise in futility.

The zone councils have certainly received technical help from the DMR in the form of the services of the resource coordinators, and the commissioner has solved certain intractable problems. If the DMR had not provided such services, it is likely the co-management effort would have failed.

The future of the Maine co-management effort will not be determined solely by actions of the lobster industry or the Maine government. Actions at the federal level will undoubtedly play a very important role in influencing the zone councils in the future.

Co-management efforts can fail if fishermen who have been competitors fail to work together in a common cause. This is certainly true as well. The zone councils are composed of members from communities with a history of territorial conflict, and no cooperative tradition. Nevertheless, council members have been able to overcome such barriers to accomplish the council's business. Had town rivalries resulted in a lot of conflict between council members, the operation of the zone councils would have been seriously undermined.

PROBLEMS NOT FORESEEN IN THE
CO-MANAGEMENT LITERATURE

In the literature on co-management, there is little mention of four issues that have posed major problems for the lobster zone management process in Maine. First, social scientists concerned with co-management have paid little attention to boundary issues. If we can judge by the Maine lobster case, they deserve a lot of attention. Co-management governance structures will have to wrestle with such issues. Rules cannot be applied in general; they can only be enforced within a given area. Boundaries are inevitable. However, the imposition of boundaries with one set of rules on one side and another on the other side inevitably causes enforcement problems and administrative costs. Bureaucrats, enforcement officers, and fishermen hate boundaries, and with good reason. Is the solution to the problem to have as few boundaries as possible? Large zones will minimize administrative costs, all other factors remaining equal. However, small zones have the virtue of making it easier for fishermen to monitor each other's behavior, which is likely to result in lower enforcement costs and the enhancement of a sense of stewardship for the resource (Coleman 1990). The size of management areas and the number of boundaries is likely to remain a central and tricky issue for those designing co-management governance structures.

Second, those concerned with co-management have ignored the enormous amount of time, effort, and cooperation necessary to make co-management work. Overcoming the barriers to effective communication between people from different towns within zones has taken its toll. The fact that council chairs and members have had to play a particularly complex and confusing role as intermediaries between two different subcultures has added to their burdens. Dealing with complex federal initiatives has been very frustrating. Some council members and chairs are feeling overwhelmed and burnt out.

Third, generating a rule to solve one problem leads to other problems, which necessitate further action. Solving the problem of trap congestion and run-away costs with a trap limit caused the big fishermen to support limited entry by zone. Imposition of limited entry brought about the 49/51 percent rule, which intensified zone boundary disputes. No doubt attempts to solve this problem will cause others.

Fourth is the issue of conflict of interest. Most of the people elected to the zone councils have performed well. However, a few acted with their own interests or those of their friends in mind. Most of the latter were voted out of office. Conflict of interest, as we shall see, is a far more serious issue for the New England Regional Fisheries Management Council, an organization that is sometimes described as a co-management institution. Both of these situations point out that co-management depends on people working for the long-run benefit of their communities and the fish stocks. It is not at all clear how to keep officers of co-management institutions from working with their own rational short-run interests in mind. Conflict of interest poses still another collective action dilemma.

In conclusion, there can be little doubt that the co-management effort in the Maine lobster industry has had a high degree of success so far. The zone trap limits and limited-entry rules attest to that. All of these rules demonstrate that under certain conditions, users of resources can and do generate governance structures to constrain their own effort for the common good. Another measure of success is that the organizations charged with co-management in Maine have encountered a number of problems, and have been able to move very effectively to solve most of them.

CHAPTER 6

Science and Local Knowledge

*I*n many fisheries, members of the industry and scientists working for management agencies are at odds. All too often, each group tends to regard management options proposed by the other as ineffective, unnecessary, counterproductive, and sometimes plain silly. Sometimes this results in regulations that one side or the other regards as undesirable. In other instances, it results in political stalemate, with no effective management program being passed.

Scientists and managers tend to view the cause of the problem in terms of the self-serving activities of members of the fishing industry, who they feel cannot conserve the resources on which their livelihood depends. Fishermen, for their part, wonder about the quality of the science behind management proposals, and are very suspicious of the motivations of scientists.

In the lobster fishery, the same gulf exists between fishermen and scientists (e.g., Stecklow 1991). Both biologists and fishermen want to promote policies that have a favorable effect on stocks. The problem is that their assessments of the state of the stocks, and their ideas about what causes changes in stock sizes are very different. As a result, fishermen and the federal and state biologists have found themselves on opposite sides of virtually every management issue in the past forty years. As we shall see, the politics of fisheries management largely revolves around fishermen lobbying to get one set of these rules passed into law to affect lobster stocks positively, and the biologists lobbying for other rules based on another set of ideas about what controls stocks.

Recently, a number of social scientists have pointed out that fishermen and scientists have two different views of the oceans and the way they work (Palsson 1994; E. Smith 1990). It is these differences of world view that underlie prescriptions for management. This certainly appears to be the case in Maine, where competent biologists and experienced fishermen have constructed what amount to different realities of the fishery, which are at the root of many of the disagreements between them. In 1996, Robin Alden, who was then Maine's Commissioner of Marine Resources, nicely summarized the situation when she said: "fishermen and scientists are two groups of people with very high respect for their own knowledge and little understanding of what the other knows" (Alden 1996).

Fishermen and biologists consider to be factual their own world view about what controls stock size. These ideas are not opinions, in the view of the respondents. It was relatively easy to find out what fishermen and biologists believe influences catches and thus what they think should be done to improve the fishery. Getting at the underlying world view proved to be much more difficult. The scientists were much more articulate than the fishermen about the reasons they promoted various kinds of policies and the science underlying their policy prescriptions. Their view of the ocean emerged during the course of two studies that focused on a topic of great interest to them, namely what influenced catches.

Some of the explanations offered by fishermen and biologists are well buttressed by data. A surprising number are not. Separating fact from fancy proved to be a difficult, but very illuminating, task.

This chapter addresses three questions: (1) What factors are identified by fishermen and biologists as influencing the behavior of lobsters, stocks sizes, and lobster catches? (2) To what extent are these explanations supported by data and thus objectively account for changes in stock sizes observed? (3) Which of these explanations about changes in stock sizes have been translated into strategies that fishermen and biologists push for in the political arena?

Data Sources

Much of the information about the ideas of fishermen and biologists about factors influencing stock sizes was obtained during a study of the changes that have occurred in the lobster fishery in the last century, especially the "bust" of the 1920s and 1930s and the "boom" of the late 1980s and 1990s. The bust and boom are well known to experienced fishermen and biologists, and asking them to explain these phenomena proved to be a very useful tool in getting them to reveal ideas and beliefs about what controlled lobster catches and what should be done to manage the fishery. In these interviews, people were not being asked about politics and management, topics that elicit emotional and guarded reactions.

Information on the opinions of fishermen about the bust and the boom were obtained in 1993 and 1994 from sixty lobster fishermen during the course of a study of attitudes toward management and the social organization of the industry. I carried out all of the interviews, administering a questionnaire featuring both structured and open-ended questions. All sixty were full-time, experienced fishermen in Knox, Lincoln, and Sagadahoc counties, and represented approximately 10 percent of the full-time fishermen in those counties. A large number of those interviewed were people who had been interviewed before; they were not selected by random sample. Nevertheless, we believe this questionnaire elicited information that accurately reflects the opinions of experienced, full-time fishermen in this part of the coast. The questions that elicited the most pertinent data were: "What caused the low lobster catches of the 1920s and 1930s?" and "What caused the high catches of the 1990s?" Other useful questions were: "What needs to be done to ensure the future success of the lobster fishery?"; "What laws, if any, have helped to increase lobster catches?"; and "Will lobster catches remain high in the future? Explain."

The views of biologists were obtained from a wider variety of sources, including publications, public presentations, unstructured interviews, depth interviews, and participant observation in which emphasis is placed on asking general questions and not suggesting answers. No survey instrument was administered to the biologists. Additional information on the views of biologists about the bust and the boom was obtained on a ten-day cruise in July 1996 on the research vessel *Sea Diver*. The scientific crew on this cruise all had done extensive work on lobster and the lobster fishery, which turned the cruise into a floating lobster seminar.

Everyone familiar with the lobster industry knows that it is presently in a period of unusually good catches. All of the fishermen and biologists have been able to observe the boom. Fishermen have a variety of explanations for their good fortune, which only partially coincide with the explanations offered by the biologists. Only the press is ignorant of the "boom."

Only two older fishermen interviewed had any direct experience with the bust, and they were boys when it occurred. However, every experienced lobster fisherman has heard of the bust and is aware of the disaster it brought people who lived through it. They would like to avoid another occurrence. The bust of the 1920s and 1930s is one of the few experiences that has been impressed in the memory of the lobster industry.

The vast majority of fishermen interviewed in the 1990s had different kinds of explanations for the bust of the 1920s and 1930s than for the boom of the 1990s. Any single individual interviewed might have offered one explanation or a combination of explanations for the bust, and mention another factor or set of factors to explain the boom. Their explanations differed substantially from those of the biologists interviewed. In some cases, a few fishermen and biologists agreed on the factors causing either the bust or the boom, but where fishermen and biologists identified the same variable, they usually gave them different emphases and had a different slant on their effect.

In the following section, the variables that fishermen identified as causing the bust and the boom are identified, and the data supporting each is assessed. Then the same type of analysis is done concerning the explanations of biologists for the bust and the boom.

The Bust and the Boom: Views of the Fishermen

THE BUST

Most fishermen interviewed had three explanations for the bust.

First is the *poverty-gauge hypothesis*. According to this hypothesis, the minimum gauge in the 1920s and 1930s was so large that the vast majority of lobster caught were illegal. This lowered catches so much that many fishermen were impoverished.

The poverty-gauge hypothesis is not supported by the data for two reasons. Fishermen assert that gauge sizes were very high in the past, reaching a maximum of 4.75 inches. They are assuming that the 4.75-inch measure was the modern carapace measurement (from the eye orbit to the back of the shell). It was not. The 4.75-inch measure that was in force between 1907 and 1919 was a total body length measurement, which was equivalent to only 3.65 inches carapace length. In short, no 4.75-carapace measure ever existed. If such a measure had been enforced, it would have made illegal 98 percent of the lobsters caught today.

Also, if the poverty-gauge hypothesis were correct, we would expect the largest minimum gauge size to have been in the 1920s and 1930s when catches were lowest, and for catches to be relatively high when the gauge was at its lowest level. This did not occur. As can be seen from table 6.1, the minimum gauge size was gradually reduced from 1895 to 1942; from 1942 to the present it was gradually raised again.

If a large minimum gauge were the cause of reduced catches, those smaller catches should have been experienced between 1895 and 1919, not in the 1920s and 1930s when the gauge was actually much smaller. Moreover, if the large gauge had been the source of the decline in catches, then one would expect that when the legal minimum size was reduced, catches should have increased. This did not happen either. In 1919, the legal minimum size was reduced another .15 inches, and instead of increasing, the total Maine catch fell to 5.8 million pounds. The legal minimum size was reduced by another .44 inches in 1933, and that year saw still another reduction in total catch. From 1937 to the present, the gauge has increased incrementally. Rather than falling, lobster catches have increased, and that increase has been especially fast after 1988.

A second explanation that fishermen give for the bust is the *culturing hypothesis*, which asserts that lobsters obtain a large amount of their food from the bait placed in traps. In the 1920s and 1930s, the number of traps was small, decreasing the amount of food available for lobsters, which in turn, reduced the stock of lobsters. As the number of traps increased after World War II, the bait supply supported a larger population of lobsters. One fisherman in Boothbay Harbor said, "Every day, Boothbay fishermen put thousands of pounds of bait in the water. That has become a large amount of their food supply. In the Depression, the number of traps dropped off and they had nothing to eat."

Few data buttress the culturing hypothesis. It is based on the idea that the abundance of lobsters depends on the amount of food; without food supplied by humans, lobster populations decline greatly. In fact, lobsters can survive quite nicely even when there is little carrion on the bottom. They can filter plankton, and much of their food supply is marine worms. Moreover, even though the effect of the amount of bait on lobster populations has not been established, food supply is apt to affect growth rates and not abundance. Abundance is more a function of larval settlement and the percentage of larvae surviving after settlement (Wahle and Steneck 1991).

In addition, no close relationship has been established between the decline in trap numbers and the decline in the lobster population. Before World War I, about 234,000 traps were fished in Maine waters; in the 1920s and 1930s, the number of traps averaged 198,000, or 15 percent fewer (Dow 1967). In this same period, catches plummeted from an average of approximately 16 million pounds between 1906 and

Table 6.1

Table 6.1
Changes in Lobster Gauge Sizes in Maine

Year	TL in inches	CL in inches (mm)[a]	
		Minimum	Maximum
1874	10.5[b]	3.65 (92.7)	
1883	9[b]	3.32 (84.3)	
1888	9[b]	3.32 (84.3)	
1895	10.5	3.65 (92.7)	
1907		4.75 (92.7)	
1919		3.50 (88.9)	
1933		3.06 (77.7)	4.75 (120.7)
1935		3.06 (77.7)	5.00 (177.0)
1942		3.13 (79.4)	5.00 (177.0)
1958		3.19 (81.0)	5.19 (131.8)
1960		3.19 (81.0)	5.00 (177.0)
1988		3.22 (81.8)	5.00 (177.0)
1989		3.25 (82.6)	5.00 (177.0)

[a] Conversions of total length (TL) to carapace length (CL) were based on data in Herrick (1911) and analyses of Jay Krouse, Maine Department of Marine Resources (personal communication). All carapace lengths are post-orbital measures that do not include the rostrum, except for the legal English measure of 4.75 inches for 1907 to 1918, which extended from the tip of the rostrum to the end of the body. Regulations were obtained from the *Laws of Maine* and summarized by Kelly (1990).
[b] Seasonal.

1912 to 5.5 million pounds in 1924 (table 1.1). If we are to take the culturing hypothesis seriously, we must argue that a 15 percent decline in the number of traps resulted in a 50 to 75 percent drop in catches. This is a difficult argument to make.

The culturing hypothesis also ignores the fact that there were no traps in the early seventeenth century when reports indicate a great abundance of lobsters off the Maine coast (Martin and Lipfert 1985: 9–11).

Third is the *illegal activity* hypothesis. Proponents of this idea assert that in the 1920s and 1930s the conservation laws were violated so massively that the lobster population was reduced.

This hypothesis likely has some substance to it, although solid data are lacking. As I pointed out in chapter 4, there is good evidence that before World War II very large numbers of undersized lobsters were sold, eaten at home, or used for bait, and that many fishermen "scrubbed" the eggs off the berried female lobsters and then sold them (Judd 1988).

Although it is impossible to estimate the losses due to illegal practices, there can be little doubt that the short-lobster trade increased mortality on adolescent lobsters and that scrubbing and keeping berried lobsters reduced the breeding stock and the number of eggs in the water. The experienced biologists writing in the early decades of the century were convinced that such practices were causing a good deal of damage to the resource. They were probably correct.

A note of caution should be sounded. In the early years of the twentieth century, boats were small, and the lobster fishery was confined to inshore waters. The deep water habitats, where a sizeable percentage of the large reproductive-sized lobsters live, remained virtually unfished. Even if a large amount of illegal activity affected inshore stocks, the amount of damage to the reproductive potential of the resource as a whole could have been minimal.

THE BOOM

The fishermen generally had four explanations for the boom of the 1990s.

The first is *decreased predation by groundfish*. According to this hypothesis, lobster stocks were at a high in the 1990s because groundfish that feed on them are at low levels. One fisherman said "big cod eat little lobsters, and there are very few cod in the Gulf of Maine at present."

The evidence for this hypothesis is mixed. In assessing it, two biological facts are critical. Very large lobsters have no natural enemies, and are not eaten by any other species, even large cod or haddock. However, there is a good deal of evidence that big groundfish prey on small lobsters. In 1909, Dr. Francis Herrick, perhaps the most knowledgeable lobster scientist of the first half of the twentieth century, wrote "Next to man with his traps, the codfish is probably the most destructive enemy of the lobster, for it not only takes in the soft and hard shell animals alike up to 8 inches or more length, but is very partial to the young from 2 to 4 inches long" (1911: 215). Herrick's observation is buttressed by experimental work that shows that groundfish, including sculpins and sea bass, eat lobsters under 1 inch in length (Barshaw and Lavalli 1988; Wahle and Steneck 1992). When small lobsters (1.57–3.54 in.) were tethered inshore (anchored to the bottom so they could not hide or escape) where few large groundfish were found, very few were eaten (Steneck 1989b). However, 80 percent were eaten within twenty-four hours when they were tethered in offshore areas where large groundfish are more abundant.

Some historical data also buttress the predation hypothesis. In the early decades of the twentieth century, large populations of big cod and haddock were found throughout the Gulf of Maine, and groundfish catches remained high until the 1930s. At the same time, the average size of lobsters had decreased markedly from the 1860s to the 1890s due to human exploitation, and has remained relatively small ever since. This means that in the 1920s and 1930s (the bust), large stocks of big cod and haddock coexisted in the Gulf with lobsters of sizes they could easily eat. This may well have resulted in large losses to predation in those years.

In the late 1930s and 1940s, after groundfish catches had been low for several years, lobster stocks began to rise (table 1.1). In 1925, 15 million pounds of haddock and 22 million pounds of cod were caught. In 1938, only 2.5 million pounds of haddock were caught, and cod catches had declined to 6 million pounds (U.S. Bureau of Commercial Fisheries 1956). In 1949, it was reported that "groundfish stocks had been depleted" (Maine Commissioner of Sea and Shore Fisheries 1949). In 1937, catches of lobster began to rise, and the increases in catches continued through the 1940s (table 1.1). This inverse variation of lobster and groundfish catches does not prove that predation plays a important role in influencing the size of lobster stocks, but it is consistent with that hypothesis.

Some data do not support the predation hypothesis. Eighty percent of all lobsters landed are caught in inshore waters, and large numbers of big cod and haddock have not been seen within 20 miles of the Maine coast for decades. This indicates that the increases in lobster landings since the late 1980s (the boom) cannot be due exclusively to the absence of groundfish.

Recent studies show that lobsters are not found in the diets of groundfish. These data have been interpreted to show that cod do not eat lobsters (Bowman 1981; Pezzack 1992: 124). This may not be the correct interpretation. After all, most groundfish are now found in offshore areas where the average size of lobsters is so large that they cannot be eaten.

A second hypothesis is that the boom is due to *increases in lobster habitat* brought about by the sea urchin industry. Fishermen argue that kelp is ideal lobster habitat, and since sea urchins eat kelp, the amount of kelp-covered ledge varies with the size of the sea urchin population. With the success of the urchin industry since the late 1980s, the number of sea urchins has fallen, causing a great increase in lobster habitat, and thus more lobsters.

Here again, the evidence is not clear cut. Some evidence suggests that the boom might be caused, in part, by an increase in habitat. Large areas off the Maine coast are covered with ledge, and the evidence supports the idea that these ledges are much better habitat for lobsters when they are covered with kelp than when they are bare. Harvesting sea urchins has resulted in more kelp-covered areas inshore and this could have helped to produce the boom by augmenting the numbers of lobsters in inshore areas where they are available to fishermen (Bologna and Steneck 1993: 130–33; Elner and Vadas 1990; Steneck, McNaught, and Zimsen 1995).

However, again there is negative evidence. The lobster boom has occurred in all the coastal New England states as well as in Atlantic Canada. Since the sea urchin industry occurs only in Maine, the favorable effects of harvesting urchins on lobster populations (if any) would only occur locally. The advent of the urchin industry cannot be used to explain the boom in Canada. Moreover, a good deal of rockweed is harvested in Canada, and there is no evidence that this has reduced lobster populations. Timing is also a problem: The lobster boom began in the late 1980s, before sea urchin harvesting had resulted in a resurgence in kelp.

No reliable data have been collected on the interactions between the urchin and lobster populations and the amount of kelp during the early years of the twentieth century. It is possible that there were large populations of sea urchins during the 1920s and 1930s and that this may have helped to produce the bust.

The third explanation is what fishermen call *"the general cycles."* This is based on the observation that lobster populations and the population of all marine species vary over the course of time, presumably due to changes in the ecology or other "natural" phenomena. These phenomena are very complicated, and affect lobster populations in ways that fishermen admit they do not completely understand. Fishermen may have very little effect on the whole process. Red Bickford of Pemaquid Harbor, who is now in his eighties, spoke for many in the industry when he said: "It's all a cycle. Sometimes it is up and sometimes it is down. You just have to be ready for what comes." For fishermen, there is wisdom in such statements. One cannot count on any stock of fish remaining the same. One has to be prepared to switch onto those species that are doing well, and be able to make that switch on short notice.

There is little doubt that lobsters are affected by a myriad of ecological factors. In 1978, we recorded very large catches and catches per unit of effort in Bremen, while towns a few miles away had markedly lower catches. Jim Thomas, then Maine's lobster biologist, said he did not know what caused such variations, but noted that he had seen such micro-variation before (Acheson 1980).

For most biologists, statements about "cycles" are vague to the point of being meaningless. One said, "it's almost mystical." Another said, "saying it is a natural cycle is little better than saying that what goes up has to come down." They have no doubt that catches fluctuate, but noting that stocks are not stable says very little in their point of view. In the view of scientists, the natural-cycle argument is little more than a way of exonerating fishermen, who are seen as doing a lot of damage to the stocks.

We will return to the "natural cycles" argument since it goes to the very heart of the differences of viewpoint between fishermen and biologists.

The fourth and most contentious explanation fishermen give for the boom is the *conservation ethic hypothesis,* which holds that the boom is due, in great part, to increases in effective conservation legislation, which has been passed over the course of the past seventy years. In the view of fishermen making this argument, several laws have resulted in greater lobster populations. The most important of these are the V-notch and oversize (5-inch) laws. These laws, fishermen assert, have preserved more egg-bearing females and thus increased the number of eggs, and recruitment. (Remember that fishermen cannot take any egged females. They may voluntarily put a notch in the side flipper of a lobster with eggs. Such lobsters can never be taken. The 5-inch law protects all lobsters over 5 inches on the carapace. These laws are designed to protect proven breeding stock and large, reproductive-sized lobsters.)

The minimum size and escape-vent laws, which protect the juveniles, as well as the ban on taking lobsters by dragger and scuba diving have also played a role in increasing the lobster population, but are less important. In addition, fishermen argue that illegal activity has declined significantly, and that these laws are now enforced, where they were widely disobeyed in the bust years.

According to these fishermen, the result of all of these laws and law enforcement is a huge brood stock, which under the right environmental conditions results in large recruitment into the fishery. One fisherman said, "The most important conservation law is the V-notch. Do away with that law and you do away with the industry." David Cousens, president of the Maine Lobstermen's Association, said that many fishermen believe the boom is due to a large and healthy breeding stock, and the health of this breeding stock is the result of the V-notch and oversize measure. He said "the members [of the MLA] can agree on keeping the brood stock." A very large percentage of the lobster fishermen would agree with these assessments.

Unfortunately, there is strong disagreement among scientists about the effectiveness of these regulations. The effect of the V-notch and oversize laws are not known for certain. For most of the past thirty years, state and federal biologists have generally viewed these laws as ineffective. Some university scientists have agreed with the industry and argued that they are more effective in conserving the lobster resource. Recently, more scientists have become more favorably disposed toward the V-notch and oversize rules as additional information has become available. The scientific argument about these conservation measures will be covered in detail in chapter 8. For the time being, let it suffice to say that the science behind the V-notch, oversize, and minimum size measures is complicated, contentious, and in a state of flux.

The Bust and the Boom: Views of Biologists

In studying the explanations offered by biologists, it is important to note that their information on the boom was much better than on the bust.

The lobster biologists interviewed in the 1990s were very concerned with the causes of the boom and had a good deal of data on factors influencing lobster landings in recent decades. However, they had come to no strong consensus about the causes of these high catches. Interestingly enough, although the biologists interviewed in the 1990s knew about the bust, they really had not studied it thoroughly. Only biologist Robert Dow of the Maine Department of Marine Resources explored the causes of the disastrously low catches of the 1920s and 1930s in any depth.

Like the fishermen, the biologists offered a number of reasons for the bust and the boom.

First, some biologists hypothesize that the bust can be attributed to *low prices*. Those advocating this point of view argue that prices were so low during the late 1920s and the 1930s that many fishermen went out of business, and the total number of traps in use was reduced, which, in turn reduced the catch. This hypothesis is the legacy of the work of Dow, who summarized the evidence in the following words: "real landed value of Maine lobster averaged U.S. $0.023 to US $0.101 per pound below the 1915 and 1916 levels throughout the 1920s and the 1930s, and probably accounts for the low fishing effort, which averaged only 203,000 traps per year for the period, well below the 234,000 trap minimum effort of pre-World War I years" (Dow 1967: 4).

Between 1928 and 1932, the number of licenses issued declined by 32 percent, and the number of traps went from an estimated 211,000 in 1928 to 180,000 in 1933 (see table 1.1.) (Correspondence of the Commissioner 1933b). However, there is strong reason to believe that low prices alone were not the cause of the reduction in fishermen or the low catches.

First, the prices were not all that low if we correct for inflation. In 1933, the very depth of the Depression, ex-vessel lobster prices averaged about $0.18 to $0.19 per pound; in 1935 the average price was $0.23 per pound. But $0.18 in 1933 is equivalent to $2.72 in 1999 dollars; $0.23 in 1935 was worth $3.18 in 1999. In 1989, the price for lobsters dropped to $1.75 per pound in late August and early September, and averaged $2.56 for the year, not that much higher than the 1933 adjusted average ex-vessel price of $2.22 per pound. In the fall of 2001, prices paid to fishermen went as low as $2.00 to $2.25 in response to a huge catch. Prices were undoubtedly low in the Depression, but equally low prices have been seen in the recent past when measured in terms of constant U.S. dollars.

Second, the data suggest that the root of the problem was low catches due to low stock sizes. Two of the best indicators of stock size are total catch and catch per unit of effort (Campbell and Duggan 1980; Fogarty 1988). Both were down in the bust. During the 1920s and 1930s, catch levels were the lowest in recorded history, averaging 5 to 7 million pounds (see table 1.1). Moreover, catch per unit of effort (CPUE) not only was low, but fell during this time period. Between 1924 and 1934, the average trap produced 32 pounds of lobster per year; in 1932 the CPUE had fallen to an average of 29.1 pounds per trap. The fact that the CPUE was falling at a time when hundreds of people were going out of business and the total number of traps in the water was decreasing is excellent evidence that the stocks were in poor condition.

Moreover, all of the historical data on this period indicate that the catches were low as well (see chapter 4). My interviews with older people all support the idea that catches were very low. Horatio Crie, who was State Commissioner of the Department of Sea and Shore Fisheries received numerous letters concerning low catches. Llewellyn Crowley wrote: "I have known the best of fishermen to go out here this winter and haul a hundred traps or more and get only nineteen to twenty pounds of lobsters and I for one only get from six to—teen pounds [the first part of the word is obscured, 'thirteen' is likely]" (Correspondence of the Commissioner 1931b). Another wrote, "Lobsters are very scarce and the price $.25 per pound the fisherman hardly make enough to pay their expenses in catching them" (Correspondence of the Commissioner 1931f). If Crowley's figures are correct, fishermen were getting one-fifth of a pound for each trap hauled. Compare those catches with those received in the summers of 1999 and 2000, when even unskilled fishermen were getting over 2 pounds per trap hauled, and catches of 4 pounds per trap were observed.

The reason that fishermen left the lobster industry in the late 1920s and 1930s is undoubtedly due to low incomes received. Fishing income, of course, is determined by both size of catches and the prices received for them. The data strongly suggest that the low incomes fishermen received were due more to low catches than to low prices. Even if prices were on the low side, fishermen could have maintained their income levels if catch levels were high enough to compensate. The disaster of the 1930s was rooted in weak prices, coupled with phenomenally low catches.

A second explanation by biologists for the bust and the boom regards *water temperature*. Some of the most important biological processes of lobsters are controlled by water temperature, including, spawning, settling of larvae on the bottom, growth, activity levels, willingness to enter traps, and migration.

Biologists have investigated two hypotheses related to water temperature. The first relates temperature to activity levels. If temperatures are high, activity levels increase, resulting in increased catches. The second links water temperature to larval settlement success.

The first hypothesis relating temperature to activity level and catches was explored by Dow (1969), who concluded that the bust was not related to temperature. "Some other factor than temperature had limited lobster landings during the period between wars" (Dow 1967: 4). Dow's conclusion stemmed from an analysis in which he attempted to link lobster landings with mean seawater temperature. His data showed that lobster landings were maximized when mean annual seawater temperature is between 9 and 11 degrees centigrade (Dow 1969: 61–63). Since lobster landings fell sharply after 1919, while the mean seawater temperature ranges before and after the war were the same, the low landings of the 1920s had to be related to something other than seawater temperature. At this time, Dow was correlating temperature with catch in the same year, which essentially was studying the effect of temperature on activity level and trapability. Thus, this study shows that temperature as it affects trapability has little or no effect on catches.

The second hypothesis, linking lobster catches to larval settlement, is supported by far more data. Recent studies have confirmed that temperature controls the larval settlement (Boudreau, Simard, and Bourget 1991), while others demonstrate that the number of larvae that settle and survive strongly influences the abundance of adult lobsters (Campbell, Noakes, and Elner 1991; Wahle and Steneck 1991, 1992). Larval settling occurs during a two-week period, usually during August in Maine, and that settlement is most successful at temperatures of 15 degrees centigrade and above. If water temperature is above 15 degrees centigrade, then large numbers of larvae settle to the bottom in good condition; if they land on cobble or other bottom that provides good cover, large numbers survive (Steneck 1989b). Since it takes seven years for lobsters to grow to legal size, a year when August water temperatures are over 15 degrees centigrade should be followed seven years later by a large year-class of lobsters molting into legal size. Lower than average landings should occur seven years after a year when August water temperature is under 15 degrees centigrade.

To what extent can the bust and the boom be explained in terms of water temperature? If this hypothesis is correct, the bust should have followed seven years on the heels of years when Maine August water temperatures were under 15 degrees centigrade; the boom should have been preceded by years when the August water temperature was over 15 degrees centigrade.

Biologist Robert Steneck and I attempted to test this hypothesis by using regression analysis to study the relationship between state-wide landings and waters temperatures, measured in Boothbay Harbor, seven years previously. The results were mixed. The regression analysis of landings between 1946 and 1986 on August temperatures with a seven-year lag resulted in an R-square of .54, indicating that 54 percent of the total variance in landings could be explained in terms of August water temperatures (Acheson and Steneck 1997). These data give strong evidence that much of the variation in lobster catches in those years can be explained in terms of temperature. However, temperature alone cannot account for the bust, and temperature appears to have had no influence on the boom (see Acheson and Steneck, 1997 for the regression results and an explanation of them).

The third explanation offered for the bust and boom is *fishing effort.* According to the biologists offering this explanation, fishing effort is excessive in both the bust and the boom years. In the bust, overfishing led to stock failure. That is, fishing pressure was so high that the breeding stock was destroyed, resulting in poor recruitment in subsequent years. As Anthony and Caddy stated, "Landings declines are often interpreted to be stock collapse due to over fishing" (1980: 355).

The larger catches of the boom are the result of a number of innovations that allowed fishermen to place more and better traps over wider areas. Dr. Michael Fogarty of the National Marine Fisheries Service pointed out in an interview that effort has increased in a number of ways. He said that "there has been a general increase in the number of traps. Fishermen are expanding the area they fish. One fisherman is fishing basins that were never fished before. In addition, they are using 'wire gear,' which allows them to fish throughout the year and is also more efficient." In the view of biologists, the larger catches of the boom are not a cause for rejoicing. They believe that more traps can lead to increased catches in the short run, and destruction of the brood stock and stock failure in the long run. In their view, the destruction of the brood stock is far advanced, and the risk of disaster is high.

As we shall see, these predictions stem from stock-recruitment models, which posit that the size of fish stocks is strongly affected by fishing pressure. If these models are correct, then low levels of fishing effort should result in healthy stock sizes. High levels of effort should result in stock failure and low catches.

The data from the Maine lobster fishery do not support these predictions. The bust of the 1920s and 1930s was not a period of high fishing effort; rather, fishing effort was very low. In 1931 (the middle of the bust) for example, there were only 2,800 fishermen who used 168,000 traps to produce 5.3 million pounds of lobster. The boom, by way of contrast, was a period in which fishing effort was very high, and had been steadily increasing for decades. In 2000, a record high catch of 57.4 million pounds was taken by fishermen using an estimated 2,780,000 traps (table 1.1). If they do nothing else, such findings show that we cannot explain lobster catches primarily in terms of fishing effort. Other factors are clearly involved. We will discuss the implications of these finding for the state of fisheries science.

Explanations of the Bust and the Boom: An Overview

Fishermen and biologists tend to explain the bust and the boom in terms of different variables. However, some explanations were far more popular than others, and

Table 6.2

Summary of Explanations for the Bust and Boom Periods in Maine

Explanation	Number of Fishermen's Responses[a]		Number of Biologists' Responses	
	Bust	Boom	Bust	Boom
poverty gauge	46	0	0	0
illegal activity	30	0	0	0
general cycles	16	22	0	0
culturing	18	13	1	1
low prices	6	0	3	0
water temperature	2	4	1	4
predation	0	52	1	2
V-notching, venting	0	32	0	3
conservation ethic	0	24	0	2
habitat	0	28	0	2
larval and juvenile	0	0	1	4
fishing effort	0	0	5	7

[a] Data are from sixty interviews with fishermen in central Maine in 1993 and 1994. Most mentioned several causes.

there was some overlap in their explanations. Moreover, both fishermen and biologists tended to account for the bust and the boom in terms of combinations of variables. Another view of their interpretations is afforded by looking at the numbers of fishermen and biologists who gave various explanations for the bust and the boom.

Two of the most productive questions asked to fishermen on our survey were "What caused the low lobster catches of the 1920s and 1930s?" and "What has caused the high catches of the 1990s?" (The same questions were asked the biologists in open-ended interviews.) The results are summarized in table 6.2.

The favorite explanations of fishermen in the 1990s for the bust of the interwar years are the poverty gauge and illegal activity (the poverty gauge was favored by 76 percent of the fishermen interviewed). Eddie Drisko of New Harbor spoke for many experienced fishermen when he said, "What lobsters you caught, you couldn't keep because of the gauge. There weren't many lobsters out there. There was a lot of illegal activity at that time." The culturing hypothesis and "general cycles" were next-most preferred explanations. Few mentioned low prices, although this was a popular explanation during the bust and in years immediately following. No fisherman ascribed the low catches in the bust to predation by groundfish or changes in the habitat, although these ideas played a prominent role in their explanations for the boom of the 1990s.

Biologists interviewed in the 1990s generally did not pretend to be expert on the disastrous 1920s and 1930s in the Maine lobster industry. Some would not hazard a guess about the cause of the bust, although it was clear that they thought that excess effort likely played a role. Others had an interest in the subject, and their explanations involved effort in combination with temperature and prices. One National Marine Fisheries Service biologist cogently expressed this argument when he said to me: "the stocks were damaged [in many coastal areas in the years before World War I] by overfishing. The water temperatures in the late teens and 1920s were low, which prevented the population from rebounding as it might have under more ordinary conditions. In the Depression, the industry experienced marketing problems which drove large numbers of fishermen from the business."

Fishermen typically saw a number of variables as explaining the boom of the 1990s. The two most commonly mentioned were low amounts of groundfish predation (i.e., no cod and haddock) and the effects of the V-notch and oversize measures. But many mentioned the conservation ethic (closely connected to the V-notch) and "natural cycles," a vague concept summarizing changes in the environment. Only four pointed to water temperature.

The boom is an enigma to the state and federal biologists. Even the most experienced and thoughtful among them admitted they were puzzled. Given the high level of fishing effort, they believed a bust could likely have occurred. In explaining the high catches, they offered a wide variety of hypotheses, but they had not come to any definite conclusions. When asked about the boom of the 1990s, Douglas Pezzack, Regional Lobster Assessment Coordinator for the Department of Fisheries and Oceans of Canada, said "I don't know. Probably a complicated set of factors is involved." An increase in catches occurred throughout the entire northwest Atlantic (from Newfoundland to southern New England). This argues that some widespread and general factors were involved (Pezzack 1992: 115). He suspects that water temperature is responsible. But he is careful to note that there is probably a "complicated set of factors influencing lobster populations. We probably do not know how they interact," he said.

On the whole, federal and state biologists were not optimistic about the future of the lobster industry. They tend to believe that the good catches observed in recent years are the result of very special circumstances. When those circumstances change, stock sizes could be drastically reduced by the high numbers of traps in the water.

As might be expected, both fishermen and biologists discounted the explanations offered by the other group for the bust and the boom.

When questioned, no biologist thought the poverty-gauge hypothesis or the culturing hypotheses had any virtue as explanations for the bust. No biologist interviewed in the 1990s was aware of the full extent of the illegal activity that occurred in the past. It was not a factor they mentioned in the interviews until they were asked about it directly, and several said they doubted the effect of such activity on catches could be evaluated. Most important, they generally do not believe that the oversize law or the V-notch are very effective, and they certainly do not believe they are a primary cause of the boom, although when questioned directly a few said such laws might have increased catches somewhat.

The fishermen strongly disagreed with the biologists' ideas about the causes of the bust and boom. No older fishermen thought that the bust was due to stock failure brought on by fishing a large number of traps. Uniformly, they said that there were few traps fished in the 1920s and 1930s. To them, the idea that the boom was caused by a large number of traps was nothing short of ludicrous. "If a large number of traps causes overfishing, why do we have so many lobsters?" one asked. The idea that the large number of traps has temporarily increased landings and that those same traps can lead to disaster, suggests itself to biologists, but not fishermen.

Fishermen had never heard of Dow's water-temperature and activity-level hypothesis, and most dismissed it. Only the older fishermen had heard of Dow's hypothesis that the bust was caused by low prices, and the vast majority did not believe this was true.

What Did Cause the Bust and the Boom?

ASSESSING THE EVIDENCE

The objective evidence on all of the various explanations offered by the fishermen and biologists leaves us very uncertain about what really did cause the bust and the boom. Virtually all of the explanations offered by the fishermen and biologists are not well supported by the evidence, and some are flatly refuted.

In a recent article, Robert Steneck and I hazarded a guess about the causes of the bust and the boom. In our view, in the past 120 years two factors have been of overriding importance in causing the changes in lobster catches: water temperature as it affects larval settlement, and the growth of effective conservation legislation (Acheson and Steneck 1997).

Our statistical analysis suggests that recruitment is influenced by thermal controls on larval settlement. Moreover, the bust and boom occurred all over the northwest Atlantic, indicating that some very widespread phenomenon is working (Pezzack 1995). In our view, this strengthens the argument that temperature has been very influential in influencing stock sizes.

We are also convinced that changes in fishing practices have played an important role in producing the bust and the boom. Many knowledgeable observers of the industry in the late nineteenth and early twentieth centuries, including biologists Herrick and Rathbun and Commissioner Crie, argued that stocks were damaged by illegal activity. More recently, Canadian biologists have come to the same conclusion (Harding, Drinkwater, and Vass 1983). Correspondingly, we believe that a decline in illegal activity in the past several decades has increased the size of the breeding stock and recruitment. The scientific debate over the effect of the oversize measure and the V-notch law has convinced us that these measures have had a positive effect since 1950, particularly since they are virtually self-enforcing.

Furthermore, we believe the evidence supports the idea that predation by groundfish reduced lobster stocks during the bust and that increases in habitat due to the sea urchin industry may have increased lobster stocks and catches during the boom.

But these conclusions are not strongly buttressed by data and must remain tenuous. Our regression data do not support the idea that either the bust or the boom can be explained in terms of water temperature alone. In addition, the hypothesis that the bust was caused by illegal activity is not supported by statistical data (See Acheson and Steneck 1997). The idea that the V-notch and oversize measure have helped to produce the boom has been hotly contested by state and federal biologists until very recently.

World View, the State of the Stocks, and Politics

Our study of the view of the fishermen and biologists about the causes of the bust and the boom revealed some differences in intellectual commitments and an outline of the world view each has constructed about the ocean and the lobster. Their variant explanations reveal, as nothing else could, that both groups believe they know what has caused changes in lobster populations and, by implication, what should be done to conserve the lobster resource.

According to the fishermen, a variety of complex factors cause changes in lobster populations, which are not understood well. Fishermen are convinced that these variables are largely beyond the control of human beings, and that they interact in complicated ways to cause rapid and unpredictable changes in stocks of fish. Many stocks of fish vary; no stock remains at the same level for long. As a result, fishermen have to be prepared to change target species on short notice.

There is nothing that humans can do to ensure steady supplies of fish. All that can be done to conserve fish stocks is to ensure that fish are protected at vulnerable parts of their life cycle. For this reason, protecting breeding fish, breeding grounds, nursery grounds, and migration routes is especially important. This can be done by rules on "how" fishing is done. These are rules limiting where fishing can take place, when it can take place, and the technology that can be used.

In the view of the fishermen, two kinds of variables have affected lobster stocks. Some of these are environmental variables such as water temperature, predation by other fish, changes in habitat, and additional factors we know little about. Others are fishing practices that have affected lobsters at crucial parts of their life cycle. The most important of these are the laws protecting the brood stock (i.e., the ban on taking egged lobsters, the V-notch, and the oversize law), and the rules protecting juveniles (the escape-vent and the minimum-size laws). Widespread violation of existing laws in the early decades of the century made the stocks prone to crash, as occurred in the bust. Lobster fishermen are also committed to the idea of maintaining the habitat by prohibiting dragging for lobsters.

Interviews with fishermen concerning the boom revealed that they thought that catches were very large because the stocks were in very good condition. Bert Witham said, "Fishing has been wonderful. There are a lot of lobsters out there." Rusty Court of Boothbay told me "Lobstering has been good. In 2000, you could catch lobsters most anywhere from the hard bottom to mud in various depths. You didn't have to hit anything or any place in particular."

Capturing the Commons

Fishermen were especially impressed with the size of the breeding stock. Time and again, discussion of the boom would lead to enthusiastic descriptions of the vast numbers of V-notch or "seed lobsters" in coastal waters. Fisherman Brian McClain said every time he hauled his traps in the fall of 1996 he caught "at least thirty big, beautiful V-notched lobsters loaded with seed." Norbert Lemieux said that in Washington County (Zone A), "we judge the health of the fishery by the number of eggers. This year [2001], the number of eggers broke all records."

But no fisherman expects this situation to be permanent. It's all a "cycle" after all. Simply maintaining a large brood stock that produces a large amount of eggs will not guarantee good fishing forever. In the words of one man, "there are hundreds of thousands of V-notched lobsters out there producing eggs. When conditions are right, those eggs hatch and produce scads of small lobsters. Right now we have a whole lot of small lobsters in the water." But he and many other experienced fishermen are fully aware that environmental conditions will not remain ideal permanently. Some day, something will change, and stocks will fall along with the catches and incomes of fishermen. This will be true regardless of the large brood stock. (None of this is to say that fishermen think we should do away with the V-notch or oversize law. The contrary is the case.)

While fishermen did not believe that fishing effort was a primary factor in causing the boom, they were concerned about the large numbers of people and traps currently employed in the lobster fishery. Most were less concerned with danger to the stock than with overcrowding and economic losses. In their view, large numbers of traps per se will not cause a disastrous decline as long as the brood stock and juveniles are protected. More damage will be done by fishing a small number of traps while disobeying the conservation laws, than by using a large number of traps while protecting the brood stock and the juveniles.

The biologists have a different view of the ocean. Their view is dominated by a commitment to stock-recruitment models, which are perhaps the most important intellectual tool employed by population dynamicists in the past fifty years. The central idea of such models is that the level of fishing effort influences the size of the spawning stock; the size of the spawning stock determines the number of eggs in the water, and ultimately recruitment into the fishery. The relationship between fishing effort, spawning stock biomass, and recruitment can be described mathematically. If a consistent amount of fishing effort is put on a fish stock, there will be a tendency towards a predictable-sized breeding stock, yield, or recruitment. If fishing effort changes, a new equilibrium should be reached in time. A corollary is that the size of fish stocks is determined largely by the level of human predation, and that stock failure is caused by overexploitation. Environmental factors play no role in influencing stock sizes. A recent article in *Science* quotes one fisheries biologist as saying "Fish stocks collapse because of plain simple over fishing" (Barinaga 1995: 1043).

Exploitation is defined in terms of amount of fish taken. Life cycle is not taken into account. It doesn't make any difference whether these fish are adults, juveniles, or fish filled with eggs. A ton of fish is a ton of fish.

Many state and federal biologists are very pessimistic about the future of the lobster fishery. They believe that effort on the lobster stock has long been too high, and that the lobster has been overfished. In their view, high levels of effort have driven the breeding stock to low levels. As a result, the fishery is in a precarious state and could collapse at any time. The high catches of the boom are scarcely a cause for celebration, since they are the result of dangerously high levels of effort that cannot be maintained without leading to disaster (Anthony and Caddy 1980: 185). They can point to a number of textbook cases in which high levels of fishing effort resulted in good catches for a while followed by a sudden stock crash. This conviction has found its way into a large number of papers on lobster management and official stock assessments going back over the past thirty years.

Conversations with fishermen and biologists had an enigmatic quality. The biologists are quite certain about the ability of humans to control the size of fish stocks. But they are relatively pessimistic about the future of the industry because of what they see as excessive effort pushing the stock to the limit. They would like to put in place far more stringent controls on effort before the inevitable stock crash. From their perspective, the problem is not the ability to control stocks, but political will.

The fishermen have far more doubts about the ability of humans to control oceans and the fish stocks in them. They are very suspicious of the scientists' claim that all will be well if we could only control fishing effort. In their view, environmental factors have important influences on stock sizes, which shows in their penchant for explaining changes in stock sizes in terms of predation by groundfish, water temperature, habitat, and especially "natural cycles." All humans can do is to help nature take its course by avoiding damaging fish in crucial parts of their life cycles. This shows in their commitment to the V-notch and the oversize laws, and their strong condemnation for dragging for lobsters. That commitment is reinforced by their collective memory of the bust, which many believe was alleviated only when more rules to conserve the breeding stock were put in place (i.e., the oversize and V-notch programs) and vigorously enforced.

The specter of the bust and the conviction that humans cannot really control lobster stocks had an effect on the behavior of fishermen at the height of the boom. From 1995 to 2001, even as catches continued to climb, older fishermen were using their new wealth to pay off business debts, and advising younger men not to get too far into debt if possible. They were convinced that a "natural cycle" would end the boom, and perhaps very soon.

Continued Growth of the Conservation Ethic

Fishermen's ideas about what influences lobster stock sizes and catches has strongly shaped the conservation ethic that has grown in the years since World War II. Fishermen do not say they are "conservationists," and even speak contemptuously of "tree huggers," "fish kissers," and other urbanites who eat fish, but have little sympathy for those who catch them. Rather, their sense of stewardship is expressed in support for certain management measures, which they believe are effective in conserving the resource, especially the V-notch and oversize measures. It also is demonstrated in increased support for law enforcement.

There can be little doubt that support for conservation has grown over the past several decades, and that the massive violations of the law that marked the earlier decades of the century have ceased. Many observers of the industry, including Colonel Joe Fessenden, Chief of the Marine Patrol, have reported that lobster regulations are largely self-enforcing, meaning that fishermen themselves sanction people violating the conservation laws (personal communication).

My own studies have also shown a growing awareness of a need for more effective conservation and support for conservation laws (Acheson 1975a: 661–66; 1989b: 212–13; 1993: 76–77). A survey of a sample of 144 lobster fishermen interviewed in 1973 showed support for some additional laws to augment those already on the books (Acheson 1975a). There was strong interest in limited-entry legislation, providing that the law was framed in such a way as to allow people from "fishing families" to be permitted to fish. Fully 94.3 percent of the fishermen interviewed said that lobster fishing should be reserved for full-time fishermen and that part-timers (i.e., those earning most of their income in other jobs) should be prohibited from fishing for lobster. Fishermen also showed strong support for a trap limit, with 88.4 percent of those interviewed favoring such a measure. Predictably, there was strong disagreement on how many traps license-holders should be permitted to fish (Acheson 1975a: 664–66).

Moreover, this survey showed support for conservation measures that were only enacted into law years later. In 1973, there were pockets of support for an escape vent, which did not become law until 1978. Eighty-two percent of those interviewed favored an apprenticeship program (as we saw in chapter 5, this did not become law until 1995).

The same 1973 survey, however, showed that lobster fishermen would not support some proposed laws, including many that were favorites of the lobster biologists and economists interested in lobster management. They were uniformly against any plan to reduce fishing effort by a trap tax or by a moratorium and subsidy scheme. Moreover, the vast majority of those interviewed (94 percent) did not support raising the legal minimum size to 3.5 inches, as the biologists recommended. "Sixty-seven percent of those men thought that such a measure would drastically reduce their catch, and would force them to market lobsters that were too large (and hence too expensive) to be readily salable" (Acheson 1975a: 663). (As we will see, the attitudes toward raising the minimum size measure have not changed from that day to 2001.)

Support for the oversize (5-inch) law was quite weak. Seventy-two percent said they favored removing the maximum size limit because they felt "it did little to conserve the lobster and because it would open a new fishery" (Acheson 1975a: 662). We can say nothing certain about support for the V-notch program. For reasons that are now inexplicable to me, we did not include any questions on this topic in the 1973 survey.

In 1998, a questionnaire sent to half the lobster license-holders in Maine revealed continued growth of the conservation ethic. This survey, which was returned by over twelve hundred lobster license-holders, demonstrated that lobster fishermen strongly supported the lobster conservation laws, particularly the V-notch and double-gauge laws. This is perhaps best demonstrated by the answers we received to the open-ended question: "What are the most important lobster conservation laws Maine currently has on the books?" Fully 66 percent of the 993 people who answered this question identified the V-notch law as the most important; another 15 percent said the minimum measure, the maximum measure, or the double-gauge law. Smaller numbers identified the escape vent, the ban on taking "eggers," trap limits, and prohibition on taking lobsters by dragging as "most important." Eighty-one percent of those who responded (886 of 1,100) "strongly agreed" with the statement "the V-notch law is effective in conserving the lobster breeding stock." When respondents were asked whether they agree or disagreed with the statement "The oversize law (5-inch) is effective in conserving the lobster breeding stock," 73 percent (805 of 1,097) of those who answered the question either "strongly agreed" or "agreed." The answer to this question suggests that support for the maximum size measure grew substantially from the time of the 1973 survey to 1998.

Lobster fishermen also had a high opinion about the effectiveness of the escape-vent law. Eighty-three percent of those responding (908 of 1,098 respondents) "strongly agree" or "agree" that "the escape vent is effective in conserving the lobster and reducing the number of culls." Most of the respondents thought that "the current laws are being enforced adequately," but a considerable minority (30 percent) wanted law enforcement strengthened even more.

However, this 1998 survey continued to show a massive lack of support for many of the ideas of the state and federal lobster biologists. Most of those interviewed did not want the minimum size increased to 3.5 inches. Sixty-one percent either "strongly disagreed" or "disagreed" with the statement "the minimum size should be increased." Forty-five percent of those interviewed disagreed with the statement "the lobster breeding stock has been over-fished."

The growth of the conservation ethic is also apparent in the support for law enforcement. People caught scrubbing the eggs off female lobsters or taking shorts or oversize lobsters are severely sanctioned by other fishermen. "Outlaws" are not only reported to the Marine Patrol; some have been driven out of business by other fishermen (Acheson 1988: 65–67). Some harbor gangs are well known for the punishments they mete out to offenders, though others are less vigorous.

In summary, by the turn of the century, there was very strong support for certain conservation laws that fishermen considered effective and for enforcement of those laws. There was very little support for the conservation program federal biologists wanted. As we shall see, this led to a good deal of conflict.

The lobster fishery does not appear to be unique in these respects. A recent study done by Harms and Sylvia (2001) on the West Coast groundfishery also found a marked conservation ethic among fishermen, but substantial differences between fishermen and scientists concerning views of stock abundance and policy issues.

Conclusions

We can draw four important conclusions. First, fishermen and biologists have differing views on what factors control stock sizes. Fishermen explain stock sizes in terms of environmental factors (habitat, predation, general cycles) and legal factors (poverty gauge, illegal activity, V-notch, oversize measure, etc.). The state and federal biologist tend to explain the bust and the boom primarily in terms of effort.

Second, there is all too little objective evidence supporting the various arguments offered to explain the bust and the boom. The arguments concerning the causes of the bust are particularly weak; those offered for the boom have little evidence to support them. One has to conclude that many of the fishermen's explanations are based in folklore; those offered by the biologists are not as scientific as they would like to think.

Third, the fact that we have such a tenuous hold on the factors that control catches means that we are formulating policies half blind. We are working in an environment of great uncertainty.

Fourth, the idea that fishermen and biologists need to agree on policy and science for co-management to work is clearly not correct. The data from the Maine lobster industry show they can disagree about important issues, and rules can still be put in place that likely play a big role in conserving the resource. However, these disagreements between fishermen and scientists certainly increase the transaction costs involved in negotiating conservation rules.

Fifth, the differences between the fishermen and biologists about what controls the size of lobster stocks underlie the long policy dispute over the direction of lobster management during the last quarter of the twentieth century. The fishermen believe the lobster stocks are in good condition due, in great part, to the V-notch program and oversize measure; the state and federal biologists believe the lobster stocks are dangerously overfished. Their commitment to stock-recruitment models has led them to call for more controls to lower mortality and increase egg production. These ideas, even though poorly supported by the evidence, are of crucial importance, as long as people act in terms of them. As we shall see, fishermen and biologists have been acting in terms of their ideas, resulting in a long period of conflict.

CHAPTER 7

Dealing with the Feds

The advent of federal control during the last quarter of the twentieth century marked a real change in lobster management. During this period, members of the industry did not devote themselves to initiating new legislation so much as to trying to influence federal policy to get rules they could live with. They have only been partially successful. They were able to ward off some federal initiatives, accommodate to others, and help shift management authority to the ASMFC, an agency they believed would be more amenable to their ideas of effective management. In many of these activities, they were forced to challenge the federal and state scientists, whose findings dominated so much of the federal agenda.

The Coming of Federal Control

From the founding of the Republic to the 1970s, fisheries management was completely in the hands of the states. The federal government had no regulatory control over fisheries, except for rights gained under international treaties. Two laws were to change this situation. Both were to have profound implications for lobster management. The first was the formation of the Atlantic States Marine Fisheries Commission (ASMFC), an interstate compact of fifteen states designed to assist in managing shared coastal fisheries resources of the eastern seaboard. The ASMFC was created by an act of Congress in 1942, when it was ratified by Maine. It was amended in 1959 (12 M.R.S.A. Sec. 4601–4613, 4651–4656).

The other was the passage of Public Law 94-265, the Fisheries Conservation and Management Act of 1976 (FCMA). In the 1970s this law was popularly called the "200-Mile Limit Bill," because it extended U.S. jurisdiction out to 200 miles (*Maine Commercial Fisheries* 1976: A1).

The ASMFC developed one bureaucracy to manage fisheries; passage of the FCMA resulted in the development of another, the regional council system. Some fisheries are managed by the ASMFC, others by one or more of the regional councils. The National Marine Fisheries Service does stock assessments on certain species for the councils and the ASMFC; other stock assessments are done by the states. Compounding the complexity is the fact that the NMFS has some control over the management plans promulgated by both the ASMFC and the states.

Management of the lobster fishery in federal waters has alternated between control by the ASMFC and various agencies of the federal government. Until 1977, the fishery was managed by the State-Federal program, which was essentially ASMFC management. From 1977 until 1995, the fishery was managed by the New England Regional Council; from 1995 to the present, control passed back to the ASMFC.

During the 1970s, the Maine fishing industry had few problems with federal involvement in their fishery. If anything, they welcomed the intervention of the feds. The FCMA was passed by the U.S. Congress largely in response to pressure from the U.S. fishing industry, which wanted the federal government to control the activities of foreign fleets with large factory ships that had appeared off American shores in the 1960s and 1970s, severely damaging stocks of fish in international waters that had been historically fished by the American fleet. What the fishing industry did not fully appreciate was that this law gave the government of the United States the power to regulate all fishing within 200 miles of the United States—including the domestic industry. They were soon to learn (Dewar 1983).

The State-Federal Program

The State-Federal Program began in 1972. It involved coordination between the Interstate Fishery Management Program of the Atlantic States Marine Fisheries Commission (ASMFC) and the State-Federal Program of the National Marine Fisheries Service.

The first rules proposed by the State-Federal Program seemed relatively innocuous. They called for all of the lobster-producing states to have uniform rules for lobster, including a uniform minimum size of at least of 3³⁄₁₆ inches carapace length, prohibitions on landing egg-bearing lobsters or lobster meat and parts of lobsters. The National Marine Fisheries Service and many of the representatives of the state agencies were in favor of uniform laws to simplify regulations and to aid enforcement efforts. These proposals caused little consternation in Maine, primarily because all of the proposed rules were already encoded in Maine law. Moreover, the Maine lobster industry was certainly in favor of other states having to raise their legal minimum measure because this would put Maine on an equal footing in competing for the so-called "chicken lobster" market. The market for these small, cheap lobsters had been dominated by other states such as New Hampshire and Rhode Island with smaller minimum-size restrictions. In short, the leadership of the Maine industry supported the goals of the State-Federal Program primarily because they recognized that the feds might be able to accomplish what no one in Maine could, namely to force these other state legislatures to pass laws raising the legal minimum size. Vinal Look, who was commissioner of Marine Resources in 1977, "stressed that what Maine would really like to see is a uniform minimum carapace length implemented by all the states" (Donnell 1977: 28).

The State-Federal Program encountered little opposition among lobster fishermen. In the early 1970s when federal intervention in lobster management began, the offshore lobster fishery was relatively small. Most fishermen exploited state waters most of the time, where they caught most of their catches. It was only in the winter months, when lobsters migrated offshore, that any numbers of Maine fishermen fished in federal waters, and the vast majority of these fishermen only ventured 5 to 10 miles outside state territorial waters. Moreover, few if any lobster fishermen even applied for the newly required permit to fish in federal waters, since federal and state authorities did not enforce the federal licensing requirements. If the rank-and-file lobster fisherman was indifferent to the coming of the feds, the leadership of the industry tacitly welcomed federal intervention, since it was considered economically advantageous to the industry.

Unfortunately, the State-Federal Program was not successful. From 1972 to 1976, the officials of the State-Federal Program worked diligently to have the precepts of their lobster plan adopted by the states. Since they had no authority to promulgate regulations, the success of the plan depended completely on their ability to persuade the state legislatures to adopt it. They were not persuasive enough. The primary problem was opposition to the $3\frac{3}{16}$ minimum-size rule in those states with a lower size limit. These had long had a monopoly on the market for small lobsters, and raising the minimum measure, they knew, would mean sharing the "chicken market" with states with larger measures. However, the fact that states such as Maine had supported the State-Federal Program was to mark the beginning of a slide into federal management in the lobster industry.

Management Under the New England Regional Council

In 1976, lobster management in federal waters was given to the New England Fishery Management Council (NEFMC), the federal management unit established under the Fishery Conservation and Management Act of 1976 (FCMA). The State-Federal Program was considered a failure, and the newly created New England Fisheries Management Council was keen to take on lobster management. The NEFMC applied for jurisdiction over lobster management and was supported in its bid by the New England states. The Secretary of Commerce granted this request.

The FCMA had established eight regional councils charged with managing the fisheries in their zones. These councils are composed of the regional director of the National Marine Fisheries Service, a representative of the Coast Guard, and three or four members appointed by each of the governors of those states, including the chief fisheries officer of each state, a legislator, and one or two others nominated by the governor. These councils are responsible for preparing fisheries management plans for all fisheries under their jurisdiction, and for making recommendations for managing these fisheries to the Secretary of Commerce. If the Secretary of Commerce accepts these plans, they are administered and enforced by the National Marine Fisheries Service. The fisheries from Maine to Connecticut are in the jurisdiction of the New England Regional Fisheries Management Council (PL 94-265).

Under the FCMA, the fisheries in territorial waters within 3 nautical miles from shore are in the jurisdiction of the coastal states. Those from the 3-mile line to the 200-mile line are in the Exclusive Economic Zone (EEZ), which is in the jurisdiction of the federal government. In reality, the situation is by no means that simple. On most issues, the federal agencies and the states coordinate activities to avoid promulgating one set of regulations for territorial waters and another for the EEZ. The state fisheries agencies, regional council, NMFS, and ASMFC try to coordinate to produce one set of rules for a fishery. Moreover, there is an attempt to make a single agency primarily responsible for a fishery, depending on the location of that fishery. Fisheries largely carried out within the territorial waters of a state are controlled in great part by the states or the ASMFC. Those done primarily in the EEZ are largely administered by the regional council and the NMFS. Complicating this picture is the fact that the federal government has the right to pre-empt the management powers of the states in cases where it judges that the management efforts of the states are inadequate.

The FCMA puts all of these agencies in an awkward and anomalous position. Management plans for species must be developed by the regional council or ASMFC, but final approval rests with the NMFS and Secretary of Commerce. The NMFS can encourage the councils or threaten them, but it cannot directly develop plans itself until the council has demonstrated its ineptitude. In other regions of the United States, this system seems to have worked reasonably well. In New England, efforts to manage the lobster fishery led to conflict and stalemate when the council failed to act as the NMFS wished.

Initially, the job of developing a lobster plan was given to the Mid Atlantic and New England Regional Councils, which worked very closely with the scientists and bureaucrats of the National Marine Fisheries Service and the states. Tom Morrissey of the National Marine Fisheries Service was chair of the committee charged with developing the plan, which included both state and federal scientists (Donnell 1977: 28A). The first lobster fishery management plan that evolved contained all of the provisions of the older State-Federal plan (i.e., $3\frac{3}{16}$ minimum gauge, prohibitions on landing lobster meat, lobster parts, and egg-bearing females). It also included several other provisions, including a rise in the minimum measure to 3.5 inches, implementing a limited-entry program, and abolishing the V-notch and oversize measure. These latter proposals were to cause a major political battle when implementation was attempted.

If this plan were to be implemented, its provisions would have to be passed into law by the Maine legislature; and failure to pass such laws would put Maine out of compliance with the FCMA. At first, the representatives of the NMFS, the Maine Department of Marine Resources, and the political leadership of the Maine lobster industry all supported the plan. Maine Department of Marine Resources Research Director Vaughn Anthony believed passage of the rules contained in the plan would help prevent a disastrous decline in the fishery, which he predicted as imminent. Initially, Eddie Blackmore, president of the Maine Lobstermen's Association, and other leaders of the industry supported the plan, including the proposed increase in the measure beyond 3¹⁄₁₆ inches (Billings 1978: A1; Blackmore 1978: 3; *Maine Commercial Fisheries* 1978a: A12). However, trouble loomed on the horizon when a survey of the membership of the industry associations showed little support for important parts of the plan. Ninety percent of the members of the Maine Lobstermen's Association supported the current double-gauge law, indicating that they did not support abolishing the oversize law (5-inch maximum), or raising the minimum measure to 3.5 inches. Moreover, the Atlantic Offshore Fish and Lobster Association wanted an economic study completed before any change in the legal measures was contemplated (*Maine Commercial Fisheries* 1978b: 20). After this, the leadership of the industry backed away from supporting the State-Federal lobster plan.

When it became apparent that the regional council plan was solidly opposed by the industry, one group after another entered the fray with proposals for a whole series of different plans. The Maine Lobstermen's Association proposed a plan featuring a five hundred-trap limit (six hundred in boats with sternmen), and limiting entry through implementation of an apprenticeship program (Morrison 1979: 23). Spencer Apollonio, the commissioner of the Maine DMR, proposed a plan based primarily on raising the minimum measure that would not involve either limited entry or a trap limit (Larkin 1979: 4). Maine Representative Pat Jackson sponsored a bill to set up a license system in which each license class would have a different trap limit. Representative George Vincent proposed a bill implementing the length recommendations of the federal fisheries management plan. None of these plans had enough political support to be enacted into law (Connolly 1979: 22).

The Blackmore-Allen Compromise: A Most Unlikely Episode

Throughout the early 1980s, the New England Regional Council pressed ahead with the State-Federal lobster plan. They were supported by the National Marine Fisheries Service and generally had the support of the state fisheries administrators and scientists, who urged legislators to adopt the ten points in the plan (Donnell 1977: A28). Increasingly, however, they were opposed by industry.

At the root of this dispute lay a profound difference of opinion about the state of the lobster stocks, what controlled those stocks, and the proper course of management. As described in chapter 6, basically the consensus among state and federal biologists was that continually escalating fishing effort had endangered the stocks. Not only were the size of lobsters small (growth overfishing), but there were not enough lobsters surviving to a size where they could produce eggs. For this reason, the lobster scientists working for the NMFS and the states generally supported raising the minimum measure to 3.5 inches (88.9 mm), a size at which 60 percent of the lobsters could extrude eggs. The biological data supporting this position are complicated, and will be discussed in detail in chapter 8. From the 1970s to the present, raising the legal minimum size to 3.5 inches became the Holy

Grail for these biologists (Acheson and Reidman 1982: 1–2; Krouse 1972; Thomas 1973a, 1973b). It was a goal whose virtues they preached incessantly. A recommendation to increase the measure to 3.5 inches was incorporated in the Comprehensive Management Plan for American Lobster produced by the Northeast Marine Fisheries Board (Billings 1978). Biologists and administrators have argued that Maine should do away with its oversize measure and the V-notch, and that these rules should not be promulgated in other states. The oversize measure, they claim, does little to conserve the large reproductive-sized lobsters, since virtually no lobsters survive to this size. The V-notch is a source of infection, and they held that "there was a lack of concrete date to support the value of the measure" (Jones 1985b: 39). Moreover, only Maine has these two laws, and abolishing them would help the cause of obtaining uniform regulations.

A large segment of the Maine lobster fishing industry viewed these recommendations as unnecessary, costly, and not in the best interests of conservation. Maine Lobstermen's Association President Eddie Blackmore's assessment of the situation was that "the lobsters have been making damn fools out of the scientists" (Stecklow 1991). They questioned the need for drastic changes in management, since they knew that catches had been very stable since 1947 and even increasing (see table 1.1). They did not believe that the brood stock had been damaged by overfishing since they saw large numbers of V-notched lobsters in their traps, and no small number of oversize lobsters (over 5 inches on the carapace). Moreover, they were committed to the idea that the goal of management should be to conserve the large reproductive-sized lobsters, and, for this reason, they believed that the V-notch and the oversize laws were the keystone of management. They believed that the oversize law created a sanctuary size for large lobsters, and that the V-notch law permitted large number of gravid females to reach that sanctuary. They also supported the oversize law as decreasing the temptation for offshore draggers to drag for lobsters, since many lobsters caught in deep waters are over 5 inches on the carapace and cannot be landed in Maine. Some scientists agreed (e.g., Bayer, Daniel, and Vaitones 1985; Waddy and Aiken 1986). However, most dealers and offshore fishermen favored abolishing the oversize measure since they argued that these big lobsters were being caught anyway and landed in other states, and the Maine lobster industry might as well get its share of the business (Acheson 1988: 133–40).

Perhaps most important, the industry was opposed to raising the measure. In their view, this was unnecessary and would make it impossible to compete in markets for small and cheap lobsters, particularly when surrounding jurisdictions (especially Canada) have a lower minimum size. The industry also strongly suspected that raising the minimum size would result in a loss of income, their primary concern. Their concern about the move to a 3.5-inch minimum was heightened in the 1980s, a time when lobster imports into the United States from Canada were increasing rapidly, lobsters that could legally be brought into this country at a size less than Maine's legal minimum.

Within the industry, there was near unanimity on these issues. To be sure, some industry members were in favor of abolishing the V-notch, but even so, a survey of MLA members revealed that "88 percent support retaining the 5-inch maximum size" (Jones 1985b).

Throughout the late 1970s and early 1980s the National Marine Fisheries Service and the New England Regional Council continued to lobby for the State-Federal lobster plan. The debate continued in the newspapers, legislature, and scientific white papers. The industry, which had been largely apathetic about the prospects of federal intervention in the late 1970s, became increasingly concerned in the 1980s when it became apparent that the council's plan was being taken very seriously by the bureaucrats and legislators, and that this plan called for a raise in the legal minimum measure to 3.5 inches and the abolition of the V-notch law.

In the 1985 session of the Maine legislature, bills embodying various parts of the council plan had been introduced. The marine resources committee considered a bill to abolish the oversize law, which had been introduced with the support of many of the dealers. It also debated bills to impose large license fees and to impose a high tax on every trap fished. The leadership of the Maine Lobstermen's Association, and its president, Eddie Blackmore, became alarmed enough to take action. Blackmore began to lobby the regional council to include V-notch protection in the federal lobster plan (Billings 1985b). He hired a professional lobbyist to counter threats in the legislature (Jones 1985b). The MLA also put forth its own plan featuring a six hundred-trap limit and an apprenticeship program to slow entry into the industry (Billings 1985a). Other individuals and industry groups followed suit. All told, Maine's Lobster Advisory Council considered plans involving tag fees, higher license fees, closed seasons, and trap limits (Billings 1985a; Morrison 1985). Representative Scarpino introduced a single bill embodying all of these measures (Billings 1985b). All of these proposals had one common element—they were designed to circumvent the State-Federal plan by conserving the lobster resource in ways that would avoid increasing the legal minimum size while maintaining the V-notch and oversize measures, which the industry considered essential.

The 1985 session of the Maine legislature passed no lobster conservation legislation, primarily because, as Representative Scarpino said, "no bill had overwhelming support in the industry" (Morrison 1985). The legislature, overburdened with acrimonious debates, controversial proposals, and contradictory advice, voted to hire a consultant to study the lobster industry and make recommendations for future legislation. L. W. Botsford and Associates of Davis, California, was hired. The "Botsford Report," released in the spring of 1986, was diplomatically worded, to avoid exacerbating the bitterly contested debate. Botsford was clearly appalled at what he called the "adversarial struggle" surrounding the debate, and refused to side with one faction or another, concluding that "no single option clearly emerges as the best policy." However, he found virtue in all of the proposals being advocated by all of the factions, including raising the minimum measure, the V-notch, and the oversize law (Botsford, Wilen and Richardson 1986: 53–55).

Taking a clue from the Botsford report, the leadership of the industry proposed a lobster plan that embodied all of the key solutions suggested by all factions

(Plante 1985: 13; Stevens 1986:12). Throughout 1986, Eddie Blackmore, MLA president, and Dick Allen of the Atlantic Offshore Lobstermen's Association lobbied for a compromise plan in which the lobster industry would accept an increase in the minimum size from 3³⁄₁₆ inches to 3⁵⁄₁₆ inches if the regional council and the NMFS would agree to retain the V-notch and oversize measures. It was clearly understood that the new minimum size would apply to Canadian imports.

Both sides had serious reservations about this plan. Federal administrators and scientists still thought the V-notch and oversize laws were useless, and fishermen from southern New England were also leery of these rules (Layton 1987). The Maine lobster industry was worried about the increase in the minimum gauge size. Eddie Blackmore said, "We are going to recover from the wound of a small gauge increase, but we would be the longtime gainer if we do get V-notch protection for the whole range [of lobsters]. I'm not in love with [increasing the gauge], but I can accept it to get the other" (Plante 1986).

In spite of these reservations, the compromise plan had enough support to have been passed into law (Stevens 1987). The language of the bill called for the minimum size measure to be increased to 3⁵⁄₁₆ inches in four ¹⁄₃₂-inch increments, to take place in 1988, 1989, 1991, and 1992. The V-notch and oversize laws were to be retained in Maine (*Commercial Fisheries News* 1987a). The same rules were incorporated into Amendment 2 of the Federal American Lobster Plan and passed by the New England Regional Council in 1987 (*Commercial Fisheries News* 1987b). The bill moved quite quickly through the council process, largely because of efforts of leaders of the Maine lobster industry. However, it is highly unlikely that this bill would have had enough support in the industry to have been passed into law were it not for a clear understanding that the NMFS and regional council would promulgate the V-notch and the oversize throughout the range of the lobster, and that the Canadians were going to raise their minimum gauge size so that the Maine lobster industry would no longer be disadvantaged in the large market for small lobsters. The Canadians were to be prodded into action by the passage of regulations to ensure that undersize Canadian lobsters would not be imported into the United States. These two sets of factors resulted in support by the leaders of the Maine lobster industry, even though there was widespread concern among license-holders about the wisdom of the gauge increase.

In 1987, Amendment 2 of the New England Fishery Management Council's Lobster Fisheries Management Plan (FMP) was implemented, and the minimum size was increased from 3¹⁄₁₆ to 3³⁄₃₂ inches in January of 1988. However, the increase in the measure was accompanied by a considerable amount of unhappiness, which quickly was transformed into an effort to stop the minimum-gauge increase. According to Bill Brennan, who was the Maine commissioner of Marine Resources, the industry wanted to stop the gauge increase for several reasons. He said in an interview that, during 1988, "the economy began to slide toward recession and the prospect of smaller catches due to a size increase became more threatening." At this same time, a study done by Dr. Robert Steneck of the University of Maine was released that argued that there were sufficient larvae in the water to maintain the stock, and questioned the need to increase the measure.

The industry seized on this study as a further reason to delay the increase in the legal measure (Alden 1989a; *Commercial Fisheries News* 1989; Plante 1989a; Steneck 1989a). More important, the unwritten understanding that persuaded the leaders of the Maine lobster industry to support the increase in the minimum size did not result in the promised legislation. Efforts by the Canadian government to bring about an increase in the Canadian minimum measure ran into industry opposition and failed completely in June 1989 (Sonnenberg 1989c). Massachusetts and Rhode Island fishermen opposed implementing a V-notch measure and an oversize law.

Amidst a growing storm of protest, the gauge was increased again by ¹⁄₃₂ of an inch to 3¼ inches in 1989. At this point, the industry leadership united in a multi-state effort to stop the gauge increases (Alden 1989b). In the summer of 1989, the leaders of the industry from the New England states called upon the regional council to delay the increase in the minimum gauge, and a formal motion to delay was offered at the August 1989 council meeting. This motion was defeated by the council, which resulted in an angry response from the industry (Plante 1989b). The industry was not expecting the council to be so obdurate. After all, they had become very effective in influencing management decisions at the state level. This defeat drove home to the industry leadership that it would be far more difficult to change federal policy.

The long fight over the gauge increase prompted the industry to use new tactics. Even before the second gauge increase went into effect in 1989, the officers of industry groups in the New England states industry began to work together. They lobbied their respective states for legislation to halt or delay the increases in the gauge. They also became actively involved in the regional council process. They became members of the council's newly created industry advisory committee, participated in the council's lobster committee meetings, and attended meetings of the full council. At the national level, industry leaders became very familiar visitors in the Washington offices of their congressional delegations, where their first order of business was the need for a law to prevent the importation of Canadian lobsters under the legal size. They also spent a considerable amount of time fostering relationships with government officials in leadership positions at the National Marine Fisheries Service and its parent agency, the National Oceanic and Atmospheric Administration. Furthermore, industry leaders began to familiarize themselves with other fisheries management organizations, such as the Atlantic States Marine Fisheries Commission, and they developed relationships with various conservation organizations. Industry leaders also opened discussion with their Canadian counterparts in an effort to get an increase in the gauge in Canada (Sonnenberg 1989a).

These industry efforts produced two results. First, in 1989, both houses of the U.S. Congress passed the Mitchell Bill, spearheaded by Maine's Senator George Mitchell (the U.S. Senate Majority Leader), which prohibited importing lobsters smaller than the federal minimum size (Sonnenberg 1989a; 1989b).[1]

Second, the raise in the minimum gauge was halted. By the end of 1990, sentiment in the regional council and the legislatures had swung against any more gauge increases. At the January 1990 meeting, the regional council voted to delay more gauge increases, and by summer 1991, Maine passed a law fixing the minimum size of lobster at 3 1/4 inches. Shortly thereafter, Massachusetts, Rhode Island, New Hampshire, and New York did the same thing (Plante 1991: 18a).

The successful campaign to stop the increase in the minimum gauge resulted in a good deal of bitterness and cynicism on the part of some of the members of the regional council, officers of the National Marine Fisheries Service, and personnel in state fisheries agencies. They felt that the leaders of the industry had reneged on an agreement. Industry leaders point out that they had never thought that increasing the minimum gauge was a good idea, and went along with it only with a clear understanding that the Canadians would increase their minimum gauge. When the Canadians failed to increase their gauge, the leaders of the industry became convinced they had been gulled into making a bad bargain, one that severely disadvantaged their members. They had few compunctions about backing out of the deal under these conditions.

The acrimonious nature of the debate did little to facilitate future cooperation between the lobster industry and the regional council and bureaucrats. Members of the council and industry described each other in far from complementary terms.

Gridlock in the Council

The successful move to nullify the gauge increase marked the beginning of a particularly nasty fight involving the industry, the regional council, the NMFS, and the ASMFC, which resulted in five long years of bickering in which no lobster plan was accepted. Ultimately, this led to an end of federal control and a return of lobster management to the states.

In 1991, the regional council stopped the gauge increase temporarily with the passage of Amendment 3, an emergency measure. Shortly thereafter, the National Marine Fisheries Service promulgated the 602 Guidelines, which were duly published in the Federal Register. This guideline specified that all future fisheries management plans were to have a definition of overfishing. This was to result in the so called "10 percent rule," which has guided federal efforts to manage lobster ever since. That is, lobster is considered "overfished" when egg production is under 10 percent of what it would be in a completely unfished fishery. (This will be discussed in detail in chapter 8.)

In January 1992, Amendment 4 to the American Lobster Plan went into effect (Alden 1991). This amendment specified that the increase in the minimum gauge would be halted for two years while an alternative plan to reduce fishing effort was developed (Sonnenberg 1992). If no acceptable plan were developed by January 1994, then the remaining two increases in the minimum size would occur automatically. It also specified that a preliminary definition of overfishing was to be developed, and that the escape vents in traps would be enlarged to $1^{15}\!/_{16}$ (Plante 1991). Amendment 4 also gave partial responsibility for developing the plan to the industry, a novel procedure that would mean bypassing the council staff, which normally developed fisheries management plans (Stevens 1992).

Amendments 3 and 4 were the result of the work of a coalition of industry leaders, officers of the NMFS, and some members of the regional council. Eddie Blackmore, president of the Maine Lobstermen's Association, spent years persuading the regional council to protect V-notched and oversized lobsters, and to halt the increase in the minimum gauge. Dick Roe, the regional director of the NMFS, in an uncharacteristic move for an NMFS officer, voted for both amendments. He was joined by some members of the regional council, including Commissioners Bill Brennan of Maine and Phil Coates of Massachusetts, who despite their former support, had begun to suspect that raising the gauge was not the *sine qua non* of lobster management. They began to talk seriously about alternative ways of managing lobster without increasing the gauge. In the minds of many, the preferred alternative was some form of co-management. Giving some authority for management to the industry, they believed, would promote a stewardship ethic. They had also come to see that the lobster fishery was so varied that it could only be managed by dividing the lobster-producing areas into zones that had different rules.

Political pressure also played a role in building support for Amendments 3 and 4. Some of the state directors on the council were under pressure from their legislatures to halt the gauge increases, and officers of the NMFS were under pressure from the congressional delegations.

Many officers of the NMFS felt that the passage of Amendments 3 and 4 compromised the goals of lobster management. In their view, the lobster was dangerously overfished, and the only solution was to raise the minimum measure. They could not support Amendments 3 and 4, even though top officers of their agency were working to facilitate them.

After Amendment 4 was passed by the council, the "Lobster Industry Working Group" was formed to develop what would be Amendment 5. This group was composed of the directors of the various lobster industry groups (i.e., Pat White and Dave Cousens from the Maine Lobstermen's Association, Bill Adler from the Massachusetts Lobstermen's Association, and Dick Allen from the Offshore Lobstermen's Association, Maine). This group outlined their preferred lobster management plan, and then went around the regional council to Bill Fox, the Director of the National Marine Fisheries Service, to get more action on the plan than they thought they would get from the regional council. Fox agreed to help develop the plan, and gave a grant to allow the regional council to hire consultants to accomplish this task (Plante 1993a). Nikki Bane, the NMFS's liaison to industry, explained, "It's our responsibility to help develop this plan, . . . The council's against the wall. Their staff and funding are limited, and the council has so many other responsibilities"(Plante 1993a). Ominously, Douglas Marshall, executive director of the regional council, was very skeptical of this action and doubted that the consultants could put together a plan that would be passed by the council.

The grant money from the NMFS was used to hire three faculty from the University of Maine who drafted what was to become Amendment 5 of the Federal Lobster Plan.[2] The regional council received the report of the industry working

Capturing the Commons

group in the fall of 1992 and spent the next several months negotiating its various recommendations. The final plan submitted to the National Marine Fisheries Service in May 1994 called for: (1) dividing the lobster fishery into zones and establishing "Effort Management Teams" (EMTs) to reduce effort. Each of these EMTs was composed of industry members appointed from each state; (2) a moratorium on entry into the fishery for two years; (3) mandatory log books; and (4) an apprenticeship program. It also adopted a definition of overfishing in the form of the 10 percent rule. They did not incorporate into the final plan two recommendations of the consultants: a closed season for lobster fishing during the shedder season and the prohibition on dragging for lobster.

Amendment 5 never became law even though it had good support in the lobster industry itself. It fell victim to internal wrangling within the council and competition between the council and the NMFS. The history of Amendment 5 from 1992 when planning for it started to 1996, when the NMFS withdrew the plan, is one of long negotiations, innumerable proposed changes, missed deadlines, and ultimately failure.

Deep divisions in the council made it impossible to agree on the provisions and ways to implement Amendment 5 (Plante 1993b). Some members were still angry that the industry had reneged on the original agreement to increase the measure in return for support for the V-notch and oversize laws. They were also disturbed that the final plan was going to be developed by the industry working group aided by hired consultants, known to be friendly to the industry, rather than the council staff (Alden 1993). They were very reluctant to approve any plan that did not include an increase in the legal minimum size.

Those council members who had become convinced that they needed to explore ways to manage the fishery without raising the legal minimum size felt badly caught between the industry, which would go to any effort to ensure the minimum size was not raised, and the federal and state scientists and their allies on the council, who would accept no other alternative. During the negotiations concerning Amendment 5, they quietly supported some of the ideas of the lobster industry working group and the consultants hired to develop the plan.

Another source of contention between the lobster industry and the regional council was dragging for lobsters. Many in the lobster industry were increasingly committed to the idea of making it illegal to take large amounts of lobsters by draggers; the regional council, which contained many representing the draggers, was opposed to stark reductions in the by-catch of lobsters for draggers.

Top officers of the NMFS supported the development of alternative plans that did not involve raising the minimum measure, but many felt they worked in ways to make it almost impossible for such an alternative plan (i.e., Amendment 5) to succeed. The fact that they hired consultants alienated many on the council and its staff. They strongly supported the overfishing definition, but then supported the dragging interests on the council who did not want to prohibit dragging for lobsters. Once the industry working group had produced a draft of Amendment 5, the NMFS strongly urged the council to adopt it. But their primary tactic was to use threats of raising the legal measure and brinkmanship (Plante 1993b; 1993d;

1994b) in an attempt to force the regional council to agree on an acceptable implementation plan. This left many council members seething.

Timing and deadlines became important issues. From the perspective of the NMFS, the council was impossibly slow to produce a lobster management plan with the required documentation. From the perspective of many council members, the NMFS set such short deadlines that it was almost certain that the council would fail to meet them. In the fall of 1992, when the council received the draft plan of the industry working group, Dave Borden, chair of the council's lobster committee, predicted that they could not meet the deadline (Plante 1992: A14). In the summer of 1993, when the council was in danger of missing the December 31, 1993, deadline, several of the state directors, including Bill Brennan of Maine and Phil Coates of Massachusetts, adamantly insisted that the NMFS find a way to extend the timetable (Plante 1993b). The NMFS refused, with the result that the regional council passed in an incomplete plan (Plante 1993c; 1993d; 1994b). The NMFS responded by approving only that part of the plan and gave the regional council another six months to "develop a plan that would reduce fishing mortality" under the threat of having the minimum size increased (Plante 1994c).

In May, the scheduled gauge increases were rescinded, and the rest of Amendment 5 was accepted on July 20, 1994 (Plante 1994c). However, Amendment 5 was accepted with the express understanding that the effort-management teams were to be formed and make recommendations on reducing effort in each of their zones by January 20, 1995 (Plante 1994c; 1994d). Four zones were created, each with its own EMT (effort-management team). Each of these zones selected different sets of effort-management proposals. Each of the zones wanted to limit the number of traps a license-holder could use, but they favored different trap numbers. The EMT from Zone 1 (Gulf of Maine-nearshore) was persuaded by the Maine contingent to favor the V-notch and maximum size limits. Zone 3, in the offshore waters of the federal zone, proposed individual transferable quotas (ITQs). Zones 2 and 4 wanted other sets of rules (Plante 1995e). None of these rules were put into effect. That would have to await the coming of ASMFC management.

In March 1995, the Amendment 5 struggle came alive again when the NMFS called for the development of a plan that took into account the recommendations of all five of the EMTs to cut effort in the lobster fishery (Plante 1995a). Moreover, the NMFS insisted that the states administer and enforce the plan, and the state directors were not sure they had the resources to accomplish these tasks (Plante 1995b). These extra requirements caused the council to delay action on the plan so that they missed the June 20, 1995, deadline set by Amendment 4 for the council to pass a plan. In response, the NMFS threatened to take lobster management out of the hands of the council by producing Amendment 6—a new plan—which they would write. They also repeated their threat to withdraw the entire lobster fishery management plan, which would nullify those parts of Amendment 5 that had been passed and approved (Plante 1995c; 1995d). However, Bill Brennan, DMR commissioner and one of Maine's representatives to the council, said in an interview that "by this time, it was too late. Lobster management had moved in other directions." In January 1996, the ASMFC took over control of lobster management after the NMFS had agreed to withdraw the Federal Lobster Management Plan.

Changing Horses in Midstream: The ASMFC Takes Over

Assumption of power over lobster management by the ASMFC came as no sudden thing. Bill Brennan, who was DMR commissioner and chair of the council's lobster oversight committee, reports that he and other state directors on the council had begun to discuss the "possibility of moving lobster management out from under federal control" as early as 1989, and by 1992 these council members had begun to discuss other radical ideas including a form of zone management (Brennan 1992).

In 1994, as the council and NMFS came to loggerheads over Amendment 5, the ASMFC began to bring its own lobster plan up to date (Plante 1994a). In 1995, they began to develop a plan in coordination with the states that would impose one set of regulations in both state and federal waters (Stevens 1995).

By 1995, everyone concerned with the lobster industry had come to realize that management by the NMFS and council was in grave difficulty. The state directors, the industry, the regional council, and the NMFS all agreed that authority for managing lobster should be transferred from the federal system to the ASMFC. Their motives differed radically, however (Plante 1996a).

A number of factors motivated the state directors. Many had been moved to anger by the heavy-handed approach of the feds to force an increase in the minimum gauge, and their inflexible opposition to any other way of managing the fishery. The long struggle over Amendment 5, with its repeated threats to raise the gauge if deadlines were not met, did nothing to calm the waters.

The state directors also had serious questions about the science involved in lobster management. The lobster-stock assessment reports produced by federal scientists indicated that the lobster resource was overexploited, and the NMFS was very rigid in insisting that the 10 percent egg per recruit criterion be used for management. Some of the state directors were skeptical that the fishery was in a state of crisis, and they questioned the science behind the 10 percent overfishing definition.

Jurisdictional issues concerned the state directors as well. They became convinced that it had been a mistake to have given the regional council control over lobster management, and that the states should take a primary role in managing the lobster fishery since it is carried out primarily in state waters.

In December 1994, the National Marine Fisheries Service refused to accept that part of Amendment 5 limiting the amount of lobster draggers could take. For some of the state directors, this was the last straw. After that they saw no alternative to taking lobster management out of the hands of the federal government.

The leadership of the industry associations came to favor management by the ASMFC because they became convinced it offered them a better forum than the federal apparatus. After all, fisheries managed by the ASMFC were managed by the states. Moreover, under the ASMFC, lobsters would be managed by a lobster management board composed of lobster industry representatives and others who knew the industry. In this arena, the lobster industry would have more regulatory power then they had in the regional council whose membership was heavily weighted toward the dragger industry. Thus, in the mid 1990s the leadership of the lobster industry began to lobby the congress to manage the industry through the ASMFC, and end management by the apparatus set up by the FCMA (i.e., regional council and the NMFS).

The NMFS had also decided that it was in its best interest to give up lobster management. The primary motivating force was the Clinton administration's "initiative to reinvent government" which shrunk the size of the federal government and resulted in across-the-board cuts in virtually every department. As a result, the National Marine Fisheries Service withdrew six fishery management plans, effectively handing over management of those species to the states (Plante 1996b). Lobster was an obvious choice for the federal government to cease managing, for it is essentially an inshore fishery (Plante 1995f). At the time, people involved in lobster management speculated that another motive was involved as well. Officers of the National Marine Fisheries Service were very frustrated with the inability of the council to produce a workable lobster management plan. After twenty years of impasse, one NMFS officer said that the fishery could only be managed if the NMFS pre-empted the control of the states within the 3-mile line, and bypassed the council. Bill Brennan, Maine's commissioner of Marine Resources, speculated that pre-emption would almost certainly be opposed by the states in federal court. In the absence of clear evidence of mismanagement, it was likely that the NMFS would lose such an attempt. Under these circumstances, officers of the NMFS thought it better to rid the agency of a troublesome fishery and transfer lobster management to the ASMFC.

Transferring power for managing lobster from the federal system to the ASMFC did not require any new legislation. The FCMA authorized the NMFS and regional councils to manage fisheries in federal waters; the Atlantic Coastal Fisheries Cooperative Management Act authorized the ASMFC to manage some fisheries in both state and federal waters. Since both agencies are empowered to manage fisheries in federal waters, they divided the work and decided which governance structure will have primary authority for developing fisheries management plans for a species. Before 1995, the state and federal governments agreed that authority to manage lobster would be given to the NMFS and the regional council. Transferring authority for lobster management to the ASMFC merely required that the NMFS "withdraw its lobster management plan," which occurred in February 1996 (Plante 1996a). After this, the ASMFC took the lead in lobster management and proceeded to develop its own lobster plan. The NMFS was supposed to follow suit by developing comparable plans for the federal zone. As Bill Adler, president of the Massachusetts Lobstermen's Association explained the situation in an interview, "The ASMFC puts in regulations and then says to the feds 'now you follow us in your waters.'" As we shall see, it wasn't quite that simple.

Management Under the ASMFC

The Atlantic States Marine Fisheries Commission is one of those agencies that exists between the states and the federal government. It began as a compact of the states for managing Atlantic coastal fisheries in 1942. In 1993, the ASMFC was given additional authority and became more a part of the federal system by the passage by the U.S. Congress of the Atlantic Coastal Fisheries Cooperative Management Act. This latter act committed the federal government to support the efforts of the ASMFC by various kinds of partnerships and federal funding. It mandates that the Atlantic coastal states included in the compact implement and enforce the provisions of all fisheries management plans that are passed by the commission. Failure to implement these provisions may result in the Secretary of Commerce placing a moratorium on the fishing for that species in that state's waters. In this sense, the act resulted in the fifteen coastal states relinquishing a lot of power to the federal government (Berger 1999). However, in other respects, the Atlantic Coastal Fisheries Cooperative Management Act increases the power of the Atlantic coastal states in that it allows them to enforce regulations beyond the 3-mile line in federal waters.

In the ASMFC governance structure, each of the fifteen Atlantic coastal states has three commissioners, including the chief state fisheries officer, a state legislator, and a member of the public nominated by the governor. There are also boards for each species, composed of industry representatives and others familiar with these fisheries. A fisheries management plan (FMP) is developed by the appropriate board; then it is passed by a vote of the ASMFC commissioners. After this, it must be ratified by the individual states. Thus, the fisheries management plan for lobster is developed by the Lobster Management Board, passed by a vote of the commissioners, and then put into effect when it is passed by the Maine Legislature, and is ratified by the other states.

Development of the ASMFC Lobster Plan (Amendment 3)

The transfer of authority for lobster management to the ASMFC came about just before the U.S. Congress passed the Sustainable Fisheries Act in 1996. This law, which upgraded the Magnusen Fisheries Management and Conservation Act of 1976 (FCMA), made some important changes in the law. It called for managing fisheries for Maximum Sustainable Yield (MSY), a concept that most people familiar with fisheries management thought was outmoded. More important, it said that if a fishery was deemed "overfished," the stock would have to be rebuilt within ten years, and it gave the National Marine Fisheries Service additional authority to accomplish this task (PL 104-297: sec. 102, 106, and 312). The Sustainable Fisheries Act and transfer of authority for lobster management to the ASMFC radically changed the nature of lobster management.

Even before authority to manage lobster was passed to the ASMFC, the agency was hard at work revamping its own plan for the American lobster. The actions of the ASMFC were given additional impetus by the report of the Twenty-second Northeast Regional Stock Assessment Workshop, produced by scientists at the Northeast Fisheries Science Center, the NMFS laboratory in Woods Hole, Massachusetts. This report concluded that the lobster was "overfished" in that egg production did not meet the 10 percent criterion. As a result, the ASMFC was bound by the Sustainable Fisheries Act to produce a plan to "rebuild" this stock in ten years.

In the summer and fall of 1996, the lobster management board of the ASMFC began working on a management plan, taking into account the goals spelled out by the Sustainable Fisheries Act as well as the recommendations of the EMTs (effort-management teams). They held hearings on a draft plan during November 1996 to hear the reaction of lobster fishermen to them (Plante 1996c). By April 1997, the ASMFC plan, called Amendment 3, was finalized, and it was approved by the ASMFC commissioners in December (*Commercial Fisheries News* 1998a; Plante 1997b; 1998a).

Amendment 3 was a complicated plan. It established six different areas (zones), each with its own lobster conservation management teams chosen from industry, which were charged with developing the conservation rules for the zone. It called for elimination of overfishing within eight years. Each area would also have different stock rebuilding targets based on the 10 percent overfishing definition (Plante 1998a).

In order to rebuild the stock within ten years, Amendment 3 was to be implemented over the course of a number of years by imposing gradually stricter rules designed to achieve the 10 percent egg-production goal by meeting a series of benchmarks. In the Gulf of Maine, for example, the schedule was to achieve 3.25 percent of the egg production of an unfished fishery in 1998 and 1999; 4.35 percent in 2000; 5.5 percent for 2001; 6.25 percent for 2002; 7.75 percent for 2003; 8.875 percent for 2004; and 10 percent for 2005 (Plante 1998a). The schedule would be met by adding addendums to Amendment 3 in each area in every year specifying the additional rules to be imposed.

Many of the rules proposed under the ASMFC's Amendment 3 plan incorporated a good many provisions that were already in the federal plan approved by the regional council, including the prohibition on possessing lobster parts, the prohibition on taking egg-bearing females, the rules mandating the use of traps with biodegradable "ghost panels," the 3¼-inch minimum size, and the prohibition on spearing lobsters (Plante 1997a, 1998a). The 10 percent rule was maintained intact as a goal for lobster management. In addition, the idea of having lobster conservation management teams was inspired by the effort-management teams, which had been a part of Amendment 5 of the federal plan.

The ASMFC's Amendment 3 also contained other rules that had not been a part of the older federal plan. Among these were protection of V-notched lobsters, a uniform vent size, and a maximum trap size. In this category was a limit on the number of lobsters that could be caught as a by-catch by draggers: one hundred lobsters per day or five hundred per fishing trip (the so-called 100/500 rule). It created an oversize measure (5-inch rule) for ASMFC area 1 (inshore Maine, New Hampshire, and Massachusetts down to Cape Cod) (Plante 1997a, 1998a).

Further complicating Amendment 3 was the fact that its rules pertained to different segments of the industry. Some rules would be universal, including the minimum 3¼-inch gauge, the 100/500 rule for dragger by-catches, the prohibition on spearing lobsters, the ghost-panel requirement for traps, and the prohibition on taking V-notched lobsters in the entire range of the species (*Commercial Fisheries News* 1998a). Other rules would apply coast-wide, but any state or zone could promulgate different measures "as long it can be shown to the ASMFC Lobster Board's satisfaction that alternative regulations provide for equivalent conservation of the lobster resource." Included in this category was licensing for different zones, escape vent, maximum trap size, and a maximum size limit. Last, each area would have separate trap limits (*Commercial Fisheries News* 1998a).

From the perspective of the Maine lobster industry, the total plan was not as important as the plan for Area 1, which included the waters of the inner Gulf of Maine adjacent to Maine, New Hampshire, and Massachusetts to Cape Cod. When Amendment 3 was formally adopted in January 1998, the recommendations of the lobster conservation management team for Area 1 were accepted as well. Three features of the Area 1 plan were of critical importance. First, the plan gave Area 1 jurisdiction out to 40 miles (Plante 1998c). The second was the protection of oversize lobsters from the New Brunswick border to Cape Cod. The third was protection of V-notched lobsters throughout the range of the species. Representatives from Maine fought very hard to have these measures included in Amendment 3 since they did not want the V-notch and oversize laws, which are so strongly supported in Maine, to be made illegal. Area 1's plan also included a graduated trap limit going from twelve hundred in 1998 to one thousand in 1999 to eight hundred in 2000.

In negotiating this plan, Maine's delegates got what they wanted on the whole. David Cousens, president of the Maine Lobstermen's Association, said, "the most important coup was coast-wide protection of V-notched lobsters."

However, the Maine delegation had to agree to include two provisions that were unpopular in Maine: a provision to raise the escape vent from 1⅞ inches to 1¹⁵⁄₁₆, and the 100/500 rules permitting draggers to take one hundred lobsters per day or five hundred per trip. The increase in the escape vent was opposed by many fishermen, who felt this rule would allow a large number of legal-sized lobster to escape. Many lobster fishermen feel that a law similar to the Maine law prohibiting the dragging for lobsters should be passed for the entire industry.

Despite these problems, implementation of Amendment 3 to the ASMFC Interstate Lobster Fishery Management Plan went forward rapidly. The plan was approved by the commissioners on December 12, 1997, and in January 1998, the lobster conservation management teams began their work (Plante 1998a). By October 1998, the proposals made by the lobster conservation management teams of Areas 2, 3, 4, 5, and 6 had been approved by the ASMFC Lobster Management Board. Area 1 did not have to do anything at this point, since Amendment 3 contained enough provisions to meet the management benchmark for Area 1 (i.e., V-notch, maximum size, trap limit, 1¹⁵⁄₁₆ escape vent.).

In implementing Amendment 3 and the plan for Area 1 several problems were encountered. The Downeast Lobstermen's Association and a group of Maine fishermen in the Boothbay area strongly disagreed with the provision of the Area 1 plan increasing the vent size from 1 ⅞ to 1 ¹⁵⁄₁₆ inches, arguing that it would allow a large proportion of the legal lobsters caught to escape. Despite their objections, in the spring of 1998, State Senator Jill Goldthwait and Pat White of the Maine Lobstermen's Association, ASMFC commissioners from Maine, strongly supported raising the vent size, arguing that Amendment 3 gave Maine what it wanted, namely protection of the V-notch and oversize lobsters. Failure to raise the escape vent to 1¹⁵⁄₁₆ inches would endanger all of Amendment 3, which would represent a great loss for the Maine lobster industry. In February 1998, the Maine legislature approved the 1¹⁵⁄₁₆ -inch trap-vent size to keep Maine in compliance with Amendment 3 recommendations (Amory 1999a).

A far more serious problem concerned jurisdictional authority of the ASMFC. This issue was raised when the NMFS attempted to impose its own version of trap limits on the lobster industry in contradiction to the plan advocated by the ASMFC. To be sure, there was a clear understanding that the ASMFC would take the lead in developing a lobster plan and that the NMFS would withdraw its lobster management plan and implement measures similar to those of the ASMFC in the federal zone. However, passage of the Sustainable Fisheries Act in 1996 radically changed the situation, according to NMFS officials, because it mandated that the agency rebuild fisheries that were deemed to be "overfished." And since lobster was classified as "overfished," NMFS Director Andy Rosenberg refused to withdraw the regional council's lobster plan until the NMFS was convinced that it was replaced with a plan that would "address overfishing problem" (Plante 1997c). Accordingly, it readied its own plan in 1997 and 1998, which ostensibly included a build-down to 472 traps over the course of five years. Throughout New England, large numbers of fishermen were very upset by this news, fearing that such a low trap limit would make them into part-time fishermen or put them out of business altogether. As was discussed in chapter 5, the Maine lobster industry was very much against the NMFS plan, and they came to favor the ASMFC plan. If the plan proposed by the ASMFC contained some provisions about which many were not enthusiastic (e.g., increasing the escape-vent size) it was something they could live with.

The Maine lobster industry and Maine government leaders closed ranks in opposition to the NMFS plan. The hearings that were held on the plan in the spring of 1998 saw a stream of industry leaders, officers of the DMR, and zone council members and chairs testify against the plan. Their comments were low key, to the point and, I thought, very persuasive. The ASMFC commissioners also worked hard to have the ASMFC plan adopted.

After the hearings, nothing was done for months. Finally, the National Marine Fisheries Service released its final plan in December 1999. Essentially, it endorsed the ASMFC plan (Plante 2000). Only those privy to the inner workings of the National Marine Fisheries Service know for certain why the NMFS plan was withdrawn, but almost certainly massive political opposition played a role in that decision.

Capturing the Commons

While the trap-limit issue has been settled, at least for the time being, the future could see more problems between the NMFS and the ASMFC. The two organizations have differences in management philosophy and unclear jurisdictional boundaries. A basic difference is structural. The ASMFC is empowered by the Atlantic Coastal Act, which is less strict in its requirements. The NMFS operates under the Fisheries Conservation and Management Act, and the recent update of that Act (i.e., the Sustainable Fisheries Act), which impose far stricter guidelines. These differences have led to a history of tensions between the two organizations. Senator Jill Goldthwait, one of Maine's ASMFC commissioners, said in an interview, "the NMFS is supposed to cooperate with us [the ASMFC]. But often times they just do what they want in the federal zone."

Amendment 4: Revisiting Old Problems

Maine lobster fishermen and the Maine ASMFC delegation were generally very happy with Amendment 3 because it protected V-notched lobster throughout their range, protected oversize lobsters in ASMFC Area 1, and limited the number of lobsters that could be dragged based on the 100/500 rule. Unfortunately, fishermen in other areas were not happy with these aspects of Amendment 3 and set about to change them. Specifically, the fishermen on the outer part of Cape Cod had long caught large numbers of V-notched lobsters, and the Rhode Island dragger fleet had come to rely on dragged lobsters for an increasing part of their income. Both wanted to continue their current practices.

The problem came to a head immediately after Amendment 3 was approved, when the Outer Cape Lobstermen's Association sued the ASMFC in January 1998, arguing that Amendment 3 "fails to address overfishing" (Plante 1998b). The real issue was that the plan prohibited taking V-notched lobsters.

A Massachusetts judge ruled on the Outer Cape lawsuit in 1999, and ordered the ASMFC to develop a procedure to allow different areas to develop different plans to meet the egg-production goals. The ASMFC responded with Amendment 4, which contained the idea of "conservation equivalencies." That is, it specified in great detail the various combinations of minimum size, maximum size, escape-vent size, and rate of V-notch compliance that would meet the 10 percent egg-production goal. (As we shall see in the next chapter, Amendment 4 involved a real change in the science.)

The LCMT for Area 1 was not happy with the idea of conservation equivalencies, which they believed was nothing but a ploy to allow the outer Cape fishermen to take V-notched lobsters. However, they assumed that Amendment 4, for better or for worse, was going to be adopted and began working on a plan incorporating the idea of conservation equivalencies. In the planning process, they avoided raising the minimum measure, the preferred solution of the government lobster biologists. They first voted tentatively to achieve the egg-production goals by lowering the maximum limit to 4.5 inches. Later in the spring, they came up with a plan to achieve the goals with a 100 percent V-notch compliance and a zero-tolerance

V-notch measure (that is, no lobster with any damage to the flipper would be legal).[3] Jon Carter, LCMT Area 1 chairman, explained the change, saying, "from the information we had, we saw that if you went to mandatory V-notching and zero tolerance, we were at the 10 percent goal. We didn't have to fool with the gauge." When the scientists on the technical and scientific committee determined that these measures would not meet the 10 percent egg-production goal, LCMT Area 1 voted in September to increase the escape vent from $1^{15}/_{16}$ inches to 2 inches if they failed to meet the full "10 percent egg-production goal by 2008" (Plante 2001: 1).

At the same time, the Outer Cape Lobstermen's Association developed a plan under Amendment 4 to allow its fishermen to take V-notched lobsters, with the stipulation that they agree to a rise in the legal minimum gauge, which would give them the equivalent conservation effect. (Fishermen from the outer Cape have their own ASMFC area.)

Maine lobster fishermen and their leadership were very much against the Outer Cape proposal. The Maine position is that it approved Amendment 3 with the clear understanding that V-notched lobsters would be protected in the entire range, and that oversize lobsters would not be taken from Maine down to Cape Cod. Allowing the Cape Cod fishermen to take such lobsters, they said, would not only be poor conservation, but would be in violation of a signed agreement. A more serious concern is something that remains unsaid. If the Cape Cod fishermen are allowed to take V-notch and oversize lobsters, the incentive for Maine lobster fishermen to conserve these lobsters is seriously undermined. The Cape fishermen counter all these arguments by saying that they are in a different administrative area and should have the right to set their own rules, regardless of the effects of their actions on lobsters other fishermen have conserved.

The politics of Amendment 4 were further complicated by the dragging-for-lobsters issue. The Rhode Island Marine Fisheries Council voted to rescind the 100/500 lobster limit (Rheault 2000). In 2000, they were voted "out of compliance" with ASMFC rules, which forced them to retain the 100/500 bycatch standard. In 2001, the Rhode Island ASMFC delegation responded by proposing to the ASMFC a rule that Rhode Island draggermen be permitted to drag for lobsters in state waters. The Maine lobster industry and Maine DMR officials were very much against this proposal as well. In their view, it would nullify the 100/500 rule limiting the amount of lobsters that could be taken by dragging, an important part of Amendment 3. Their sentiment against the proposed Rhode Island rule reflected strong support for the Maine law outlawing dragging for lobsters.

The debate over Amendment 4 continued throughout 2001. The amendment finally came up for a vote by the ASMFC commissioners at a meeting held in Rockport, Maine, in October 2001. Before the vote was taken, several Maine lobster fishermen spoke against the proposal, including former MLA President Eddie Blackmore who gave an impassioned speech favoring protecting the V-notched lobsters. When the final vote was tallied, Amendment 4 was defeated. The vote was three against (Maine, New Hampshire, and Connecticut) and two for the proposal (Rhode Island and Massachusetts). When I asked Pat White, one of Maine's

AFMFC delegates, why he voted against the measure, he said "We opposed harvesting V-notch lobsters and dragging for lobsters."

The defeat of Amendment 4 will not see an end of the debate over the V-notch and dragging issues. Rhode Island is planning to sue to resurrect Amendment 4, and it is likely that the Outer Cape Lobstermen's Association will do the same. The Maine ASMFC delegation believes it may have only a temporary reprieve. Pat White said, " I thought we were done with the dragging issue and the V-notch problem [when Amendment 3 passed]. Now it is right back to the drawing board."

Comparing the Regional Council and the ASMFC

Despite the problems it has encountered, the ASMFC was far more effective in producing a workable management plan (Amendment 3) than the federal governance structure had been in producing a lobster management plan. The ASMFC took eighteen months from the beginning of plan development in the summer of 1996 to final approval in December 1997. To be sure, the failure of Amendment 4 means that it is unclear exactly how the Area LCMTs can meet their various management goals, but the management plan itself is very much intact. By way of contrast, the federal governance system (that is, the NMFS and the regional council) failed to produce a plan in eighteen years.

Why was the ASMFC able to produce a workable management plan in such a short time period? One reason, of course, is that the ASMFC's Amendment 3 built on the hard-won accomplishments of the regional council and incorporated many provisions that had been a part of the previous federal plan (i.e., Amendment 5). However, the major reasons are structural. Two of the most critical factors were identified in a hearing in Portland in the fall of 1999 organized by U.S. Senator Snowe of Maine, chair of the Senate Commerce Committee's Subcommittee on Fisheries and Oceans. First, the ASMFC has more independence. Spencer Apollonio, who had been executive director of the regional council in the 1970s, said that the ASMFC decisions are not "reviewed and second guessed" by another agency, referring to the fact that the NMFS reviews and approves (or disapproves) all regional council decisions. He later pointed out, "These decisions are reviewed by NOAA attorneys who are totally removed from the debates leading to the decisions." Second, the ASMFC has a more bottom-up approach to management. Pat White, executive director of the Maine Lobstermen's Association, said that the regional council process is really "top-down management," which does not include those directly involved in the decisions (Stevens 1999). The NMFS and regional council management system is heavily influenced by draggermen who generate rules for an entire region. ASMFC lobster management decisions, by way of contrast, are made by the Lobster Management Boards with the advice of the industry LCMTs, who know the industry very well and are in a position to write what they want in a plan. The rules they devise are matched to the needs of different areas. The effect of these two management structures can be seen in the way they have treated the minimum-gauge issue. The regional council and the NMFS stubbornly spent eighteen years trying to force the industry to accept an increase in the minimum-size measure, a strategy that the Maine industry considered harmful and ineffective. It failed. The ASMFC lobster management effort is organized in a way that has allowed it to sidestep this issue. In Area 1 (Maine, New Hampshire, and Northern Massachusetts), where an increase in the minimum measure is very unpopular, the goals of management can be met by using other means. In other ASMFC areas, where raising the minimum measure is more acceptable, it will be raised to meet various management goals.

Last, the regional council operates under more legal constraints. Bill Brennan, who has considerable experience in dealing with the council and the ASMFC, wrote me saying, "The council, by law, is a far more public forum than the ASMFC and the laws and regulations ensuring the public's right to participate are, in large measure, why the council process has become so tedious. The ASMFC, on the other hand, is a far less public forum and consequently is not as constrained by administrative laws and procedures."

However, the ASMFC has its own limits that could easily result in gridlock of a different kind. The ASMFC is a creature of the states and cannot enforce any rules unilaterally. All management measures recommended by the ASMFC must be implemented through the legal administrative process in each state. In some states, such as New Hampshire, where the chief fishery administrator has authority to promulgate rules of the ASMFC, this can happen quickly. In others, where management measures must be adopted as statutes by the legislature, the process is much slower.

In the regional council, conflicts are apt to be between the council members and industry, and they can be very nasty and confrontational. In the ASMFC, where state interests are paramount, severe conflict can occur between states, as was demonstrated by the battle over Amendment 4. In the ASMFC arena, policy discussions are usually held in private, but they can be just as intense, if usually more civil.

The Right Whale Controversy

Since 1996, the lobster industry has had to contend with federal regulations to preserve endangered species. The National Marine Fisheries Service is charged under the Marine Mammal Protection Act with implementing rules to reduce mortality on all "strategic" stocks of marine mammals, which includes four species of whales in the Gulf of Maine. In addition, the right whale, which has a population of only three hundred, is listed as endangered, and is thus covered by the Endangered Species Act.

Problems began in 1996 when the state of Massachusetts was sued under the Marine Mammal Protection Act by Max Strahan, representing a conservation organization called "Greenworld," seeking to invoke the act to prevent whales from being killed by becoming entangled in lobstering gear. In September 1996, a federal judge ruled in favor of the plaintiffs and ordered Massachusetts to come up with a plan within sixty days to prevent lobster gear from harming endangered right whales (University of Maine 1996). Massachusetts complied by putting into effect a number of emergency regulations designed to protect the right whale in inshore waters where they were known to congregate. They banned the use of single lobster traps, sink gill nets, and polypropylene line; and required that all buoy lines attached to fixed gear have breakaway sections (Stevens 1997).

The efforts to protect the whales left the lobster fishing industry feeling unfairly targeted. After all, most whale mortality is caused by collisions with vessels. In 1998, Terry Stockwell of the Maine DMR confirmed that in the past twenty-five years, ten right whales had died, eight from collisions with ships and only two from becoming entangled with fishing gear. Nevertheless, they recognized that the whole industry would have to respond. They were fully aware that if Massachusetts could be successfully sued under the Marine Mammal Protection Act, other states were vulnerable as well.

In April 1997, the NMFS put out its "Atlantic Large Whale Take Reduction Plan," designed to prevent death or injury to whales by fishing gear. In the weeks that followed, the Maine Lobstermen's Association, Downeast Lobstermen's Association, the DMR, and the newly formed lobster zone councils devoted considerable time to framing the state's response to the plan (*Commercial Fisheries News* 1997a). The NMFS held hearings in which the lobster fishing industry criticized many aspects of the plan. The proposed regulations concerning breakaway gear came under special attack by many fishermen, especially those from the eastern part of the Maine coast where very strong lines are needed to fish against fast-running tides (Jones 1997a).

The NMFS modified the plan with the comments of the fishing industry in mind. Essentially, the final plan, announced in July 1997, proposed modifying gear so that it would break away from entangled whales, and forming disentanglement teams to free whales that did get tangled in fishing gear. The plan also restricted fishing in critical habitat areas, and extended the emergency regulations in these areas (i.e., Cape Cod Bay and the Great South Channel area east of Nantucket and Cape Cod) (Jones 1997a, 1997b; Plante 1997d).

The fishing industry and the DMR were generally pleased with the plan. When the NMFS announced the final whale plan, Robin Alden, the Maine DMR commissioner, described the plan as "a great day for the state's more than 7,000 fishermen and a great day for the 300 right whales remaining in the endangered species population" (Jones 1997b). Some of the conservationists, however, accused the NMFS of caving in to industry pressure. Nina Young of the Center for Marine Conservation was quoted as saying "there is nothing new that prevents entanglement. It [the plan] represents retreat" (Jones 1997b).

During the next two years, the plan went into effect. Over three hundred volunteer fishermen were trained to disentangle whales. Their training was coordinated by Glenn Salvador, hired jointly by the Maine DMR and the Center for Coastal Studies.

In the spring of 2000, the whale situation heated up again. In February 2000, a consortium of conservation groups, which had been monitoring whales, readied a report documenting the number of whale entanglements in fishing gear. A total of twenty-four whales had become entangled, including six right whales in U.S. waters. In 1999 alone, two endangered right whales died, one from being struck with a ship and a second, named "2030," from being entangled with fishing gear (Stevens 2000b). The report went on to say that current gear regulations would not prevent mortality and serious injury to the whales. They recommended the removal of "all vertical and floating lines that are capable of entangling right whales" (Stevens 2000a). This, of course, would make it impossible to use traps to take lobsters. Leroy Bridges, president of the Downeast Lobstermen's Association, said that if such regulations were enacted, "it would finish us [the lobster industry]" (Stevens 2000a).

Worse was to come. In May 2000, Max Strahan sued in Maine to protect the right whale under the Endangered Species Act (Stevens 2000d.) His demands were quite dramatic. The suit held Governor King of Maine, DMR Commissioner George La Pointe, Penny Dalton, administrator of the National Marine Fisheries Service, and U.S. Secretary of Commerce William Daley "personally liable for the environmental crimes that they have committed as employees of their respective government agencies" (Stevens 2000d). The suit requested to have the court "hold [Maine Governor] King and other defendants in contempt and fine him and the other co-defendants $100,000 per day until they prove to the court that they will no longer entangle whales and sea turtles in their fishing gear." He wanted to require Daley and the NMFS to "grant Greenworld's petition for relief to adopt an emergency regulation banning vertical buoy lines on lobster gear and gillnets" and order Governor King and the other defendants to "pay $10 million per year for 10 years to the plaintiffs so that they may implement a conservation program to increase the size of the populations of the endangered whales and sea turtles devastated by the commercial fishing activities of King and the other defendants" (Stevens 2000d). Fortunately, in December of 2000, this lawsuit was postponed due to a problem in the language used in the suit; later it was dismissed. Despite the extreme demands, it was a serious threat. Max Strahan, it must be remembered, won the suit to protect the spotted owl that forever changed the timber industry in the northwest part of the United States. The kinds of penalties he called for are entirely possible under the Endangered Species Act. The ESA is written in extreme language, and makes it mandatory for federal agencies to take all steps necessary to stop any activity that could possibly cause death or injury to one endangered animal. The costs and benefits of such actions do not need to be taken into account. If timber harvesting in the northwest can be curtailed to protect the spotted owl, the lobster industry can be forced to make radical changes to protect the right whale.

The power of the Endangered Species Act was soon demonstrated. In March 2000, the Conservation Law Foundation and Humane Society gave the NMFS sixty days notice of intent to sue under the Endangered Species Act (Stevens 2000c). They wanted the NMFS to take additional steps, including the development of safer gear, to protect the right whale. The Conservation Law Foundation and the Humane Society did file suit in federal court. In the spring of 2001, the court ruled in favor of the plaintiffs. As a result of this suit, the National Marine Fisheries Service issued four "biological opinions" calling for changes in four fisheries management plans to protect the right whale (Stevens 2001: B1). One of these was the lobster management plan for federal waters.

The NMFS is proposing new rules for the lobster industry, which were announced in September 2001. These rules included gear modifications, closed areas, and "seasonal dynamic closures," that is, rules requiring gear to be moved when whales are in the area. Moreover, these rules hold in both state and federal waters. The future may well see more restrictions, including a complete closure of certain areas where whales are known to congregate, such as Cape Cod Bay and Jeffrey's Ledge.

The response of the Maine lobster industry and the DMR was to put in place a state plan, which is strongly supported by the leadership of the DMR, Maine Lobstermen's Association, Downeast Lobstermen's Association, and Maine Gillnetters Association. This plan calls for hiring a "whale take reduction coordinator" who will oversee all efforts of volunteer fishermen and Maine Marine Patrol officers to monitor the movements of all whales in areas where fishing gear is placed. This system was developed by DMR resource coordinator Terry Stockwell, who was successful in obtaining grants to support the program from the Sea Grant Program and the National Marine Fisheries Service (Stevens 2001: B1). At this writing, it is uncertain how well this program will work. It is obvious that its degree of success will depend greatly on the willingness of fishermen to volunteer. Regardless of how well it works, the fact that a suit under the Endangered Species Act has succeeded signals a permanent change in lobstering.

Conclusion

During the course of the 1980s and 1990s the leadership of the lobster industry became fairly adept at working in the federal management arena, and they had an appreciable effect on federal lobster management policy. Nevertheless, it proved much more difficult to influence federal policy than state policy. Most of the time, the industry did not initiate changes. Rather, it responded to federal actions and tried to modify the way federal policies were implemented to make them more amenable to the industry. In the 1980s, the lobster industry could not stop all gauge increases, but they were able form a coalition with federal and state officials to stop the last two increases and to save the V-notch and oversize laws. They lobbied hard to pass the Mitchell bill. If they could do nothing about forcing the Canadians to raise their legal minimum measure as promised, the Mitchell bill ensured that small Canadian lobsters would not enter the U.S. market. In 1998 and 1999, they also worked hand in hand with officials of the Maine Department of Marine Resources and others to persuade the NMFS to endorse the ASMFC trap-limit proposal, which they saw as the lesser of two evils. In the late 1990s, lobstermen supported a program to monitor right whales using industry volunteers in the hopes that this would stave off very restrictive federal rules. They also supported moving lobster management from the regional council to the ASMFC, an organization that is having more success in managing the lobster resource. While they could not have affected this move alone, they were part of a coalition that did.

Perhaps most important, the leadership of the lobster fishermen's associations had a strong influence on the development of the lobster management plan in the 1990s. In 1992, they were able to persuade NMFS officials and the regional council to permit the industry working group (i.e., officials of the fishermen's associations) to frame a lobster management plan, which was to become Amendment 5 of the federal lobster plan. They got the NMFS to finance consultants to work out the details of that plan. While Amendment 5 was not passed as originally conceived by the industry working group, much of it was eventually ratified by the regional council and became part of the ASMFC lobster management plan (Amendment 3).

Why was it more difficult to influence federal policy? One factor is that federal scientists have had a good deal of influence over lobster management policy. They and the industry have very different conceptions about the state of the lobster stocks and how they should be managed. In addition, the federal laws affecting lobster management give federal agency officials great power to manage the stocks, and little leeway in how this will be accomplished.

CHAPTER 8

The Politics of Science

*I*n the past fifty years, lobster science has been highly politicized. At times, ideas of scientists have been judged in a cool, calm, objective atmosphere, and these ideas were either accepted or rejected by managers with political goals and realities in mind. Most of the time, scientific debates are linked with policy discussion that have been carried on in a far more public arena where various groups of scientists, administrators, and industry members have debated. The findings of scientists have influenced the discussion and the political agenda, and science has been influenced by politics. Those engaged in policy discussions are fully aware that "scientific facts" are rarely completely neutral. They tend to favor some policy positions and undermine others. How successful stakeholders are in this arena depends, in great measure, on their ability to influence what facts are presented and even to influence what the "facts" are.

We know little about the politics of science in the nineteenth century when the first laws were developed. We know much more about the scientific issues behind the development of the double-gauge law in the early decades of the twentieth century. During this period, the validity of the work of biologists Field and Herrick was apparently never seriously questioned, although it did not influence the development of legislation for a long time. The period from 1970 to the present is different. Since the passage of the FCMA in 1976, one management effort has followed another at very close intervals. The accompanying scientific debate has been constant, increasingly complicated as simulation modeling gained ascendancy, and sometimes quite unfriendly. The findings of scientists have been challenged routinely.

In the past thirty years, the politics of science have involved two factions. One is the conservative faction of state and federal biologists and their scientific allies. The second is the industry and its allies. The state and federal biologists, who devote so much of their lives to lobster research and management, put out various studies and suggested policies. These have almost invariably been contested by members of the lobster fishing industry, who have been informed by their own version of the biological facts. University biologists and social scientists have periodically entered the fray, and on some occasions, have sided with the industry.

Since the early 1970s, lobster management has revolved around two issues. One is the state of the stocks. The second is the proper way to manage stocks. This second issue, more specifically, concerned the effectiveness of the minimum gauge, the V-notch, and the oversize measure.

The politics of lobster science took place in two stages. The first stage, which began in the 1970s and lasted to the early 1990s, concerned the second question. Federal and most state biologists favored raising the minimum gauge, and became committed to undermining the industry's claims about the effectiveness of the V-notch and oversize measures. Those favoring the V-notch and oversize countered by seriously questioning the validity of federal science. This fight over the "politics of the gauge" has resulted in a series of political battles intertwined with scientific debates that have not ceased to this day.

In the second stage (early 1990s to 2001), the debate concerned both the state of the stocks and the effectiveness of changes in the gauge and the V-notch program.

Stage I: The Politics of the Gauge

THE POSITION OF FEDERAL AND STATE SCIENTISTS

Over the course of the past thirty years, state and federal biologists have remained convinced that the lobster stocks are overfished and subject to sudden collapse. As early as 1973, Jim Thomas of the Maine Department of Marine Resources wrote that the lobster "population has been at a precarious limit to ensure an adequate parent-progeny relationship or derivatives thereof along the coast of Maine" (1973b: 8). In 1978, Vaughn Anthony, who was director of research for the DMR at the time, told an audience at the Fisherman's Forum, "In the lobster fishery, the effort is increasing, and it now seems probable that our inshore lobsters are from offshore parents; this loss of seed lobsters is alarming. Coupled with this, the water temperature is cooling so stocks are apt to drop through natural causes as well." He concluded, "we could be headed for a 'crisis'—and soon" (*Maine Commercial Fisheries* 1978a: 12). The same theme is found in more recent reports. The report of the Twenty-second Northeast Regional Stock Assessment Workshop (22nd SAW) concluded that "fishing effort is intense throughout the range of the species and previous stock assessments have warned that the stock is overfished and vulnerable to collapse" (Stock Assessment Review Committee 1996: 47).

The solution, from the perspective of many biologists, is to increase the numbers of eggs produced by increasing the minimum size measure. Much of the early work supporting this point of view was done by Jim Thomas and Jay Krouse, biologists working for the Maine Department of Marine Resources. Their reasoning is that mortality is so high that only a very small proportion of female lobsters survive to a size at which they can extrude eggs. They base their conclusions on the fact that at least 90 percent of all lobsters are caught in the first year after they molt into legal sizes, when they are between 81 and 92 millimeters (at that time, the Maine legal minimum measure was 3¾₆ inches or 81 millimeters). Only 6 percent of the females are sexually mature at 81 millimeters (3¾₆ inches), whereas nearly all females are sexually mature at 98 millimeters, at least two years later (Krouse 1973). Thus, Thomas and Krouse concluded that 90 percent of female lobsters do not survive to extrude eggs even once. An increase in the legal measure to 88.9 millimeters (3.56 inches) would ensure that at least 60 percent of female lobsters would have an opportunity to extrude eggs. Thus, a small increase in the minimum size measure would greatly increase the number of eggs in the water and would have a profound effect on the future prospects for the industry. These insights strongly affected the position of most federal and state lobster biologists for more than twenty years. In 1996, the Report of the Stock Assessment Workshop states that "since over 90 percent of the landings come from lobsters within 10 to 11 mm CL of the minimum legal size," it follows that the vast majority of lobsters that are caught cannot extrude eggs (Stock Assessment Review Committee 1996: 55).

These federal and state scientists also believe that both the oversize measure and the V-notch are ineffective. Thomas (1973a: 55) said the "maximum size regulation of 127 mm [5 inches] carapace length is biologically unsound." A Maine DMR biologist said in a meeting in December 1996 that "the V-notch is not based on science." They reason that since more than 90 percent of the lobsters are caught before they can extrude eggs, the percentage that could possibly be protected by the V-notch law is very small as well. Moreover, they assert that since virtually no lobsters have survived to be 5 inches on the carapace, the oversize measure is virtually useless since it protects no lobsters. Thomas concluded that if the minimum measure were raised to 3.5 inches, "the maximum size regulation of 127 mm [5 inches] carapace length is unnecessary" (1973a: 1). These biologists buttress their findings with data from trawl surveys that turned up very few V-notch and oversize lobsters. In the 1970s and early 1980s they offered two additional indictments of the V-notch: (1) it is a voluntary program, and few fishermen really put a notch in the egg-bearing females they catch, and (2) it is a source of infection. In sum, these data have led most federal and state scientists to conclude that the minimum gauge should be increased, preferably to 3.5 inches, and that both the oversize measure and the V-notch should be abolished.

THE POSITION OF THE INDUSTRY AND ITS ALLIES

The fishermen responded by arguing that the lobster stock is in good condition, and that the reproductive stock is high. The secret of maintaining it is to protect the large, reproductive-sized lobsters, not increasing the minimum gauge.

From the perspective of the industry, a 3.5-inch measure was unacceptable because it would result in large lobsters that could not be sold competitively. A 3.5-inch minimum size would do nothing but give much of the market to the Canadians. Moreover, the 3.5-inch minimum is not necessary, from the industry point of view, since the V-notch and oversize laws are effective in conserving large lobsters that produce most of the eggs.

The difference between the position of the government lobster biologists and the industry was forcefully underscored in two conversations that I had concerning the V-notch. One well-known federal biologist told me in 1996 that the V-notch was ineffective, and that very few fishermen really V-notched many lobsters. When I asked him how many V-notched lobsters he thought there were in the Gulf of Maine, he said "No more than ten thousand." When I told this to David Cousens, president of the Maine Lobstermen's Association, he was incredulous. He said (expletive deleted) "I V-notch four thousand a year myself."

The problem was that the industry had little proof that its position was correct. However, a number of scientists took the side of the industry in these matters. Some university and government biologists argued that oversize lobsters are especially valuable since the number of eggs extruded increases exponentially with the size of the lobster (see chapter 1). A female measuring 3¼ inches on the carapace might be able to extrude five hundred eggs; one 5 inches on the carapace can extrude one hundred thousand at once. Moreover, large lobsters can extrude eggs twice on a single molt or copulation (Botsford, Wilen, and Richardson 1986; Waddy and Aiken 1986). In this, they echo the ideas of biologists John Field and Francis Herrick at the beginning of the twentieth century who advocated protecting very large lobsters, arguing that these lobsters were especially prolific. These scientists believe that protecting all lobsters over 5 inches in carapace length does a great deal to protect the breeding stock and ensure egg production.

The claims of the conservative faction of federal and state biologists regarding the desirability of raising the minimum measure were also questioned. Biologist Robert Steneck argued in the late 1980s that a raise in the legal measure was not necessary since the breeding stock was large enough and the bottleneck in lobster production was adequate habitat, not an inadequate-sized brood stock (Plante 1989a). My own studies of the economic effect of raising the minimum size measure substantiated the fishermen's claim that raising the measure would have mixed effects. This study showed that both catches and income to fishermen would decline in every year that the measure was raised incrementally, and would only result in a modest return thereafter (Acheson and Reidman 1982: 10–11.).

In order to show the effectiveness of the V-notch law, the Maine Lobstermen's Association has run V-notch surveys in which they request that fishermen collect and record data on the V-notched lobsters they catch. Dr. Robert Bayer and his students analyzed these data and concluded that "data gathered by the Maine Lobstermen's Association showed that compliance with the V-notch is very high among fishermen" and that "over 60 percent of the egg-bearing females had a V-notch" (University of Maine Lobster Institute 1995). Other studies further supported the effectiveness of the V-notch (Bayer, Daniel, and Vaitones 1985; Daniel, Bayer, and Waltz 1989). A more recent study completed in 2000 showed that the number of egged lobsters with a V-notch had grown to 80 percent (personal communication, Carl Wilson, DMR).

In addition, the idea that the V-notch is a source of infection was undermined by a study by Department of Marine Resources scientists (Maine Department of Marine Resources 1987).

The NMFS trawl data were also attacked. Dr. Robert Bayer's migration studies showed that large numbers of large lobsters migrated offshore. He argued that

Capturing the Commons

these offshore lobsters continued to produce a lot of eggs, which replenished the stock inshore, and that migration, not overexploitation, likely accounted for the absence of these large lobsters in sea samples.

Many federal and state biologists were not impressed by these arguments, since they did not see them as conclusive. Indeed, they were not. These scientists have unceasingly advocated for increasing the minimum gauge. If they have not yet succeeded in having a 3.5-inch measure adopted, they have kept the issue on the table. In 1978, a recommendation to raise the minimum measure to 3.5 inches (88.9 millimeters) was made a part of the federal lobster management plan (Northeast Marine Fishery Board 1978). Throughout the early 1980s, the regional council and NMFS attempted to make an increase in the minimum gauge to 3.5 inches the mainstay of their lobster management plan. After primary authority for lobster management was transferred to the ASMFC, most federal and state biologists still favored raising the minimum measure. As a result, an increase in the legal measure was made part of the management plans put forth by the lobster conservation management teams in all the areas. The single exception was Area 1 (inshore Maine, New Hampshire, and Massachusetts to Cape Cod) where an increase in the measure is almost unthinkable due to the massive industry opposition (Plante 1999).

As we have seen, the federal and state scientists were not able to persuade administrators and legislators to abolish the V-notch and oversize measures, and they were only able to get the minimum size increased from $3\frac{3}{16}$ inches to $3\frac{1}{4}$ inches with the passage of Amendment 2 to the regional council's fishery management plan for lobster. As we saw in chapter 7, the primary reason for their failure was the effective political campaign of the Maine lobster industry and its leaders, whose arguments had enough scientific backing to be credible.

Stage II: The Politics of Modeling

Since the early 1990s, the debate over the quality of science has taken a different direction. It has largely focused on the adequacy of the models used by the federal and state scientists.[1] Until very recently, the conservative faction of federal and state scientists remained devoted to the same policy prescriptions. They espoused an increase in the minimum size measure, and were opposed to managing the resource by using the V-notch program and oversize measures. They remained adamant that the lobster fishery was badly overexploited and subject to a crash. However, now they buttressed their arguments with data produced by the simulation model developed by scientists at the Woods Hole laboratory of the National Marine Fishery Service. Federal policy is based largely on the reports of the stock assessment workshop issued every four years and written by a committee of the top federal and state population dynamicists working with each species. These data produced by the federal model became the primary evidence informing the reports of the lobster stock assessment workshops in 1992, 1996, and 2000.

People in the industry and some university and state scientists came to have deep misgivings about the models, the science on which they are based, and the political goals of those using them. In recent years, those reservations have been shared by legislators as well.

In the eyes of the detractors of federal lobster science, there are two problems. Over the course of the past thirty years, it has become very apparent that state and federal lobster scientists cannot predict changes in lobster stocks. Since the 1970s, state and federal biologists have consistently said that the stocks were at risk, and could fall precipitously. Rather than falling, catches have risen dramatically in the boom years. Second, federal and state scientists are accused of having consistently underestimated the size of the breeding stock. Fishermen say they have never seen so many V-notched and egged lobsters. Both of these criticisms have a good deal of substance. Nevertheless, the state and federal biologists do not think their models are seriously flawed. In public at least, they admitted to very little skepticism about their models. They believe it is their duty to sound a warning about the state of the lobster stocks. After all, population dynamicists have noted many cases where increases in effort have preceded stock crashes, and there is no denying that fishing effort in the Maine lobster industry has increased greatly in the past few decades (see table 1.1). Dr. Colin Bannister, chairman of the advisory panel of the American Lobster Management Board, expressed this view well when addressing the record-high catches after the 1996 report of the stock assessment workshop was released. He was quoted as saying, "The responsibility to constrain effort is still there. What happens if the recruitment mechanism reverses? The more effort, the bigger the crash when it happens. We don't know how far down the stock can go before affecting the survival of the population." He emphasized the need for a "precautionary approach" (Plante 1996d: A10).

In the recent past, the conservative faction of lobster scientists have had a strong influence on the lobster management agenda, especially since 1996 with the passage of the Sustainable Fisheries Act. Fishermen find that maddening.

The late 1990s saw a marked change in federal lobster science and policy. First, there was a tacit admission that the V-notch and oversize law are effective in conserving the lobster. Second, there was a growing consensus among scientists, including many who worked for federal and state government, that the fishery was not as dangerously overfished as previously thought and that the reproductive stock was in reasonably good condition.

Support for the V-notch program and oversize measure have grown in the scientific community, even among federal scientists. The change became obvious with the advent of Amendment 4 incorporating the idea of conservation equivalencies. On January 8, 2001, LCMT Area 1 received the report of the lobster scientific and technical committee concerning the various combinations of minimum sizes, maximum size, V-notch percentage, and vent sizes and the various egg per recruit values associated with these measures. For example, table 4 of the technical committee report shows that 10.4 percent of the eggs produced by an unfished stock (the goal is 10 percent) could be achieved by a combination of a $1^{15}/_{16}$-vent size, a $3\frac{1}{4}$-inch minimum lobsters measure, a 73 percent V-notching rate, and a $4\frac{1}{4}$-inch maximum size; lobster measure. In short, all that LCMT1 would have to do to achieve the 10 percent goal was keep all current regulations and lower the maximum size from 5 inches to 4¼ inches (Lobster Technical Committee 2000). This report was introduced with little fanfare, but it openly admits that the V-notch and oversize measures are effective management tools. The idea of "conservation equivalencies," making use of V-notch and oversize protection, represents a major change for the federal and state biologists. Most of them are still firmly convinced that the best way to increase eggs is to increase the minimum gauge, but many have come around to admitting that the fishermen have been right on the value of the V-notch and oversize.

Another major change in federal science and policy concerns estimates of the state of the stocks. In 1996, the stock assessment committee came to the conclusion that the lobster fishery was overfished according to the 10 percent egg-production criteria (Stock Assessment Review Committee 1996: 47).

The 2000 stock assessment report is more tentative in its conclusions. No alarming predictions were made of impending disaster. The authors of the report conclude that in all areas the lobster stock is overfished according to the 10 percent egg-production criteria, more so in some areas than others. However, in all areas, they conclude that the stock is "growth overfished," but not "recruitment overfished." This means that mortality is high enough that lobsters are less than optimal weight (growth overfished), but that the spawning stock is of adequate size and the lobster resource should be able to sustain itself (i.e., not "recruitment overfished") (American Lobster Stock Assessment Sub-committee 2000: i–iv). In short, this stock assessment report, unlike some of the earlier ones, is reporting an unhealthy situation, but not a terminal illness.

After the 1996 report concluded that the lobster fishery was "overfished," the Sustainable Fisheries Act left the ASMFC no choice but to "rebuild the stock in ten years." Accordingly, Amendment 3 of the ASMFC set up a series of "benchmarks" for each area and a timetable specifying the egg-production goal each area was to reach in each (Stock Assessment Review Committee 1996: 47). After the 2000 report, the original egg-production benchmarks were retained as the goals for management. The lobster industry conservation management teams (LCMTS) began to ask, if the lobster stock isn't "overfished," why are we being asked to stick to the original schedule to rebuild the fishery?

What Changed Federal Science?

These changes in federal scientific prescriptions for lobster management are not the result of any fundamental change in the federal lobster model, but were produced by three different kinds of changes.

First, the conclusions of the stock assessment committee were influenced as much by a change in the composition of the committee as by the scientific facts presented. The 1992 and 1996 stock assessments were done primarily by committees made up of state and federal scientists in the conservative faction. After years of interacting with each other within a closed network, they had come to the conclusion that the lobster was overfished, the brood stock was in poor condition, and the solution is to raise the minimum measure. The 2000 stock assessment report was produced by a committee composed of federal and state scientists and university faculty members, including some who had been quite critical of the efforts of past stock assessment efforts.

However, the conclusions of the 2000 report are not the result of a consensus of the scientists on the committee. This report is a political document, and was produced by a committee that could not reach consensus on many issues in spite of months of negotiations. The minority reports contained in the manuscript make it clear that some of the university scientists on the committee believe the data do not support the idea that the stock is in imminent danger of collapse. The minority reports by some of the biologists from the National Marine Fisheries Service indicate that they feel the lobster stock is in a far more precarious position, and they are urging a "more precautionary approach" and more regulations (American Lobster Stock Assessment Sub-Committee 2000).

Second, the anomaly of the boom motivated some top federal scientists to re-think what controls stock sizes. They know their modeling efforts have not allowed them to accurately predict changes in stocks. They are aware that predicting a bust only to see the boom occur has hurt their credibility with the industry and others. This clearly set many of them to thinking in innovative ways.

In 1996, when I asked Dr. Michael Fogarty, a very experienced lobster biologist and modeler, to explain the boom, he said in essence that several factors were involved. He stressed the "increases in effort due to more traps, better technology, and more area being fished." He went on to say "recruitment is up, there has been a change in predator populations, the habitat has been enhanced, and water temperature has increased." He also said that "changes in the law [escape vents, increases in the minimum measure, and the V-notch program]" were having a favorable effect on egg production. He finished by saying "all of this is a way of saying, 'I don't know which of these factors is more important.'"

The anomaly of the boom also influenced the official stock assessment reports. The authors of the report of the Twenty-second Northeast Regional Stock Assessment Workshop wrote:

> The daunting question, 'Why are there so many lobsters landed?' Explaining increases in recruitment and catch after years of extremely intense fishing mortality is difficult. However, recruitment increased in the late 1980's throughout the range of the lobster, and catch is now decreasing in many areas. Some reasons offered were environmental factors, an ever-expanding fishery (e.g., longer fishing seasons, increased effort, expanding fishing areas), and decreased predation. The stock-recruit relationship is apparently quite flat. (Stock Assessment Review Committee 1996: 69)

What is most notable is the fact that the explanations of the federal and state biologists and the fishermen are starting to converge. The biologists are saying that the lobster stock is overfished, and maybe will crash, but that factors such as water temperature, predation by groundfish, habitat, the V-notch program, and others have compensated for the high amount of effort, at least temporarily, resulting in high stock levels, and good recruitment (American Lobster Stock Assessment Sub-Committee 2000: 140–83).

A third force for changing policy prescriptions was the fact that other scientists had begun to model the lobster fishery with very different results. Jim Wilson of the University of Maine School of Marine Science used a version of the federal model to show that the V-notch and oversize rules greatly affected egg production (Wilson 1997). Three years later, the lobster technical committee produced a report in connection with Amendment 4 that includes the V-notch and oversize measures as optional ways to manage the resource (Lobster Technical Committee 2000). I suspect the committee members were prodded to change their minds about the effectiveness of the V-notch and oversize measures when independent evidence was produced about these measures and conveyed to the ASMFC representatives from Maine.

Current Problems Facing Lobster Scientists

At any given time, any science has problems that must be solved if progress is to be made. At this juncture, several problems face lobster scientists; some are more intractable than others. Laura Taylor, assistant to the commissioner of the Maine Department of Marine Resources, summarized the problems facing lobster scientists in 2000 by saying, "They haven't got the models to work right. Even if they fix the model, they haven't got the right data to put into it."

MODELING

At this time, it is apparent that the models being used by federal scientists are flawed. Why doesn't the model used by federal and state scientists to assess lobster populations have better predictive value? I can identify several factors.

First, federal and state biologists do not have actual figures substantiated by research on several parameters used in the model, and the model may be very sensitive to these parameters. The two most important are growth and natural mortality. For example, biologists usually assume that natural mortality is 10 percent, but little evidence supports this figure (Conser and Idoine 1992). Real mortality might be much higher or lower, and may vary considerably from one time and place to another. If the 10 percent figure is off by any appreciable amount, this can have a substantial effect on fishing mortality estimates, which, in turn, can strongly affect the results coming out of the eggs per recruit model. The same problem exists with virtually all other parameters used in the federal model.

Second, the model does not take into account all of the factors, such as changes in temperature and predation, which can cause substantial changes in lobster populations in the juvenile and early adolescent stages.

Third, stock-recruitment models are based on the assumption that recruitment is a function of brood-stock size. Dr. Douglas Pezzack (1992) has shown that "no clear stock-recruitment relationship has been found in lobsters." In this regard, scientists in the United States have concluded that the recruitment curve is "quite flat," implying that recruitment remains constant over a wide range of stock sizes (Stock Assessment Review Committee 1996: 69). This means that large numbers of lobsters can be produced by relatively small brood stocks, and that large brood stocks can result in small amounts of recruitment if conditions are poor. It also suggests that other factors are more important in influencing recruitment than size of the breeding stock alone.

By 2000, scientists were beginning to address problems in the model. According to reports, federal scientists and administrators are aware of the deficiencies of the model and are determined to make improvements. Moreover, university scientists are beginning to look at the lobster modeling problem and are beginning to make suggests that will likely improve their predictability. Professors Robert Steneck and Cathy Castro, newly appointed members of the lobster technical committee, are arguing that additional data and variables need to be considered in the federal models, such as water temperature and changes in habitat (American Lobster Stock Assessment Sub-Committee 2000). Dr. Yong Chen, a population dynamicist employed by the University of Maine, has studied the federal models with a view toward improving them. By September 2001, he had tentatively concluded that the existing model has some very serious problems. He is proposing that a new model be developed, one that is based on "more realistic assumptions" and one that is able to incorporate more data from sources other than the federal trawl survey. In short, some very serious rethinking of the federal modeling effort is underway. These studies will almost certainly result in improvements in the model.

QUALITY OF DATA

The data going into the model come from several sources, some of dubious quality. Much of the data on the state of the stocks is derived from trawl surveys done offshore by National Marine Fisheries Service personnel. Fishermen have complained that the NMFS was under-reporting the number of reproductive-sized lobsters because few of the sites being sampled are within 20 miles of shore, where lobsters are concentrated. Carl Wilson, Maine's DMR lobster biologist and chair of the technical committee, points out that the problem is compounded by the fact that the federal trawl survey turns up very few lobsters—approximately 146 lobsters per year—which means that the parameters going into one of the federal lobster models are based on a very small sample.

By 2001, three different efforts were underway to improve the quality of the data on lobster abundance and the state of the breeding stock. The Department of Marine Resources is doing a coast-wide inshore trawl survey financed by DMR and the Northeast Consortium (Sea Grant). A sea sampling survey is being done under the supervision of Carl Wilson of the DMR using monies provided by the U.S. congress obtained by U.S. Senator Olympia Snowe. Still a third is being done by Thistle Marine Company, using funds from the NMFS and the Maine State Technical Foundation to hire fishermen to record data using electronic log books.

Lobster fishermen have long been concerned about the quality of data being used by the federal scientists. They have strongly supported efforts to improve the data. The Maine zone councils have helped to ensure that gear is removed from the areas where the inshore trawl survey will take place. Fishermen are directly involved in collecting data for the other two surveys.

Preliminary data coming from the DMR trawl survey strongly suggest that the National Marine Fisheries Service has severely underestimated the size of the reproductive stock due to the sampling locations selected and the technology used. In February 2001, Carl Wilson reported that the trawl survey completed in one location in eastern Maine turned up only twenty egged lobsters out of a total of seven hundred landed, a very low number. However, he said that he was on a boat fishing nearby that found three hundred egg-bearing lobsters in the three hundred traps hauled. These results suggest that egged lobsters do not turn up in large numbers in trawls, but are caught in large numbers in traps, which may be sampling different habitats. If this is any indication, the NMFS scientist have underreported the population of egged lobsters because they are using a technology that is not sampling habitats where lobsters are concentrated.

Goals of Management

The 10 percent egg-production goal has long been criticized. Several scientists have made the point that fish stocks cannot be assessed adequately using a single index, and that if we had to pick one, eggs per recruit is the wrong one. University of Maine biologist Robert Steneck said "we are not meeting the 10 percent egg-production goal, which means we must rebuild the stock in ten years. But how do you rebuild the stock from record-high levels?"

What should the goals of management be? There is serious talk in the ASMFC lobster board about supplanting the 10 percent egg-production goal with other means of assessing the goals of management. In the spring of 2001, four optional "reference points" were under discussion. Using several different means to assess the state of the fishery will undoubtedly result in a good deal of lively discussion in the lobster technical and scientific committee and in the ASMFC itself.

Politics and the Interpretations of Biologists

Several different kinds of social and cultural factors also influence the quality of the science. Government agencies and their scientists can be notoriously secretive about their activities. Position papers are often kept in house, and the data and models used in lobster management are guarded closely.

Much of the work on which lobster management (and fisheries management in general) is based is never published in scientific journals and consequently never subject to peer review. Scientists in the National Marine Fisheries Service and the states often are not involved in the critical give and take of the publishing process that helps to improve the quality of academic papers and ensures that the worst work is not published at all.

In addition, some state and federal scientists become wedded to their models and scientific findings and the science behind them. They often work on the same model or problem for years on end. In some cases, their entire career is tied up with a particular line of research and the policies stemming from it. Several have devoted much of their careers to furthering the cause of increasing the minimum gauge. Devoting one's career to furthering a policy does not lead to the kind of skepticism and open-mindedness that produces the best science.

Last and most important, lobster science has become heavily politicized. This is not to suggest that lobster biologists are dishonest or crooked. In fact, they are bright, well educated, and devoted to saving the species. The basic problem is that there is a high degree of uncertainty in the science. This means that results of models and other studies are open to a wide range of interpretations. That is, scientists can legitimately interpret the data in several different ways. The interpretation they choose can be strongly influenced by political considerations. One example will demonstrate the point. Between 1997 and 1999, the lobster technical and scientific committee devoted much of its time to the problem of Long Island Sound. The essence of the issue was that if the federal model were applied without change to Long Island Sound, fishing effort would have to be drastically cut because egg-production figures in that area were a long way from the 10 percent egg-production goal. As a result, representatives from states bordering on the Sound devoted considerable time to attacking the parameters used in the model. Their message was that Long Island Sound was different, and thus the same assumptions about lobster size at sexual maturity, mortality, and the like could not be used there. There is no question that the data could be legitimately interpreted as they said. However, there is little doubt that the motive to change the parameters used in the model was political and economic.

Politics and the Interpretations of Fishermen

On the whole, fishermen have been very astute observers of the lobster and ocean, and some of their conclusions about the causes of stock fluctuations have a lot of merit, as we saw in chapter 6. However, it is very clear that some of their interpretations are influenced by political interpretations as well. The "poverty gauge" and "culturing hypothesis," the most popular arguments advanced by the fishermen for the bust, are excellent cases in point.

Why do large groups of fishermen espouse ideas that are demonstrably false? Part of the reason is that these ideas have a strong ideological component, and have practical value in the political arena (Geertz 1973).

The poverty-gauge hypothesis asserts that the bust of the 1920s and 1930s was due in large part to a very large gauge that made it impossible for fishermen to keep most of the lobsters they caught. The idea of the poverty gauge apparently gained widespread popularity in the late 1960s and early 1970s as a means of countering pressure from biologists to raise the minimum legal size. Raising the minimum gauge was very unpopular with most members of the Maine lobster industry, and the poverty-gauge myth found favor as a means of demonstrating that large gauges could be very damaging. It is still used in this way by many members of the industry when the topic of increasing the gauge is broached. Jim Thomas, who did a lot of work on lobsters in the 1960s and 1970s for the DMR, said that he never heard the poverty-gauge idea raised until the early 1970s when the idea of raising the gauge was first proposed.

The culturing hypothesis was advanced as a cause of the bust long after that event was over. The basic idea behind this explanation is that fishing activity does more good than harm to the size of the stock because lobsters depend on the bait in traps for a high proportion of their food. My interviews suggest it is popular among those wishing to counter the idea that high fishing pressure automatically causes disaster. One fisherman wrote: "We have a great stock of lobsters on bottom due to the fact of their getting fed daily. Reason is the amount of bait being dumped to the bottom by fishermen hauling gear! If the law is passed to lower the limit of traps to 472 by 2003, Maine as a unique state will collapse."

CHAPTER 9

Conclusion

*T*he Maine lobster fishery is one of the world's most successful fisheries. It is distinguished by a sense of stewardship, political support for conservation rules, and effective fisheries conservation legislation. In these respects, it is different from most other fisheries in the industrialized world.

At root, what differentiates this industry is an ability to solve a whole series of collective action dilemmas. Members of the industry have been very effective in organizing themselves to lobby for legislation with the state government to obtain rules they wanted, and they have had some success in influencing the federal fisheries management agencies, including the National Marine Fisheries Service, New England Regional Fisheries Management Council, and the Atlantic States Marine Fisheries Commission. In other cases, where the government would not or could not act, lobster fishermen have been able to generate rules on an informal basis. Some harbors have provided themselves with informal trap limits. All over the state, fishermen have been able to coordinate efforts to defend territories. In all cases, they have had to overcome a strong tendency for people to free ride on the efforts of others.

Talking about collective action dilemmas in general obscures the fact that four different arenas are involved. Each arena has different organizational characteristics and poses different kinds of collective action problems which have been solved with different degrees of success. One is the arena of the government of Maine, where groups of fishermen at the community level and industry factions and units of the state government have fashioned rules. The rules established are the result of a conscious, deliberate, and completely legal effort—a "visible hand" process. Another is the level of the local harbor gang, where informal rules are developed purposefully. Still a third arena is the informal territorial system, where rules are the result of an "invisible hand" process, unplanned by anyone. In this arena, the rules that have evolved are the result of an accidental aftereffect of competition. The final arena is that of the federal government, involving a bewildering array of federal and state agencies, fishermen's lobbying groups, legislatures, and the United States Congress. In this arena, fishermen can do little more than react to initiatives of others, and their efforts to solve collective action dilemmas have been far less successful.

Data on the Maine lobster industry will allow us to make contributions to three different bodies of theory. First, the Maine lobster case allows us to add to our understanding of collective action dilemmas in general. The data that are most applicable here are those concerning the ways that people generated rules informally and at the state level. Second is a body of theory concerning threat systems, and the relevant data concerns the territorial system. The third is a body of theory about resource management. Data concerning all four arenas bear on management issues, but data on the federal level are of special importance.

Collective Action Dilemmas and Establishing Rules

Scholars interested in the new institutionalism have developed a large body of theory to account for the generation of rules and institutions. One theme in the literature concerns the prerequisite conditions that are conducive to collective action. The emphasis is on the characteristics of groups and resources that are likely to give rise to rules and institutions (E. Ostrom 2000a; 2000b). Another body of theory has been developed on the mechanisms by which rules are generated, which focuses on the types of interactions between people that give rise to rules and norms (e.g., Knight 1992; Lewis 1969; North 1990a; Sugden 1986). These interactions can be modeled as different types of games. Still another concern is the historical aspects of developing rules (see, for example, Axelrod 1986; Bates et al. 1998). Some scholars have contributed primarily to one of these sets of ideas; others, such as Douglass North, to several. I argue that all of these perspectives are necessary if we are to understand the development of rules to manage the lobster. I will cover each of these bodies of theory separately and then bring them together in the final section entitled "The Evolution of Rules and a Conservation Ethic in the Lobster Industry."

PREREQUISITE CONDITIONS NECESSARY TO DEVELOP INSTITUTIONS

Scholars interested in delineating the background circumstances allowing groups to devise institutions informally assume that if the right combination of characteristics is present, the probability is high that rules can be produced by groups working independently of the government. Implicit in this analysis is the idea that rules or norms result from a number of variables working in tandem. No single variable alone will result in the production of norms. A number of other people who have attempted to understand the conditions under which groups are able to generate rules have come to a similar conclusion, including Libecap (1995), E. Ostrom (1990: 90; 1999a; 2000b: 138), Pinkerton and Weinstein (1995: 178ff), and Wade (1994: 215–16).

The efforts of many of these scholars have gone into developing a number of lists of variables that, they argue, give rise to informal or "decentralized" rules to manage common pool resources. While there is some overlap in the lists, many variables mentioned by one analyst do not match those of others. Agrawal (2000) points out that Wade (1994), E. Ostrom (1990), and Baland and Platteau (1996) have contributed the most important analyses in this body of literature. He concludes, "but the most significant issues of method stem from the sheer number of conditions that seem relevant to the successful management of common-pool resources. Wade, Ostrom, and Baland and Platteau jointly identify 36 important conditions. On the whole there are relatively few areas of common emphasis among them. If one compares across their list of conditions, interprets them carefully, and eliminates the common conditions, 24 different conditions are still to be found" (Agrawal 2000: 16). Whether it will be possible some day to develop a list of factors that everyone agrees are responsible for the generation of rules is debatable. Among these scholars there is a consensus that the generation of rules is very complicated, and that the problem cannot be reduced to a simple elegant solution.

Elinor Ostrom, who has done as much thinking as anyone about the evolution of norms and rules, recently produced the following list of variables affecting the ability to cooperate to produce rules:

> the type of production and allocation functions; the predictability of resource flows; the relative scarcity of the good; the size of the group involved; the heterogeneity of the group; the dependence of the group on the good; common understanding of the group; the size of the total collective benefit; the marginal contribution by one person to the collective good; the size of the temptation to free ride; the loss to cooperators when others do not cooperate, have a choice of participating or not; the presence of leadership; past experience and level of social capital; the autonomy to make binding rules; and a wide diversity of rules that are used to change the structure of the situation.(E. Ostrom 2000b: 148)

She goes on to list five design principles for "Self-organized Resource Regimes": (1) "the presence of clear boundary rules," (2) "that local rules in use restrict the amount, timing, and technology of harvesting the resource; allocate benefits proportional to required inputs; and are crafted to take local conditions into account," (3) "that individuals affected by a resource regime can participate in making and modifying their rules,"(4) "that resource regimes select their own monitors, who are accountable to the users or who are users," (5) "use graduated sanctions that depend on the seriousness and context of the offense" (E. Ostrom 2000b: 148–51). Many of these variables are involved in the production of rules for the lobster industry.

The problem with this approach to the production of rules is that it does not make clear how those rules come about. As Esther Mwangi says of this school, "The issues concerning why and how institutions change are neglected while the beginning and end points in institutional evolution are overemphasized" (Mwangi 2001). The problem of the production of rules has been approached by another group of scholars concerned with the mechanism of social change.

Capturing the Commons

Another group of scholars has focused on the mechanisms that bring about rules. They have studied the interactions or relationships that provide incentives for people to agree to constrain themselves. The most important mechanisms are those proposed by North and Alchian, Lewis and Sugden, and Knight. All of these theorists assume that change stems from the rational actions of individuals, and that the development of rules or norms will generate mutual benefits. Beyond that, their analyses differ greatly.

North and Alchian: Competitive Selection. Douglass North (1990a; 1990b) and Armen Alchian (1950) see norms as emerging from voluntary contracts to facilitate exchange. They assert that when people can benefit from an exchange, they must agree on the terms by which that exchange will take place, including rules guaranteeing the compliance of both parties and the sanctions that will be imposed if either party reneges on their duties toward the other. The rules embodied in contracts can benefit both parties even though they are engaged in a prisoner's dilemma interaction. Over the course of time, it is widely recognized that these contracts give superior results, and thus they are adopted widely. In time, they become norms and institutions.

According to North (1990a: 86), institutional change ultimately results from changes in prices. When the price of technology, information, enforcement, or production changes, the parties to an exchange may decide that they can do better with a new contract. Sometimes they can negotiate a new contract within existing norms. In other cases, negotiating a contract may necessitate changing or ignoring more basic norms or structural principles upon which the contracts depend.

New institutions come into being as a result of competitive selection. Individuals choose to enter into contracts with the goal of overcoming high transaction costs. As a result, they select those organizational forms that reduce the cost of getting the information necessary for negotiating an agreement, negotiating the exchange, and enforcing the exchange. These choices produce a range of organizations. The kinds of organizations that prevail in the long run depend on relative efficiency. Competition will drive out of existence those organizations that are inefficient and thus less profitable, a theme that was first found in the work of Alchian (1950), and later echoed in the early work of North (1990a). The organizations that survive provide maximum joint benefits for those involved in the exchanges, as well as an efficient use of resources for the society.

Lewis and Sugden: The Theory of Social Conventions. According to David Lewis and Robert Sugden, the need to coordinate activities gives rise to norms, which are, in essence, social conventions. Lewis and Sugden assume that all actors have an equal amount of power and are involved in a coordination game. Under these conditions, all actors would prefer to cooperate because cooperation provides better outcomes than any non-cooperative solution. In a pure coordination game, "a coincidence of interest predominates" (Lewis 1969: 14). A good example of a social convention is driving on one side of the road. Equally good results can be had from a rule specifying that everyone will drive on either the right or the left. Failure to agree on one or the other will result in bad outcomes in the form of high collision rates.

It presumably would be relatively easy for the parties to recognize what the rule should be if only one equilibrium or solution exists in the game. If two or more solutions are available, the actors might enter into an agreement to select one of them. If they cannot do this, the actors will seize on any salient information in their environment to aid in selecting one of the available solutions. Over a period of time, some of the actors focus on one solution and the others emulate them, which gradually establishes a convention (Sugden 1986: 73). Once the convention is established, it will tend to be self-reinforcing, since no actor can better his own position by defecting from it (Knight 1992: 99).

Knight: Conflicts over Distribution of Resources. Jack Knight (1992) argues that norms come into being as an aftereffect of strategic conflict over assets and rewards. He begins with the assumption that the goal of actors is to attain a reward; rules are created to facilitate that goal. That is, rules rarely distribute rewards equally; they often result in parties or groups gaining differential rewards. In some cases, people are fully aware of this and consciously lobby and maneuver to create rules that will give them a distributional advantage. In other cases, rules are generated as the unplanned byproduct of a struggle over rewards, or of attempts to resolve conflicts over rewards. In both cases, the goals of actors are to obtain resources; the rules that emerge facilitate this goal.

The rules are created through a process of negotiation. The parties involved have different amounts of power in the negotiations because they have different assets. The actors with more assets have a distinct advantage in the negotiations because they are in a position to accept more risk, because they have more withholding power, and because people are less willing to sanction them if they violate a norm. As a result, the rules that result from negotiation sessions are apt to favor the more powerful; the less powerful have no option but to accept those rules since they cannot do better (Knight 1992: 128). If the creation of a rule is the result of a centralized, collective decision-making process, the resulting rule will reflect the asymmetries in the actors' resources. That is, we would expect those with more resources to succeed in negotiating the establishment of a rule beneficial to themselves.

If the norms come about via an informal or "decentralized" process, we would expect a different sequence of events to occur. Over time, actors with more resources will be able to resolve negotiations in ways favorable to themselves. Others with similar resources will be able to do the same, establishing a pattern. As people recognize that they are dealing with someone with superior resources, they will adjust their strategies to achieve their own best outcomes. In time, they will alter their strategies to converge on a particular outcome, thus establishing a norm.

Of these three theories, only Knight's will help to explain the development of a large number of rules and institutions. Virtually all of the interactions and negotiations leading to the development of rules for the lobster industry involve conflicts over who is going to get the lobster resource. The theory of *social conventions* is only useful in explaining the development of one rule, namely the escape vent.

In the last analysis, it is difficult to make the case that *competitive selection* can explain any rules or institutions. North's theory might be used to explain the decision to transfer control of lobster management in the federal zone from the New England Regional Fisheries Management Council to the ASMFC. The fact that the ASMFC was able to produce an acceptable lobster management plan in eighteen months when the NEFMC could not do so in eighteen years might be interpreted as an instance in which a less efficient organization was supplanted by a more efficient one. However, there are problems with this interpretation. Neither the NEFMC nor the ASMFC are especially efficient organizations. If the NEFMC is hampered by federal rules concerning public hearings and oversight by the National Marine Fisheries Service, the ASMFC must contend with interstate rivalry and the fact that none of its rules is enforceable without being ratified by all of the states involved.

Moreover, efficiency was not the motivation to switch governance of the lobster industry to the ASMFC. The change was motivated by the fact that the NMFS was in a financial bind, and because of the desire of industry and the state directors for more influence on the policy process.

KEY VARIABLES IN THE PRODUCTION OF RULES

A number of variables play some role in producing both formal and informal rules for the lobster industry, but a few appear to be of crucial importance.

First is the existence of *distribution fights*. Virtually every lobster conservation or management rule came about as a result of a fight between various factions over control of the resource. Chapter 2 documents the rules stemming from competition over productive fishing areas.In chapter 4, we saw that the first size limits and the prohibition on taking egg-bearing females came about during the course of a vicious fight between the canners, who wanted rules allowing them to take any size lobster, and the live-lobster industry, which wanted rules to conserve lobsters until they reached "dinner lobster" size. The double-gauge law was the result of a struggle between the fishermen in the western part of the state, who were allied with the dealers and Commissioner Crie, against fishermen in the eastern part of the state. What was at stake here was control over export, with the fishermen in the west wanting to increase exports of lobsters to other Atlantic coast states, while fishermen in the east wanted to prevent an avalanche of imported lobsters from Canada, which they feared would lower the prices they received. The motive to pass a trap limit (chapters 3 and 5) was a desire on the part of fishermen with small and medium-sized operations to increase their catches and incomes by establishing rules to constrain those with large numbers of traps. In chapter 5, we saw that the recent zone boundary disputes were rooted in a conflict over access to productive lobster bottom, while the struggle over the limited-entry rules was fought over who would get access to the lobster at all. Chapter 6 described the decades-long resistance of the Maine lobster industry to efforts to increase the minimum size measure to 3.5 inches, which was rooted in the fear that such an increase would result in an increased share of the market going to other jurisdictions, including Canada. The conflict between Maine and the outer Cape Cod lobster fishermen concerned whether V-notched lobsters will be conserved, as was agreed in Amendment 3 of the ASMFC, or whether fishermen south of Cape Cod will be permitted to take them. Every one of these issues involved a dispute over rules that would have a differential effect on people's income. It would not be far wrong to say that rules in the lobster industry are the result of distributional issues. Again, the two exceptions are the escape-vent law and the V-notch program.

The second crucial factor influencing the generation of both informal and formal rules in the lobster industry is *political entrepreneurship*. None of the informal rules or conservation laws were put in place without some person, or a very small group, mustering support in the industry and/or lobbying officials. These individuals often had to work for long periods to change the values and attitudes of large numbers of people. Such people as Sonny Sprague, Oscar Simpson, and Alfred Stanley worked for years to negotiate informal trap limits on the islands where they live. Biologist Francis Herrick and Commissioner Horatio Crie were instrumental in obtaining support in the industry and legislature for the double-gauge law that was finally passed in 1933, after decades of discussion and debate. MLA President Eddie Blackmore and DMR Commissioner Spencer Apollonio lobbied mightily for the escape-vent law of 1978; and Blackmore lobbied against the increase in the minimum gauge in 1985. It is very unlikely that the zone management law or the concept of effort management teams and lobster conservation management teams of Amendment 3 of the ASMFC would have come about if people such as Commissioner Robin Alden, Commissioner Bill Brennan, and MLA Executive Director Pat White had not changed people's ideas about co-management. While only a few scholars have stressed the importance of political entrepreneurship in overcoming collective action problems, it appears to be a key variable in the Maine lobster industry. Russell Hardin (1982: 35–37) argues that entrepreneurs must be present if latent possibilities are to be turned into rules. Miller (1992) and Kuhnert (2001) echo this theme.

A third factor behind the production of rules is a *low discount rate*. A low discount rate refers to the fact that people have a long-term perspective and are willing to sacrifice to maintain the lobster resource in the long run. Without this interest in conserving the resource for the future, no conservation rules will be developed. Nevertheless, this factor has not received much attention from theorists. A few exceptions, including E. Ostrom (1990: 34–37, 188, 206–209; 1998: 2–4; 2000a: 34) and Singleton (1998: 24), stress that people's willingness to sacrifice present harvest levels for future gain increases with their dependence on the resource in question.

A low discount rate, however, is not a variable such as group size or heterogeneity. It is a summary statement about the values of a group of people, which is the result of their experience and prospects for the future.

In the lobster fishery, people have come to assume that reasonable numbers of lobsters will be available in the future. Not only have catches been remarkably steady since 1947, but the territorial system has worked to control entry into the industry, especially on the perimeter-defended islands, so that established fishermen are assured that they will not have to share their largesse with new entrants. The new zone limited-entry rules have further raised the barriers to new entrants. Under these conditions, one can afford to sacrifice present catches for future gains (E. Ostrom 1990: 34–35). Conservation rules make less sense if future returns are more problematic due to the probability of stock failure or actions of other fishermen.

Ironically, this long-term perspective includes memories of the bust period. Older fishermen, especially, are very aware of the disastrously low catches that occurred in the 1920s and 1930s, and they are convinced that some of the conservation efforts put in place since that time have helped to prevent a reoccurrence. Their support for the V-notch and oversize measures stems in part from such concerns, along with their support for law enforcement. Vivid memories of the bust also give rise to a *sense of mutual vulnerability,* which motivates fishermen to cooperate now.

CENTRALIZED VERSUS DECENTRALIZED SOLUTIONS TO
COMMUNAL ACTION DILEMMAS

Social scientists appear to consider "centralized" and "decentralized" solutions to communal action dilemmas as very different phenomena. Rules generated by the state are normally studied by political scientists, while those produced informally (decentralized) are in the purview of anthropology and sociology. However, the case of the Maine lobster fishery points out that the circumstances surrounding the production of both have many similarities (see table 9.1).

As we saw in chapter 3, the variables allowing the small, perimeter-defended islands to produce trap-limit rules informally included bargaining over distributional issues, small size, perimeter-defended territoriality, limited-entry rules, a low discount rate, high dependence on the resource, a homogenous fishing population, a sense of community and social capital, and political entrepreneurs.

Some, but not all, of these same variables lie behind the production of rules at the state and federal level. Most of the formal rules came about when political entrepreneurs from the industry associations or legislature were able to negotiate solutions to distributional conflicts. In the industry as a whole, there is a moderately low discount rate. In harbor gangs most people know everyone in the gang at least by reputation, and they have a good idea about who can be trusted and who is likely to cause problems. One thinks twice about violating rules when one is likely to be caught, when that will mean alienating long-standing friends and work groups whose opinion one values and upon whom one is dependent for help in emergencies. Last, the interaction in harbor gangs is intense enough to facilitate consensus on laws that members would like the legislature and zone councils to pass.

However, the industry as a whole lacks many of the characteristics that help the fishermen on small islands to develop rules for themselves. The industry is quite heterogenous. Most fishermen, especially in the western part of the coast, come from communities with relatively little dependence on the lobster resource, and with no effective means of limiting entry into the industry. In these areas, harbor gangs do not have exclusive ownership over much lobster bottom. Few mainland harbor gangs have developed much social capital or a strong sense of community. Even so, there are striking similarities between the characteristics of the small islands, where decentralized rules are devised, and the characteristics of the industry as a whole, where dependency on centralized rules is the norm (see table 9.1).

It is the prerequisite conditions that make it possible to generate rules informally, that is, to produce "decentralized" solutions. If the community is small and homogeneous, with a strong sense of community, and the harbor gang can keep interlopers from taking the lobsters in their area, then political entrepreneurs will have a high probability of being able to persuade other members of their harbor gang that enforcing local rules is in their own best interests. If those prerequisite conditions are not present, then political entrepreneurs have no other recourse than to approach the legislature or other formal body to establish those rules.

It might take very little for a group that had been trying to obtain a rule informally to turn to the legislature. The factors motivating them to take either approach are largely the same. In this sense, the state is a substitute for the kinds of social characteristics that would allow people to generate rules informally.[1]

Is there a single prerequisite variable that can be considered the most important in making possible the production of rules at the informal level? If we can judge by the data in chapter 3 on the factors producing informal trap limits, no single variable stands out. Small size is certainly important in the production of trap-limit rules in that it facilitates monitoring and enforcement. Taylor and Singleton argue that groups with a strong sense of community are apt to be able to solve their "CAP [collective action problem] endogenously," and some of these islands do have a strong sense of community (1993: 204–205). However, boundaries and limits on entry play an even more important role. There would be no sense in having a local trap-limit rule if the benefits went to free riders (i.e., fishermen from other harbors who did not make the sacrifice).

The advent of the trap-limit law provides an excellent example of the ways in which formal rules come about in the aftermath of a failure to produce rules informally. In chapter 3, I argued that informal trap limits were essentially the product of a distribution battle between fishermen with a lot of traps and fishermen with small and medium-sized operations who wanted rules to constrain the "big fishermen." However, these informal trap limits only came into being on a few islands with a number of prerequisite characteristics. Even though the majority of the lobster fishermen in the mainland harbors of the state could have benefitted by a trap-limit rule, they had to wait decades before the leadership of the Maine Lobstermen's Association could persuade the legislature to act on trap limits.

Formal rules can also come about through the erosion of informal rules and practices. For example, when Swan's Island and Monhegan found that traditional

Table 9.1
Summary of Variables Involved in Producing Decentralized and Centralized Rules

Decentralized	Centralized
Distribution conflicts	Distribution conflicts
Political entrepreneurship	Political entrepreneurship
Very low discount rate	Low discount rate
Small-sized gangs	Moderate-sized gangs
Perimeter-defended areas and limited entry	Nucleated areas and little control on entry
Strong sense of community and much social capital	Low sense of community and moderate amounts of social capital
High dependence on resource	Moderate dependence on the resource
High level of homogeneity	Moderate heterogeneity

means of protecting lobstering area were no longer sufficient, they lobbied the legislature to pass laws, which effectively help them maintain their traditional areas and self-imposed trap limits. Another example is afforded by the erosion of informal barriers to entry and lack of mechanisms to limit the number of traps. In order to deal with burgeoning numbers of fishermen and massive escalation of trap numbers, the industry began calling for limited-entry and trap-limit laws. The eventual result was the zone management law.

ENVIRONMENTAL KNOWLEDGE AND
COLLECTIVE ACTION PROBLEMS

In addition to all of the usual problems encountered in generating rules to overcome collective action problems, the situation in Maine presented some unusual obstacles. A good deal of empirical research indicates that it is easier to devise rules to conserve common pool resources when the factors controlling stock size are well understood (Dolsak and Ostrom in press). This means that a key to understanding the solution of collective action problems is knowledge about the environment. Humans are capable of learning a great deal about their environment and can manage it well. Unfortunately, they can also misunderstand their environment and make serious errors in managing it.

The Maine lobster industry provides examples of both incredible insight and serious errors in understanding the environment and ways to manage it. Fishermen have insisted for several decades that the V-notch and the oversize measure were effective in conserving the lobster. They are probably right. Only in 2000 have federal and state biologists come around to this point of view, and not all of them are convinced yet. However, many members of the industry are convinced that the bust was caused by the poverty gauge and the lack of bait in the water (i.e., the culturing hypothesis). These ideas are almost certainly wrong.

There is nothing unusual about this situation. Anderson observes that "folk beliefs are a melange of truth and inaccuracy" (1996: 101). "It is a major task, there-fore, to seek out ecologically sensible practices and knowledge from the mixture of superstition, beliefs and folk-science." However, it does underline the problems people have acquiring accurate information about a very complex environment.

Both Bennett (1976: 253) and Wilson (2001) trace the difficulties in identifying correct solutions to environmental problems to a lack of understanding of the feedback mechanisms in socio-ecological systems. Another source of error is that the lessons of the past may be forgotten by later generations. Both authors stress that separating fact from fantasy poses major difficulties for humans.

This suggests that a major impediment for humans seeking to solve collective action problems concerning natural resources is the tremendous difficulty we have in understanding the socio-ecological environment. This problem deserves a good deal more research.

CASCADING COLLECTIVE ACTION DILEMMAS

Solving one collective action dilemma often involves the solution of others. Two different kinds of phenomena are involved. First, in some circumstances one can-not solve one collective action dilemma until others are solved first. (In the litera-ture this is usually referred to as a first-order, second-order, etc. "free-rider prob-lem" [Hechter 1990: 246] or "collective action problem.") The result is a cascade of rules in which the solution of one problem depends on the prior solution of oth-ers. In chapters 2 and 3, we saw how informal trap limits could only be devised in those few island communities that had devised strict limited-entry rules, while also having perimeter-defended areas. The perimeter-defended areas, in turn, could not be maintained unless political teams could be organized to defend those boundaries. Each one of these types of problems could not be solved unless peo-ple overcame the tendency to free ride on the efforts of others and devised rules to constrain themselves. Fishermen could informally devise trap-limit rules only after two previous collective action dilemmas had been solved. Organizing the po-litical team for boundary defense is a first-order collective action dilemma; devis-ing limited-entry rules and boundaries is a second-order collective action di-lemma; devising the trap-limit rules is a third-order collective action dilemma.

Second, in other circumstances, solving one collective action dilemma passes on externalities to other people, who, in turn, demand rules to solve the problem created by the first rule. This can create another type of cascade. For example, chapter 5 describes the way in which trap limits were created by Maine's new zone councils, which passed costs on to the "big fishermen" and benefited the "small fishermen." The big fishermen, in turn, demanded rules to constrain the small fishermen. The result was limited-entry rules passed by the zone councils and rules to limit the speed with which small fishermen could add to their trap num-bers. However, limited entry could not be effective if people could fish in the wa-ters of other zones. Thus, Commissioner LaPointe of the DMR promulgated the so called "49/51 percent rule." This, in turn, caused conflicts over boundaries, which were only solved in 2000 and 2001 by the zone councils and the DMR negotiating "buffer zones." No doubt, the buffer zones will cause problems for some groups of fishermen, who will demand still other rules to solve them.

EVOLUTION OF RULES AND A CONSERVATION ETHIC IN THE LOBSTER INDUSTRY

One of the most remarkable features of the Maine lobster industry is its strong conservation ethic. Fishermen are genuinely concerned with the state of the resource, and have supported legislation to conserve that resource and efforts to enforce those laws. Under the right conditions, as we saw in chapter 3, some groups of fishermen have been able to generate rules informally. It is this sense of stewardship that separates the lobster fishery from so many others.

How did this sense of stewardship come into being? I argue that it represents a genuine cultural change that occurred as a result of technological, biological, historical, and social factors interacting and reinforcing each other over the course of much of the twentieth century. To be sure, the conservation ethic has an ideological element. Like all aspects of culture, the conservation ethic is a set of ideas that exist in the symbolic realm (Geertz 1973). However, changes in this cultural system are the result of long-term experience of people in the industry. It is a very practical adaptation to the world in which they live. It is also part of an evolutionary process, in which the people of the lobster fishery are reacting to and affecting the environment in which they exist.

Rational choice theorists argue that the nature of the resource and the technology in use themselves can affect the development of rules (E. Ostrom 2000a; Schlager, Blomquist, and Tang 1999). Certainly, technology and biology have made it easier to manage the lobster fishery than other fisheries. Lobsters can be brought to the surface and returned to the water without harm. Moreover, one can see the reproductive status of lobsters. Eggs attached to the belly of a female lobster are obvious to all. In addition, lobster traps are highly selective. What this means is that a lobster trap can be pulled to the surface where the legal-sized lobsters can be retained while the illegal ones (juveniles, egged females, oversized, and V-notched lobsters) can be selected out and released unharmed. By way of contrast, fin-fishing technology is far less selective. A very high percentage of the fish caught come aboard dead, either smothered in the cod end of a net or killed by a burst swim bladder. Even if fin-fishermen wanted to return egged females to the water, they would have difficulty selecting out an appreciable percentage of such females.

Moreover, *social and organizational factors* of the lobster fishery should make it relatively easy to enforce rules once they are in place. After all, the entire Maine lobster industry is organized into small harbor gangs whose members have interacted over long time periods, who are dependent on each other, and who know who can be trusted. Individuals can monitor each other's behavior relatively easily. All of these factors make defection from norms less advisable, and facilitate sanctioning people who do (E. Ostrom 1990; 2000a; 2000b). In addition, the lobster industry is relatively homogenous. Even in mainland harbor gangs, lobster fishermen all use boats in a narrow size range with much the same electronic gear and operate with one- or two-man crews. They all use traps to fish inshore waters on one-day trips. As a result, rules proposed for the lobster industry are more likely to give a much higher percentage of fishermen the same costs and benefits, which means they are less likely to generate opposition from disadvantaged license holders.

In addition, the *kinds of rules* that have been put in place in the lobster fishery are favored by the industry and fit fishermen's ideas about the way the ocean works. As we have seen in chapter 6, lobster fishermen see the ocean as an environment in which fish stocks can change rapidly and unpredictably in response to a myriad of environmental and biological factors. From their perspective, the best kind of rules are those that protect the fish in critically important parts of their life cycle—during reproduction, migration, spawning, on nursery grounds—by enacting rules about how to fish—rules concerning when, where, and with what technology. (We call these "parametric rules"; Acheson & Wilson 1996; Wilson et al. 1994.) As we have seen in chapters 4, 5, and 6, most of the conservation rules are of this type.

In large measure, the success that the lobster industry has had in devising parametric rules is due to historical accident. These rules were put in effect when the fishery was completely controlled by the state of Maine. The minimum and maximum size laws and the V-notch program came about long before scientists, enamored of stock-recruitment models, had much influence on legislation. It is doubtful if such laws would have been put into effect if initial efforts to get them enacted had come about after the passage of the Fisheries Conservation and Management Act of 1977. As it is, the industry has had to fight to retain such rules and to avoid having more costly rules imposed, such as an increase in the minimum gauge or a quota system.

There can be little doubt that the biological, technical, organizational, and historical factors discussed above have made it easier to formulate effective, enforceable rules for the lobster industry. Nevertheless, it is easy to make too much of them. After all, none of these factors has changed much from the beginning of the century to the present. In the lobster industry, the biology and technology, harbor gang organization, and the general nature of lobstering rules have not changed from 1900 to the present. Throughout the century, lobster management has been based on rules designed to protect small lobsters and the breeding stock.

What has changed is fishermen's compliance with these rules and their willingness to generate new conservation rules. The key question is why the lobster industry changed from violating the conservation rules to supporting them and adding more.

I argue that ideology, rules, and changes in catches, along with biological, technical, and organizational factors, affected each other in an interactive way to produce what we call the conservation ethic, a massive change in the culture of the industry. In the late nineteenth and early twentieth centuries, the lobster conservation rules were extensively violated, and violations of these laws were condoned by both people in coastal communities and the courts. The painful experience of the lobster bust of the 1920s and 1930s caused a change in people's perceptions about the value of the conservation laws. Many became convinced that cheating was doing a good deal of damage to the resource, and that compliance with the rules would result in collective benefits. An increasing number of these people began to obey the rules themselves and began to report flagrant violators (Acheson 1997: 8–10). Arguments in favor of conservation were buttressed by the modest increases in landings that occurred in the late 1930s and early 1940s.

After World War II, many (but not all) returning veterans became convinced that conservation would benefit the resource. They wanted to make a living in the lobster industry and did not want it to return the dismal conditions of the 1930s. Eddie Blackmore, past president of the Maine Lobstermen's Association, stated, "Many people came back from the war and wanted to go fishing. We knew that if we took care of it [the fishery] it would be there." Beginning in the 1940s, increasing numbers of fishermen became convinced that the fishery would be enhanced by protecting the breeding stock, and that the best way to accomplish this goal was to voluntarily support the V-notch program. The popularity of V-notching grew continually from the late 1940s onward.

Success fed on success. During the 1950s, 1960s, and 1970s, catches were very stable, averaging 20 million pounds, three times what catches had been in the lobster bust years of the 1920s and 1930s. The stable catches hardened the conviction of many fishermen, including industry leaders, that their view of the ocean was correct and that the lobster conservation laws were effective and were playing a key role in producing relatively high catches and incomes for them. This conviction, in turn, led to increased efforts to sanction those who violated the law. "Bandits" now had an unsavory reputation in coastal communities, and fishermen increasingly felt justified in helping the Marine Patrol obtain evidence against them. Taking "shorts" (undersized lobsters) was now viewed by most as a crime, not a necessity.

The increased faith in conservation regulations led to the development of further regulations. In 1978, the industry supported legislative initiatives for an escape-vent law, and in 1995 the zone management law, a co-management initiative, received excellent support from the industry. The record-high lobster catches experienced from the late 1980s on have buttressed belief in the effectiveness of the conservation laws, and in the fishermen's view of the ocean that make such laws seem so sensible. Many lobster fishermen now are convinced that the success of the industry is due, in great part, to their own effort in supporting passage and enforcement of conservation laws.

The development of lobster conservation laws reveals a high degree of *path dependency*. Choices that were made in the nineteenth century opened some avenues for regulation and closed off others. In the late nineteenth century, it became axiomatic among early biologists (e.g., Francis Herrick) and fishermen that the key to conserving the lobster resource was the preservation of lobsters in critical parts of their life cycle, namely juvenile and reproductive-sized lobsters. This became part of the ideology of the industry. The first rules in the 1870s accomplished these goals by a minimum size measure and a prohibition against taking egg-bearing females. These laws set a precedent that has not changed to this day. All of the important legislation that followed was built on the same principle and was designed to protect the breeding stock (i.e., the 1917 seeder law, the 1933 double-gauge law, and the V-notch program), or to protect the juveniles (i.e., the escape vent and the increase in the legal minimum size). Once large numbers of people in the industry became convinced such rules were effective, any attempt to change them would likely have resulted in a political firestorm.

In summary, the rules that have solved the collective action dilemma for the lobster industry are the result of a seventy-year-long process in which stable and higher catches have buttressed faith in lobster conservation laws and reinforced a view of the ocean and the lobster on which those laws are based. This faith in conservation, in turn, has led to passage of more parametric laws and increased support for enforcement efforts. Once the upward spiral began, technology, biology, social organization, and the parametric nature of the rules helped to continue it. The selective gear (traps), and the biology of the lobster made it possible to put juveniles and breeding-sized lobsters back in the water without harm, bolstering stock sizes, while the harbor gang organization made it easy for fishermen to monitor each other and aided enforcement of the rules. Changes in practice, values, catches, and a view of the ocean all worked to reinforce each other over the course of decades in a way that has allowed this industry to solve its collective action dilemmas to establish desirable legislation and ward off less desirable rules.

Events in the lobster industry are not unique. Axelrod argues that norms evolve over time in a process in which success plays a crucial role. "This approach is based on the principle that what works well for a player is more likely to be used again while what turns out poorly is more likely to be discarded" (1986: 1097). Lin Ostrom expanded on this insight in a conversation with me. She pointed to the "importance of slow but steady changes" in establishing norms. "Instead of creating a big set of rules and trying to get everyone to cooperate under them, it is important to find some new set of rules or norms that people can understand and follow, taking small steps, showing them to be successful and slowly building on that history." The lobster industry demonstrates how those who faced a catastrophic loss in the "bust" came to recognize some of the problems, make sequential changes, learn from those changes, and gradually develop a sustainable industry over the long run. Robert Bates and his co authors (1998) describe a number of other historical cases that are similar in many respects.

A warning needs to be sounded, however. If upward spirals are possible, leading to increased conservation, downward spirals are also possible. It might take very little to tip a system from one to the other. In the lobster industry, where people are relatively sure that the resource will be there in the future, and the rules are well enforced by both the Marine Patrol and other fishermen, people sacrifice to conserve the resource. However, where discount rates are high and enforcement is less certain, people compete to get as much of the resource as possible, and a tragedy of the commons ensues. Chief Marine Patrol officer Joe Fessenden points out that this has occurred recently in the Maine scallop and groundfish industries, which are currently in very poor condition.

In the lobster industry, a number of possible changes could converge to produce a downward spiral. Lower water temperatures could reduce larval settlement success; a resurgence in the populations of large groundfish inshore could reduce lobster populations; rules to protect the right whale and "closed areas" could raise costs and reduce the space and time available for lobster fishing; an influx of "hog groundfishermen" into the lobster industry and allowing outer Cape Cod fishermen to take V-notch lobsters could undermine incentives to participate in the V-notch program; and a rise in air freight costs could reduce demand and prices for lobsters. If all of these events happened at once, enough Maine lobster fishermen might come to believe that they would not be able to earn a living in the lobster fishery in the future, and that their best course of action would be to take as much of the resource as possible. Under these circumstances, a downward spiral could begin and gain momentum as catches fell.

CONSERVATION ETHIC AND DISCOUNT RATE

I see little to distinguish what in the literature is called a conservation ethic from a low discount rate. The first stresses a culture of conservation; the second places value on future rewards. The essence of both is the willingness to sacrifice present gains for future rewards. The data on the Maine lobster industry lead to two observations concerning these concepts. First, a conservation ethic or low discount rate is crucial for the development of institutions to conserve resources. Second, the higher the probability that people will be able to harvest all or most of a resource in the future, the more willing they will be to devise rules to conserve those resources. This means that people will be more willing to invest in rules when: (1) the resource is sedentary; (2) harvest levels are relatively stable or rising; (3) the area exploited by a group is reserved for that group and there are limits on entering that group; (4) the group knows enough about the resource to be assured that the rules will aid in conserving it, if not biologically, at least for themselves; and (5) there is the ability to enforce rules, which, in turn, depends on group size and heterogeneity.

Territoriality and Rules

The territorial system is the root institution governing the lobster industry, making possible the generation of other kinds of rule systems. Despite the fact that every society makes territorial claims on the land it occupies, and large numbers of fishing societies have systems of riparian rights (Acheson 1981; Acheson and Wilson 1996; Schlager 1994), there have been comparatively few analyses of how territorial systems come into being and change.

An unusual system of social relationships is involved in the territorial system. Alan Page Fiske (1991) argues that there are four elementary forms of human relations, which he calls communal sharing, authority ranking, equality match, and market pricing. None of these comes close to describing the territorial system. There is still another basic system of relations—a threat system. These are systems where social relationships are ordered through the threat or actual use of force. The outcomes depend completely on the decision of combatants to fight or submit.

The territorial system of the Maine lobster industry is a threat system used to regulate access to ocean territory. It is an informal system of rules, which are unenforceable by third parties such as the state. Two sets of rules should be distinguished: boundary rules, defining where different groups of fishermen have rights regardless of how temporary, and rules-of-the-game, defining how these territorial rights are to be defended, or new territories generated.

No system of rules will exist for long if the rules cannot be enforced. For most of the past one hundred years, violators of the territorial rules could be sanctioned at low cost. Almost anyone could get away with sanctioning violators of territorial "boundaries" if they used minimal care. It is entirely probable that the territorial system would not have come into being at all if the costs of sanctioning had been high. Indeed, in the past twenty years when the activities of the Marine Patrol and changing values in the industry have made large numbers of fishermen more reluctant to cut traps, boundary defense has languished. As a result, the entire territorial system is changing and may go out of existence.

In an article I wrote with Roy Gardner (n.d.), we use evolutionary game theory to describe the factors producing changes in the Maine lobster territorial system over the course of one hundred years. Our analysis builds on the observation of Demsetz (1967), who argued that territories are established when the benefits of maintaining territories outweigh the costs, a theme echoed in the work of Dyson-Hudson and Smith (1978) and others. In the Maine lobster industry, territorial rights are established when it is worthwhile for groups of fishermen from one harbor to dislodge people from other harbors from fishing in an area. What is unusual about the lobster industry is the large number of variables affecting costs and benefits of territorial defense and offense, and the fact that these factors can combine in ways that produce at least three different patterns of territorial usage. No single factor by itself consistently results in territoriality.

In the lobster industry, the factors influencing the decision to defend or invade an area are the value of the fishery, trap congestion, monitoring costs, the costs of transportation, trap losses that occur in trap-cutting incidents, and risks of prosecution. Early in the century, it was worthwhile to defend inshore areas close to home since the value of the fishery was high, congestion was high, cost of monitoring one's own traps were low, and chances of being apprehended were small.

Over the course of the twentieth century, at least four different changes have strongly affected the costs and benefits of territorial incursion and defense, tipping the decision to defend or invade areas in different ways in different stages. These changes are trap escalation, new technology, changing perceptions of the risk of trap cutting, and ecological changes along the central coast that increased the lobster catches on mud bottom in deep water fished in the winter. No territories developed in offshore areas that began to be extensively used by more fishermen in the 1980s and 1990s. Traps were not so congested in these deep water areas that what one person caught subtracted much from others' share of the catch, and fear of losing one's license dissuaded many fishermen from indulging in a lot of trap cutting. In the middle of bays, it is likely that for some time there has been trap congestion during the fall months when large numbers of fishermen concentrate their traps in these zones. However, no attempt to develop exclusive territories has occurred here, because any attempt to dislodge fishermen from adjacent harbors would like result in a "Mexican standoff," an expensive fight with no clear winner, or a Pyrrhic victory.

There are several aspects of the lobster territorial system about which current theory provides few insights. One issue is what maintains the peace in such systems? In the past two decades, the increasing influence of the Marine Patrol makes it risky to violate laws. However, before 1980, the amount of violence was low, even though law enforcement was less effective and there was no means of settling disputes once they started. Why violent episodes were relatively rare is not completely clear. Some clue to the answer might be found in the data on territorial systems maintained by the threat of force that have been described in some detail in Africa, Afghanistan, and other parts of the world. In those societies, several mechanisms have been identified as maintaining order, including a system of "conflicting allegiances" (Gluckman 1956).

A second, and closely related, question concerns the stability of threat systems. As Boulding (1963) has pointed out, threat systems can be very unstable. Once one party defies another or uses force, it is difficult to predict what will happen. Conflict can quickly escalate into a confrontation in which both sides can lose heavily. Under other circumstances, such systems can be very stable and operate as systems of deterrence. Threat systems can work to maintain the peace if conditions are right. In the long standoff between the United States and the Soviet Union in the Cold War, the technology of offense and defense and second strike capability prevented an outbreak of war for decades. Similar mechanisms are apparently working to prevent escalating violence among lobster fishermen. Several fishermen and Marine Patrol officers have said that having territories limits competition for space, thereby reducing the likelihood of violence. Political scientist Mike McGinnis (personal communication) points out that the territorial system likely helps lobster fishermen avoid the level of conflict that might occur under other circumstances. What those circumstances are deserves extensive analysis.

A third question concerns political alliances. In large numbers of systems around the world where relationships between groups are dominated by the threat of force, groups in conflict will form alliances with other groups against a common enemy. The most famous of these systems are probably those described by Evans-Pritchard (1969) among the Nuer of the Sudan and by Barth (1959) for the Swat Pathans.

In the lobster industry, by way of contrast, such alliances do not form. If two harbor gangs X and Z are both having a territorial conflict with harbor Y between them, they have an interest in defeating a common enemy, and thus might profit by an alliance between them. However, no such alliances apparently have existed.

Why not? The reason might be clarified if we knew more about the operation of the political teams that are involved in territorial defense and invasion.

Answering these questions presents an opportunity to make some contribution to our understanding of threat and territorial systems in general.

Implications for Fisheries Management

SIZE OF GOVERNANCE UNITS AND POLICY

One of the insights provided by rational choice theory is that people in small social units are more able to provide themselves with rules in the common good than those in large units where people are less able to come to consensus and monitor each other's behavior (Coleman 1990; North 1990a: 12; Ostrom 1990, 2000, 2001). Policy makers have been persuaded to take advantage of this insight in devising both the Maine lobster zones (chapter 5) and the ASMFC areas (chapter 7). In both cases, the fishery was divided into smaller units to facilitate establishing rules tailored to local ecological conditions and to reflect the wishes of the local constituents. Both of these efforts have been reasonably successful.

The territorial system also involves small units that have been conducive to achieving the goals of effective management. The territorial system, I have argued, has helped produce a sense of stewardship and one of the most effective conservation programs in any fishery in the industrialized world. If the territorial system has bolstered efforts to generate rules to conserve the resource and enforce those rules, why hasn't the state of Maine formalized these territories to ensure their continued existence? In fact, it has not and is not likely to do so in the near future. The issue came to a head in 1998 when the legislature was asked to pass a law creating a "conservation zone" for Monhegan Island, similar to the one that had been established around Swan's Island in 1984. As we saw in chapter 3, one of the primary motives for establishing such a zone was to prevent fishermen from the mainland harbor of Friendship from encroaching on Monhegan's traditional territory. But the Monhegan fishermen also wanted some very special rules for their zone. This law was passed, with the result that Monhegan has the most stringent conservation laws of any harbor in the state. Swan's Island also successfully petitioned the commissioner of Marine Resources in 1984, and the fishermen in this zone enforce the most restrictive trap limit in the entire state. When other harbors, especially Isle au Haut, also wanted to establish conservation zones, the legislature established a sub-zone task force to study the issue. As we saw in chapter 5, this task force advised against establishing more sub-zones of any kind, including conservation zones. This decision reflected the wishes of the majority of fishermen from mainland harbors, a group that for the past forty years had been expanding the amount of area in which the members placed traps. The recommendation of the task force also pleased members of the marine resources committee of the legislature who wanted to avoid more lengthy and divisive fights such as the one that occurred concerning the establishment of the Monhegan conservation zone, as well as officials of the DMR who feared having to enforce the boundaries of a large number of conservation zones, each with different rules. Although preventing the proliferation of more small management zones made sense from the point of view of enhancing political support and reducing enforcement costs, it is ironic to see government officials dedicated to the cause of "conservation" working against the establishment of local-level conservation zones, especially when the fishermen in the two existing zones have proven able and willing to impose very restrictive conservation rules on themselves. In summary, in some cases those making policy for the lobster industry have been able to take advantage of the idea that small-sized units are more effective, but not in others.

POLICY FAILURE AND SUCCESS

Efforts of various branches of government to manage the lobster industry have met with mixed success. Some of the laws first enacted by Maine, such as the prohibition on taking egg-bearing females, the double-gauge rule, and the V-notch program have almost certainly helped to conserve the breeding stock and are well supported by industry. The zone management law was perhaps the most successful state law in that it quickly led to both trap limits and limited-entry rules for most of the zones.

Efforts by the federal government to manage the lobster fishery have been far more mixed.[2] The New England Regional Council and National Marine Fisheries Service failed to produce a lobster management plan that would obtain political support in the industry. Their attempts to increase the minimum gauge and do away with the V-notch and oversize measures led to years of political stalemate. These attempts did nothing so much as pose another collective action dilemma for the industry.

After 1995, when primary authority for managing the lobster in federal waters was assumed by the Atlantic States Marine Fisheries Commission, management efforts went ahead much faster. As we have described, Amendment 3 to the ASMFC lobster management plan was adopted in eighteen months, and all of the areas are on track for imposing regulations to meet the egg-production goals specified by this plan. Still, ASMFC management leaves much to be desired in the view of many industry members. The V-notch and oversize rules are still contentious, as the 2001 struggle over Amendment 4 demonstrated.

In short, the best example of policy success is Maine's zone management law. Management by the regional council between 1977 and 1995 is probably the best example of policy failure. This is not to suggest that all of Maine's lobster management efforts work flawlessly, or that federal management has had no successes.

The literature on policy failure and success does not provide a very clear picture of the reasons for this differential success. A very large number of explanations have been offered for cases where the government does not do its job. Policy failure is a number of diseases, not just one. Moe (1990) argues that government inefficiency can be the product of deliberate design; others stress agency problems such as the self-serving behavior of politicians and government officials (Cook and Levi 1990: 411; Moberg 1994; Shleifer and Vishny 1998: 4). A number of authors, including Miller (1992: 140–42), Tullock (1965: 142–93), and Williamson (1970: 25–27) trace the failure of bureaucracies to asymmetrical information flows that leave top administrators without adequate information upon which to make decisions. Others see the source of government failure in the activities of "winning majorities" (Buchanan and Tullock 1962) and "pressure groups (Becker 1983; Olson 1965), which force governments to redistribute goods and services to them at enormous cost to the public. A closely related phenomenon is "rent seeking," which occurs when an interest group "colonizes a government bureau so that the bureau promotes the specific interests of the organized group at the expense of the public as a whole" (Bickers and Williams 2001: 194).

Some of these ideas help to explain the failure of federal fisheries policy and some of the actions of the regional council, but none of them fits the case precisely. For example, a variation on rent seeking took place. Most of the members of the regional council were groundfishermen who wanted to impose rules with short-run goals in mind, to the long-run detriment of their own fishery and those of others. A good example is the council's refusal to pass rules outlawing dragging for lobsters, a proposal much favored by the lobster industry.

However, none of these ideas in the policy-failure literature adequately pinpoints the underlying causes of the failure of federal management efforts. I believe two reasons underlie the problems federal management agencies have had in devising institutions to manage the lobster. One involves the problems of science and of applying knowledge to policy. The second relates to problems stemming from the imposition of a top-down, highly centralized management structure.[3]

THE PROBLEMS OF SCIENCE

We have discussed the problems with science in some detail in chapters 6, 7, and 8. The basic issue is that scientists are using stock-recruitment models, which are considered state-of-the-art techniques. Unfortunately, dependence on such models has not permitted fisheries scientists to predict changes in lobster stocks. Even worse, it has led them to state that the breeding stock is at low levels, the stock is overfished, and the fishery is prone to disaster. This has led the NMFS to advocate policies that have seriously damaged the credibility of government scientists with the industry and other observers of the scene, including the author. Inadequate science played no small role in undermining the whole federal management effort.

The problems that fisheries scientists are having in predicting stock changes have been widely noted both in academic circles and within the bureaucracy itself. William Fox, director of science and technology for the National Marine Fisheries Service, said in speaking of fisheries science, "It's not really science; its

Capturing the Commons

like an artist doing it—so a large part of your scientific advice comes from art" (Appell 2001: 19).

Increasing numbers of people experienced in fisheries management are beginning to suspect that stock-recruitment models are fundamentally flawed and cannot be cured by fine-tuning the models and gathering more data (Berkes and Folke 1998: 2) . We may never be able to predict changes in fish stocks or the outcomes of management options. The problems are so basic that we may need a whole new approach to management.

The critics of standard scientific management say that the basic problem is that fisheries science is built on a inaccurate view of the ocean. Fisheries science assumes that oceans are relatively simple linear systems that tend toward equilibrium. In reality, oceans are very complex, and very likely are chaotic systems (see Hastings and Higgins 1994). This conclusion is buttressed by the work of our research group at the University of Maine, which used a simulation model to show that even simple communities of fish vary unpredictably with limits, even though they are bounded within a range (Acheson and Wilson 1996; Wilson et al. 1991a; 1991b). However, there is no consensus on the matter, and none is likely to emerge for some time.

Even if fisheries are not chaotic, they are certainly complex and therefore highly unpredictable (Ludwig, Hilborn, and Walters 1993). In either case, accurate prediction would be very difficult or impossible. Two factors make it very difficult to predict changes in stocks or the effects of a management policy. First, although there are regularities in such complex systems, such a large number of nonlinear relationships exist, and the feedback mechanisms in the system are so complicated, that a huge amount of accurate, fine-grained, continuously updated data would be necessary to make accurate prediction possible. Second, non-linearity of these systems means that models of the systems must almost be complex duplicates of the systems themselves. Otherwise, small variations or inaccuracies in measurement would result in great errors in prediction. Under these conditions, accurate prediction is a practical impossibility.

If this is correct, then fisheries management is bound to be a highly uncertain enterprise. This poses tremendous problems for policy makers, because under conditions of uncertainty, many different interpretations can plausibly be made of the same data, a number of policies can be supported, and controversy is inevitable. In this regard, Jasanof (1998: 154) says, "in complex systems under study, enough suggestive and even persuasive evidence can be found to sustain very different overall stories about what is really going on. Lacking ways of testing or falsification, neither theoretical position is able to deal a body blow to the other. Ideology and politics thus become the primary determinants of choosing among competing scientific accounts of felt reality." In lobster management, scientific uncertainty has certainly given rise to a good deal of political controversy.

Problems with science have quickly led to problems with policy. In the absence of credible scientific explanations, the lobster industry has adhered to its own version of the biology of the lobster. The views of the scientists and those of the industry compete for influence in the policy arena. Even in simpler situations where all parties share a common understanding, implementing effective policy can be very difficult, but the situation in the lobster fishery is made especially contentious by the fact that the competing sides not only have different interests, but also fundamentally different conceptualizations of the lobster and the ocean. This makes for a difficult policy problem, but one, I suspect, that is found in other situations.

THE SUCCESS OF PARAMETRIC MANAGEMENT

If fisheries are complex, and possibly chaotic, then the key questions for fisheries managers are: How do we manage under conditions of extreme uncertainty? What can be done to conserve stocks when we really do not know what affects stock sizes and cannot predict the effects of policies?

The way that the lobster has been managed provides a clue to the answers to these questions. As we saw in chapter 8, there is increasing evidence that the lobster management rules are effective in conserving the stocks. These rules are unusual in that they are designed to maintain critical life processes. They preserve the reproductive stock and proven breeding stock (the prohibition on taking egg-bearing females, and the V-notch and oversize laws), and juveniles (i.e., the escape-vent and minimum size law). The rules are not designed to limit fishing effort. No quotas on lobster exist.

Moreover, the same kinds of management rules are found in many tribal and peasant societies in the world. As in the lobster industry, these rules limit how fishing is done by specifying where fishing will be done, the techniques that will be used, and the times when fishing shall be allowed (Acheson and Wilson 1996; Wilson et al. 1994). The fact that such rules are used so widely suggests that fishing peoples in a wide variety of societies have hit on some kind of universal set of general principles that appear to be effective in conserving fish stocks.

These kinds of rules are used so widely, we argue, because they are consistent with the chaotic nature of fisheries. In simulating fisheries under conditions that approximated real life conditions, it became apparent that the outputs of the models vary unpredictably, but they varied within certain ranges. These ranges are set by the parameters of the model, which were assumed to be constant. In the model, these parameters were stable biological processes such as growth potential, migration, growth rates, and habitat. The fact that the populations of fish vary within specifiable limits when these parameters were held constant suggests that fisheries can be managed by maintaining these parameters.

This suggests that other fisheries could be managed by similar kinds of rules. These rules would be designed to maintain habitats necessary for the well being of these species (e.g., spawning grounds, breeding grounds, nursery areas, migration routes, etc.), and to limit taking fish in crucial parts of their life cycle (e.g., egged females, spawning congregations, etc.). This can be done by rules limiting the techniques of capture, where fishing is done, and when it is done.

Managing fisheries by the use of parametric rules would not result in constant

Capturing the Commons

stock sizes or catches. Cyclical fluctuations would occur as they have in the lobster industry. However, the use of such rules presumably would prevent stock failure. This may be all that can be expected of such rules. It may be enough.

Even if we choose to manage fisheries using parametric rules, it may be too much to expect that one set of rules could be put in place that would solve the problem for all time. Hollings (1978) and Walters (1986) have suggested that fisheries be managed by what they term "adaptive management." Adaptive management is predicated on the idea that ecosystems are not only complex, but that they are marked by a number of feedback mechanisms and irreversible processes. Under these conditions, interactions between people and ecosystems cannot be predicted and result in a number of "surprises." As a result, resource managers should treat policies as experiments from which they can learn. Management from this point of view is a kind of iterative process in which policies are enacted, their effect observed, and the policies changed repeatedly to obtain better results. However, policies can never be matched perfectly to ecological conditions because those conditions change, sometimes rapidly and in ways that are impossible to predict. Thus, the process of developing effective policies is continual.

PROBLEMS WITH TOP-DOWN MANAGEMENT

Elinor Ostrom (2000b: 138) argues that one important source of government failure is top-down management policies that "frustrate, rather than facilitate the private provision of public goods." This, I believe, lies at the heart of the problem of the failure of the federal fisheries management system.

The federal system of fisheries management is, at root, a highly centralized, top-down management system. To be sure, the fisheries management system is not presented in this way. Federal officials have even used the word "co-management" in describing the regional councils set up under the Fisheries Management and Conservation Act, and point out that the councils do have industry members. But the FCMA gave the Secretary of Commerce and the National Marine Fisheries Service ultimate control over fisheries management rules for the federal zone. The Sustainable Fisheries Act passed in 1996 greatly strengthens those powers of the National Marine Fisheries Service and the Department of Commerce by giving them the right to pre-empt the management authority of the regional councils, the states, and the Atlantic States Marine Fisheries Commission if it is judged that they are doing a poor job in managing "overfished species." In addition, while the ASMFC began as a compact of the states, it too became part of the top-down federal management system when Congress passed the Atlantic Coastal Fisheries Cooperative Management Act in 1993, making it mandatory for all signatory states to enforce the plans of the ASMFC under threat of having the Secretary of Commerce place a moratorium on the fishing for species not managed in compliance in the waters of the affected states.

The Marine Mammal and Endangered Species acts are written in very extreme language, and make it mandatory for federal agencies to take strong unilateral action when such species are threatened. These acts do not allow states to manage these species even in state waters. All lower-level governmental units are literally at the mercy of the federal court system in such matters.

What are the problems inherent in top-down management? First and foremost, top-down management leaves lower-level government units without clearly defined rights. Any action they take can be overruled by a higher-level unit under the right conditions. This problem has occurred repeatedly in the annals of lobster management at the federal level. In dealing with the regional council, the NMFS repeatedly acted in a very heavy-handed manner, especially in the late 1980s and early 1990s when it attempted force the council to increase the lobster minimum gauge and refused to consider other ways of managing the fishery. During the long Amendment 5 fight, officials of the NMFS even went so far as threatening to take over lobster management and write Amendment 6 to the federal lobster plan with no input from the council. In 1998, the NMFS was seriously contemplating using its powers under the Sustainable Fisheries Act to pre-empt the powers of the states and the ASMFC by imposing a 475-trap limit on the lobster industry. In the end, they were persuaded not to impose such a stringent trap limit, but no one questioned their right to do so. Had they imposed this limit by fiat, they would have seriously undermined the authority and effectiveness of the Maine zone management process and the ASMFC.

A second problem is that top-down federal management attempts to enact uniform rules, regardless of local social or ecological conditions. Beginning with the advent of the State-Federal Program in 1972, the NMFS administrators have wanted to do away with the V-notch and oversize measures in the cause of regulatory uniformity. Since Maine was the only jurisdiction that had these rules, they would have to be abolished to produce a single regulatory regime. This caused a decades-long battle with the Maine industry, which insisted that these rules were the backbone of lobster conservation. Another example is the insistence of federal scientists on the lobster technical and scientific committee on applying the federal lobster model to both the Gulf of Maine and Long Island Sound, despite obvious differences in the ecologies of these two areas.

A third problem is that top-down federal management becomes obsessed with symbolic goals. An excellent example is the effort to save the "sacred" right whale. Programs to save the three hundred remaining right whales are going forward despite the very high costs to the fishing industry and the probability that these efforts will not prevent the whale from going extinct anyway. Another example is the insistence on using the "best science" to manage fisheries, a goal enshrined in the FCMA. This is the goal of management even when it is clear that the "best science" is not very good and that a better course of action is to question seriously what we consider the "best science."

Another problem is that federal management has become ensnared in very complex bureaucratic procedures required by federal law.

In order to manage fisheries, we need to know what controls stock sizes, be able to identify management strategies that have a favorable effect on stock sizes, and be able to garner the political support necessary to develop the organizations and rules to sustain those stocks. To date, the federal fisheries agencies have had major problems accomplishing any of these tasks.

THE SUCCESS OF BOTTOM-UP MANAGEMENT EFFORTS

All of the more successful lobster management efforts have in common that they have embodied many of the elements of bottom-up or co-management. Most of the important Maine lobster conservation laws began as bills that had political support from strong factions in the industry, and they were revised with the ideas of the industry in mind. This includes the oversize law, the V-notch program, and the escape-vent law. The Maine lobster zone management bill embodies a co-management program in which authority to manage important aspects of the industry in each zone is shared between the zone councils and Maine Department of Marine Resources. The ASMFC lobster management program divides the lobster-producing waters off the northeast coast into areas. Each area has a lobster conservation management team, composed of industry members, who propose management rules for the area.

The fact that such bottom-up programs work better will come as no surprise to rational-choice theorists. In fact, a good deal of evidence supports the idea that rules devised by local-level units or user groups are more effective at managing resources than those imposed by a top-down process (Baland and Platteau 1996; E. Ostrom 1990: 90, 101; 2000b: 41; Wade 1994: 216). E. Ostrom (2000b: 148) says: "A frequent finding is that when the users of a common-pool resource organize themselves to devise and enforce some of their own basic rules, they tend to manage local resources more sustainably then when rules are externally imposed on them."

Bottom-up approaches are successful largely because people support them so that enforcement costs are lowered. When people devise their own rules, they will formulate ones they consider sensible, effective, and low-cost. They will also frame rules that embody local knowledge, that are designed to be adapted to local conditions, and that avoid conflicting with basic norms. They are far more likely to obey such rules than those imposed by outside authorities, which, all too often, are framed in ways that impose high economic costs on users, promote conflict, and are seen as ineffective in helping to maintain the resource.

Bottom-up management has another advantage, namely that the management units are small and local in nature. This means that a mistake made by one management unit in one area will have limited repercussions. Moreover, a number of redundant management units each carrying out its own experiment enhances the opportunities to learn about what is effective.

Conversely, a good deal of evidence exists to demonstrate that top-down management by central governments is not especially effective. Wunsch summarizes this literature by saying "Numerous scholarly studies have come to this conclusion: the centralized, hierarchical, bureaucratic administrative model has failed. Indeed, to many, it appears to be a wasteful enterprise . . . " (1999: 244).

If the problems with federal efforts to manage the fishery stem from poor-quality science and top-down governance structures, the way to solve the problems is to improve the quality of science and promote co-management. There are serious efforts underway to do exactly this. At this writing, efforts are being made to improve the lobster model produced by federal scientists and to improve the quality of the data to be used in the model. More important, the entire scientific enterprise behind fisheries management is being questioned, and some radically new approaches are being discussed.

Co-management has been introduced successfully in the Maine lobster industry in the form of the zone management initiative. It has also been tried in several different countries with notable success, including Canada, Japan, Norway, New Zealand, and Australia (Pinkerton 1989; Pinkerton and Weinstein 1995). There are undoubtedly many other areas where conditions will allow people to successfully generate their own rules for management. Almost certainly some of these governments, noting the success of co-management, will follow suit in the near future.

However, it may not be as easy to improve science as we have hoped. Despite the problems that federal and state scientists have had in predicting changes in lobster, they appear to be wedded to stock-recruitment models. Most fisheries scientists have assumed that the basic precepts of population dynamics are correct, and that our ability to predict changes in stock can be greatly enhanced by improving the models of the fisheries and by gathering better information to put in them.

Faith in these models is bolstered by the fact that they are considered state-of-the-art science. Scientists know that these models have not helped to predict changes in stock sizes, but they believe these anomalies can be explained. The idea that we may not be able to model phenomena as complex and rapidly changing as marine species does not suggest itself easily. Among scientists, the idea that management should depend on crude rules about *how to fish* finds very little support.

Nevertheless, there has been a move toward a form of parametric management in the efforts to establish marine reserves. Those advocating marine reserves are, in essence, admitting that our knowledge is inadequate to manage marine species, and that the best policy is to leave certain critical areas completely alone in the hope that natural processes will result in rejuvenated fish populations. The rules involved are parametric in the sense that they specify where fishing cannot take place, and call for a ban on the use of all gear in those areas.

Moreover, serious impediments to imposing co-management or bottom-up management do exist, especially at the federal level. If co-management is going to succeed, governments must be willing to share power with groups of resource users, and government officials must be constrained from dictating to local groups. Co-management would presumably be most easy to establish in governments with the traits of what Vincent Ostrom calls a polycentric system. These are systems with "many centers of decision making that were formally independent of each other" (V. Ostrom 1999: 52). In such systems, units of government perform different functions and can maintain their independence from other branches of government because each unit has "veto capabilities in relation to other decision structures" that are guaranteed by constitutional level rules (1999: 64). In a polycentric system where power is traditionally shared, it presumably would be easier to establish a co-management system than it would be in a monocentric system where all power to determine and enforce laws is centered in one dominant government unit.

The United States Constitution establishes a polycentric system in which a few powers are given to the central government and the rest automatically are the prerogative of the states. If the United States were operating as the framers of the Constitution envisioned, co-management might be established more easily. However, in the past eighty years the United States has moved away from this polycentric model, as the federal government has come to dominate vast areas of the society.

The federal government now provides a huge number of services affecting every aspect of life ranging from health care (Medicare and Medicaid), retirement funding (social security), and education (both elementary and higher education) to environmental protection, agriculture, transportation, and community development. At the same time, Congress has passed innumerable laws giving the federal government power to regulate an enormous number of activities and products (e.g., workplace safety, automobiles, food products, consumer advertising, rules to prevent discrimination, to mention just a few). All of these services and regulations are in addition to those that have long been the traditional functions of the federal government such as defense, the post office, and foreign policy.

The federal agencies developed to provide services did not supplant local governments. Rather, they generally work through local-level units to provide services and funds to the ultimate recipients. In the process, the state and local governments lost a lot of autonomy, and became cogs in a system dominated by the central government.

Over the course of time, the federal government has developed a number of mechanisms to influence and control the activities of these lower-level governmental units. They give funds and tax incentives to encourage desirable behavior. They also have developed sanctions to punish lower-level governmental units that do not behave in accordance with federal law, including withholding of funds (Bickers and Williams 2001: 156–53).

In short, top-down management by agencies of the federal government is now our standard way of governing the country. It should come as no surprise to us that the laws passed by Congress to manage fisheries (such as the Fisheries Conservation and Management Act and the Sustainable Fisheries Act) as well as laws designed to protect various marine species (including the Endangered Species and Marine Mammal acts) have given federal agencies a good deal of authority to manage in a top-down fashion.

In summary, co-management or bottom-up governance structures appear to be more effective than top-down management structure in managing fisheries. If we are going to develop co-management, we need to evolve polycentric systems, which are amenable to bottom-up, power-sharing arrangements. For the past eighty years, however, we have been moving in exactly the opposite direction, toward top-down management. It would take a major change in the laws to reverse direction.

The Maine lobster industry has succeeded, in part, because it has been able to circumvent many of the problems inherent in the federal management system. The industry has stubbornly insisted on maintaining sets of rules that they are certain are effective, even though those rules have been opposed by the majority of lobster scientists working for government agencies. The fishermen do not believe that the resource has been dangerously overfished, and they have been able to counter some of the policy recommendations of scientists who believe it is in danger of collapse. They often have been aided in this endeavor by officers of the Maine Department of Marine Resources, members of the legislature, and some non-government scientists. Their case has been strengthened by record-high stock sizes and catches, which have posed real anomalies for scientists. History has also played an important role. Most of the state lobster conservation laws were in place before the federal government played any role in management.

The Future

There can be little question that the lobster industry is living in unusually good times. The high catches are due to the parametric rules that have been put in place, in combination with favorable ecological circumstances. It is tempting to say that as long as the existing system is maintained, all will be well. That may be true. However, it is all too easy to imagine changes that could bring disaster too.

Destabilizing shocks to the existing system could occur in the form of changes in government policy. The industry has become very adept in working with state officials to establish the rules they want. However, they are having far more difficulty working with officials at the increasingly important federal level. In order to develop rules in this political arena, they must encompass the divergent interests of a much larger number of stakeholders (industry factions from different states, multiple legislatures, federal agencies, and the ASMFC) and deal with scientists with different conceptualizations of the problems of management. It is all too easy to see how this very complex structure could break down.

The chaotic nature of the fishery presents other possibilities for problems. In such systems, population levels will vary considerably, but always within certain limits, as long as the parameters of the system are maintained. I have argued that this is what the parametric rules do by regulating "how" fishing is done. But if a change occurred in the parameters within which the system operates, or a shock occurred that moved the system into a different parameter space, then drastic changes in stock levels could occur suddenly. Economic changes could also help to move the system in a different direction. It is conceivable that a number of such changes could happen at once with disastrous results for the stocks.

I believe the rules governing lobster fishing are working well and will prove to be very resilient. However, there is reason for caution in predicting long-term trends in this fishery and the future evolution of its governance structure. For the present, we are witnessing the unparalleled success of an industry in which people are determined to capture the lobster commons for themselves and future generations.

Notes

1. Introduction

1. Throughout this book I am using the terms "fisherman/men," "lobsterman/men," and "sternman/men" rather than "fisher(s)." Although the majority in the industry are men, there are some women who have their own boats and others who work as sternmen on the boats of others. Men and women alike prefer to be called fishermen, lobstermen, or "lobster catchers," not "fishers." The term "fisher" has a negative connotation. A fisher is a fierce brown animal in the weasel family that has eaten many pet cats in Maine and regularly kills dogs.

2. Rosen (1995: 4) says of professional fishery managers, "Our role in debate before public and political bodies should be as professionals who serve as objective interpreters and purveyors of scientific information." He quotes Livingston as writing, "In conservation we have always assumed a dealing between ourselves and everyone else; a civilized, adversary proceeding in which reason, logic and meticulous argument, liberally laced with horrible precedent, would persuade just men and women to our position. Unfortunately, for reasons and resources, it has not worked" (ibid.).

2. Spatial Strategies and Territoriality

1. Maine has a long tradition of holding all fish in lakes and rivers, and other animal resources, in public trust. The "great ponds" law allows anyone to travel over privately owned property to any pond over 10 acres in size to fish and "fowl." All these laws have been tested in court in recent years; all have been upheld. By law, people are allowed to hunt on private property without permission of the landowner.

2. Several factors make it difficult for people from nucleated areas to describe fishing territories. One is the variation in where people from the same harbor can fish. They know how far they can go personally before they lose traps, but they know others can range greater or shorter distances, and they often are not aware of the outer limits where all people from their harbors have traps. Then, some areas have no traps at all since there are no lobsters to be caught there. Most important, these fishermen know that mixed fishing is allowed in a large portion of the area in which they fish. For these reasons, defining a harbor's fishing areas in terms of a single continuous line around the periphery of the area they fish does not get at the reality of the situation in their minds.

3. The Island Game

1. In the discussion that follows, I will be describing four of these five islands in some detail. The fifth, Metinic, is not included here in detail, but has a history similar to that of Green Island.

2. According to Maine law, ocean is owned by the government, but as we have described, all groups of lobster fishermen have territories. Moreover, in Penobscot Bay, local custom upholds the rights of landowners to fishing rights in waters near their property; here, there are instances in which people have purchased islands to gain the right to fish in the waters nearby.

3. Recently there has been a considerable divergence of opinion on the importance of property rights in ensuring cooperation solutions. Michael Taylor (1990: 236–38) strongly argues that property rights are not necessary to solve collective action problems. Elinor Ostrom (1992: 69) argues that "clearly defined boundaries" are necessary if institutions to manage irrigation systems are to be developed, which of course involves solving a collective action problem. Ostrom's position reflects that of theorists concerned with common-pool resources in general (see Acheson 1989a). The data on the trap limit in the Maine lobster industry reinforce the case that Ostrom is making concerning the importance of boundaries and property rights.

4. Although fishermen speak of "full-time fishermen" and "part-timers," it is very difficult to accurately define a full-time fishermen. Very few fishermen exploit only lobster throughout the year and have no other source of income. What full-time generally means is that lobstering is the most important source of income.

4. The Genesis of State Laws for the Lobster Industry

1. To read some of the testimony and debate, one would have thought that the life blood of the industry was lobsters 13 inches and over.

2. In the years between World War I and World War II, catches ranged between 5 and 7 million pounds in most years, one-fourth of what they had been in the 1890s (Maine Department of Marine Resources 1995) (see table 1.1). The causes of this decline are complex; and there is little consensus on the cause (see Acheson and Steneck 1997).

3. The double-gauge law appears in Maine Public Law, 1933, c.2, sec.89. It was amended in 1935 (Laws of Maine 1935, Chapter 294, "An Act Relating to Measurement of Lobsters").

4. The V-notch will last through several molts and serves to protect egg-producing females for a period of several years. This rule is thought to be especially effective in conserving the largest females, which may not extrude eggs every year. Such animals may extrude over one hundred thousand eggs every other year.

5. Apparently some unscrupulous dealers and fishermen continued to scrub the eggs off berried females and sell them. When caught with egged lobsters in their possession, they would claim they were saving them for the "seeder program."

6. In this sense, the establishment of the escape-vent and the V-notch laws are not really a collective action problem as defined by Elster where rational action (i.e., defection) by an individual can lead to a Pareto inferior outcome (1989: 24–27).

5. Co-management in the Maine Lobster Industry

1. The Maine Fisherman's Forum is a unique institution. Since 1972, fishermen, bureaucrats, representatives of companies serving the fishing industry, and a few academics and politicians meet annually in Rockport and participate in four days of sessions on various topics of interest to the fishing industry. The forum makes Maine the only state in which an ongoing discussion of fisheries policy issues takes place. It is attended by a serious group of people.

2. This committee was composed of Penn Estabrook of the Maine Department of Marine Resources; Patten White and David Cousens, officers of the Maine Lobstermen's Association; Junior Backman, president of the Downeast Lobstermen's Association; fisherman John Williamson; and three academics from the University of Maine, Jim Wilson, Alison Rieser, and myself.

7. Dealing with the Feds

1. The Mitchell bill originally had been written by members of Representative John McKernan's (R-Me) staff, and was originally known as the McKernan bill. It was designed to ensure that if the Canadians were going to catch lobsters under the federal minimum size, at least they were not going to import them into the United States.

2. The three consultants were Professors James Wilson, Robert Steneck, and the author. Wilson took the lead in producing the draft plan.

3. Achieving a 100 percent V-notch compliance rate might be achieved more easily than one might think. An egged lobster not V-notched by one fisherman presumably would be returned to the water and caught by others who would put a notch in her.

8. The Politics of Science

1. In reality, three different models are used jointly. A "DeLury" model looks at size frequencies of lobsters to provide information on mortality and lobster abundance. The "length cohort" analysis examines changes in number of lobsters caught in different size ranges to estimate fishing mortality. Most important is the "eggs per recruit" model, which, as the name suggests, estimates the number of eggs produced by legal-sized lobsters, and the yield of those eggs. It is this model that is used to determine whether the egg production goal of 10 percent of an unfished fishery has been achieved.

9. Conclusion

1. Knight (1990) and Singleton and Taylor (1992) also argue that communities may be able to use the government to establish the rules they want when they cannot devise those rules informally.

2. The success of federal programs varies considerably. Some programs work well, and the agencies that run them are highly efficient. Few people these days would want to do away with the social security system. Moreover, the federal government has done jobs that the states could not or would not do themselves. A prime example is in ending discrimination against Blacks. In other areas, centralized control by the federal government of the

United States has not been very successful. This certainly includes federal management of fisheries in New England under the regional council system.

3. Finlayson (1994) points to the same two factors as causing the mismanagement of the cod stocks of Newfoundland in the past three decades. In the Newfoundland case, the results were devastating. James Scott's (1998) analysis echos this theme. He argues that the most devastating failures of policy in state societies in general have occurred when autocratic governments have foisted "high modernistic" schemes ostensibly based on "rationality" and "science" on a public that was powerless to resist.

References Cited

Acheson, James M. 1972. "Territories of the Lobstermen." *Natural History* 8 (4): 60–69.

———. 1975a. "Fisheries Management and Social Context: The Case of the Maine Lobster Industry." *Transactions of the American Fisheries Society* 104 (4): 653–68.

———. 1975b. "The Lobster Fiefs: Economic and Ecological Effects of Territoriality in the Maine Lobster Industry." *Human Ecology* 3 (3): 183–207.

———. 1980. "Factors Influencing Productivity of Metal and Wooden Lobster Traps." Maine Sea Grant Technical Report no. 63. Orono: University of Maine Sea Grant.

———. 1981. "Anthropology of Fishing." *Annual Review of Anthropology* 10: 275–316.

———. 1988. *The Lobster Gangs of Maine*. Hanover, N.H.: University Press of New England.

———. 1989a. "Management of Common Property Resources." In *Economic Anthropology*, ed. Stuart Plattner, 351–78. Stanford: Stanford University Press.

———. 1989b. "Where Have All the Exploiters Gone? Co-management of the Maine Lobster Industry." In *Common Property Resources: Ecology and Community-based Sustainable Development*, ed. Fikret Berkes, 199–217. London: Belhaven.

———. 1992. "Maine Lobster Industry." In *Climate Variability, Climate Change and Fisheries*, ed. Michael H. Glantz, 147–65. New York: Cambridge University Press.

———. 1993. "Capturing the Commons: Legal and Illegal Strategies." In *The Political Economy of Customs and Cultures*, ed. Terry L. Anderson and Randy Simmons, 69–83. Lanham, Md.: Rowman and Littlefield.

———. 1994. "Welcome to Nobel Country: An Overview of Institutional Economics." In *Anthropology and Institutional Economics*, ed. James M. Acheson, 3–42. Monographs in Economic Anthropology no.12. Lanham, Md.: University Press of America.

———. 1997. "The Politics of Managing the Maine Lobster Industry: 1860 to the Present." *Human Ecology* 25 (1): 3–27.

———. 1998. "Lobster Trap Limits: A Solution to a Communal Action Problem." *Human Organization* 57 (1): 43–52.

Acheson, James M., and Ann Acheson. 1998. "Report of the Lobster Questionnaire Project: Selected Results as Requested by the Department of Marine Resources." In *A Report Regarding Limited Entry into Maine's Lobster Management Zones: Presented to the 119th Legislature's Joint Standing Committee on Marine Resources.*" Augusta, Maine: Lobster Advisory Council.

Acheson, James M., and Roy Gardner. n.d. "The Origins of Territoriality: The Case of the Maine Lobster Fishery." Submitted to *American Anthropologist*.

Acheson, James M., and Robert L. Reidman. 1982. "Biological and Economic Effects of Increasing the Minimum Legal Size of American Lobsters in Maine." *Transactions of the American Fisheries Society* 111 (1): 1–12.

Acheson, James M., and Robert S. Steneck. 1997. "Bust and then Boom in the Maine Lobster

Fishery: Perspectives of Fishers and Biologists." *North American Journal of Fisheries Management* 17 (4): 826–47.

Acheson, James M., and James A. Wilson. 1996. "Order Out of Chaos: The Case for Parametric Fisheries Management." *American Anthropologist* 98 (3): 579–94.

Agrawal, Arun. 2000. "Common Resources and Institutional Sustainability." Unpublished ms. Department of Political Science, Yale University.

Agrawal, Arun, and Clark Gibson. 1999. "Enchantment and Disenchantment: The Role of Community in Natural Resource Conservation." *World Development* 27 (4): 629–49.

Alchian, Armen. 1950. "Uncertainty, Evolution and Economic Theory." *Journal of Political Economy* 58: 2311–21.

Alden, Robin. 1989a. "Lobster Industry: Adapting to Meet the Challenges of the 1990's." *Commercial Fisheries News*, April, 6.

——. 1989b. "Lobster Politics: Go Slow, Stay Cool, Keep Listening." *Commercial Fisheries News*, July, 6.

——. 1991. "Lobstering: 100-year-storm, New Management Challenges." *Commercial Fisheries News*, December, A6.

——. 1993. "Why Manage Lobsters, What Should the Fishery Be?" *Commercial Fisheries News*, September, A6.

——. 1995. "DMR Commissioner Initiates Monthly Report." *Commercial Fisheries News*, November, B4.

——. 1996. "What Policy Makers Want and Expect from Scientists." Speech at Marine Policy Symposium, November 13, 1996, University of Maine.

American Lobster Stock Assessment Sub-Committee. 2000. *Draft American Lobster Stock Assessment Report for Peer Review*. Washington, D.C.: Atlantic States Marine Fisheries Commission.

Ames, Ted. 1999. "How to Fix Maine's Lobster Zone Council System." *Maine Commercial Fisheries*, October, C14.

Amory, Joan. 1999a. "Maine Approves 1–15/16" Lobster Trap Vent Size." *Commercial Fisheries News*, February, A15.

——. 1999b. "Maine Legislative Update." *Commercial Fisheries News*, May, B6.

Anderson, Eugene, N. 1996. *Ecologies of the Heart*. New York and Oxford: Oxford University Press.

Anderson, T. L., and R. T. Simmons, eds. 1993. *The Political Economy of Customs and Culture: Informal Solutions to the Commons Problem*. Lanham, Md.: Rowman and Littlefield.

Anonymous. [1907]. "Clans of Lobstermen Threaten Bloodshed." Newspaper article from the files of the *Brunswick Times Record*. No author or newspaper identification. Probable date is 1907.

Anthony, Vaughn, and J. F. Caddy. 1980. "Proceedings of the Canada–U.S. Workshop on Status of Assessment Science for N.W. Atlantic Lobster *(Homarus americanus)* Stocks." Canadian Technical Report of Fisheries and Aquatic Sciences no. 9312. Saint Andrews, New Brunswick.

Appell, David. 2001. "The New Uncertainty Principle." *Scientific American* 284 (1): 18–19.

Arrow, Kenneth. 1971. "Political and Economic Evaluations, Social Effects and Externalities." In *Frontiers of Qualitative Economics*, ed. Michael D. Intriligator, 3–25. Amsterdam: North-Holland Press.

Axelrod, Robert. 1986. "An Evolutionary Approach to Norms." *American Political Science Review* 80 (4): 1095–111.

Bailey, Frederick G. 1969. *Stratagems and Spoils*. Cambridge, Mass.: Schocken Press.

Baland, J. M., and J. P. Platteau. 1996. *Halting Degradation of Natural Resources: Is There a Role for Rural Communities?* Oxford, U.K.: Clarendon.

Bangor Daily News. 1996. "Lobster Conservation Law Opposed." April 18, 1996, B1.

Barinaga, Marcia. 1995. "New Study Provides Some Good News for Fisheries." *Science* 269: 1043.

Barshaw, D. E., and K. L. Lavalli. 1988. "Predation upon Postlarval Lobster *Homarus americanus* by Cunners *Tautogolabrus adspersus* and Mud Crabs *Neopanopi sayi* on Three Different Substrates: Eelgrass, Mud and Rocks." *Marine Ecology Progress Series* 48: 119–23.

Barth, Fredrik. 1959. *Political Leadership among the Swat Pathans.* London: Athlone Press.

———. 1981. *Process and Form in Social Life.* London: Routledge and Kegan Paul.

Bates, Robert. 1994. "Social Dilemmas and Rational Individuals." In *Anthropology and Institutional Economics,* ed. James M. Acheson, 43–66. Monographs in Economic Anthropology no.12. Lanham, Md.: University Press of America.

Bates, Robert, Avner Greif, Margaret Levi, Jean-Laurent Rosenthal, and Barry Weingast. 1998. *Analytic Narratives.* Princeton: Princeton University Press.

Bayer, Robert, Peter C. Daniel, and Scott Vaitones. 1985. "Preliminary Estimate of Contributions of V-Notched American Lobsters to Egg Production along Coastal Maine Based on Maine Lobstermen's Association V-Notch Survey: 1981–1984." *Bulletin of the Department of Animal and Veterinary Sciences.* Orono: University of Maine.

Becker, Gary. 1983. "A Theory of Competition among Pressure Groups for Political Influence." *Quarterly Journal of Economics* 98 (3): 371–400.

Bennett, John. 1976. *The Ecological Transition: Cultural Anthropology and Human Adaptation.* New York: Pergamon Press.

Berger, Tina. 1999. "ASMFC Part II." *Commercial Fisheries News,* July, B10.

Berkes, Fikret. 1989. *Common Property Resources: Ecology and Community-based Sustainable Development.* London: Belhaven Press.

Berkes, Fikret, and Carl Folke. 1998. *Linking Social and Ecological Systems: Management Practices and Social Mechanisms for Building Resilience.* New York: Cambridge University Press.

Bernard, H. Russell. 1988. *Research Methods in Cultural Anthropology.* Newberry Park, Calif.: Sage.

Bickers, Kenneth, and John T. Williams. 2001. *Public Policy Analysis.* Boston: Houghton Mifflin.

Billings, Betty. 1978. "Feds Aim at Lobster: Entry Moratorium, Minimum Size Increase Pushed." *Maine Commercial Fisheries,* August, A1.

———. 1979. "MLA Plan." *Maine Commercial Fisheries,* February, 23.

———. 1985a. "Will Trap Tags Work." *Commercial Fisheries News,* June, 42.

———. 1985b. "Tallying Trap Tags on Bottom." *Commercial Fisheries News,* May, 29.

Blackmore, Eddie. 1978. "Needed: A Raise in the Small Measure." *Maine Commercial Fisheries,* June, 3.

Bologna, P. A., and R. S. Steneck. 1993. "Kelp Beds and Habitat for American Lobster *Homarus americanus.*" *Marine Ecology Progress Series* 100: 127–34.

Botsford, Louis, James E. Wilen, and E. Richardson. 1986. "Biological and Economic Analysis of Lobster Fishery Policy in Maine." Unpublished ms. submitted to the Commissioner of Marine Resources. Study commissioned by the 112th Legislature of Maine.

Boudreau, B., Y. Simard, and E. Bourget. 1991. "Behavioral Responses of the Planktonic Stages of the American Lobster *Homarus americanus* to Thermal Gradients, and Ecological Implications." *Marine Ecology Progress Series* 76: 12–23.

Boulding, Kenneth. 1963. "Towards a Pure Theory of a Threat System." *American Economic Review* 53: 424–34.

Bowman, R. E. 1981. "Food of 10 Species of Northwest Atlantic Juvenile Groundfish." *Fisheries Bulletin* 79: 200–206.

Brennan, William J. "Lobsters." Maine Department of Marine Resources. June 23, 1992. Memo to David Borden, Director of Fish and Wildlife, R.I., and Phil Coates, Director, Division of Marine Fisheries, Mass.

Buchanan, James, and Gordon Tullock. 1962. *The Calculus of Consent.* Ann Arbor: University of Michigan Press.

Business Week. 1984. "The Lobster Business is Going to Pot." October 1, 1984, 42.

Campbell, A., and D. R. Duggan. 1980. "Review of the Grand Manan Lobster Fishery with an Analysis of Recent Catch and Effort Trends." *Canadian Technical Report Fisheries and Aquatic Science* 997: 1–20.

Campbell, A., D. J. Noakes, and R. W. Elner. 1991. "Temperature and Lobster, *Homarus americanus,* Yield Relationships." *Canadian Journal of Fisheries and Aquatic Sciences* 48: 2073–82.

Clifford, Harold. 1961. *The Boothbay Region: 1906–1960.* Freeport, Maine: The Cumberland Press.

———. 1974. *Charlie York: Maine Coast Fisherman.* Camden, Maine: International Marine Publishing Co.

Coase, Ronald. 1937. "The Nature of the Firm." *Economica* 4 (3): 386–404. Reprinted in *The Nature of the Firm: Origins, Evolution, and Development,* ed. Oliver E. Williamson and Sidney G. Winter, 1977. New York: Oxford.

———. 1960. "The Problem of Social Costs." *Journal of Law and Economics* 3:1–44.

Cobb, John N. 1901. "The Lobster Fishery of Maine." In *Bulletin of the United States Fish Commission,* vol. XIX for 1899, 241–65. Washington, D.C.: U.S. Government Printing Office.

Coleman, James. 1990. "Norm Generating Structures." In *The Limits of Rationality,* ed. Karen Cook and Margaret Levi, 250–73. Chicago: University of Chicago Press.

———. 1994. "A Rational Choice Perspective on Economic Sociology." In *The Handbook of Economic Sociology,* ed. Neil J. Smelser and Richard Swedberg, 166–80. Princeton: Princeton University Press.

Colson, Elizabeth. 1974. *Tradition and Contract: The Problem of Order.* Chicago: Aldine.

Commercial Fisheries News. 1987a. "Lobster Plan Amendment Receives Approval." November, 24.

———. 1987b. "Lobster Amendment Set for Council Vote." June, 29.

———. 1989. "Gauge Tools and Gauge Increases: Inshore Lobstering Reaches Winter Hiatus." February, 22.

———. 1997a. "DMR Turns to Lobster Councils for Help with Whale Response." June, B4.

———. 1997b. "Lobster Zone E to Vote on Trap Limit." September, B5.

———. 1998a. "ASMFC Lobster Provisions—At a Glance." January, B9.

———. 1998b. "Subzone Taskforce Wraps Up Deliberations." December, C21.

Commons, John R. 1934. *Institutional Economics: Its Place in Political Economy.* New York: MacMillan Company.

Connolly, Maureen. 1979. "Maine Legislative Update." *Maine Commercial Fisheries,* May, 22.

Conser, R. J., and J. Idoine. 1992. "A Modified DeLury Model for Estimating Mortality Rates and Stock Sizes of American Lobster Populations." Papers of the Northeast Regional Stock Assessment Workshops. Appendix to CRD-92–07. Research Document of the 14th Stock Assessment Workshop. Northeast Fisheries Science Center, Woods Hole, Mass.

Cook, Karen, and Margaret Levi. 1990. *The Limits of Rationality*. Chicago: University of Chicago Press.

Cooper, Richard A., and Joseph R. Uzmann. 1971. "Migration and Growth of Deep-Sea Lobsters." *Science* 171: 288–90.

———. 1980. "Ecology of Juvenile and Adult Homarus." In *The Biology and Management of Lobsters*, ed. J. S. Cobb and B. F. Phillips, vol. 2, 97–141. New York: Academic Press.

Correspondence of the Commissioner of Sea and Shore Fisheries 1930–1934. Maine State Archives. Augusta, Maine. Correspondence is filed by date.

———. 1931a. Vernon Gould to Horatio Crie, February 16, 1931.

———. 1931b. Llewellyn Crowley to Horatio Crie, February 2, 1931.

———. 1931c. Alton Dobbins to Horatio Crie, February 9, 1931.

———. 1931d. Draft of Speech Given by Horatio Crie, in folder for January 3, 1931.

———. 1931e. Zenas Howe to Horatio Crie, November 20, 1931.

———. 1931f. Letter from Mr. Woodward to Commissioner Horatio Crie, February 22, 1931.

———. 1932a. Horatio Crie to Walter Donnell, March 19, 1932.

———. 1932b. Judge William Whiting to Horatio Crie, December 30, 1932.

———. 1932c. Walter H. Donnell to Horatio Crie, March 17, 1932

———. 1933a. F. E. Peabody to Horatio Crie, February 27, 1933.

———. 1933b. Horatio Crie to Russell Turner, September 23, 1933.

———. 1933c. J. M. Jasper to Horatio Crie, May 1, 1933.

———. 1933d. Horatio Crie to U.S. Representative E. C. Moran, May 31, 1933.

———. 1933e. U.S. Representative Edward Moran to Horatio Crie, April 10, 1933.

———. 1933f. Henry J. Flint to Horatio Crie, July 13, 1931.

———. 1933g. Horatio Crie to Alton Dobbins, December 16, 1933.

———. 1933h. C. S. Beale to Horatio Crie, March 11, 1933.

———. 1934. Horatio Crie to Joseph Wallace, telegram in box 54, no date (probably April or May).

Crie, Horatio. 1933. Speech to the Honorable Sea and Shore Fisheries Committee, Maine Legislature. Typed manuscript. Maine State Archives. Correspondence of the Commissioner of Sea and Shore Fisheries, December 11, 1933.

Daniel, Peter C., Robert C. Bayer, and Cheryl Waltz. 1989. "Egg Production of V-notched American Lobsters *Homarus americanus* along Coastal Maine." *Journal of Crustacean Biology* 9 (1): 77–82.

Demsetz, Harold. 1967. "Towards a Theory of Property Rights." *American Economic Review* 62: 347–59.

Dewar, Margaret. 1983. *Industry in Trouble: The Federal Government and the New England Fisheries.* Philadelphia: Temple University Press.

DMR News. 1997. *Commercial Fisheries News,* June, B4.

———. 1998a. *Commercial Fisheries News,* April, B4.

———. 1998b. *Commercial Fisheries News,* June, B4.

Dolsak, Nives, and Elinor Ostrom. In press. "The Challenges of the Commons." In *The Commons in the New Millennium: Challenges and Adaptations.* Cambridge: MIT Press.

Donnell, Bill. 1977. "The Feds and Lobsters." *Maine Commercial Fisheries,* December, A28.

Dow, R. L. 1967. "Temperatures, Fishing Effort Point Up Growing Problem." In *The Influence of Temperature on Maine Lobster Supply,* Sea & Shore Fisheries Research Bulletin no. 30, Augusta, Maine.

———. 1969. "Cyclic and Geographic Trends in Seawater Temperature and Abundance of American Lobster." *Science* 164 (1060): 3.

Dyer, Christopher, and James R. McGoodwin. 1994. *Folk Management of the World's Fisheries: Lessons for Fisheries Management.* Niwot: University Press of Colorado.

Dyson-Hudson, Rada, and Eric Alden Smith. 1978. "Human Territoriality: An Ecological Assessment." *American Anthropologist* 80: 21–41.

Eggertsson, Thrainn. 1993. "Economic Perspectives on Property Rights and the Economics of Institutions." Paper given at the Beijer International institute of Ecological Economics, The Royal Swedish Academy of Sciences.

Elden, A. 1931. "Lobster Dealers Interested in Fast Transportation to Big Centers." *Atlantic Fishermen,* November, 12.

Elner, R. W., and R. L. Vadas. 1990. "Inference in Ecology: The Sea Urchin Phenomenon in the Northwestern Atlantic." *American Naturalist* 136: 108–25.

Elster, Jon. 1989. *The Cement of Society.* New York: Cambridge University Press.

Elton, Alfred. 1933a. "Maine Lobster Law Remains Unchanged." *Atlantic Fisherman,* March, 8.

———. 1933b. "Maine Lobster Fishermen Polled for Views: Asked Whether They Favor Present Law, Nine Inch Law, or Double Gauge." *Atlantic Fisherman,* February, 9.

———. 1934. "Double Gauge Law Passed." *Atlantic Fisherman,* January, 7.

Ensminger, Jean. 1992. *Making a Market: The Institutional Transformation of an African Society.* New York: Cambridge University Press.

Evans-Pritchard, Edward E. 1940. *The Nuer.* Oxford: Clarendon Press.

———. 1969. *The Nuer: A Description of the Modes of Livelihood of a Nilotic People.* Oxford: Oxford University Press.

Fallers, Lloyd. 1955. "The Predicament of the East African Chief: An Instance from Uganda." *American Anthropologist* 57: 290–305.

Ferejohn, John, and Barry Weingast. 1997. *The New Federalism: Can the States be Trusted.* Stanford, Calif.: Hoover Institution Press.

Finlayson, Alan Christopher. 1994. *Fishing for Truth: A Sociological Analysis of Northern Cod Stock Assessment from 1977 to 1990.* St. John's, Newfoundland: Institute of Social Economic Research, Memorial University of Newfoundland.

Firmin-Sellers, Kathryn. 1996. *The Transformation of Property Rights in the Gold Coast: An Empirical Analysis of Applying Rational Choice Theory.* New York: Cambridge University Press.

Fiske, Alan Page. 1991. *Structures of Social Life: The Four Elementary Forms of Human Relations.* New York: The Free Press.

Fogarty, Michael J. 1988. "Time Series Models of the Gulf of Maine Lobster Fishery: The Effect of Temperature." *Canadian Journal of Fisheries and Aquatic Sciences* 45: 1145–53.

Fromm, Erich. 1941. *Escape from Freedom.* New York: Farrar and Rinehart.

Garcia, S. M., and C. Newton. 1997. "Current Situation, Trends and Prospects in World Capture Fisheries." In *Global Trends: Fisheries Management,* ed. Ellen K. Pikitch, Daniel A. Huppert, and Michael Sissenwine, 3–27. Bethesda, Md.: American Fisheries Society.

Geertz, Clifford. 1973. "Ideology as a Cultural System." In *The Interpretation of Cultures: Selected Essays by Clifford Geertz,* 193–233. New York: Basic Books.

Gluckman, Max. 1956. "The Peace in the Feud." In *Custom and Conflict in Africa,* 1–26. London: Blackwell.

Greenlaw, Lawrence. 1978. "Act on Lobster Management." *Maine Commercial Fisherman,* October, 1.

Griffin, Walter. 1998. "Monhegan, Friendship Lobstermen Press Views." *Bangor Daily News,* January 28, B1, B6.

Hardin, Garrett. 1968. "The Tragedy of the Commons." *Science* 162: 1243–48.

Hardin, Garrett, and John Baden. 1977. *Managing the Commons*. San Francisco: W. H. Freeman.

Hardin, Russell. 1982. *Collective Action*. Baltimore: Johns Hopkins University Press.

Harding, G. C., K. F. Drinkwater, and P. Vass. 1983. "Factors Influencing the Size of the American Lobster *(Homarus americanus)* Stocks along the Atlantic Coast of Nova Scotia, Gulf of Saint Lawrence, and Gulf of Maine: A New Synthesis." *Canadian Journal of Fisheries and Aquatic Sciences* 40: 168–84.

Harms, John and Gil Sylvia. 2001. "A Comparison of Conservation Perspectives between Scientists, Managers and Industry in the West Coast Groundfishery." *Fisheries* 26 (10): 6–15.

Hastings, Alan, and Kevin Higgins. 1994. "Persistence of Transients in Spatially Structured Ecological Models." *Science* 263: 1133–36.

Heath, Anthony. 1976. *Rational Choice and Social Exchange*. New York: Cambridge University Press.

Hechter, Michael. 1990. "Comment: On the Inadequacy of Game Theory for the Solution of Real-World Collective Action Problems." In *The Limits of Rationality*, ed. Karen Cook and Margaret Levi, 240–49. Chicago: University of Chicago Press.

Herrick, Francis H. 1911. "Natural History of the American Lobster." *Bulletin of the Bureau of Fisheries* 29: 153–440. Washington, D.C.: U.S. Government Printing Office.

Hodgson, Geoffrey. 1988. *Economics and Institutions: A Manifesto for a Modern Institutional Economics*. Philadelphia: University of Pennsylvania Press.

Hoffer, Eric. 1951. *The True Believer: Thoughts on the Nature of Mass Movements*. New York: Harper and Row.

Hollings, C. S. 1978. *Adaptive Environmental Assessment and Management*. London: Wiley.

Huq, A. M., and H. I. Hasey. 1973. *Socio-economic Impact of Changes in the Harvesting Labor Force in the Maine Lobster Fishery*. Washington, D.C.: National Marine Fisheries Service, Economic Research Division.

Jasanof, Sheila. 1998. "Skinning Scientific Cats." In *Green Planet Blues*, ed. Ken Conca and Geoffrey Dabelko, 153–56, Boulder: Westview Press. .

Jentoft, Svein. 1989. "Fisheries Co-management: Delegating Government Responsibility to Fishermen's Organizations." *Marine Policy* 13: 137–54.

Jentoft, Svein, and Anthony Davis. 2000. "Self and Sacrifice: An Investigation of Small Boat Fisher Individualism and its Implications for Producer Cooperatives." http://www.sffx.ca/people/abayesp/selfscarifice-report.ht.

Jones, Susan. 1985a. "Lobstermen Endorse More than 1 Vent for Wire Traps." *Maine Commercial Fisherman*, May, 12.

———. 1985b. "Okay to Sell V-notched Males." *Commercial Fisheries News*, August, 39.

———. 1995a. "Me. Marine Resources Committee Deliberates over Lobster Plan." *Commercial Fisheries News*, June, A22.

———. 1995b. "Lobster, Urchin Legislation Pending in Maine." *Commercial Fisheries News*, July, A8.

———. 1996a. "Maine Lobster Law Comes on Line: Discussion Opens on Zones, Councils." *Commercial Fisheries News*, February, A1.

———. 1996b. "Lobster Trap Tag Rules Take Effect in Maine." *Commercial Fisheries News*, March, B3.

———. 1996c. "Maine Plans May Hearings on Lobster Zone/Council Rules." *Commercial Fisheries News*, May, A22.

———. 1996d. "Maine Launches Lobster Zone Management Councils." *Commercial Fisheries News*. November, A11.

———. 1996e. "Maine Lobstermen File Court Action to Halt Trap Limit." *Commercial Fisheries News,* May, A22.

———. 1997a. "Whale Take Reduction Plan Proposed Rule." *Commercial Fisheries News,* June, A15.

———. 1997b. "NMFS Plan Balances Whale Protection, Fishing Needs." *Commercial Fisheries News,* August, A1.

———. 1997c. "Pork Group Sues Promotion Council." *Commercial Fisheries News,* April, A18.

———. 1998a. "DMR Proposes Regulation to Reduce Zone G Trap Limit to 800." *Commercial Fisheries News,* March, A16.

———. 1998b. "Maine Judge Puts Hold on Zone G Trap Limit." *Commercial Fisheries News,* August, A9.

———. 1998c. "Me. Commissioner Certifies Lobster Zone Vote." *Commercial Fisheries News,* February, A14.

Jones, Susan, and Janice M. Plante. 1996. "Maine Schedules Lobster, Urchin Hearings." *Commercial Fisheries News,* July, A17.

Judd, Richard W. 1988. "Saving the Fisherman as Well as the Fish: Conservation and Commercial Rivalry in Maine's Lobster Industry: 1872–1933." *Business History Review* 62: 596–625.

Kapferer, Bruce. 1976. *Transactions and Meaning: Directions in the Anthropology of Exchange and Symbolic Behavior.* Philadelphia: Institute for the Study of Human Issues.

Keiffer, Elizabeth. 1993. "Where Have All the Lobsters Gone?" *New York Times,* November 18.

Kelly, Kevin H. 1990. *A Summary of Maine Lobster Laws and Regulations: 1820–1990.* Lobster Informational Leaflet no. 19. Augusta: Maine Department of Marine Resources.

Kinzie, Susan. 1998. "Monhegan Lobstering Zone Passes the Senate." *Bangor Daily News,* February 26, A1.

Knight, Jack. 1992. *Institutions and Social Conflict.* New York: Cambridge University Press.

Krouse, Jay S. 1972. *Size at First Sexual Maturity for Male and Female Lobsters Found along the Maine Coast.* Lobster Information Leaflet no. 2. Augusta: Maine Department of Sea and Shore Fisheries.

———. 1973. "Maturity, Sex Ratio, and Size Composition of the Natural Population of American Lobster, *Homarus americanus,* along the Maine Coast." *Fishery Bulletin* 71: 165–73.

———. 1977. *Lobster Tagging Study.* Lobster Information Leaflet no. 5. Augusta: Maine Department of Marine Resources.

Krouse, Jay S., and James C. Thomas. 1976. "Effects of Trap Selectivity and Some Population Parameters on Size Composition of American Lobsters Catch along the Maine Coast." *Fishery Bulletin* 73 (4): 863–71.

Kuhnert, Stephan. 2001. "An Evolutionary Theory of Collective Action: Schumpeterian Entrepreneurship for the Common Good." *Constitutional Political Economy* 12: 13–29.

Kyle, Bruce. 1996. "Helping a Sinking Ship." *Bangor Daily News,* May 21, 1.

Landa, Janet T. 1997. *Trust, Ethnicity and Identity.* Ann Arbor: University of Michigan Press.

Larkin, Alice. 1979. "Apollonio to Propose New Lobster Plan." *Maine Commercial Fisheries,* April, 4.

Laws of Maine
1874, Chapter 210. "An Act for the Better Protection of Lobsters in the Waters of Maine." Augusta: Office of the Secretary of State, 146–47.
1879, Chapter 96. "An Act for the Protection of Lobsters." Augusta: Office of the Secretary of State, 114.

1883, Chapter 138. "An Act for the Protection of Lobsters." Augusta: Office of the Secretary of State, 115–16.

1885, Chapter 275. "An Act to Amend Chapter Forty of the Revised Statues, Relating to Fish and Fisheries." Augusta: Office of the Secretary of State, 224–26.

1889, Chapter 292. "An Act for the Regulation of the Lobster Industry." Augusta: Office of the Secretary of State, 258–60.

1899, Chapter 172. "An Act Establishing a Close Time on Lobsters in Pigeon Hill Bay in the Towns of Milbridge and Steuben." Augusta: Office of the Secretary of State, 225.

1907a, Chapter 49. "An Act to Amend Section Seventeen of Chapter Forty-one of the Revised Statutes Relating to Measurement of Lobsters." Augusta: Office of the Secretary of State, 49–50.

1907b, Chapter 61. "An Act to Better Protect the Lobster Industry within Two Miles from the Shore of Monhegan Island between the First Day of June and the Twenty Fifth Day of November of Each Year." Augusta: Office of the Secretary of State, 273.

1911, Chapter 260. "An Act Establishing a Close Time on Lobsters in the Waters of Winter Harbor, in Hancock County." Augusta: Office of the Secretary of State, 584.

1915a, Chapter 154. "An Act Establishing a Close Time on Lobsters in the Towns of Cutler, Trescott and Lubec." Augusta: Office of the Secretary of State, 498.

1915b, Chapter 122. "An Act Establishing a Close Time on Lobsters in the Waters of Jonesboro and Roque Bluffs, in Washington County." Augusta: Office of the Secretary of State, 464.

1915c, Chapter 121. "An Act Establishing a Close Time on Lobsters in Machias Bay and Adjacent Waters in the County of Washington." Augusta: Office of the Secretary of State, 463–64.

1925, Chapter 14. "An Act to Establish Close Time on Lobsters West of Petit Manan Point." Augusta: Office of the Secretary of State, 236.

1931, Chapter 47. "An Act Relating to Lobster Fishing in Waters Adjacent to Criehaven." Augusta: Office of the Secretary of State, 39.

1935, Chapter 294. "An Act Relating to Measurement of Lobsters." Augusta: Office of the Secretary of State, 54–55.

1947, Chapter 332. "A Law to Revise the Sea and Shore Fisheries Laws." Augusta: Office of the Secretary of State, 408.

1978, Public Law 1977, Chapter 385. "An Act to Allow the Escape of Sublegal Lobsters from Lobster or Crab Trap."

Layton, Arthur B. 1987. "Marshall Says V-notch Acceptance Likely." *Commercial Fisheries News,* August, 23.

Legislative Documents

1872, House no. 54. "An Act to Protect the Spawn or Egg Lobsters in the Waters of Maine."

1935, House no. 503. "An Act Relating to Measurement of Lobsters." February 12.

Legislative Records

1915a. Senate, March 30, 1165.

1915b. Senate, March 30, 1160.

1915c. House, March 25, 1070; Senate, March.

1917. House, March 8, 1917, 486.

Lewis, David. 1969. *Convention: A Philosophical Study.* Cambridge: Harvard University Press.

Libecap, Gary. 1989. *Contracting for Property Rights.* New York: Cambridge University Press.

———. 1995. "The Conditions for Successful Collective Action." In *Local Commons and*

Global Interdependence: Heterogeneity and Cooperation in Two Domains, ed. Robert O. Keohane and Elinor Ostrom, 161–90. London: Sage Publications.

Lobster Technical Committee. 2000. "Management Measures that Can Be Evaluated on an Area-by-Area Basis: Report to the ASMFC American Lobster Board." Washington, D.C.: Atlantic States Marine Fisheries Commission. Unpublished manuscript.

Ludwig, Donald, Ray Hilborn, and Carl Walters. 1993. "Uncertainty, Resource Exploitation and Conservation: Lessons from History." *Science* 260: 17–36.

Maine Commercial Fisheries. 1976. "200 Mile Limit is Law." May, A1.

———. 1978a. "The Maine Forum." April, A12.

———. 1978b. "Comparison of Lobster Management Plan Positions." December, 20.

———. 1978c. "Retain Measure, Heed our Experience—Fishermen Say." October, 1.

Maine Commission of Sea and Shore Fisheries. 1926. *Fourth Biennial Report of the Commission of Sea and Shore Fisheries of the State of Maine.* Rockland, Maine.

Maine Commissioner of Sea and Shore Fisheries. 1949. Annual Report. Augusta, Maine.

Maine Department of Marine Resources. 1987. "Little Chance of Infection for V-notching." *Commercial Fisheries News,* April, 10.

———. 1995. *Summary of the Maine Lobster Industry.* Hallowell, Maine.

———. 1999. *Summary of the Maine Lobster Fishery: 1880–1994.* Manuscript of the Department of Marine Resources, Augusta. Originally published 1995, and updated annually thereafter.

Maine Department of Sea and Shore Fisheries. 1936. *Ninth Biennial Report of the Department of Sea and Shore Fisheries of the State of Maine.* Thomaston, Maine.

Martin, Kenneth R., and Nathan R. Lipfert. 1985. *Lobstering and the Maine Coast.* Bath: Maine Maritime Museum.

Mattocks, Luther. n.d. *Looking Backward: Memories From the Life of Luther Mattocks.* Undated typescript, Special Collections, Fogler Library, University of Maine, Orono.

McCay, Bonnie. 1988. "Muddling through the Clam Beds: Cooperative Management of New Jersey's Hard Clam Spawner Sanctuaries." *Journal of Shellfish Research* 7 (2): 327–40.

———. 1992. "Everyone's Concern, Whose Responsibility? The Problem of the Commons." In *Understanding Economic Process,* ed. Sutti Ortiz, 189–210. Lanham, Md.: University Press of America.

McCay, Bonnie, and James Acheson, eds. 1987. *The Question of the Commons.* Tucson: University of Arizona Press.

McCay, Bonnie, and Svein Jentoft. 1996. "From the Bottom Up: Participatory Issues in Fisheries Management." *Society and Natural Resources* 9: 237–50.

McFarland, R. 1911. *A History of the New England Fisheries.* Philadelphia: University of Pennsylvania Press.

McGinnis, Michael D. 1999. "Introduction." In *Polycentric Governance and Development: Readings from the Workshop in Political Theory and Policy Analysis,* 1–28. Ann Arbor: University of Michigan Press.

McGoodwin, James R. 1990. *Crisis in the World's Fisheries: People, Problems and Policies.* Stanford: Stanford University Press.

McLane, Charles B. 1982. *Islands of the Mid-Maine Coast: Penobscot and Blue Hill Bays.* Woolwich, Maine: Kennebec River Press.

Miller, Gary. 1992. *Managerial Dilemmas: The Political Economy of Hierarchy.* New York: Cambridge University Press.

Moberg, Mark. 1994. "An Agency Model of the State." In *Anthropology and Institutional Economics,* ed. James M. Acheson, 213–31. Monographs in Economic Anthropology no.12. Lanham, Md.: University Press of America.

Moe, Terry. 1990. "The Politics of Structural Choice: Toward a Theory of Public Bureaucracy." In *Organization Theory*, ed. Oliver Williamson, 116–53. New York: Oxford University Press.

Morrison, Susan. 1979. Lobster Management—More Views Revised Plan." *Maine Commercial Fisheries*, February, 23.

———. 1985. "No Decisions Yet on Controversial Lobster Proposals." May, 43.

Murawski, Steven A., Jean-Jacques Maguire, Ralph Mayo, and Fredric M. Serchuk. 1997. "Groundfish Stocks and the Fishing Industry." In *Northwest Atlantic Groundfish: Perspectives on an Industry Collapse*, ed. John Boreman, Brian S. Nakashima, James A. Wilson, and Robert Kendall, 27–70. Bethesda, Md.: The American Fisheries Society.

Mwangi, Esther. 2001. "Fragmenting the Commons: The Transformation of Property Rights in Kenya's Masai Land." Unpublished manuscript, Department of Political Science, Indiana University, Bloomington.

National Research Council. 1986. *Proceedings of the Conference on Common Property Resource Management*. Washington, D.C.: National Academy Press.

North, Douglass. 1990a. *Institutions, Institutional Change and Economic Performance*. New York: Cambridge University Press.

———. 1990b. "Institutions and their Consequences for Economic Performance." In *The Limits of Rationality*, ed. Karen S. Cook and Margaret Levi, 383–401. Chicago: University of Chicago Press.

Northeast Marine Fishery Board. 1978. *American Lobster Fishery Management Plan*. Gloucester, Mass.: Northeast Marine Fishery Board.

O'Leary, Shawn. 2000. "Avoid Eating Lobster, List Says." *Bangor Daily News*, February 24, 1A.

Olson, Mancur. 1965. *The Logic of Collective Action: Public Goods and the Theory of Groups*. Cambridge: Harvard University Press.

Ostrom, Elinor. 1990. *Governing the Commons: The Evolution of Institutions for Collective Action*. New York: Cambridge University Press.

———. 1992. *Crafting Institutions for Self-Governing Irrigation Systems*. San Francisco: ICS Press.

———. 1998. "A Behavioral Approach to the Rational Choice Theory of Collective Action." *American Political Science Review* 92 (1): 1–22.

———. 1999a. "Coping with Tragedies of the Commons. *Annual Review of Political Science* 2: 493–535.

———. 1999b. "Institutional Rational Choice: An Assessment of the Institutional Analysis and Development Framework." In *Theories of the Policy Process*, ed. Paul A. Sabatier, 35–71. Boulder: Westview Press.

———. 2000a. "Reformulating the Commons." *Swiss Political Science Review* 61 (1): 29–52.

———. 2000b. "Collective Action and the Evolution of Social Norms." *Journal of Economic Perspectives* 14 (3): 137–58.

Ostrom, Elinor, Roy Gardner, and James Walker. 1994. *Rules, Games, and Common-Pool Resources*. Ann Arbor: University of Michigan Press.

Ostrom, Vincent. 1999. "Polycentricity (Part 1)." In *Polycentricity and Local Public Economies: Readings from the Workshop in Political Theory and Policy Analysis*, ed. Michael D. McGinnis, 52–74. Ann Arbor: University of Michigan Press.

Palmer, Craig. 1994. "Are Folk Management Practices Models for Formal Regulations? Evidence from the Lobster Fisheries of Newfoundland and Maine." In *Folk Management in the World's Fisheries*, ed. Christopher L. Dyer and James McGoodwin, 237–49. Niwot: University of Colorado Press.

Palsson, Gisli. 1994. "Enskilment at Sea." *Man* 29: 901–27.

Pezzack, Douglas S. 1992. "A Review of Lobster *(Homarus americanus)* Landing Trends in the Northwest Atlantic, 1947–1986." *Journal of the Northwest Atlantic Fisheries Society* 14: 115–27.

———. 1995. "Scotia-Fundy Region: Lobster Summary Sheets, 1993–1994 Season." Halifax Fisheries Laboratory, Fisheries and Oceans.

Pezzack, Douglas S., and Dr. R. Duggan. 1986. "Evidence of Migration and Homing of Lobsters *(Homarus americanus)* on the Scotian Shelf." *Canadian Journal of Fisheries and Aquatic Science* 43: 2206–11.

Pinkerton, Evelyn. 1989. *Cooperative Management of Local Fisheries: New Directions for Improved Management and Community Development.* Vancouver: University of British Columbia Press.

Pinkerton, Evelyn, and Martin Weinstein. 1995. *Fisheries that Work: Sustainability through Community Based Management.* Vancouver: The David Suzuki Foundation.

Plante, Janice M. 1985. "Maine Lobstermen Consider Compromise." *Commercial Fisheries News,* March, 13.

———. 1986. "In Maine, It's Been Lobsters, Lobsters, Lobsters." *Commercial Fisheries News,* April, 18.

———. 1989a. "Scientists Question Me Lobster Researcher." *Commercial Fisheries News,* July, 7.

———. 1989b. "Council Vetoes Lobster Size Delay." *Commercial Fisheries News,* September, A1.

———. 1991. "Charge to Lobster Industry: Reach Consensus." *Commercial Fisheries News,* A18.

———. 1992. "Industry Pushes for Action on Lobsters." *Commercial Fisheries News,* November, A14.

———. 1993a. "Fox Agrees to Bankroll Lobster Amendment." *Commercial Fisheries News,* January, A1.

———. 1993b. "Council Inaction May Thwart Lobster Plan." *Commercial Fisheries News,* May, A17.

———. 1993c. "NE Council Considers Framework Amendment to Beat Lobster Gauge Increase Deadline." *Commercial Fisheries News,* September, A16.

———. 1993d. "Frameworked Lobster Proposal Draws Fire." *Commercial Fisheries News,* October, A11.

———. 1994a. "Roe Gives Council Heads Up on Lobster Amendment." "What ifs." *Commercial Fisheries News,* March, A12.

———. 1994b. "NE Council Approves Lobster Amendment." *Commercial Fisheries News,* January, A12.

———. 1994c. "Lobster Amendment Draws Partial Approval." *Commercial Fisheries News,* June, A1.

———. 1994d. "Lobstermen Involvement Crucial to Success of Self-management Effort." *Commercial Fisheries News,* July, A8.

———. 1995a. "NMFS Warns: Approvals of Lobster Package Contingent on States's Setting Compatible Regs." *Commercial Fisheries News,* March, B1.

———. 1995b. "Lobster Plan Hits Snag: Council Delays Action." *Commercial Fisheries News,* June, A11.

———. 1995c. "Lobster Amendment Falters: NMFS to Solicit Comments on Plan Withdrawal." *Commercial Fisheries News,* September, A1.

————. 1995d. "NMFS/ASMFC Probe Lobster Options; Mitchell Bill Concerns." *Commercial Fisheries News,* September, A15.

————. 1995e. "Trap Limits Leading Choice of Lobster EMTs." *Commercial Fisheries News,* January, A9.

————. 1995f. "States Agree to Develop Inshore Lobster Regs." *Commercial Fisheries News,* April, A11.

————. 1996a. "ASMFC Takes Lead." *Commercial Fisheries News,* April, A1.

————. 1996b. "Lobster Management Shifts to Interstate Arena." *Commercial Fisheries News,* April, A1.

————. 1996c. "ASMFC Lobster Plan Open to All Suggestions." *Commercial Fisheries News,* November, A16.

————. 1996d. "Review Panel Concurs: Lobsters Overfished." *Commercial Fisheries News,* August, A10.

————. 1997a. "ASMFC Interstate Lobster Plan Takes Shape." *Commercial Fisheries News,* April, A11.

————. 1997b. "ASMFC Readies for Lobster Plan Hearings." *Commercial Fisheries News,* August, A14.

————. 1997c. "NMFS, ASMFC Butt Heads Over Lobsters." *Commercial Fisheries News,* November, B1.

————. 1997d. "Federal Large Whale Regulations Imminent." *Commercial Fisheries News,* May, B1.

————. 1998a. "ASMFC Signs Off on Lobster Amendment: Industry Teams to Guide Effort Reduction." *Commercial Fisheries News,* January, B8.

————. 1998b. "Outer Cape Lobstermen to Sue ASMFC over Amendment 3." *Commercial Fisheries News,* January, B10.

————. 1998c. "NMFS Seeks Comment on Federal Lobster Measures." *Commercial Fisheries News,* March, A1.

————. 1999. "ASMFC Splits Lobster Management Proposals." *Commercial Fisheries News,* March, A1.

————. 2000. "Federal Lobster Rules Brings New Trap Limits." *Commercial Fisheries News,* January, A14.

————. 2001. "LCMT1 Needs 'More' to Meet 2008 Lobster Egg Production Target." *Commercial Fisheries News,* August, A1.

Plante, Janice M., and Susan Jones. 1995. "Maine Confirms Alden: Lobster Bill to be Filed." *Commercial Fisheries News,* March, A21.

Portland Sunday Telegram. 1933. "Machiasport Lobster Fishermen in Favor of Double Gauge Law." December 31, 2a.

Proper, Ida S. 1930. *Monhegan, the Cradle of New England.* Portland, Maine: Southworth Press.

Public Law 94–265. 1976. "An Act to Provide for the Conservation and Management of the Fisheries, and for Other Purposes." 94th Congress, April 13, 1976.

Public Law 1995, Chapter 468. "An Act to Establish a Management Framework for the Lobster Fishery within State Waters."

Public Law 104–297. The Sustainable Fisheries Act. 1996. "An Act to Amend the Magnuson Fishery Conservation and Management Act to Authorize Appropriations, to Provide for Sustainable Fisheries, and for Other Purposes." 104th Congress, October 11, 1996.

Public Law 1997, Chapter 693. "An Act to Establish a Requirement that Holders of Lobster Fishing Licenses Must Own or Control the Vessel from which They Conduct Authorized Activities."

Public Law 1999, Chapter 397. "An Act to Establish a Lobster Trap Tag Freeze to Limit Effort in the Lobster Fishery."

Public Law 1999, Chapter 508. "An Act to Limit Entry into the Lobster Fishery by Zone."

Rathbun, Richard. 1887. *The Lobster Fishery: The Fisheries and Fishery Industries of the United States.* Section V: *History and Methods of the Fisheries,* vol. II, ed. George Brown Goode, 658–794. Washington, D.C.: U.S. Government Printing Office.

Rheault, Ann Kane. 2000. "R.I. Hangs Tough, Rejects Lobster Limits." *Commercial Fisheries News,* June, B18.

Rosen, R. 1995. "Advocacy for Fishery Professionals." *Fisheries* 20 (7): 4.

Ruddle, Kenneth, and Tomoya Akimichi, eds. 1984. *Maritime Institutions in the Western Pacific.* Senri Series in Ethnology, no. 17. Osaka: National Museum of Ethnology.

Ruddle, K., and R. E. Johannes. 1985. *The Traditional Knowledge and Management of Coastal Systems in Asia and the Pacific.* Jakarta Pusat, Indonesia: United Nations Educational Scientific and Cultural Organization.

Schlager, Edella. 1994. "Fishers' Institutional Responses to Common-Pool Resource Dilemmas." In *Rules, Games, and Common-Pool Resources,* ed. Elinor Ostrom, Roy Gardner, and James Walker, 247–65. Ann Arbor: University of Michigan Press.

Schlager, Edella, William Blomquist, and Shui Yan Tang. 1999. "Mobile Flows, Storage, and Self-Organized Institutions for Governing Common-Pool Resources." In *Polycentric Governance and Development: Readings from the Workshop in Political Theory and Policy Analysis,* ed. Michael D. McGinnis, 114–47. Ann Arbor: University of Michigan Press.

Scott, Anthony D. 1955. "The Fishery: The Objectives of Sole Ownership." *Journal of Political Economy* 63: 187–99.

Scott, James C. 1998. *Seeing Like a State.* New Haven: Yale University Press.

Sharp, David. 2000. "Retrial Ordered for Lobsterman Convicted in Fishing Rights War." *Kennebec Journal,* Augusta, Maine, November 15.

Shleifer, Andrei, and Robert W. Vishny. 1998. *The Grabbing Hand: Government Pathologies and their Cures.* Cambridge: Harvard University Press:

Simpson, Dorothy. 1960. *The Maine Islands in Story and Legend.* Philadelphia: J. B. Lippincott.

Singleton, Sara. 1998. *Constructing Cooperation: The Evolution of Institutions of Comanagement.* Ann Arbor: University of Michigan Press.

Singleton, Sara, and Michael Taylor. 1992. "Common Property, Collective Action and the Community." *Journal of Theoretical Politics* 4 (3): 309–24.

Skud, B. E., and H. C. Perkins. 1969. "Size Composition, Sex Ratio, and Size at Maturity of Offshore Northern Lobsters." *U.S. Fish and Wildlife Service Special Scientific Report* 598: 1–10.

Smith, Courtland. 1988. "Conservation and Allocation Decisions in Fishery Management." In *Salmon Production, Management, and Allocation: Biological, Economic and Policy Issues,* ed. William J. McNeil, 131–38. Corvallis: Oregon State University Press.

Smith, Estellie. 1990. "Chaos in Fisheries Management." *MAST* 3 (2): 1–13.

Sonnenberg, Liz. 1989a. "Industry Plans Two-pronged Attack." *Commercial Fisheries News,* November, 17.

——. 1989b. "Bill Targets Ban on Sale of Undersized Lobsters." *Commercial Fisheries News,* November, 16.

——. 1989c. "Canadians Give Gauge Increase Thumbs Down." *Commercial Fisheries News,* October, 12.

——. 1991. "Maine Lobster Gauge Moving, Scallops on Hold." *Commercial Fisheries News,* March, A22.

———. 1992. "Lobster Industry: Name Your Plan." *Commercial Fisheries News,* February, A25.

Stecklow, S. 1991. "Lobster Scientists in over their Heads." *Lewiston Sun Journal,* September 16, 17–18.

Steneck, Robert S. 1989a. "Ecological Considerations on Increasing the Minimum Legal Size of Lobsters." Summary paper sent to the New England Regional Council in support of Amendment 5 of the American Lobster Plan.

———. 1989b. "The Ecological Ontogeny of Lobsters: In Situ Studies with Demographic Implications." In *Proceedings of the Lobster Life History Workshop 1,* ed. Irving Kornfield, 20–22. Orono, Maine.

Steneck, Robert S., D. McNaught, and S. Zimsen. 1995. *Spatial and Temporal Patterns in Sea Urchin Populations, Herbivory and Algal Community Structure in the Gulf of Maine.* Proceedings of the Sea Urchin Conference, Boothbay Harbor, Maine.

Stevens, Lorelei. 1986. "A Deal? Gauge Increase for V-notch Protection." *Commercial Fisheries News,* March, 12.

———. 1987. "Council Clears Lobster Plan Amendment." *Commercial Fisheries News,* July, 16.

———. 1992. "Lobster Industry Working Group Wrestles to Find Management Common Ground." *Commercial Fisheries News,* March, B6.

———. 1995. "MLA Lobster Seminar Looks at What's Ahead." *Commercial Fisheries News,* March, A1.

———. 1997. "Multitrack Right Whale Protection." *Commercial Fisheries News,* March, B1.

———. 1998. "Trap Tags." *Commercial Fisheries News,* March, A16.

———. 1999. "Maine Industry Details What's Wrong with Magnuson." *Commercial Fisheries News,* November, B9.

———. 2000a. "Whale Report Triggers Alarm among Lobstermen." *Commercial Fisheries News,* February, A8.

———. 2000b. "NMFS Reports 24 Whales Entangled in 1999." *Commercial Fisheries News,* March, A16.

———. 2000c. "Whale Fears Confirmed: CLF to Sue NMFS." *Commercial Fisheries News,* April, A8.

———. 2000d. "Strahan Sues Maine, Demands 'Whale Safe' Gear." *Commercial Fisheries News,* June, A16.

———. 2001. "TRT Takes Hard Look at Fixed Gear Restitutions." *Commercial Fisheries News,* August, B1

Stock Assessment Review Committee. 1996. *Report of the Twenty-second Regional Stock Assessment Workshop (22nd SAW).* Northeast Fisheries Science Reference Document 96–13. Woods Hole, Mass.: Northeast Fisheries Science Center/NMFS.

Sugden, Robert. 1986. *The Economics of Rights, Cooperation and Welfare.* London: Basil-Blackwell.

Taylor, Larry. 1987. " 'The River Would Run Red with Blood': Community and Common Property in an Irish Fishing Settlement." In *The Question of the Commons,* ed. Bonnie J. McCay and James Acheson, 290–307. Tucson: University of Arizona Press.

Taylor, Michael. 1982. *Community, Anarchy and Liberty.* New York: Cambridge University Press.

———. 1990. "Cooperation and Rationality: Notes on the Collective Action Problem and Its Solutions." In *The Limits of Rationality,* ed. Karen Cook and Margaret Levi, 222–49. Chicago: University of Chicago Press.

Taylor, Michael, and Sara Singleton. 1993. "The Communal Resource: Transaction Costs and the Solution of Collective Action Problems." *Politics and Society* 21 (2): 195–214.

References Cited 255

Thomas, James. 1973a. "An Analysis of the Commercial Lobster *(Homarus americanus)*, August 1966 though December 1970." National Oceanic and Atmospheric Administration, Technical Report. Washington, D.C.: National Marine Fisheries Service.

———. 1973b. "Ecological Considerations on Increasing the Minimum Legal Size of Lobsters." Summary paper sent to the New England Regional Council in support of Amendment 5 of the American Lobster Plan.

Tierney, John. 2000. "A Tale of Two Fisheries." *New York Times Sunday Magazine*, 38–43.

Tullock, Gordon. 1965. *The Politics of Bureaucracy*. Washington, D.C.: Public Affairs Press.

University of Maine. 1996. "Adler Chosen for Right Whale Commission." *Lobster Bulletin of the University of Maine* 9 (2): 1.

University of Maine Lobster Institute. 1995. "V-Notching Then, Now and Around the World." *Lobster Bulletin* 8 (2): 3. Orono: University of Maine, Lobster Institute.

U.S. Bureau of Commercial Fisheries. 1956. *Historical Fisheries Statistics of the United States: 1895–1998*. Washington, D.C.

Waddy, Susan, and D. E. Aiken. 1986. "Multiple Fertilizations and Consecutive Spawning in Large American Lobsters, *Homarus americanus*." *Canadian Journal of Fisheries and Aquatic Sciences* 43: 2291–94.

Wade, Robert. 1994. *Village Republics: Economic Conditions for Collective Action in South India*. San Francisco: ICS Press.

Wahle, R. A., and Robert S. Steneck. 1991. "Recruitment Habitats and Nursery Grounds of the American Lobster (*Homarus americanus* Milne Edwards): A Demographic Bottleneck?" *Marine Ecology Progress Series* 69: 231–43.

———. 1992. "Habitat Restrictions in Early Benthic Life: Experiments on Habitat Selection and in situ Predation with the American Lobster." *Journal of Experimental Marine Biology and Ecology* 157: 91–114.

Walters, C. J. 1986. *Adaptive Management of Renewable Resources*. New York: McGraw Hill.

Westbrook, Perry D. 1958. *Biography of an Island: The Story of a Maine Island, Its People and Their Unique Way of Life*. New York: Thomas Yoseloff.

Williamson, Oliver. 1970. *Corporate Control and Business Behavior*. Englewood Cliffs, N.J.: Prentice-Hall.

———. 1975. *Markets and Hierarchies: Analysis and Anti-trust Implications*. New York: The Free Press.

Wilson, James A. 1997. "Reducing Maximum Size Could Help Industry." *Lobster Bulletin* 10 (1): 4–5. Orono: University of Maine, Lobster Institute.

———. 2001. "Scientific Uncertainty, Complex Systems and the Design of Common Pool Resources." In *Institutions for Managing the Commons,* ed. Thomas Deetz, Paul Stern, Nives Dolsak and Elinor Ostrom, 327–59. Washington, D.C.: National Research Council.

Wilson, James A., James Acheson, Peter Kleban, and Mark Metcalfe. 1994. "Chaos, Complexity and the Communal Management of Fisheries." *Ocean Policy* 18 (4): 291–305.

Wilson, James A., John French, Peter Kleban, Susan McCay, and Ralph Townsend. 1991a. "Chaotic Dynamics in a Multiple Species Fishery: A Model of Community Predation." *Ecological Modeling* 58: 303–22.

———. 1991b. "The Management of Chaotic Fisheries: A Bio-economic Model." In *Proceedings from Symposium on Multiple Species Fisheries,* ed. Michael Sissenwine and Nils Daan, 287–300. Copenhagen: International Council for the Exploration of the Sea.

Wunsch, James S. 1999. "Institutional Analysis and Decentralization: Developing an Analytical Framework for Effective Third World Administrative Reform." In *Polycentric Governance and Development: Readings from the Workshop in Political Theory and Policy Analysis,* ed. Michael D. McGinnis, 243–68. Ann Arbor: University of Michigan Press.

Index

Bourget, E., 155
Bremen, 32, 37, 43–44, 48, 51, 52
Brennan, William, 173, 176, 178–80, 188, 212
Brewer, Jennifer, 13, 53
Bridges, Leroy, 190
Bristol, 114. *See also* New Harbor; Pemaquid
    Harbor; Round Pond
Buchanan, James, 226
"bust and boom," 16–18, 147–65; assessing
    causes of, 159–60. *See also* law enforce-
    ment; lobster measure; lobster stock size

Caddy, J. F., 156, 162
Campbell, A., 154–55
Canada, 13, 84, 87, 94, 171, 173–75, 191, 195,
    211–12
Cape Elizabeth, 47
Casco Bay, 32, 37, 42, 47, 51, 77, 98, 100–101
Chebeague Island, 51
Clifford, Harold, 81–82
Coase, Ronald, 5–6
Coates, Phil, 176–78
Cobb, John M., 82, 84–85
Coleman, James, 7–8, 69, 71, 98, 143, 224
collective action, 215–16; cascading dilemmas
    in, 77–78, 216–17; dilemmas, 7, 8, 77–79,
    206–7; and escape vent and V-notch, 238n;
    four types of, 206; free-rider problem, 7–8,
    216; influence of property rights on, 238n;
    rational action, 7; secondary and tertiary,
    216. *See also* institutions; institutions, de-
    vising; institutions, mechanisms produc-
    ing; rules
Colson, Elizabeth, 5
co-management, 10, 97–144, 229, 232;
    fishermen's views on, 133–37; future of,
    137–41; impediments to, 232–34; sea ur-
    chin, 99; theoretical issues in, 142–44. *See
    also* management, bottom-up; parametric
    management; zone management
common-pool resources, 2, 7, 8–11, 55, 235;
    controlled access to, 11
common property resources. *See* common-
    pool resources; property
commons. *See* common-pool resources
Commons, John R., 5
communal action. *See* collective action
Conser, R. J., 201
conservation, 1, 18–19. *See also* conservation
    ethic; conservation organizations; conser-
    vation zones

conservation ethic, 3, 81–92, 95–96, 143, 152–
    53, 161–64, 217, 221. *See also* fishermen, pol-
    icies advocated by; institutions, prerequi-
    sites conditions, discount rate; spirals, up-
    ward and downward
conservation organizations: Center for Ma-
    rine Conservation, 189; Conservation Law
    Foundation, 189–90; Humane Society, 190
conservation zones, 61, 67–68, 224–25. *See also*
    Monhegan Island; Swan's Island; territo-
    ries (lobstering), conservation zones
Cook, Karen, 226
Cooper, Richard A., 15
cooperation. *See* collective action
Cousens, David, 31, 37, 129, 152–53, 176, 183, 196
Crie, Horatio, 87–88, 92, 94–96, 154, 159, 211–
    12; Correspondence of the Commissioner,
    80–81, 87, 153–54
Crie, Robert, 61–62
Criehaven, 29, 53, 57, 62–64, 69–71, 89
Cundy's Harbor, 51
Cushing, 32, 37, 47, 50, 51–52, 72–75

Damariscotta, 37, 73
Damariscotta River, 37, 38, 45
Daniel, Peter C., 171, 196–97
Davis, Anthony, 141
Demsetz, Harold, 222
Department of Marine Resources. *See* Maine
    Department of Marine Resources
distribution fights, 2–3, 6, 8, 69, 75, 77–79, 86–
    88, 105–6, 133, 138, 142. *See also* institutions,
    mechanisms producing, distributional is-
    sues
DMR. *See* Maine Department of Marine Re-
    sources
Dolsak, Nives, 215
double gauge. *See* lobster measure, double
    gauge
Dow, Robert, 137, 148, 153, 155, 159
Downeast Lobstermen's Association, 100, 108,
    137, 189, 191
Drinkwater, K. F., 153
Duggan, R., 16, 154
Dyer, Christopher, 1, 10
Dyson-Hudson, Rada, 222

effort. *See* fishing effort
Elner, R.W., 151, 155
Elster, Jon, 7–8
encapsulated systems, 24

Endangered Species Act. *See* federal laws, Endangered Species Act
Ensminger, Jean, 6, 94
escape vent. *See* lobster traps, escape vent on
Esterbrook, Penn, 112
Etnier, David, 99, 111, 113
Evans-Pritchard, Edward E., 29, 223
exclusive areas. *See* territories (lobstering), exclusive areas
Exclusive Economic Zone (EEZ). *See* federal laws, Exclusive Economic Zone (EEZ)

Fallers, Lloyd, 125
FCMA. *See* federal laws, Fisheries Conservation and Management Act (FCMA)
Federal American Lobster Plan: Amendment 2, 173; Amendment 3, 175; Amendment 4, 175–77; Amendment 5, 99–100, 177–79; Amendment 6, 178. *See also* federal laws, American Lobster Plan
federal laws: American Lobster Plan, 90, 99, 169–70; Atlantic Coastal Fisheries Cooperative Management Act, 181, 185, 229; Endangered Species Act, 19, 140, 142, 190, 230, 233; Exclusive Economic Zone (EEZ), 100, 169; Fisheries Conservation and Management Act (FCMA), 19, 24, 140, 166–79, 181, 185, 218, 230, 233; Marine Mammal Protection Act, 19, 105, 125, 140, 188, 230, 233; Mitchell Bill, 174, 191, 239n; Sustainable Fisheries Act, 19, 105, 140, 181, 229–30, 233. *See also* Atlantic States Marine Fisheries Commission; National Marine Fisheries Service; New England Fisheries Management Council; right whale issue
Ferejohn, Jon, 140
Fessenden, Joseph, 163, 220
Field, George, 85, 196
Finlayson, Christopher, 240n
Fisheries Conservation and Management Act. *See* federal laws, Fisheries Conservation and Management Act
fisheries management, 224–34; government units in, 224–25; new approaches to, 4; and territorial unit size, 224. *See also* co-management; institutions, mechanisms producing; management; management goals (federal and ASMFC); parametric management; policy failure; science; scientists
fisheries science. *See* science
fisheries scientists. *See* scientists

fishermen: attitudes of, 89–90, 129, 162–63, 168, 170; conflicts with scientists, 3, 145, 158–59, 164, 195–96; eastern Maine, 101, 116; folklore, 3, 215; full-time and part-time, defined, 238n; policies advocated by, 89, 91–93, 165, 170–72, 177, 183, 186, 195–96, 204–5; world view of, 145–46, 160–62, 234. *See also* politics, industry influence on
fishing effort, 156, 194–95; escalation in traps, 128–29, 138. *See also* Atlantic States Marine Fisheries Commission, effort management teams; New England Fisheries Management Council, effort management teams
Fiske, Alan Page, 221–22
Five Islands, 26, 44–45, 51
Fogarty, Michael, 154, 156, 200
Folke, Carl, 227
free rider. *See* collective action, free-rider problem
Friendship, 25, 29, 32, 35, 44–45, 48–53
Fromm, Erich, 141

game theory. *See* territoriality, and game theory analysis
Gardner, Roy, 9, 55, 70, 222
gauge. *See* lobster measure (gauge)
Geertz, Clifford, 204, 217
Gibson, Clark, 71
Gluckman, Max, 223
Goldthwaite, Jill, 61, 137, 184
goods. *See* property
Green Island, 25, 29, 35–36, 45, 50, 53, 57, 64–65, 69–71
Greenlaw, Lawrence, 9, 99
Greenworld. *See* Strahan, Max
groundfishing, 25, 177. *See also* Atlantic States Marine Fisheries Commission, 100/500 rule

harbor gangs, 21–23; entry into, 30–31, 34; political teams in, 38–40. *See also* Criehaven; Green Island; Monhegan Island; Swan's Island; territories (lobstering)
Hardin, Garrett, 7, 10
Hardin, Russell, 212
Harding, G. C., 153
Harpswell, 51
Harms, John, 164
Hastings, Alan, 227
Heath, Anthony, 4
Hechter, Michael, 70, 216

Herrick, Francis H., 81, 86, 149–50, 159, 196, 212, 219
Higgins, Kevin, 227
Hilborn, Ray, 227
Hoffer, Eric, 141
Hollings, C. S., 229

Idione, Joseph 201
illegal activity, 27–29, 80–81, 149–50, 159, 164. *See also* law enforcement; Marine Patrol
institutional economics. *See* new institutionalism
institutions: characteristics of, 5–6; definition of, 5; externalities, 7, 10, 98; non-market, 6, 10; risk, 5; and types of rules, 2. *See also* collective action; institutions, devising; institutions, mechanisms producing; institutions, prerequisite conditions for; rules
institutions, devising, 2, 4, 57–59, 68–72, 144, 191–92, 206–21, 234; effect of biological, technical, and organizational factors on, 218. *See also* institutions, mechanisms producing; institutions, prerequisite conditions for; rules; spirals, upward and downward
institutions, mechanisms producing, 8, 93–95, 209–11, 215; competitive selection, 209–11; distributional issues, 69, 75, 79, 93–94, 210–14, 216; political entrepreneurs, 2, 8, 72, 77–79, 87–88, 91–93, 312–13; social conventions, 94–95, 209–11. *See also* collective action; distribution fights; institutions; institutions, devising; institutions, prerequisite conditions for; rules
institutions, prerequisite conditions of, 68–72, 75–77, 93–96, 207–8, 214–15; boundaries, 70, 76–78; community, 8, 71, 74, 76, 78, 213; dependence on resources, 71, 74, 76, 78; discount rate, 8, 71, 75, 95, 212–13, 221; entry limits, 70, 74, 78; group size, 8, 69, 76, 217; homogeneity, 8, 213–14; monitoring, 78; Ostrom's design principles, 208; rule changing ability, 8, 74, 76; social capital, 8, 71, 74, 76, 78. *See also* collective action; institutions; institutions, devising; institutions, mechanisms producing; rules
Interstate Lobster Fishery Management Plan: Amendment 3, 181–86, 212; Amendment 4, 185–87; conservation equivalencies, 185, 199; lobster dragging, 186. *See also* lobster measure, maximum; lobster traps, escape vent on; V-notch
Isle au Haut, 224

Jackson, Pat, 99, 170
Jasanof, Sheila, 227
Jentoft, Svein, 139, 141–42
John's River, 32
Jonesboro, 89
Judd, Richard, 80, 83, 85, 87, 91, 93, 149

Kapferer, Bruce, 4
Kelly, Kevin H., 85, 89, 91
Kennebunk, 112
Kennedy, Lyman, 106
King, Angus, 190
kinship, 21
Kittery, 107
Knapp, Larry, 107, 126
Knight, Jack, 8, 69, 93–94, 207, 209–11
Krouse, Jay S, 15–16, 90, 149, 171, 194–95
Kuhnert, Stephan, 212

Landa, Janet, 6
LaPointe, George, 111, 124, 137, 190, 216
law enforcement, 46, 54. *See also* illegal activity; Marine Patrol; territoriality
Lemieux, Norbert, 115
Levi, Margaret, 226
Lewis, David, 8, 94, 207, 209–10
Libecap, Gary, 70, 207
limited entry: formal, 57, 98, 100, 108–12, 144, 163; informal, 60, 62, 65–66. *See also* territories (lobstering); trap limits
Lipfert, Nathan R., 81–82, 85, 90, 149
Little River, 26, 37, 44, 51
Lobster Advisory Council. *See* zone management, Lobster Advisory Council
lobster, biology of: diet, 15; habitat, 15, 47; life cycle, 15; migration, 15–16, 36; reproduction, 15
lobster conservation management teams (LCMTs). *See* Atlantic States Marine Fisheries Commission, effort management teams
lobster fishermen. *See* fishermen
lobster fishery: canners, 82–84; catch statistics, 14, 16–18; future of, 234–35; license numbers, 14, 16–18; success of, 1, 4, 11, 101, 137–38, 144, 213, 218, 232–34
lobster gangs. *See* harbor gangs
lobstering: annual round, 19–20; sales, 13, 128–

29; technology, 14, 37. *See also* harbor gangs; territories (lobstering)

lobster management: Atlantic States Marine Fisheries Commission, 167–68, 179–88; federal, 169–71, 193–201; local, 57–79; state, 80–144; State-Federal Program, 167–68, 170, 172, 230. *See also* Federal American Lobster Plan; Interstate Lobster Fishery Management Plan

lobster measure (gauge), 149; double gauge, 85–88, 238n; maximum (oversize), 18–19, 86, 88, 153, 159, 163–64, 171–73, 182, 185–86, 194–97, 199, 215; minimum, 18, 82–86, 88, 153, 163–64, 170–75, 182–83, 218; "poverty gauge," 86, 147–48, 157, 204–5

lobster stock size, 3, 16–18, 80, 170, 204, 226, 234; culturing hypothesis, 140–49, 157, 204–5; effect of conservation ethic on, 145–53, 156–61, 165; and environmental factors, 160–62; fisherman's views on, 145–53, 156–61, 165; general cycles in, 151–52, 157; and groundfish predation, 150–51, 159; habitat change, influence on, 151; low prices, influence on, 153–54; scientists' view on, 145–46, 153–59, 161–63, 165, 200; water temperature, effects of, 155–56. *See also* "bust and boom"; illegal activity; law enforcement

lobster traps: biodegradable panel on, 182–83; escape vent on, 90–91, 95, 153, 164, 175, 184, 186, 212, 238n; traps-only law, 19

lobster wars. *See* territories, "lobster wars"

Look (Senator), 87, 88

Look, Vinal, 90, 92, 167

Loud's Island, 37

Lubec, 89

Ludwig, Donald, 227

Machias Bay, 89

Maine Department of Marine Resources (DMR), 2, 12–13, 87, 90–93, 97, 103, 107–8, 113–14, 116, 119, 122–23, 126, 135, 139–40, 143, 169, 189, 191

Maine Fisherman's Forum, 99, 103, 106, 239n

Maine lobster laws and regulations, 18–19; Administrative Procedures Act, 140; egg-bearing females, 83–84; export ban, 85; Great Ponds Law, 234n; owner-operator law, 119; public trust, 24, 234n; seasonal closures, 84–85; traps only, 18. *See also* conservation zones; law enforcement; limited entry; lobster measure, lobster traps; Ma-

rine Patrol; territories; trap limits; V-notch; zone management

Maine Lobstermen's Association, 37, 91, 98, 100–101, 123, 170, 189, 191

Maine State Archives, 12

Maine State Legislature, 2–3, 83, 91–93, 97–101, 107–8, 113, 119, 139, 172; Sub-zone Task Force, 12, 51, 224. *See also* Botsford Report; Maine lobster laws and regulations

management: bottom-up, 187, 231–32; polycentric governance, 232–34; top-down, 187, 226, 229–33, 239n. *See also* co-management; fisheries management; institutions, mechanisms producing; management goals (federal and ASMFC); parametric management

management goals (federal and ASMFC): 10 percent rule, 182, 186, 199, 203; benchmarks, 182, 199; "best science," 230; maximum sustainable yield (MSY), 181; over fished fishery, 184, 199; overfishing, definition of, 175, 179, 181–82

Marine Mammal Protection Act. *See* federal laws, Marine Mammal Protection Act

Marine Patrol, 40, 46, 55

markets, 85–86, 128, 167, 195

Marshall, Douglas, 176

Martin, Kenneth R., 81, 82, 85, 90, 149

Martinsville, 49

Matinicus Island, 49, 50, 63, 112–13

Matinicus Rock, 47

Mattocks, Luther, 82

McCay, Bonnie, 1, 9–10, 35, 99, 139, 142

McGinnis, Michael, 10, 223

McGoodwin, James, 1, 7, 10, 142

McNaught, D., 151

Medomak River, 44

Metinic Island, 25, 35, 50, 53, 238n

methodology, 11–13, 117, 133, 146–47

Milbridge, 89

Miller, Gary, 212, 226

Mitchell Bill. *See* federal laws, Mitchell Bill

mixed fishing. *See* territories, "mixed fishing" areas

Moberg, Mark, 226

Moe, Terry, 226

Monhegan Island, 22, 29, 35, 41–42, 50–53, 55–61, 69–71, 84, 214–15

Murawski, Steven A., 128

Muscle Ridge Channel, 45

Muscongus, 25

Rosenberg, Andrew, 184
Round Pond, 32, 37, 44, 48, 52
Ruddle, Kenneth, 1, 10
rules, 1, 4; centralized and decentralized, 2, 212–13, 215; definition of 5; formal and informal, 2, 80–96; 206, 215, 239n. *See also* federal laws; institutions; institutions, devising; institutions, mechanisms producing; limited entry; Maine lobster laws and regulations; territories, rules regarding; trap limits, informal

Saco, 107
Scattergood, Leslie, 81, 89
Schlager, Edella, 217, 221
science: chaos, 228–34; conceptual problems in, 227; lobster data, 196–97, 202–3; of lobster measure (gauge), 170–71, 193–95; modeling, 197–99, 201–2, 239n; predicting lobster stock size, 198; problems in, 3, 179, 204, 226–28; stock-recruitment models, 156–61, 201, 227
scientists: attitudes of, 170, 195, 199–201; conflicts with fishermen, 145, 158–59, 193, 195–96; early, 81, 85–86, 151, 159, 193, 196; factions of, 153, 193, 198, 200, 202; policies advocated by, 85–86, 90, 163–65, 170–73, 182, 191, 194–99, 203–5, 227–28; world view of, 3, 145–46, 161–62, 227, 234. *See also* politics, scientist's influence on
Sea Grant. *See* University of Maine Sea Grant
Searsport, 43, 53
Sebasco Estates, 45, 51
Sheepscot River, 45
Shleifer, Andrei, 226
Simard, B, 155
Simmons, Randy, 1, 10, 99
Simpson, Dorothy, 66
Singleton, Sara, 11, 71–72, 111, 212, 214
size laws. *See* lobster measure
Skud, B. E., 15
Small Point, 52
Smith, Courtland, 142
Smith, Eric Alden, 222
Smith, Estellie, 145
Snowe, Olympia, 187, 202
South Bristol, 26–27, 32, 37–38, 45, 49, 51–52
Southport, 51–52, 74
South Thomaston, 37
spirals, upward and downward, 218–21, 234–35
Sprague, Myron "Sonny," 67–68, 212

Spruce Head, 45, 47, 50, 52–53, 72–75, 112
State-Federal Program. *See* lobster management, State-Federal Program
Steneck, Robert, 4, 12, 15, 148, 150–51, 155, 159–60, 173–74, 196, 202–3
Steuben, 89
St. George, 25
Stock Assessment Review Committee, 199, 202
stock-recruitment models. *See* science, stock-recruitment models
Stockwell, Terry, 107, 110, 124, 138, 189, 191
Stonington, 29
Strahan, Max, 188, 190
study area, 11
Sub-zone Task Force. *See* Maine State Legislature, Sub-zone Task Force
Sugden, Robert, 8, 94, 207, 209–10
Sustainable Fisheries Act. *See* federal laws, Sustainable Fisheries Act
Swan's Island, 50, 51, 55, 57, 66–71, 214–15
Sylvia, Gil, 164

Tang, Shui Yan, 217
Taylor, Laura, 110, 115, 139, 201
Taylor, Michael, 7, 8, 69, 71–72, 95, 214
Teel's Island, 37
Tenant's Harbor, 25, 29, 38, 45, 49, 64
territoriality, 221, 224; competition, 26, enforcement of, 222; factors changing, 222–23; and game theory analysis, 222; offense and defense, costs and benefits of, 222; riparian rights, 221; scale, 24; threat system, 222–23. *See also* law enforcement; territories (lobstering)
territories (lobstering): boundaries of, 25, 54; boundary defense and offense, 27–29, 31–32, 34–35, 37–40, 47, 60, 63, 65, 68; boundary movement, 37–51; conservation zones, 51, 55–56, 61, 67–68; consolidation of, 43–45; construction of, 53–55, 237n, 238n; economic and biological effects of, 35–36; exclusive areas, 49; factors influencing, 26, 55; "lobster wars," 28; "mixed fishing" areas, 42, 45, 47, 51, 54; Monhegan-Friendship dispute, 49–50, 61; nucleated, 29–32, 54–56, 237n; open areas, 47, 52–53, 70; origins of, 40–42; perimeter-defended, 29, 33–36, 45; problems describing, 53–55, 237n; recent changes in, 46–51; rules regarding, 24–36; 55–57. *See also* harbor gangs; territoriality

Thomas, James, 90, 152, 171, 194–95, 205
top-down management. *See* management, top-down
transaction costs, 70, 75–76, 209
trap cap law. *See* zone management, trap cap law
trap limits: formal, 97–100, 103–7, 144, 163, 214; informal, 57, 61–63, 65, 67–72, 75–78, 191, 214; responses of fishermen to, 126–32. *See also* politics, of local trap limit; politics, of state trap limit
Trescott, 89
Tullock, Gordon, 226

United States laws. *See* federal laws
University of Maine Sea Grant, 12, 124
Uzmann, Joseph R., 15

Vadas, R. L., 151
Vaitones, Scott, 171, 196–97
Vass, P., 153
Vinalhaven, 45, 50, 53, 113
Vincent, George, 170
Vishny, Robert W, 226
V-notch, 18–19, 88–90, 95, 152, 159, 164, 171–74, 182–87, 194–97, 199, 212, 215, 238n, 239n; origin of, 88; and "seeder program," 89, 238n. *See also* Maine lobster laws and regulations, egg-bearing females

Wade, Robert, 8, 69–70, 207–8, 227
Waddy, Susan, 171
Wahle, R. A., 148, 150, 155
Walker, James, 9, 55, 70
Walters, Carl, 227, 229
Weed, Gerald, 116
Weingast, Barry, 140
Weinstein, Martin, 10, 207, 232

Westbrook, Perry D., 66
West Point, 45
Wheeler's Bay, 25, 49, 50, 112
White, Pat, 101, 176, 184, 186–87, 212
White, William, 87
Williams, John T., 226, 233
Williamson, Oliver, 6
Wilson, Carl, 196, 202–3
Wilson, James, 4, 99, 102, 201, 216, 218, 221, 227–28
Winter Harbor, 89
Wiscasset, 43
Wunsch, James S., 231

Zimsen, S., 151
Zone G lawsuit. *See* zone management, Zone G lawsuit
zone management: apprenticeship program, 97, 100, 102, 115–16; Department of Marine Resources resource coordinators, 120, 125–26; enforcement, 143; fishermen's views on, 133–37; 49/51 percent rule, 112–14, 144; implementation committee, 101–3, 239n; implementation problems, 123–26; in/out ratios, 108–9; law, 19, 97, 100–101, 133, 225, 230, 232; license moratorium, 115; Lobster Advisory Council, 107–8, 119, 122–24, 135, 138–41; role of government in, 138–40; trap cap law 107–8; traps per boat, 119; zone boundaries, 102, 104, 112–14, 142–43; zone bylaws, 102–3; zone districts, 97, 102, 121–23; Zone G lawsuit, 103, 106–7; zone meetings, 120–21
zones (Maine lobstering): Zone A, 111–12, 120; Zone B, 114, 116–17, 120; Zone C, 111–14, 116, 121; Zone D, 109–14, 116–17, 121; Zone E, 107, 109–11, 113–14, 121; Zone F, 109–13, 120; Zone G, 103, 106–7, 109–13, 121

DATE DUE		
OCT 1 7 2003	7-6-10	
DEC 2 6 2003		
R APR 1 5 2004		
JUL 2 7 2004		
DEC 2 1 2004		
AUG 0 4 2006		
MAR 0 3 2007		
MAY 2 0 2008		